Making Fine Furniture

Perfect Results with Power Tools

Peter Anderson

Sterling Publishing Co., Inc.
New York

Library of Congress Cataloging-in-Publication Data

Anderson, Peter (Peter C.)

Making fine furniture : perfect results with power tools / Peter Anderson.

p. cm.

Includes index.

ISBN-13: 978-1-4027-3964-4

ISBN-10: 1-4027-3964-8

1. Furniture making—Amateurs' manuals. 2. Power tools—Amateurs' manuals. I. Title.

TT195.A64 2007

684.1'04—dc22

2006029292

10 9 8 7 6 5 4 3 2 1

Published by Sterling Publishing Co., Inc.

387 Park Avenue South, New York, NY 10016

© 2007 by Peter Anderson

Distributed in Canada by Sterling Publishing

c/o Canadian Manda Group, 165 Dufferin Street

Toronto, Ontario, Canada M6K 3H6

Distributed in the United Kingdom by GMC Distribution Services,

Castle Place, 166 High Street, Lewes, East Sussex, England BN7 1XU

Distributed in Australia by Capricorn Link (Australia) Pty. Ltd.

P.O. Box 704, Windsor, NSW 2756, Australia

Book design and layout: *tabula rasa* graphic design

Printed in China

All rights reserved

Sterling ISBN-13: 978-1-4027-3964-4

ISBN-10: 1-4027-3964-8

For information about custom editions, special sales, premium and corporate purchases, please contact Sterling Special Sales Department at 800-805-5489 or specialsales@sterlingpub.com.

Author's Web site: www.andersonfurniture.com

To Janet
For being a partner in everything

Thank you!
To my friend Mary Boulanger, who made this book more readable
by vetting it with the eye of an English teacher, and to the staff at
Sterling Publishing Co., Inc. for their professional guidance.

Contents

Introduction

VISITORS TO MY SHOWROOM OFTEN tell me they dabble in woodworking. My response is always, "Why not do it properly?" The idea that working wood to high standards is only for experts has not been true since power tools for the home workshop became affordable. These tools enable any woodworker to produce first-class results immediately: Lack of experience is no longer an obstacle.

Power tools do much more than replace muscle power. They offer advantages that enable a novice to undertake the construction of fine furniture and be confident of success. Perfect results can now come from correct procedures rather than skill; if you can follow instructions, you can use power tools with precision from the outset. While skills with hand tools may take years to learn, good procedures with power tools can be applied immediately: to produce straight edges, true surfaces, accurate dimensions, and precise joints every time. The way to learn fine woodworking is to start with a worthwhile project and a determination that only first-class results will do. Anything less would not justify the investment in tools, time, or materials; nor will it bring satisfaction.

To make fine furniture, you must learn how good design and construction allow for the behavior of wood. You must learn what to look for when buying lumber and how to prepare it so that subsequent operations will give you the desired results every time. Then the finer points of woodworking become simple. You will see that perfect joints are easy to make with power tools guided by simple jigs. The tools themselves are easy to use. They do not require finely honed skills; they just require an understanding of good procedures.

It is easy to see why many amateur woodworkers lack confidence: Information about woodworking is readily available but is often poorly presented. Books and articles that offer simple projects reinforce the belief that serious woodworking should be left to the experts. Other publications go to the opposite extreme by stating what has to be done rather than how to do it, leaving the inexperienced reader with more questions than answers. Even woodworking shows on television offer little help. They present what appear to be beautiful pieces of furniture, but either most of the work has been done off-screen or the construction methods are inferior. You could watch these shows for years without gaining an understanding of real woodworking. It all adds to a belief that fine furniture cannot be made without first spending years acquiring experience. As a result, woodworking enthusiasts may find the prospect of making a major item of fine furniture daunting because they have an inflated concept of what is involved—so many operations, so many parts. In reality, fine woodworking is entirely within the average person's ability, and perfect results can be obtained from the outset.

This book shows you how to take advantage of power tools to make furniture like mine and to achieve excellence even if you are not skilled with hand tools. It also contains all the information essential to a fundamental understanding of the craft. Chapter 1 describes the characteristics of wood and basic approaches to safety; chapters 2–18 go on to explain the principles of furniture construction and the proper use of all necessary tools and techniques. Lastly, chapters 19–21 present projects that show in fine detail exactly how to make three major items from my range of furniture.

Some hand tools are important—even to the power tool user. Chapters on those hand tools have been included because it would be foolish not to use them for very simple tasks.

The introductions to each of the projects reinforce what earlier chapters have taught and explain the procedures in detail. You will see the big picture clearly before you begin to work, and every stage in the projects will be described step by step.

Even if you are a complete beginner, you can experience the satisfaction of uncompromising workmanship in wood.

Part 1
Wood & Woodworking

The Woodworking Process

IF YOU ARE NOT AN EXPERIENCED woodworker, this brief description of how lumber is turned into furniture will help you see the big picture. Aside from special techniques such as veneering or bending wood, the operations involved are surprisingly consistent regardless of what piece you are making.

When you have a design and know roughly how much material you require, each project will begin at your local hardwood lumber retailer's yard, where you will select suitable boards from storage racks. To do this you, will need two things: knowledge of lumber (provided in this book), and a retailer who will allow you to sort through the yard's stock. If the retailer is not helpful, try to find one who is. Some sources are mentioned in the text and you can consult my Web site (see the copyright page or the last page at the end of "About the Author") for an updated list of sources.

After bringing the lumber home, you will plan the cutting of boards in order to minimize waste while obtaining the characteristics each component of the project requires. Next, you will cut the boards into pieces that are a little longer and wider than the required parts, and then make one face of each piece absolutely flat, using an important item of home workshop machinery called a jointer. With one face of each piece flat, you will

pass the parts through a planer to make the opposite faces flat and parallel to the first ones, and to bring each piece to the right thickness.

Now that you have pieces that are flat and smooth on two faces, and are of the required thickness, you will use the jointer again to make one edge of each piece perfectly straight and perpendicular to the faces. These straight edges simplify the next step: using a table saw to cut the parts to their final widths, resulting in pieces that are flat, have straight edges, and are the right width but still a little longer than required and have rough ends. You will then use the table saw again, first to make one end of each piece square to the side edges, and second to cut them to exact lengths. None of the operations so far require special expertise, just knowledge of how to use your power tools safely and accurately.

The parts that you first cut from the boards were rough blanks; now they are finished blanks, perfectly flat and straight, of the right thickness and length and with all surfaces parallel or perpendicular to each other. Such pieces make subsequent work very straightforward.

Other parts may need to be wider than your original boards and must be made by gluing pieces together side by side. The straight edges produced by the jointer, combined with an understanding of how to match the pieces, will make the seams almost invisible.

The next step is likely to be joinery work—shaping the ends so they will fit together to make the framework of the piece you are building. These end shapes are usually either dovetails, in which the ends of two pieces are formed into interlocking shapes, or some form of mortise-and-tenon joint, which allows one piece to be inserted into another and glued in place. All these joints are easily made with a router, plus jigs that guide it. After the joinery work, some tasks remain that are best done before the parts are fixed together. These include sanding and shaping.

Sanding used to be tedious and time consuming. Now it can be done quickly with small power tools. Shaping operations might include forming a decorative bead on the edges of table legs, tapering them, or cutting curves along the edges of a table's aprons. The router, bandsaw, and jigsaw are the most commonly used tools for these operations. Sanding is usually needed again to finish the shaped edges. For this task, sanding by hand is sometimes the quickest method, although inexpensive devices are available to reduce even this effort.

After shaping and sanding, most of the work on individual parts will have been completed. However, some work may remain before the parts can be assembled. This may include making holes or slots that will be used later for fixing a top to the piece.

Assembly involves applying glue to the joinery surfaces and then clamping the parts together until the glue hardens. This stage requires careful planning to ensure that all the necessary facilities are ready. These usually include an adequate number of clamps, some pieces of wood to protect the parts from damage by the clamps, and a means of checking that the clamped assembly is straight and square. Once the glue is applied, your time is limited, so you should try out the procedure first without glue to make sure that your preparations are complete and that everything goes together easily.

Large pieces of furniture may comprise a number of subassemblies, in which case the procedures described above will be repeated for each one. Even the most complex items should be thought of in terms of repeating the series of steps just described. Some items may involve additional work (drawer parts, for example, require grooves cut in the sides to accommodate the bottoms), but everything is done one step at a time. If you follow good procedures, your power tools will produce the desired results.

After assembly, some final work will be necessary. This may include further edge-shaping, more sanding, fixing beading around the drawers to highlight them, or fixing supports and guides for the drawers. Here, too, following simple procedures is enough to produce perfect results. When the work has been done, you will spend some time inspecting the piece closely to find any dents, surface flaws, or glue stains that need yet more sanding. Then you will be ready for what can be the most satisfying part of the job—applying a finish to bring out the beauty of the wood.

Furniture-making can involve specialized techniques such as carving, bending, veneering, inlay work, etc. These specialized techniques can be learned from specialized books; from this volume, you will learn all that you need to know to make furniture like mine. In all of this work, you will also need to be aware of dangers and work safely in a systematic manner.

SAFETY

Woodworking tools are dangerous. They can cut tough material at speeds that are faster than we humans can react. Power tools can also throw out heavy pieces of wood or grab hair or loose clothing and pull them into the cutters. Some hand tools even resemble weapons designed to kill. Anything that is sharp is dangerous, and anything can become dangerous when it is being machined. Screwdriver blades can puncture flesh, and chisels are prone to penetrate any object that gets in their way.

You can work safely only by taking a systematized approach that involves reading manufacturers' safety recommendations and never, ever taking shortcuts. Most woodworking activity requires concentration; and with so much mental capacity occupied, one cannot always be thinking about safety. For this reason, safety depends upon becoming habituated to safe procedures.

Tool manufacturers carry a great deal of liability for safety, so they try to cover their bases by providing comprehensive warnings. Studying the safety instructions in their equipment manuals is an important step toward avoiding accidents. No matter how dull this may seem, reading all the safety notes and thinking about them are important ways to become aware of the risks.

Many hazards are not obvious. For example, inexperienced woodworkers may not be aware that certain tools can catapult a workpiece with dangerous force; many machine guards are designed to prevent this as well as to protect against direct contact with a blade. Use the guards and resist the temptation to take shortcuts. Look at it this way: Every time you omit a safety precaution, the odds against you get worse. You might be unlucky the first time, so don't take risks.

Personal protection, such as safety goggles or glasses, hearing protectors, or dust masks, can be uncomfortable in hot weather. Whenever you are tempted to work without them, remember that they have saved many woodworkers from loss of sight, impaired hearing, or even disease. Even common sawdust has now been classified as a carcinogen.

Sometimes a machine guard will prevent you from carrying out a task. If you decide to remove a guard, take alternative precautions even if you have to spend considerable time on them. Safe procedures must become second nature to you. If you don't think you can use them one hundred percent of the time, then you really should not be working with wood.

1 About Wood

NO MATTER HOW MUCH EFFORT and care you expend on a project, the results will be disappointing unless you allow for the behavior of wood. To obtain satisfaction by producing fine work, you must be confident that it will stand up to the changes that affect wood before and after it is made into furniture. The next few pages go on to explain the remarkable way that wood reacts with its environment, and why understanding these changes is so important.

HOW WOOD CHANGES

Wood shrinks or swells whenever the humidity of the air around it changes. Wood absorbs moisture from humid air. When it absorbs moisture, it expands. In drier air, it loses moisture and shrinks. "Seasoning" does not prevent this process, which persists even after the wood has been dried and made into furniture.

In extreme circumstances, wood can expand or shrink by more than an inch for every foot of its width. In typical circumstances, furniture parts will seasonally expand and shrink by up to $\frac{1}{8}$" per foot of width: A tabletop might shrink to 48" in width in winter and expand to $48\frac{1}{2}$" width in summer. Not all species of wood will change this much, but they all shrink or swell to some degree.

Sometimes the effects are trivial; perhaps drawers or doors will stick only slightly in summer. However, wood's tendency to change its size might also cause parts to split or drawers to jam solid. Joints can be broken because of pressure from expanding parts. Whether trivial or serious, changes in size all result from changes in the amount of water in the wood.

When wood is first taken from a drying kiln, it has a moisture content (MC) of about 6 percent. In this condition, a cherry board that is 2" thick, 12" wide, and 10' long will contain nearly five pints of water. No matter how wet or dry the wood is when you buy it, its MC will change later on. Much of the work involved in furniture design stems from the requirement to accommodate these changes.

The furniture-maker has to contend with expansion that varies with direction. Wood expands or shrinks across the grain, but it does not change significantly in the direction of the grain. The direction of the grain is along the length of a log, or along the length of a board cut from the log. *Across the grain* means across the diameter of the log or across the width of the board. The length of a piece of wood is always measured in the direction of the grain; width is the larger dimension across the grain; thickness is the smaller, third dimension, also across the grain.

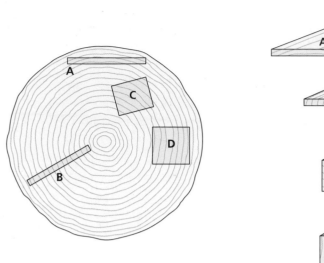
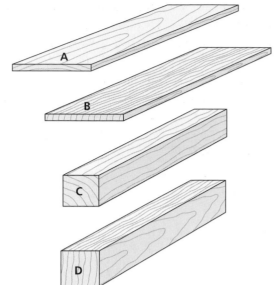
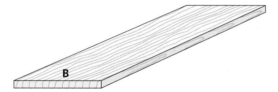

1.1 Four boards with different growth-ring orientations

1.2 Cathedral figure grain pattern

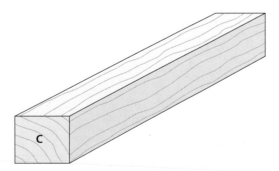

1.3 Quartersawn, or radially sawn, board

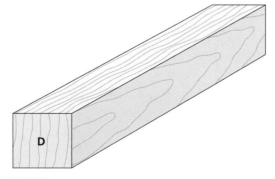

1.4 Diagonal end-grain pattern

1.5 Board with two faces flatsawn and two quartersawn

A log or a board can be thought of as a long bundle of fibers with open ends arranged in rings of annual growth. This concept is useful for understanding why wood absorbs or loses moisture very rapidly from its end surfaces but only slowly through its side faces. The surface pattern (grain pattern or figure) on boards is determined largely by the way the growth rings intersect the surfaces. This intersection is in turn determined by the way the boards were cut from the log.

The growth-ring orientation is extremely important to furniture-makers because it also determines how the boards react to changes in MC. Four ways that boards might be cut from a log are shown in **1.1**.

Board A (**1.2**) is cut so that the growth rings on the end are either almost parallel to the top and bottom faces of the board or tangential to them. Boards cut this way are said to be flatsawn or tangentially sawn. The grain pattern on the faces of such boards is often a series of arches that is sometimes referred to as cathedral figure.

Board B (**1.3**) is cut so that the growth rings on the ends are approximately perpendicular to the faces. This board is said to be quartersawn, or radially sawn, and the grain pattern is a series of straight lines along the face of the board.

Board C (**1.4**) has been cut so that the growth rings are diagonal on the ends. All four faces have a similar grain pattern.

Board D (**1.5**) has two faces that are flatsawn and two that are quartersawn. The growth rings are perpendicular to the top and bottom faces but parallel to the side faces—or vice versa if the board is turned 90 degrees.

How logs can be sawn into flatsawn and quartersawn boards is shown in **1.6**.

In addition to shrinking across the grain but not along it, the circumference of a log shrinks disproportionately to its diameter. The corresponding effect in cut boards is that the distance along the growth rings changes more, proportionately, than the distance between them.

It is these directional differences that cause trouble. If wood expanded or contracted equally in all directions, furniture would simply get larger or smaller—doors and drawers would expand or shrink in proportion to the frames around them, cabinet carcasses would increase in size to keep pace with their tops, and furniture-making would be altogether easier.

The nonproportional aspects of wood's expansion and shrinkage result in the following phenomena:

- In **1.7**, two pieces of wood are glued together with their grain directions crossed. Piece A will shrink across its grain as it loses moisture, but this effect will require piece B to change along its grain. At the same time, piece B tends to shrink across its grain, but piece A (plus glue) prevents piece B from doing so.

- If nails, screws, or other nonrigid fixings were used instead of glue, the joint might have enough flexibility to resolve

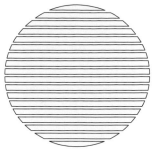

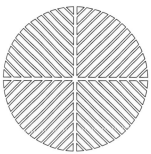

1.6 How logs can be sawn into flatsawn and quartersawn boards

1.7 A joint with crossed grain directions

this conflict. But glue can produce a situation in which an irresistible force meets an immovable object: Something has to give, and the give may be a split in one or both pieces.

Indoors, flatsawn wood typically changes its width seasonally by around 1 percent. For pieces that are 12" wide, the method of fixing them would have to allow for $\frac{1}{8}$" of movement to avoid problems. If the pieces are only 2" wide, they will tend to change by less than $\frac{1}{32}$" in width, and problems are unlikely even with rigidly glued joints.

Methods of construction must allow for crossed-grain situations. In **1.8**, a headboard that expands in height (across its grain) must fit into bedpost slots that are a constant distance apart (along the grain of the posts). The conflict is resolved by gluing only the top horns of the headboard into the posts, leaving the bottom ones free to move within oversized slots.

Because dimensional changes are not proportional in all directions, wood will change shape. How boards that are square or round when cut from a log will change as they dry is shown in **1.9**. When the distances along the growth rings change more than the distances between them, the shapes alter as shown—the square

becomes rectangular or diamond shaped, depending on the ring orientation, and the circle becomes oval. If the shapes were holes in the wood, instead of solid pieces, the same changes would occur. Similar effects occur in shapes cut from board faces, where changes in width are not accompanied by changes in length.

When a piece of wood fits into an opening, it may change size more than the opening. For example, a drawer front, which expands and shrinks in width, fits into an opening that is fixed by the lengths of the pieces that form it. For that reason, drawers must not be fitted too closely into their openings. Room must be left for expansion; otherwise, the drawer may jam when the indoor humidity is high.

Wide pieces such as a tabletop or a chest top must be joined to the table base or the chest carcass in a way that allows the top to expand and shrink. A wide tabletop might expand by more than $\frac{1}{2}$" from winter to summer, but the frame to which it is fixed will not.

Mitered frames **(1.10)** pose their own problems. If the miters are made tight in winter when the wood is very dry, they will open at the outside corners in summer, when the wood expands in width but not in length. If the miters are made in

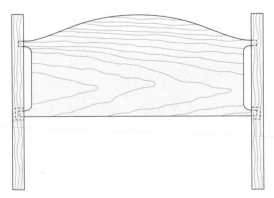

1.8 Headboard with room to expand

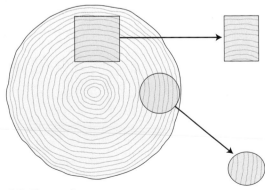

1.9 Shape changes

summer, the inside corners will open up in winter, when the pieces shrink in width. The seriousness of the problem depends on the width of the pieces; when they are narrow, the problem is usually not serious.

When the circumference of a log shrinks disproportionately to its diameter, the log will split from the outside to the center (1.11). Splitting will occur first at the ends because end-grain surfaces lose moisture much faster than side-grain surfaces.

Splitting occurs at the ends of sawn boards (1.12) because moisture loss here takes place much faster than from faces or edges. The ends are shrinking in width but are unable to shrink fully because, just a few inches from the ends of the boards, the wood is still full width. The conflict is resolved by the split.

Flatsawn boards tend to "cup" as they dry. They become concave on the bark side, convex on the pith side, and reduce the curvature of the rings. In this photograph of a cupped board (1.13), note that the cupping is not circular; rather, it almost forms a sharp bend at the center. Cupping will be greatly reduced by cutting the board along its length, through the center of the curve.

Boards will also cup if opposite faces have different moisture content. If you

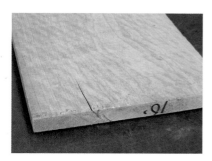

1.11 A split caused by nonproportional shrinkage

1.12 Split ends

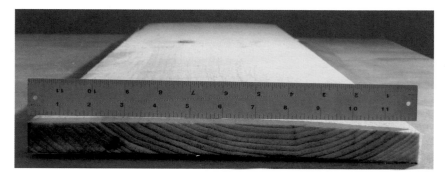

1.13 Cupped board

leave boards lying on a bench overnight, the faces exposed to the air may expand or shrink in width while the faces on the bench do not. The boards will cup, and the drier faces will become concave. Although this cupping can often be reversed by turning the boards over, it is far better to avoid the problem in the first place by allowing air to circulate over all the faces. If the pieces are not too large, an even better short-term practice is to put them in plastic bags so that their moisture content cannot change.

A similar effect occurs when finish is applied unequally to two sides of a large panel. Applying finish only to the visible face will result in warping because the two faces will not absorb atmospheric moisture equally.

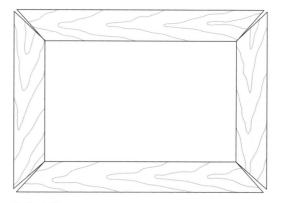

1.10 Miter gaps

MOISTURE CONTENT

Wood retains water in two ways. In a growing tree, the cell cavities are filled with so-called free water. When the tree is cut down, the cavities begin to lose this water. Eventually, if the log is stored under cover, the only remaining water is that which is held in the cell walls—the solid material of the log. This is called bound water.

When the free water has evaporated from the cell cavities but the fibers still contain the maximum amount of bound water, the log is said to be at its fiber saturation point (FSP). At FSP the bound water typically accounts for nearly one-fourth of the weight of the log! If the log continues to be stored under cover, some of the bound water will evaporate until the remaining bound water accounts for about one-eighth of the log's total weight, depending on the average humidity of the air around it. The log is then said to be air-dried, and the water in it will increase or decrease seasonally as the humidity of the air changes.

The moisture content (MC) of wood is defined as the weight of water divided by the weight of dry material. The MC is around 30 percent at FSP in most wood species. MC can be measured by cutting off a small piece of wood, weighing it, and then heating it in an oven to remove all the water. The wood is taken from the oven periodically and weighed until there is no further reduction in weight. At this point, it is oven-dry, and the original MC of the piece equals the change in weight divided by the final weight. For example, if the piece weighed 10 ounces before drying and 9 ounces afterwards, the original MC was $1/9$, or 11 percent.

RELATIVE HUMIDITY

Humidity is a broad term meaning the dampness of the air. However, wood absorbs or loses water until its moisture content is in balance with the *relative humidity* (RH) of the air—the amount of water in the air as a percentage of the maximum that the air is capable of holding.

Suppose the air in a room can hold a maximum of two pints of water but actually holds only a half-pint: The relative humidity would be 25 percent because the air could hold four times as much moisture. If the air actually held nearly two pints, the RH would be close to 100 percent.

When the RH is low, at 25 percent, the air can easily absorb more water, and any water in the room will rapidly evaporate. If wood furniture in the room has a high MC, the air will draw moisture out of it until the MC is in balance with the 25 percent RH.

By contrast, if the RH is close to 100 percent, the air is unable to absorb much more moisture. Water will evaporate very slowly, if at all, and wood will absorb water from the air.

The capacity of air to hold water depends on air temperature: The higher the air's temperature, the more moisture it can hold. If the temperature drops, but the amount of water in the air stays the same, the RH immediately becomes higher because its water content is now closer to the limit. Conversely, when the air temperature rises faster than the amount of water in it, its RH must drop. This is why RH in heated houses is very low during cold weather—the incoming cold air is heated and becomes capable of holding much more water.

EQUILIBRIUM MOISTURE CONTENT

To summarize, wood will lose or gain moisture until its MC is in balance with the RH of the air around it. This is the equilibrium moisture content (EMC) for that RH. For all hardwoods, the EMC is zero when the air is totally dry and rises to about 30 percent when the RH is 100 percent.

Table 1 shows the EMC of wood for various RHs at a temperature of 70 degrees Fahrenheit.

In many regions of the United States, the outdoor RH averages 70 percent. The corresponding EMC (from Table 1) is 13.1 percent. In other regions, the RH and EMC averages are higher or lower. Thus, the MC of lumber that has been stored in unheated sheds or garages may be very different from the 6 percent MC it had when it left the kiln.

Table 1 applies to wood that is drying out for the first time. During subsequent increases in RH, the MC changes will be somewhat smaller.

MEASURING MOISTURE CONTENT AND RELATIVE HUMIDITY

There are two types of moisture meters on the market, and both work by exploiting properties of wood that change with MC. One type employs a pair of steel pins that have to be driven into the wood so that electrical current can flow between them. The other type, called pinless meters, do not penetrate the surface but measure either the electrical capacitance of the wood or the amount of radio frequency energy it absorbs.

RELATIVE HUMIDITY (%)	EQUILIBRIUM MOISTURE CONTENT (% AT 70°F)
5	1.3
10	2.5
15	3.5
20	4.5
25	5.4
30	6.2
35	6.9
40	7.7
45	8.5
50	9.2
55	10.1
60	11.0
65	12.0
70	13.1
75	14.4
80	16.0
85	17.9
90	20.5
95	23.9

Source: USDA Forest Products Laboratory. *Wood Handbook—Wood as an engineering material.* Madison, WI: USDA; 1999. Available at: www.fpl.fs.fed.us/documnts/fplgtr/fplgtr113/fplgtr113.htm

Table 1. Relative Humidity (RH) and Equilibrium Moisture Content (EMC) of Wood at 70°F

There are disadvantages to both types; on balance, the pinless meters are probably best because they do not make holes in the wood. Meters that mar the wood do not encourage frequent testing because, no matter where you test a board with them, you often find later that it was the worst possible place to have made pinholes. A further disadvantage of pin-type meters is that the readings depend on depth of penetration—wood usually doesn't have the same MC near the surface as it does in the center. It may even have different MCs on each face. What you really need to know is its average MC, and this may be difficult to deduce.

This last problem also applies to pinless meters because they are calibrated to measure at a certain depth and may not give the average MC. Their readings are affected by the thickness of the wood, so they may be calibrated for either 1"-thick or 2"-thick lumber, but not for both. The density of the lumber also affects these meters. Although simple correction factors can be applied to allow for the average densities of each species, they do not correct for density variations within a species.

In addition to these limitations, pin-type meters and many pinless ones cannot measure MCs lower than about 7 percent. Nevertheless, you should obtain either type of meter and use it often enough to develop a feel for the way the MC of wood in your shop changes with the seasons.

I think that a hygrometer (RH meter) is even more important than an MC meter, although ideally you should have both. You can buy an accurate digital hygrometer for about $25, and with one of these you will always know how moisture is affecting your lumber.

Even if your lumber has only recently been brought into your shop, you can still estimate its MC without having a moisture meter by using a hygrometer and a plastic bag. When you start cutting wood for a new project, take a few slices from the middle parts of some boards and put these into a small plastic bag together with your digital hygrometer. The wood will raise or lower the RH of the air in the bag to a value consistent with the MC of the wood. Reading the hygrometer after a few hours will enable you to estimate the MC using **Table 1**.

Table 1 pertains to wood that is drying out for the first time; your lumber will not follow quite the same MC/RH relationship. Nevertheless, the hygrometer can tell you whether or not your lumber is acclimated to the prevailing RH, and what stage of its seasonal shrinkage and expansion cycle it has reached. For example, if the hygrometer in the bag reads 50 percent and the annual range of indoor RH that you expect is from 20 to 70 percent, the MC of the lumber is more than halfway to its annual maximum level. Also, if the RH in your shop is very different from the RH in the bag, you will know that the lumber MC is changing rapidly.

HOW MUCH EXPANSION?

Furniture manufacturers have advantages over individual craftspeople in avoiding problems caused by seasonal wood movement. They can buy lumber with an MC that represents the average of the values that will occur after it is made into furniture. Also, their factories are climate-controlled to keep the wood at this MC. These measures reduce the shrinkage and swelling they need to allow for because the difference between the manufacturing MC and future MCs will equal no more than half of the MC range.

Individual woodworkers do not have these advantages. The MC of their lumber will depend first on the RH at the supplier's storage facility and then will change in response to the working conditions. For example, if the RH in the workshop is only 20 percent, the wood's MC may drop to around 5 percent before a project is completed.

Manufacturers usually also minimize future MC changes by applying heavy coats of finish to slow the penetration of atmospheric moisture. Although individual craftspeople can do the same, they often prefer a wipe-on, wipe-off oil finish, which is not an effective barrier against moisture.

As an individual furniture-maker, you need to anticipate the future expansion or shrinkage of your material. A good starting point is to look at the maximum shrinkages that occur the first time wood is dried after being cut from the log. **Table 2** shows the shrinkages that occur in some commonly used species when they first go from FSP (about 30 percent MC) to totally dry. Note that these are the averages of many samples; it is impossible to predict exactly what any individual piece of wood will do.

The table shows, for example, that flatsawn beech shrinks 11.9 percent, which is nearly 1½" per foot of width. By contrast, quartersawn cherry shrinks 3.7 percent, little more than $\frac{7}{16}$" per foot.

Stability problems caused by differences in changes along and between the growth rings are smallest in species such as mahogany, where the flatsawn and quartersawn changes are similar. **Table 2** can be used to show which species perform best in this respect. For instance, beech shrinks 116 percent more along the rings than between them, while the difference for mahogany is only 37 percent.

SPECIES	QUARTERSAWN SHRINKAGE (%)	FLATSAWN SHRINKAGE (%)
American beech	5.5	11.9
Black cherry	3.7	7.1
Sugar maple	4.8	9.9
Northern red oak	4.0	8.6
White oak	5.6	10.5
Black walnut	5.5	7.8
True mahogany	3.0	4.1

Source: USDA Forest Products Laboratory. *Wood Handbook—Wood as an engineering material*. Madison, WI: USDA; 1999. Available at: www.fpl.fs. fed.us/documnts/fplgtr/fplgtr113/fplgtr113.htm

Table 2. Shrinkage of Quartersawn and Flatsawn Lumber Dried to 0 Percent Moisture Content (MC)

After wood has been dried, it will expand and shrink again as the RH of the air around it changes. However, after the first drying, the dimensional changes are smaller because wood becomes more stable. There are two reasons for this, and I am indebted to The Wood Doctor* for explaining them to me.

The first reason is that when the RH rises, the MC of dried wood does not begin to change until the RH has increased by a few percent. Then, when the RH drops, the wood MC does not respond to the first part of that change either. This type of effect is called hysteresis, and it reduces all future MC changes. The second reason is

---

*Gene Wengert, Professor Emeritus, University of Wisconsin–Madison. President, The Wood Doctor's Rx, LLC. Available at: www.woodweb.com/gene_wengert

that when the MC of dried wood does change, the wood does not swell or shrink in response to the first few percent of that change. This is another hysteresis effect, which combines with the first to reduce dimensional changes.

Even so, the swelling and shrinking that does occur after the first drying depends on changes in RH. The extent of the dimensional changes in lumber and furniture therefore varies from region to region. The RH in my New Hampshire workshop and house drops to around 20 percent for a couple of months each winter and rises to above 70 percent for a few weeks in summer. In some years it peaks briefly at or above 80 percent.

For 10 years I have had a very wide, very short strip of cherry wood affixed to the wall of my workshop. Every year its width changes by more than an inch. It was made by gluing together several pieces side by side cut from different boards. All the pieces are 1" long, and the strip is 87" wide. The pieces are approximately flatsawn, so the strip represents typical flatsawn cherry boards. Because no part of it is more than $\frac{1}{2}$" from end grain, it reacts quickly to changes in humidity. I can almost see it move when the weather changes. The change is similar every year, varying between 1.1 percent and 1.3 percent of the average width. Maximum width occurs in years when there is an extended period of high humidity.

For several years I monitored the top gaps of more than 20 cherry drawer fronts (which have an oil finish) in my house to record how they change in width. The changes ranged from 0.6 percent to 1 percent (for 8" fronts, the gaps changed by $\frac{1}{16}$" to $\frac{3}{32}$").

These measurements, and many others, indicate that the annual expansion of unfinished flatsawn cherry will be less than 1.5 percent (about $\frac{3}{16}$" per foot of width) when the range of relative humidity is from 20 percent to 80 percent. The expansion of quartersawn cherry is lower still. For other species, the expansion may be higher or lower, and can be estimated by comparing expansion figures in **Table 2** with those for cherry. The figures for regions with other RH ranges will be different, but most craftspeople consider 1.5 percent to be a more than safe allowance for expansion in nearly all circumstances.

If your furniture designs allow every part to expand and shrink by 1.5 percent of its width, you do not need to know the present or future MC of the lumber (assuming that it has been kiln-dried and kept under cover). This is a practical and sensible approach in many instances. However, some expansion allowances, such as drawer top gaps, need to be more carefully controlled because they are aesthetically important. If you used the simple 1.5 percent approach to allow a 9"-wide drawer front to expand, you would leave a gap of more than $\frac{1}{8}$" above it. But the front might already be at maximum MC, so the only future change would be shrinkage. The gap would become excessive and ugly because it needlessly allowed for expansion that had already occurred. In situations like this, you should realistically assess future expansion; this requires knowledge of roughly where your lumber stands in its cycle of seasonal MC changes.

When I make drawers from cherry, I assume that their seasonal expansion will not exceed 1.5 percent. Next, I estimate what part of that 1.5 percent will occur after construction: This is the part that I allow for.

If you know the RH to which your wood has become acclimated, you can derive its future expansion from **Table 3.**

ACCLIMATED RH (%)	FUTURE EXPANSION (%)
20	1.5
30	1.28
40	1.08
50	0.89
60	0.65
70	0.38
80	0.0

Table 3. Future Expansion of Wood, Based on 1.5% Expansion for a Relative Humidity (RH) Change from 20% to 80% with Expansion Proportional to Moisture Content

The table shows that when wood is acclimated to an RH of 20 percent, all the expansion will take place in the future. When the wood is acclimated to 80 percent RH, the expansion has already occurred. If you know the RH to which the wood is acclimated, you can use the table to find the expansion allowance to use. You can increase the allowance for species that expand more than cherry, and for situations where RH might remain above 80 percent for a considerable time.

Table 4 uses the data in **Table 3** to show the required expansion gaps for cherry drawer fronts of various widths and MCs.

Any finish applied to wood will slow down the absorption of moisture. Several coats of lacquer or polyurethane will have a significant effect, but a wiped-on oil finish will not, and neither will wax. Regardless of the finish, the wood will eventually arrive at an MC (and width) appropriate to the RH—that is, if the RH remains constant for long enough.

BUYING LUMBER

Hardwood lumber is graded for quality according to rules established by the National Hardwood Lumber Association. The top grade, called Firsts, is followed by Seconds, Selects, No. 1 Common, No. 2 Common, and No. 3 Common. Firsts and Seconds are always combined and sold as a single grade, imaginatively called FAS

ACCLIMATED RH (%)	FUTURE EXPANSION (80%)	DRAWER WIDTHS (INCHES)					
		4"	5"	6"	7"	8"	9"
		EXPANSION GAPS (THOUSANDTHS OF AN INCH)					
80	0.0	0	0	0	0	0	0
70	0.38	15	19	23	27	30	34
60	0.65	26	32	39	45	52	58
50	0.89	36	44	53	62	71	80
40	1.08	43	54	65	76	86	97
30	1.28	51	64	77	90	102	115
20	1.5	60	75	90	105	120	135

Table 4. Recommended Initial Expansion Gaps for Cherry Drawers, Based on the Relative Humidity (RH) to Which the Wood Is Acclimated at the Time of Construction

(Firsts and Seconds). This is the grade you will usually be looking for, although you can often find suitable lumber in the other grades.

One approach to buying lumber for a project is to work out a combination of board sizes that should provide all the parts and then to look for those boards. This method can work for a small project, but not for a large one because you will not find boards of just the right size, and the boards you do find will contain defects that result in varying degrees of waste. An alternative approach is to calculate the volume each individual component requires, and then to total these up, adding a generous allowance for wastage. With future projects in mind, you can make the allowance 50 percent or more, knowing that any leftover material will be used another time.

You could calculate the volume in cubic feet, but it is better to work in board feet because this is how lumber is sold. A board foot is the volume of a piece of wood that is 1" thick, 1' wide, and 1' long. To calculate board feet, just multiply the thickness in inches by the width and length in feet. For example, a board 1" thick, 6" wide, and 8 feet long contains $1 \times 6/12 \times 8 = 4$ board feet. A board 2" thick, 15" wide, and 12 feet long contains $2 \times 15/12 \times 12 = 30$ board feet.

The thickness of sawn lumber is stated not in inches but in quarter inches: 1"-thick boards are called four-quarter lumber (written as 4/4), while 2"-thick boards are eight-quarter lumber (8/4). You should get used to using quarter terminology when specifying lumber. You can also use it in your calculations of board footage. For example, our 2" × 15" × 12' board contains $8/4 \times 15/12 \times 12 = 30$ board feet.

You will be buying unplaned lumber that has been sawn from the log and then dried in a kiln to a moisture content of about 6 percent. When you are sorting through the supplier's stock looking for good boards, certain defects such as large knots and splits will be obvious. However, you will have to examine them carefully for other problems. The rough surface of the boards can make it difficult to spot worm holes and rotted or discolored areas. Sapwood and warp might also be reasons to reject a board.

Sapwood refers to the outer growth rings of a tree; it therefore appears on the edges of boards. Sapwood is the living tissue of the tree—the part that conducts sap. It is not a defect, and is usually almost as strong as the heartwood, but it may be a different color. It is a particular problem with cherry, in which the sapwood is almost white. In recent years it has become difficult to find cherry boards without a high proportion of sapwood in them. Although sapwood is not a defect, and while it may be acceptable in commercial furniture (often disguised by the finish), it is not desirable for visible parts of fine furniture unless it is a deliberate feature of the design. Any sapwood is likely to end up in the scrap bin, so you should reject boards that contain a lot of it on both faces. If sapwood is showing only on one face, it may be possible to use that board where the sapwood will not show. However, if you are considering boards with a lot of sapwood on one face only, remember that although you may keep it to the underside, it will still show on the ends of table and chest tops. On the other hand, sapwood is desirable in some species of wood because it constitutes the largest part of the tree. In these species, it is the small heartwood area that has the "wrong" color.

Warp is any deviation from flatness in the surface of a board. It includes bowing along the length, cupping across the width, and twist (or wind, as it is also called). It can present a serious problem because the only way to flatten a board is to cut away the surface of both faces until they are flat. Sometimes your biggest challenge will be to find boards that can be flattened without leaving them too thin for your project.

Suppose you are choosing 4/4 lumber for a table with a ¾"-thick top. You pick up each board and sight along its edge to judge the flatness and find that every board is visibly bowed. How do you know whether you can produce a flat tabletop from them? By estimating what thickness of material will have to be removed in order to leave a flat surface. You can do this by placing something with a long, straight edge along the length of the board on the concave side of the bow. The deepest part of the gap between the straightedge and the board is the amount of bow that must be removed to flatten the entire board. If the original board is a generous 4/4, and the gap is ¼", then you just might be able to finish with a flat, ¾"-thick board for your tabletop.

Boards that are twisted pose a bigger problem. If a board appears to have significant twist, you can use winding sticks to estimate the amount (winding sticks are straight strips of wood with parallel edges). Lay one stick across each end of the board, and then stand back and sight across both of them (1.14). If the board is twisted, the winding sticks will lie at different angles, as illustrated in 1.14.

You can measure the twist by raising the low end of one winding stick to make it parallel to the other one. The distance you have to raise the stick equals the thickness you would have to remove to make the entire board flat. In 1.15, the twist is almost an inch, so this 6/4 (1½"-thick) board would be reduced to ½" thickness.

Twist and bow will be automatically reduced when the boards are cut into

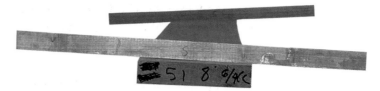

1.14 Twisted board

1.15 Measuring twist

smaller pieces. The projects in this book do not require any pieces wider than about 7" or longer than 4 feet. Finding boards to yield flat pieces with these dimensions will not be difficult.

Curvature across the width can be severe; it can be assessed by laying the straightedge across the width of the board. It will present a problem only if you want to use the board as a wide piece. If you can use it to make narrow pieces, the curvature will be dramatically reduced as soon as the board is cut (1.16 and 1.17).

Insufficient flatness is the reason for not buying ready-planed lumber: It will almost certainly still be warped to some extent, and since it is already planed to thickness, there is nothing left to remove and thus no possibility of flattening it to a useful thickness. Deceptively, the stated thickness of planed lumber often refers to

1.16 A wide cupped board

1.17 Cupping has been reduced by cutting the board

FURNITURE STABILITY

Some furniture parts cannot be restrained mechanically from warping. For example, the top of a pedestal table is fixed only at its center, and a cabinet door is fixed only at its hinges. Components like these must be made from lumber that is unlikely to warp. A good starting point is to choose lumber that is reasonably flat. As a general rule, boards that are badly warped before flattening are likely to warp again after flattening.

A change in internal stresses is one of the factors that can cause wood to change shape after flattening. As trees grow, stresses become locked into their trunks as layers of growth accumulate. When a tree is sawn into boards, the stresses may become unbalanced and cause the boards to warp. When the boards are recut in the workshop, the balance of stresses may change again to cause more warping. This is why some boards distort as they are being worked on. Changing stresses within the wood is also a reason for cutting components to rough size before they are flattened.

Warping due to sawing or planing away some of the stressed wood that had been in equilibrium will usually emerge in time for you to make a replacement piece. However, the possibility of future wood movement caused by changes in MC remains.

Changes in MC are inevitable. When stability is a major concern, one option is to choose quartersawn boards or a stable wood species such as mahogany. Alternatively, you might select parts of boards that approach the quartersawn condition. For example, while true quartersawn lumber has growth rings that meet both surfaces at 90 degrees, the growth rings of some wide flatsawn boards are angled at between 90 degrees and 45 degrees to both faces for a

the thickness of the rough boards before planing, which may be $\frac{1}{4}$" more than the actual thickness of the boards being sold.

Most rough boards have discernible warp when they leave the drying kiln. When you sort through boards at the lumberyard, you should be pleased to find any large boards that have no more than $\frac{1}{8}$" of bow and $\frac{1}{16}$" of cup or twist. Among any stack of dried boards, you are likely to find some with cupping of up to $\frac{1}{4}$" and bow or twist of more than $\frac{3}{8}$". Fortunately, depending upon the job, all boards are usable. Even the most warped ones can be used to make small, flat components. By carefully selecting boards and employing a good flattening technique, you can produce flat components of all sizes.

few inches near each edge (**1.18**). Strips cut from these edges will have roughly parallel ring sections, and their faces will be less likely to cup. Also, since the rings create straight lines on the top and bottom faces, bow and twist are less likely to occur. The opposite conditions exist near the center of flatsawn boards. Here, the growth rings are significantly more curved on the face that was closest to the pith; on the bark side, the rings are flatter. This configuration is likely to cause cupping when the MC changes.

When tabletops and the like are made from several boards glued edge to edge, cupping due to MC changes will be minimized when adjacent boards have opposite ring orientations, that is, when the inner (pith-side) face of one board is facing up and the inner face of the next is facing down, and so on. Then, if cupping occurs, it will be in opposite directions on adjacent boards. A trade-off is involved in this arrangement: Although the panel will not have a deep curve across the whole width, it may develop a rippled surface instead. A single curve can be controlled by fixing the panel to a base frame or by screwing stiff battens (cleats) to the underside, but it is difficult to do much about an undulating surface. Furthermore, arranging the boards with their pith-side faces either all up or all down might produce a more attractive panel.

Sometimes the need for stability overrides all other concerns, and you may need to combine all available stability-friendly measures. These include choosing a stable species and using quartersawn boards or the edges of boards where the growth rings are oriented at between 45 degrees and 90 degrees to the faces. You could also cut the wood into narrow strips and glue these together with the bark-side and pith-side faces alternating. Since all the strips would be straight-grained, they would not be visibly mismatched.

After you have milled pieces that must stay flat and straight without restraints, leave them for as long as possible before using them. Doing so will provide a final opportunity for you to discard any pieces that have unsuspected warping tendencies. Place the milled pieces on wood strips (stickers) to allow air to circulate all around.

1.18 Growth rings at the edges of a wide flatsawn board may be similar to those of a radially sawn board

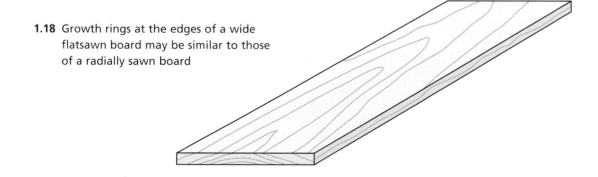

Any board, even a quartersawn one, may become cupped or bowed whenever the MC of one face changes more than that of the opposite face. Unlike the changes that occur when moisture is evenly distributed, the direction of cupping does not depend on the orientation of growth rings. If only one face shrinks, that face will become concave; if it expands, it will become convex. This can happen with completed work if an applied finish insulates one face more than the other against changes in humidity. Therefore, finishes that form a surface film should always be applied equally to all faces.

Take precautions with a work in progress; otherwise, it may warp between operations. If flattened components are left overnight with only one face exposed, they may cup. The precautions are simple: Just sticker them or stand them on edge to provide all-around air flow. Items that are especially vulnerable, such as thin resawn boards, should be wrapped in plastic or placed in a large plastic bag so changes in MC cannot occur.

Part 2
Starting a Project

2 Flattening Lumber

DOING FINE WOODWORKING IS impossible unless you start by making one face of every workpiece absolutely flat. You could flatten a board and bring it to the desired thickness using a hand plane, but it is hard work, requiring constant checking with a straightedge and winding sticks. This book is about getting first-class results easily with power tools, the most fundamental of which are the jointer and the planer.

Jointers and planers both create flat ("plane") surfaces. A jointer can flatten any face of a board, but a planer can flatten a face only if the opposite face is already flat. As well as flattening the second face, the planer makes the second face parallel to the first one and thereby gives the board a uniform thickness.

Planers have automatic feed systems, whereas jointers, by contrast, demand more operator control.

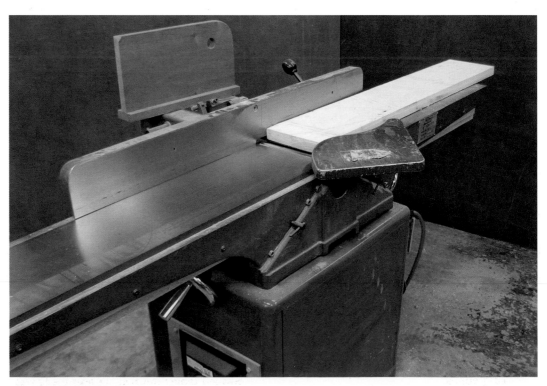

2.1 Eight-inch jointer

JOINTER AND PLANER SAFETY

Always follow the instructions in the machine manuals. Do not joint workpieces that are too short, too thin, or too narrow for safe handling. Never feed pieces through the planer unless they are longer than the distance from the infeed to the outfeed rollers.

THE JOINTER

The jointer's most important functions are to flatten one wide face of a board and to make an adjacent edge flat, straight, and perpendicular to it. If two opposite faces were flattened on the jointer, they might not be parallel, in which case the board would have uneven thickness.

A jointer that can flatten 8"-wide boards will be about 7 feet long and cost upward of $700. Four-inch and 6" machines are much cheaper and shorter. They will give you a 4"- or 6"-wide flat area that reduces handwork and provides a guide for flattening the rest of the board. It is important to be aware that on most machines it would be necessary to remove the guard in order to flatten boards that are wider than the jointer. You must never attempt this unless you can fit a temporary replacement guard that allows you to work safely. An 8" jointer with a board on its infeed table is shown in **2.1**.

The basic elements of a jointer are as follows:

1) a rotating cutterhead, typically with three blades, or knives;
2) an infeed table in front of the cutterhead and lower than the cutting edges;
3) an outfeed table level with the cutting edges;

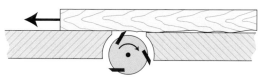

2.2 A board moving over the knives from the infeed to the outfeed table

4) a fence at 90 degrees to the tables; and
5) a pivoting guard over the cutters.

In **2.1**, a board has pushed aside the guard and is about to encounter the knives. A board moving over the knives, from the infeed to the outfeed table is shown in **2.2**.

The operator pushes the board being jointed along the infeed table and over the cutters. The difference between the heights of the infeed table and the cutters determines the depth of the cut. The outfeed table is level with the cutting edges, and the leading end of the board slides onto it after being cut. The operator's job is to push the board along the infeed table and over the knives while keeping the flattened end firmly on the outfeed table.

In **2.3**, the leading end of a board rests on the outfeed table after passing over the knives. Its cut surface will lie on the outfeed table and will be flat—provided that no

2.3 The leading end of a board rests on the outfeed table after passing over the knives

2.4 Using a pushstick at the jointer

rocking motion occurred during the forward movement. Even if the knives cut only parts of the board (because it is warped), those parts will make contact with the outfeed table, all in the same plane; subsequent passes will flatten the entire face. The process sounds simple, and it usually is.

Face Jointing

When you use a jointer for the first time, start with medium-size pieces of wood about 4" wide and up to 3 feet long. Make a pushstick similar to the one shown in **2.4**, and always keep it within reach.

Set the depth of cut to about $\frac{1}{32}$"; then, place your wood on the infeed table and start the machine. If the board is short, move it with the pushstick only. If it is longer, put the fingers of your left hand on the piece, well back from the knives, to hold it down, and use the pushstick at the trailing end to push it forward. You may have to push a long board forward with both hands at first, but always switch to the pushstick before your hands get near the cutters.

Listen to the sound of the knives. If the board is reasonably flat, you will hear the leading end being cut; if it is bowed, the ends may be higher than the knives, and cutting will begin farther back along the board. When a few inches have been cut, move your left hand forward to apply pressure above the cut surface on the out-

feed table. Never apply pressure with your hand above the knives: As your left hand approaches them, raise it, and replace it on the board safely beyond the blades. Always bear in mind the possibility of a kickback that might shoot the board backwards, leaving the knives exposed. I have never experienced a kickback from a jointer, but it could happen and I would not want to be pressing down above the knives when it does.

Apply enough pressure on the outfeed side to keep the cut surface on the outfeed table, but allow the board to slide under your hand. Apply less pressure on the infeed side. At the end of the cut, use the pushstick to push the board well past the knives and allow the guard to close. Then inspect the cut face and, if any of the original surface is still there, make another pass.

When a board is significantly bowed, it is usually best to cut it into smaller pieces. If you have to joint it in one piece, you may need to use a special technique to minimize loss of thickness. In these cases, first make one pass with the convex face of the bow down, and then inspect the cut face. If the start and finish of the cut are at roughly equal distances from each end, proceed as normal. If the cut area is close to one end but stops well short of the other, making more passes to extend the cut surface may produce a board that is too thin at one end. One end may even become too thin for jointing to continue safely. To prevent this, you need to make a tapered cut that extends to the rough end without removing any more material from the flattened end.

Tapering is actually easy to do; it is the way that items such as table legs can be shaped on the jointer. The technique involves laying the flattened end of the board on the outfeed table before starting a cut. If you do this, the flat end cannot be cut any more, but as you push the board forward, the cut will become progressively deeper, reaching full depth at the part that was touching the infeed table. If the cut still does not reach the rough end, you can repeat the procedure until it does without removing any more material from the front end. The procedure is as follows:

- Judge whether the piece you are about to joint can be flattened to an adequate thickness. Use a straightedge to help with your assessment. Substitute another piece if necessary.
- Joint the convex face and inspect it. If the cut area extends to about the same distance from each end, continue until the whole face is flat.
- If only one end has been flattened, stop the jointer and place about an inch of the flattened area on the outfeed table.
- Hold the board on the infeed table; start the jointer and push the board forward as normal to make a cut that becomes deeper as the board moves ahead.
- Make further taper cuts if necessary, stopping the machine each time until the cut surface is the same distance from each end. Then make full-length passes.

In all situations, you must prevent any rocking movement of the board when it is being jointed. The plane of the cut will change if any side-to-side or front-to-back rocking motion occurs after cutting has started. Any board that cannot be moved without rocking should first be made stable by removing its high spots with a hand plane. Alternatively, the board should be cut up and used for smaller components.

Edge Jointing

When one wide face of a board is flat, the edges can be jointed straight, flat, and

perpendicular to it. The procedure resembles face jointing, except that the board is on edge and its flattened face is held against the jointer fence while the edge is passed along the table and over the knives. As in face jointing, it is essential to prevent the workpiece from rocking, and taper cuts will sometimes be necessary.

If the boards are planed to thickness before the edges are jointed, you can place either face against the fence. This is essential when boards are going to be glued edge to edge (see Chapter 13, "Making Wide Panels"). Planing to thickness also allows you to minimize tear-out by choosing which end of the board should lead.

It is customary to joint only one edge initially and to rip the other edge parallel to it with a table saw. You may decide not to joint the ripped edge afterwards, depending on the purpose of the piece.

Jointing End Grain

Rarely, you will want to joint the end of a board. Two safety considerations are particularly important here:

1. If the piece is narrow, it could tip into the jointer throat, causing a kickback; and
2. Long pieces on end are difficult to control. I would advise against jointing the end of any piece that

2.5a Jointing end grain

2.5b Chamfered corner at trailing edge

2.6a Backing piece prevents end grain from splitting

2.6b Splitting occurs only on the backer board

is longer than 12" or any piece that is not at least 3" wider than the jointer throat.

Start by setting the infeed table for a very light cut. Hold the end of the workpiece on the infeed table, with a wide face against the fence; put downward pressure at the trailing edge to prevent the front edge from tipping down into the jointer throat. Move the workpiece slowly over the knives. Transfer the downward pressure to the leading edge when it is on the outfeed table.

Jointing the end grain will always cause some splitting at the trailing edge unless measures are taken to prevent it. If the end is jointed while the piece is at least a quarter of an inch too wide, the splitting can be removed afterward. Alternatively, a small chamfer sanded onto the trailing corner will prevent splitting (**2.5a** and **2.5b**).

If the piece is thick, a third option is to clamp a backer board to it. Splitting then affects only the backer board (**2.6a** and **2.6b**).

PLANING

A planer's main function is to reduce stock to an even thickness. It accomplishes this by cutting the upper face of a board to make it parallel to the lower face. Planer knives are mounted above a flat bed, and boards are moved over the bed by means of powered drive rollers, which pass the boards under the cutters and out the other side. If the distance between the bed and the knives is less than the thickness of the board, the upper surface will be planed. A single pass through the machine will reduce the board to an even thickness and give it a smooth upper surface. If the thickness is still greater than required, the knives can be lowered (or the bed raised, depending on the planer design) and further passes made.

The planed board will be flat only if its lower face was flat to start with. A planer may reduce cupping across the width to some degree, but it will have little effect on twist and no effect on bow in the length. Therefore, standard procedure is to flatten one face of every piece before planing it to thickness.

After the second face is made flat, the board can be turned over for subsequent passes. If several passes are necessary, planing each face alternately has advantages. By removing equal portions from each face, the internal stresses may remain in better balance; more importantly, equal planing will avoid exposing two faces with markedly different MCs. However, often it is necessary to preserve one good face and remove all excess thickness from the other, for example, when surface tear-out is likely or when further planing from the good face might expose defects or sapwood that should be confined to the back face.

DIRECTION OF FEED

Every board should be oriented in the direction of cutting so that the knives will not tend to lift the grain. This is called cutting with the grain. A board oriented so that the grain is sloping away from the rotation of the jointer knives is shown in **2.7**. A similar arrangement for a planer is shown in **2.8**. These orientations minimize any tendency for the cutters to lift the grain and produce tear-out.

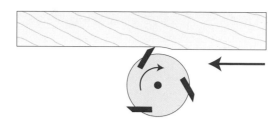

2.7 Jointing with the grain

2.8 Planing with the grain

Unlike hand planes, planing machines and jointers do not allow you to change the direction of a cut halfway along a board; thus, there is no correct orientation when the board has grain that reverses its slope halfway along its length. Even when the grain angle is constant, the apparently correct direction does not always give the best results.

On average, the best results come from feeding in the boards as illustrated in **2.7** and **2.8**. However, there will be many exceptions when you will get better results by reversing the boards end for end. So start off with the "correct" orientation, and then reverse it if the first pass produces bad tear-out.

When you are using a jointer, you can feed the work over the cutters slowly to reduce tear-out, but with a planer the speed is usually fixed. If planing causes tear-out on a board regardless of which way the board is fed into the cutters, you may be able to repair the best face by jointing it again and then continuing to plane it to thickness on the less important face.

JOINTER ADJUSTMENTS

Many woodworkers do not feel confident about adjusting a jointer and consequently tolerate less than ideal performance from their machine. This is a shame, because adjusting a jointer is not difficult, just a matter of following a simple procedure that anyone can carry out. With luck, your jointer will give perfect results for a long time before you need the information in this section, but you will need it when the knives have to be replaced. Even before then, it is worthwhile to check the adjustments to be sure you are getting optimum performance from the machine.

Two requirements mainly determine jointer performance: The knives must be set to the correct height in relation to the outfeed table, and the infeed and outfeed tables must be parallel to each other. It is important to be aware of the problems that result when either of these requirements are not being met.

Consider what happens when the outfeed table is significantly lower than the knives: As you begin to joint a board, the leading end will be higher than the outfeed table. Eventually, that end will tip downward. When this happens, the plane of the cut will change. Finally, the trailing end may drop when it leaves the infeed table, producing an extra-deep cut (snipe) for a short distance. The opposite situation—outfeed table too high—may result in the leading edge hitting the edge of the table, which will force you to stop and make adjustments. If the outfeed table is only slightly high, the board will ride up on the table's front edge, getting higher and higher until it eventually tips downward.

Problems will also occur if the outfeed table is not parallel to the infeed table. When this is the case, one table is either angled up or droops, so the cutters are at the trough or peak of a shallow V or

inverted V. In either situation, a board cannot make proper contact with the outfeed table. If the tables are drooping, the leading end of the board will at first touch only the edge of the outfeed table, but eventually will tip down and its trailing end will rise. If the tables slope upward from the knives, the depth of the cut will change as the leading end of the board climbs up the outfeed table.

If you suspect that your jointer is not performing optimally, you should check for all the above problems. Often, all that is needed is a small adjustment to the outfeed table height. Jointer geometry is complex and cannot be analyzed by simple trigonometry because small errors produce effects that change as the cut progresses. Thus, the solution lies not in analysis, but in rigorously checking the factors mentioned above and correcting them where necessary.

Checking That Tables Are Parallel

You will need a long straightedge and some feeler gauges to check whether the infeed and outfeed tables are parallel to each other. A straight aluminum rule the length of the jointer is ideal. Hold or clamp one-half of the straightedge to the outfeed table while the other half is projecting out over the infeed table. Raise the infeed table until it touches the straightedge, that is, to the level of the outfeed table. Check with the feeler gauges that both tables are making contact with the full length of the straightedge. If the tables are not, then corrective action is necessary.

Jointer tables are typically set into dovetail-shaped grooves machined into their base. The grooves are at an angle, so the height of either table can be adjusted by sliding it along the grooves. The tables fit loosely into the grooves, but metal plates called gibs are inserted between the tables and the groove walls to make the fit tighter. Gib screws are used to force the gibs against the tables and the groove walls; this controls tightness and possibly increases or decreases the table's droop. The amount of droop adjustment the gib screws yield is limited, so your jointer may incorporate other means of making the tables parallel. In any event, little adjustment should be necessary; if the jointer manual doesn't specify any other method, then gib screw adjustment is the first option. You will probably have to further adjust the infeed table height after each adjustment of the gib screws. If this doesn't do the trick, you can insert shims between a table and its grooves to lift either end. Thin metal is the proper material for shims, but layers of thin card will also work.

Setting the Knives

In typical cutterheads, each knife is held in a slot by a metal plate (another gib) that is jammed against it by screws. The heads of the screws push against one wall of a slot so that the knife is jammed against the opposite wall **(2.9)**. Larger machines may feature screws that force wedges in between the knives and the slot walls. Instruction manuals usually state that knives must be removed and replaced one at a time; that is, one replacement knife must be installed before loosening the next set of screws because a single slot should not be stressed while the others stand empty. Some cutterheads incorporate screws that adjust the knife height, and these are very helpful. Others have springs under the knives (I find these a nuisance and have discarded mine).

A jointer will work well only when the knife edges are almost exactly level with the surface of the outfeed table. Problems are likely to occur if the knives are $\frac{1}{1000}$" below the table, though there seems to be

2.9 Cutterhead, knife, gib, and gib screws

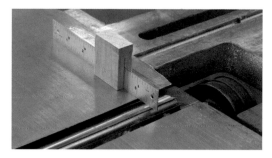

2.10 A small slotted block supports a straight-edge

more leeway if they are slightly higher than the table. The knives must be parallel to the outfeed table, so every part of an edge must be at the same height relative to the table. Also, each knife must reach the same height at the top of its arc.

Commercial devices are available to help adjust the knives' setting; they include devices that employ magnets to hold the knives level with the table while the knife-fixing screws are tightened. My preferred method, described herein, is to use a simple straightedge laid across the table that projects out over the knives. With any method, it is best to remove the jointer fence before starting to make the adjustments.

For the straightedge, you can rub the edge of a 6" steel rule on sandpaper taped to a flat surface, as described in Chapter 8 for straightening the edge of a card scraper. You will need to make a small wood block with a narrow slot in it, as shown in **2.10**, to hold the rule loosely on edge. Two other necessities are a thin

2.11 A flashlight illuminates the surface of the table near the cutterhead opening

2.12 Using backlight and a ruler to adjust the cutterhead height

screwdriver or similar device for levering the knives up and a small stick of wood for tapping them down.

Before you replace knives, you should check the replacements for straightness. To do this, place them on a flat surface and bring two edges together. If the edges are straight, check that the jointer is unplugged and then remove one of the old knives and its clamp plate. Remember— the old knives are still sharp enough to be dangerous. Clean out the knife slot and the plate; then insert a new knife, with the plate, into the slot.

Tighten the screw at each end of the plate just enough to hold the knife in place against gravity, but not enough to prevent it from being levered up or tapped down. Do not tighten the other screws, or they will become pivot points for the knife.

Arranging all the knives at the right height relative to the outfeed table is essential. By shining a light on the table at a low angle, you can see when a knife is just raising the rule. A flashlight positioned to illuminate the surface of the table near the cutterhead opening is shown in **2.11**.

Adjust the new knife with your levering device and wooden tapper until the rear edge of the bevel projects out of the cutterhead by $\frac{1}{16}$" or by the amount recommended in your jointer's manual. Place the rule and block on the table and extend the rule over the knife. If your outfeed table is adjustable, adjust it until it is approximately level with the edge of the knife.

Next, lever up and tap down the knife until just a tiny glimmer of light shows under the rule when it is raised by the knife at the top of its arc as you move the cutterhead by hand (**2.12**).

If your outfeed table is not adjustable, you should aim for the smallest gap you can achieve. If your hearing is good, you can set the knife so that no light is showing, provided you can hear it scrape under the rule. With an adjustable table, you can set larger gaps and reduce them later by raising the table.

Carry out this procedure at both ends of the knife, and make sure that the knife raises the rule the same distance in both places.

When the knife touches the rule the same way at either end of the blade, it is time to tighten all the clamping screws. This step could set you off on another round of adjustments because cutterhead knives have a habit of shifting as the screws are tightened. Your best chance of preventing this is to tighten the intermediate screws gently to the same degree as the end screws, and then to tighten the end screws a little more, and so on. By tightening each screw in stages, the knife is held at several positions before heavy pressure is applied at any one of them.

Once the first knife is set, repeat the procedure with the others, but do not adjust the table height. Set the other knives so that each of them raises the rule by the same amount as the first one.

If your outfeed table is adjustable, you can make further adjustments for accurate jointing. As a guide to table height, you can replace the rule with a small stick of wood, about $\frac{3}{8}$" × $\frac{3}{4}$" × 6". Place it on its narrow edge on the table and over the knives, and then rotate the cutterhead by hand. Adjust the table height until the knives drag the wood by less than $\frac{1}{8}$" as they pass. Find the best knife-to-table height by edge-jointing some boards that are about as long as your infeed table. Place the jointed boards edge to edge to see if they meet perfectly. When the jointer is edge-jointing perfectly, once again test how far the knives drag the stick and note this measurement for future reference.

PLANER PRACTICALITIES

A 12" planer is large enough for any amateur shop. Prices range from under $300 to around $2,000. The less expensive ones can give excellent results, but you will probably have to make lighter cuts than you would with a heavy-duty model. When choosing a machine, you should inquire about the ease of replacing the knives and whether it has facilities for making the bed parallel to the cutterhead.

When you use a planer for the first time, start with a test piece that is at least 6" wide and 12" long, with one flat face. Lower the planer bed (or raise the cutterhead, depending on the planer design) and insert the board under the cutterhead, flat face down. Raise the bed or lower the cutterhead until the infeed roller grips the board, and then loosen the grip enough to allow you to remove the board. Now raise the bed or lower the cutterhead by about $\frac{1}{8}$", start the planer, place the test piece on the bed, and allow the infeed rollers to pull it into the machine.

If any of the original rough surface remains after the board has passed through, adjust the bed or cutterhead for a further $\frac{1}{16}$" cut and then pass the board through again. Using measuring calipers or a micrometer, measure the thickness of the planed board at each edge. If the thicknesses differ, the board is tapered across its width and you should adjust the planer to correct this. Refer to the manufacturer's instructions to see what facilities your machine has for changing the height of one side of the bed or cutterhead. Of course, the problem might be a result of knives that are poorly installed.

Sometimes an overly deep cut occurs a few inches from the trailing end of the board. This is called snipe, and it occurs if the trailing end rises slightly when it leaves the infeed roller and is no longer held down. The problem is common to all planers; however, it is usually only a couple of thousandths of an inch deep and can be removed very quickly by sanding. You can often prevent snipe by stopping the trailing end from rising: Simply lift the leading end as it leaves the planer bed. Snipe can also occur at the leading end of a board before it reaches the outfeed roller. The solution here is to pull up on the trailing end of the board until it is under the control of both feed rollers.

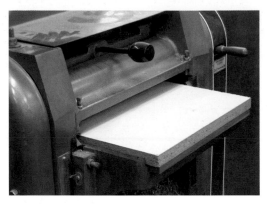

2.13 Auxiliary bed for planer

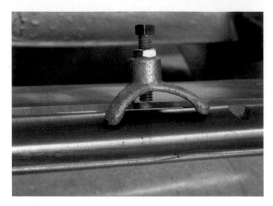

2.14 Planer knife-setting gauge

Some machines have rollers set into the bed to help feed boards that are rough on both faces. Because you will never plane a board without first jointing one face, you do not need them. They can be a positive nuisance, especially when planing thin material; even if they are set level with the bed, the discontinuity in the bed may cause thin material to flex. Therefore, I keep my bed rollers level with the bed. When I plane anything less than $\frac{1}{2}$" thick, I install an auxiliary bed to cover the roller openings. The auxiliary bed is a simple piece of $\frac{3}{4}$" melamine-faced chipboard that covers the planer bed and has a cleat underneath to stop it from being pulled into the machine **(2.13)**. Plain chipboard, plywood, or MDF (medium-density fiberboard) can also be used if the face is smooth. The easiest way to smooth the face is to give it a couple of coats of shellac and then to sand it with fine sandpaper. Shellac dries so fast that you could make and finish an auxiliary bed in a few minutes.

Adjusting the Planer Knives

It is not necessary to reference planer knives to the bed if the cutterhead and the bed can be made perfectly parallel. However, the knives must all project exactly the same amount from the cutterhead, from end to end. Some devices for setting them incorporate a dial gauge in a special base, but these are unnecessarily sophisticated. You need only ensure that the knife projection is the same for them all, a task that can be done without a dial gauge. An adequate setting gauge can consist of a simple carrier for a screw, as shown in **2.14**. The carrier rests on the cutterhead at each side of a knife slot, and the rounded head of the screw points down from it to the edge of the knife. When the knife is set correctly, the screw just touches it. The gauge shown here has a tripod base and a central screw and locknut.

When you install or adjust a knife, set it to project from its slot by an amount recommended by the manufacturer—typically about $\frac{1}{4}$". Then, place the metal carrier on the cutterhead at one end and adjust the screw until you feel it lightly contacting the edge of the knife when you move the carrier. Lock the screw at this setting, and adjust the knife until the screw lightly touches it at any position. A change in height of as little as $\frac{1}{1,000}$" produces a marked change in the sound and feel of the screw tip scraping over the blades. Use the same screw setting for the other knives.

Part 3
Working on Flattened Parts

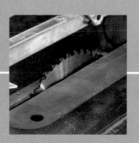

3 The Table Saw

ON A GOOD TABLE SAW, FINE WORK almost happens by itself. When the saw is properly adjusted, the right procedures guarantee straight and accurate cutting. A quality machine is easy to set up initially, and will hold its settings; bargain basement alternatives, on the other hand, can make life difficult, so give the table saw priority when planning the workshop budget.

The machine is used for many different operations, but its two most important functions are making straight cuts down the length of a board (rip cuts) and across a board (crosscuts).

In ripping operations, as shown in **3.1**, a guiding fence (the rip fence) is a straight-edge that can be fixed at any position parallel to the blade. The distance between the fence and the blade determines the width of the board after ripping.

In **3.1**, the workpiece is being pushed forward with a pushstick, and its right-

3.1 Using a rip fence

3.2 Splitter and anti-kickback pawls

3.3 Blade guard and splitter seen from behind

hand edge slides against the fence. The blade cannot be seen because it is covered by a guard.

In **3.2**, the guard has been raised to show the blade. The large black plate behind the blade is the splitter, which prevents the cut from closing on the blade. The semi-circular piece against the splitter is one of the anti-kickback pawls that prevent the workpiece from being thrown back, toward the operator.

During normal use, as in **3.3**, the guard is down to protect the operator from making accidental contact with the blade. Note the table surface behind the table saw meant for the workpiece to rest on after it is cut.

In crosscutting operations, boards are held against a miter gauge, a short sliding fence perpendicular to the blade. The miter gauge can be moved only in a straight line toward and away from the blade; it is limited to straight-line movement by a bar that slides within a slot in the saw table. The miter gauge in use is shown in **3.4**; how it looks when removed from the table saw is shown in **3.5**.

3.4 Miter gauge in use

3.5 Miter gauge removed from the table saw

3.6 Miter gauge fence set at an angle to the miter bar

3.7 Making an angled crosscut with the miter guage

3.8 Pushstick for rip cuts

A variation on crosscutting, called mitering, is carried out with the miter gauge fence at an angle other than 90 degrees to the blade (**3.6** and **3.7**). The miter gauge still moves in the same straight line, guided by the table slot.

For much of table-saw work, the blade is kept vertical, though most machines are equipped with a tilting-arbor facility that enables the blade to be set at any angle up to 45 degrees from vertical. This facility provides an alternative method of mitering, as well as a way of cutting a beveled edge.

If the blade height is less than the thickness of a board, it will cut a groove; if the groove is cut across the grain, it is called a dado. Grooves wider than the normal blade thickness can be made with special blades or by making repeated cuts.

A pushstick should always be used when you are ripping material to less than 8" in width. A simple and effective pushstick that can be made in a few minutes with a bandsaw or jigsaw is shown in **3.8**. Its shape allows for two sticks to be cut from a single rectangular piece of wood. It stands about 6" high and 15" long, with a $\frac{3}{8}$" $\times$ 10" step at the front to give more control than a short notch would provide. The edges at the handle end are sanded smooth for comfort, and a circular depression cut into each side of the handle improves the grip.

TABLE-SAW SAFETY

A table saw looks dangerous—unlike some tools—but not all its dangers are obvious. The inexperienced operator may not realize that the blade can throw out a workpiece toward the operator. These kickbacks occur at such high speed that the operator has no chance of dodging the missile. Such things happen in an instant: The teeth of a typical table-saw blade may be moving at more than 100 mph, and an object thrown at this speed would take less than one-hundredth of a second to travel the short distance needed to hit the operator. Failure to follow safety instructions might even result in a kickback that drags a hand into the blade.

All table saws have safety devices to protect the operator against kickbacks or contact with the blade. However, certain tasks cannot be accomplished unless these devices are removed, and in such cases, shop-made alternatives are necessary. The standard devices then need to be reinstalled for normal work. As a result, it becomes tempting to operate the table saw routinely with neither standard nor shop-made safety devices in place. Obviously, this is a dangerous way of working and should not be allowed in any workshop.

Sometimes manufacturers do not clarify the reasons for particular safety instructions. For example, instructions that the rip fence must be carefully aligned with the blade might not explain that otherwise the fence could force a workpiece against the blade and cause a kickback. Other circumstances that can induce kickbacks are described in the following list to reinforce the fact that safety instructions should be followed at all times, regardless of convenience.

- Contact with the back of the blade: At the front of the blade, the teeth are moving downward and tend to hold the work against the table; teeth at the back are moving upward, and neither the workpiece nor the off-cut should ever be allowed to press against them or ride up onto them.
- Reaching over the blade while it is running presents an obvious danger of accidental contact. Also, the blade may make contact with the work the operator is retrieving from behind it.

In this event, the operator's hand might be pulled into the blade.
- If work is not pushed clear of the blade after being cut, it may become trapped between the blade and the fence. This could cause a violent kickback.
- The blade exerts a backward force (toward the operator) on work being cut. This force can cause the trailing end of the workpiece to pivot against the rip fence, pushing the leading end against the blade and resulting in a kickback.
- The tendency to pivot is greatest with short workpieces. Therefore, work being ripped should always have its longest edge to the fence, and the rip fence should not be used with workpieces shorter than the blade diameter. Extra care should be taken when ripping any piece that is less than twice as long as it is wide.
- A pushstick should make contact with the workpiece closer to the blade than to the fence; otherwise, the piece's tendency to pivot will be made worse.
- If the saw is used with the blade cover removed, objects are at risk of being dropped onto the blade and thrown forward.
- Guarding arrangements should include a splitter (sometimes called a spreader) behind the blade. When wood is ripped, its inner equilibrium is changed. This can cause the wood to distort and to press against the blade, or to pinch the blade if the kerf (the slot cut by the blade) closes up. Splitters reduce these risks.
- The edge of the workpiece against the fence must be straight. If the edge is convex, the work may pivot in toward the blade; if the edge is concave, the cut will not be straight if the points of contact change at either end of the fence.

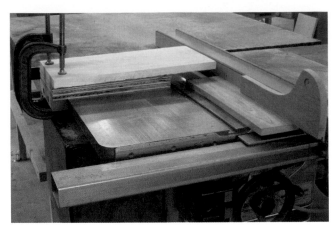

3.9 An example of special guarding arrangements

- If the bottom surface of the workpiece is not flat, it may wobble and put pressure on the blade, or it may become jammed between the blade and the fence, possibly resulting in kickback.

This list is by no means complete. It simply illustrates the fact that hazards are not always apparent, and therefore following manufacturers' instructions is doubly important.

It is inadvisable for the operator, or anyone else, to stand directly in front of the blade in case a kickback occurs.

GUARDING ARRANGEMENTS

Standard guards, supplied by table-saw manufacturers, cover the blade to protect the operator from making contact with it. They incorporate devices that will dig into the workpiece if it begins to move backward along with a splitter, which is a thin sheet of metal behind the blade that holds the work to the fence and keeps the kerf from closing. Standard guards generally incorporate the blade cover and the splitter into a single device; consequently, if the blade cover has to be removed, so must the splitter (and vice versa).

Table-saw manufacturers' standard guards leave much to be desired. In response, an aftermarket in improved guards has developed. Separate blade covers and splitters are available, which allows at least one of the safety measures to be used even if the job requires the other to be removed. They are usually less cumbersome and much easier to fit than all-in-one arrangements. In addition, advantages usually include better visibility of the work and the blade.

To allow certain cuts to be made, the guards may have to be removed. Examples of such cuts are narrow rip cuts (because the blade cover can impede the fence and the pushstick), cuts that do not go completely through the work (grooves and dadoes), and some beveled cuts. In all such cases, special guarding arrangements can be made to provide protection against kickback as well as to minimize the possibility of contact between hand and blade. In **3.9**, three boards have been clamped to the saw table, with the top one overhanging the blade. The arrangement offers some protection against kickback and prevents contact with the blade while allowing narrow rip cuts to be made. Just enough space remains between the top board and the rip fence for the pushstick to pass through.

Special guarding arrangements, like the one shown here, must be clamped to the saw table. However, doing this securely may be difficult if the underside of the table is not suitable for clamps. A block of wood bolted to the table edge can provide a clamping point. When using screw clamps on the saw table, check that vibration does not begin to loosen them.

When the pushstick is thicker than the distance between blade and fence, it must be modified to push the workpiece forward without touching the blade. The one shown in **3.10** has been shaped to facilitate the narrow rip cut mentioned above.

Featherboards, which have flexible fingers, can be fixed to the fence or saw table to hold work down or push it to the fence. They increase the accuracy of certain cuts and provide some protection against kickback by resisting any backward movement of the workpiece (**3.11** and **3.12**).

In **3.11**, the featherboard is locked into the miter slot. In **3.12**, it is screwed to a board that has been fixed to the rip fence.

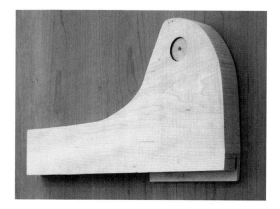

3.10 Pushstick shaped to make a narrow rip cut

TABLE INSERTS

An opening in the table surface gives access for changing the blade. In **3.13**, a removable plate with a slot for the blade is fitted in the opening during use. The insert plate features leveling screws that allow it to be made flush with the table surface. Occasionally, the standard insert has to be replaced with a shop-made version with a slot of exactly the same width as the blade teeth, to prevent narrow off-cuts from slipping down into the gap (**3.14**).

To make a zero-clearance insert (as these replacement plates are called), plane a piece of hardwood to a thickness $\frac{1}{8}$" less than the depth from the table surface to the lugs that the leveling screws rest on. First, draw the shape of the standard insert onto the wood; then cut the shape on a bandsaw, and sand it to fit freely in the opening. Screw a small flathead wood screw (e.g., #4 × $\frac{1}{2}$") into the underside at each leveling position to allow the new insert to be made flush with the table surface.

With the table-saw blade fully lowered, place the insert into the opening and make it level with the table. Lock the rip fence in position over it to hold it down, and then start the saw. Raise the blade slowly to cut a slot that is exactly as wide as the teeth. Stop the saw and remove the insert;

3.11 Featherboard holding work to the rip fence

3.12 Featherboard used as a hold-down

3.13 Table-saw insert

3.14 Zero-clearance insert

next, make another slot in it with either a bandsaw or a handsaw and chisel to accommodate the guard and splitter.

BLADES

Medium- and high-quality blades usually have tungsten-carbide teeth that will cut cleanly and sharply for a long time. Blades with high-quality steel teeth can give a superior cut, but they require frequent sharpening. Most craftspeople prefer carbide-toothed blades on account of their long service between sharpenings. Tooth designs that are best for cutting with the grain are different from those intended for cutting across the grain. Although combination blades have teeth that can work for both ripping and cross-cutting, the best results come from using separate rip and crosscut blades.

The teeth of most medium-quality rip blades are about $\frac{1}{8}$" thick and produce a $\frac{1}{8}$" kerf. Narrow-kerf rip blades make a cut that is only $\frac{3}{32}$" wide; they will cut with less resistance and can significantly reduce waste when multiple narrow strips are ripped from a board. However, narrow-kerf blades are more prone to flexing and vibration, which can result in rough surfaces. Another drawback is that

many splitters are too thick to be used with a narrow-kerf blade.

Wide grooves and dadoes can be made by repeated cuts with an ordinary rip or crosscut blade, but it is more convenient to make them with a dado cutter. Dado cutters come in two varieties, and the better type is a set of blades that can be stacked together to increase their tooth width. The other type is a blade that is designed to wobble as it rotates. The degree of wobble determines the width of cut and is adjustable. Note that you must install a table insert with a wider opening before using a dado blade.

RIP FENCES

A rip fence should be aligned parallel to the blade so that the workpiece does not push against the back of the blade. Although aligning a rip fence is easy, cheap rip fences may need to be realigned every time they are moved. Because few woodworkers are willing to check the alignment repeatedly, these fences are inherently dangerous. They may also tend to move out of position as their locking handle is operated, making precision work tedious and frustrating. The solution to these problems is to throw away the cheap fence and to buy a better one. A good-quality fence is a sensible investment if your table saw can accommodate one.

The best-known type of quality rip fence is the T-square fence, shown in **3.1**. It has a crosspiece of heavy-duty metal rigidly fixed to its front end at a 90-degree angle to its length. A locking handle clamps this crosspiece against an equally heavy-duty bar, which attaches to the front of the table. After being adjusted once, such a fence will align perfectly every time. And when necessary, this type of fence can be lifted off the table and replaced instantly on the other side of the blade without requiring further adjustment.

For some jobs, you may need to increase the fence height by fixing a piece of wood or plywood to it. This addition can improve safety for certain jobs and provide a surface to which featherboards and other items can be screwed.

MITER GAUGES AND CROSSCUT SLEDS

The metal fence of the miter gauge is usually about 8" in length and 2" in height. It has holes bored through it to allow a wooden supplementary fence to be screwed to its face. Such added fences can be made longer or higher to suit the job at hand. While the metal fence may reach no closer than an inch or so from the blade, a longer fence fixed to it, and then cut off by the blade, will show the exact location of the cutting line **(3.15)**.

An extended miter gauge fence offers other advantages: It can have a stop block fixed to it for cutting a series of pieces to identical lengths, and it will help hold a workpiece steady during a cut. This increased stability is particularly important when the fence is angled, because the blade will tend to push the workpiece

along, or away from, the fence. Sandpaper glued to the wood fence will further improve the workpiece's stability. (For the sake of the blade, however, sandpaper should not extend to the cutting line.)

Extended fences may need to be shaped (as is the one in **3.15**) so they can pass under the blade cover. This will probably require a simple notch at the blade end of the fence.

Whenever a stop block is fixed to the miter gauge, the work must be held firmly

3.15 A miter gauge fence extension shaped to pass under the blade guard; the end of the fence has been cut off by the blade to provide an exact cutting line

3.16 Miter gauge used in conjunction with a stop block on the rip fence

against the fence; otherwise, kickback could result. Of course, this system cannot be used for cutting short pieces, because it would require the operator's fingers to come dangerously close to the blade.

For repeated short cuts, a better method is to use a stop block clamped to the rip fence, as shown in **3.16**. The rip fence can then be locked in a position such that the work butts up against the block before the miter gauge pushes it forward.

Position the block on the rip fence sufficiently forward of the blade for the workpiece to move beyond the block before it reaches the blade. In this way, you avoid any possibility of the cut-off piece being trapped between the block and the blade. The block must also be wide enough so that the distance from the rip fence to the blade is greater than the diagonals of the cut-off piece; otherwise, the piece might become trapped between the blade and the fence. The rip fence must never be used as a length stop without the stop block.

A stop block can be made more easily adjustable by inserting a machine screw into it and butting the workpieces against the screw head, as shown in **3.17**. By turning the screw, fine adjustments can be made. A screw will cut its own thread in a hole that is about one drill-size smaller than the screw diameter. Putting furniture wax in the hole and the screw threads will make it easier to install the screw.

For crosscutting square to the blade, an alternative to the miter gauge is a shop-made device called a crosscut sled. It is a baseboard with a miter bar fixed under it and a fence screwed to it (**3.18**). The sled functions much like a miter gauge, with the major difference being that the baseboard straddles the blade to carry off-cuts past it and bring them back again. A second advantage is that the baseboard eliminates drag between the workpiece and the table. The two sides of the baseboard are held together by the fence at the back and a hardwood block at the front. Both the fence and the block are tall enough to remain sturdy after being cut by the blade at full height.

The saw kerf in the sled can be an accurate guide for positioning a workpiece at the cutting line, that is, until the kerf edges become worn or a different blade is installed. You can obtain a fresh cutting line by screwing a piece of $\frac{1}{8}$" MDF to the baseboard. The cutting line can be regularly renewed by shifting the MDF closer to the blade.

Guarding must be installed where the blade emerges behind the sled fence. A box structure fixed to the back of the sled

3.17 Screw adjustment for a stop block

3.18 Crosscut sled

will do the job, in conjunction with stop blocks on the sled and saw table to arrest the sled before the blade cuts into the box (**3.19** and **3.20**).

The sliding bar for the sled can consist of a length of hardwood, planed and sanded to run smoothly within the miter slots. A metal bar would be better, however, because its fit will not change when the relative humidity changes.

When a crosscut sled is used, standard blade guards must be removed. It is possible to devise alternative guards that fit the sled, but I usually avoid the problem by using a sort of hybrid miter gauge and crosscut sled: a miter gauge with an added fence that has a piece of MDF screwed to the bottom (**3.21**). It gives me an accurate cutting line, eliminates drag between the workpiece and the table, and can be used with the standard guard in place.

USING THE TABLE SAW

Never cut anything freehand on a table saw: Always use a fence to guide the workpiece.

Material to be cut must be flat enough to be stable as it is pushed along. In addition, the edge that goes toward the fence must be straight. Therefore, every workpiece should be checked for stability on the table and against the rip fence or miter gauge. Any instability should be corrected by jointing, by removing the high spots with a hand plane, or by cutting the material first with a bandsaw or jigsaw.

In the special case of a workpiece that is badly cupped but stable when its concave face is down, you should be aware that when it is ripped, it will drop closer to the table and may press against the blade. To prevent this, first improve the flatness of the piece with a hand plane or jointer. A cupped board should not be cut with its convex face down.

3.19 Box guard at back of sled

3.20 Sled travel is stopped when a block fixed to the sled meets a block fixed to the table

3.21 A miter gauge with an extended fence and a baseboard

Provide a support surface level with the outfeed side of the saw table so you do not have to worry about catching workpieces after they are cut. Provide extra outfeed support for very long workpieces.

If all necessary adjustments have been made, and the guard system is in place, prepare to make a rip cut by clamping the fence in position and setting the blade height to $\frac{1}{8}$" more than the thickness of the workpiece. Use one hand to push the board forward and the other to keep it down and pushed to the fence. While the trailing edge of the workpiece is on the saw table, use a pushstick to move it forward; if the workpiece is long, use the pushstick when the trailing end reaches the saw table. Position the pushstick closer to the blade than to the fence, but always between them—never push on the off-cut side of the work. Do not allow the hand without the pushstick to come closer than 6" to the blade.

Keep the workpiece moving until it completely passes the blade. Do not attempt to remove workpieces or cutoffs while the blade is moving, and never reach over the moving blade even though it is guarded.

If the blade is tilted to make beveled rip cuts, place the fence on the side away from the direction of the tilt. If the blade is tilted for making cuts with the miter gauge, use the miter slot also on the side away from the direction of the tilt.

To make 90-degree crosscuts with the blade vertical, the miter gauge is usually installed in the left-hand miter slot. When using the miter gauge in this slot, hold the workpiece down and toward the gauge fence with the left hand while pushing the gauge forward with the right. Reverse hand positions whenever the right-hand slot is used. Do not crosscut short workpieces that would require bringing a hand too close to the blade.

Whether you are ripping or crosscutting, do not push directly in line with the blade. You should not have to push the work with significant force: If force is necessary, something is wrong. A clean, sharp blade will cut with minimal resistance unless the workpiece is binding somewhere, whereas blunt or dirty blades require more feed force. Pushing hard is dangerous.

CUTTING ROUGH LUMBER

As a general rule, parts should always be cut to rough size before being flattened because this minimizes the amount of flattening required. Exceptions would be parts too small to be flattened safely as individual pieces. However, sawn boards from the lumberyard are often neither flat enough nor straight enough to be ripped safely on a table saw. At the same time, they are too long for crosscutting on a table saw. Crosscutting them on a bandsaw would be safer, but long boards are too unwieldy for the process, and any attempt would probably result in a broken blade.

Before parts can be cut from a sawn board, some of the board's length has to be sacrificed to remove any splits. When lumber is first dried, it usually develops splits in the ends. These splits may be very short or several inches long, and they may close up and become invisible. To detect them, you must cut short pieces from the ends and then rap the pieces hard on the workbench. If the end pieces break, cut more pieces further down until rapping hard does not break them.

Several types of saw are available for crosscutting long boards to rough length: These include the circular saw, the hand-held jigsaw, the radial arm saw, and the sliding miter saw (if it has adequate width capacity). If necessary, you can obtain the rough parts by making complex cuts along and across the grain with a jigsaw.

After the boards have been cut into manageable lengths, the parts can be cut to rough widths with a bandsaw. They can be cut to length and width on the table saw after they have been given at least one flat face and one straight edge.

ADJUSTING THE TABLE SAW

Your table saw should be adequately adjusted by the manufacturer. But in case it isn't, or in case a part has shifted, you should carry out some tests before using it for serious work.

Before starting any adjustments, mill a couple of strips of wood to about $\frac{3}{4}$" × 2" × 20" for use as test pieces. Make a third piece that is $\frac{3}{8}$" × $\frac{3}{8}$" × 6". Except for when test pieces are being cut, the table saw should be unplugged during all the following procedures.

To start, make the miter bar fit properly into the slots so that it slides freely but without too much play. The initial fit is unlikely to be too tight; instead, it may well be too loose. To correct this, make a series of dimples along one side of the bar with a hammer and a pointed nail punch. The raised edges of the dimples will make the fit tighter. If the fit becomes too tight, file down the dimples lightly until the bar runs easily in the slot.

The next step is to check the slots for parallelism with the blade:

- Set the blade to vertical at its maximum height.
- Hold the $\frac{3}{8}$" × $\frac{3}{8}$" × 6" test piece against the miter gauge fence and have it make light contact with a tooth at the front of the blade. Mark the tooth with crayon or a felt-tip pen, and turn the blade backward and forward so you can feel the tooth rubbing on the wood.

- Hold the piece of wood at the same place on the fence, and rotate the blade backward until the marked tooth is at the same height at the back end of the opening in the table-saw insert.
- Push the miter gauge and test piece to the back of the blade, and move the blade backward and forward to rub the marked tooth against the wood again. If the blade touches the wood in the same way it did when it was at the front, the miter slot is parallel to the blade. If it misses the wood, or rubs harder than it did at the front, the slot and blade are not parallel.

If the slots are not parallel, the table must be moved slightly, relative to the blade, until the feel of the marked tooth touching the wood is the same when the tooth is at the back as when it is at the front of the insert slot. Procedures for adjusting the table should be detailed in the setup instructions supplied with the saw. A rubber hammer or a block of wood and a hammer will be useful for shifting the table position when its fixing bolts are loosened.

This is a suitable point at which to check and adjust the splitter alignment (the manufacturer's instructions for this may involve using the miter slots, which are now aligned with the blade). The procedure may vary from one splitter to another, so follow the manufacturer's instructions.

Check the accuracy of the blade tilt adjuster at its blade-vertical setting:

- Turn the tilt control fully to the stop at the 0-degree end of its scale.
- Place a square on the table, against the fully raised blade between the teeth, so that the square touches only the disc of the blade.
- If the blade is not vertical, adjust the stop and the tilt wheel until it is.

This straightforward method depends on the blade disc being perfectly flat. Another simple method is to rip a thick piece of wood, or crosscut a piece on edge, and then check that the cut face is square with the bottom face.

A more accurate method of checking blade verticality involves crosscutting one of the ¾" × 2" × 20" test pieces with the miter gauge. To use this method, follow these steps:

- Set the miter gauge to its square-cutting position, and hold a 2" face of the test piece against it while cutting about 3" from the end.
- Stop the saw and leave one piece standing on the edge that is already on the table. Flip the other piece onto its opposite edge and push the cut ends together, as in **3.22**.
- Inspect the junction of the two pieces: If the blade is vertical, there will be no gap between the two ends. If it is not vertical, there will be a gap at the top or bottom of the abutting ends. Any angle between the ends will be double the angle error of the blade, making this an accurate method of testing.
- Adjust the blade angle if necessary, and repeat the test until the two ends butt together perfectly.

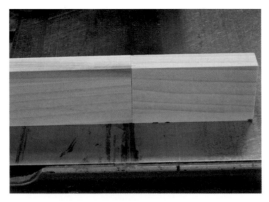

3.22 Aligning two crosscut pieces of wood to test blade verticality

- Adjust the 0-degree-tilt stop so that the setting can be quickly restored after future changes.

Use the same principle to check the 45-degree setting of the blade:

- Turn the tilt adjuster until it hits its 45-degree stop; then crosscut a test piece on edge.
- Lay both pieces on their wide faces, with one piece flipped over, and bring the cut ends together to make a corner.
- Check the corner angle with a square (**3.23**). If it is 90 degrees, the blade was at 45 degrees.
- If the corner angle is not 90 degrees, adjust the blade angle. It may be necessary to adjust the angle stop screw first. Repeat the test.
- Lock the 45-degree stop at the correct position.

Check the miter-gauge fence angle at its 90-degree setting. A quick method is to use a square to check the angle between the fence and the miter bar; a more accurate test is as follows:

- Set the blade to vertical at maximum height, and set the miter gauge to its square-cutting position.
- Crosscut another test piece, this time with a ¾" edge held against the miter gauge and a 2" face on the table.
- Stop the saw, and stand both pieces on the table on the edges that had been toward the gauge.
- Flip one of the cut pieces over onto its opposite edge, and bring both cut ends together. If the miter gauge was square to the miter slots, there will be no gap between the two ends. If it was not, there will be a gap at the top or bottom of the abutting ends. The angle between the two ends will be double the setting error.

- Adjust the setting and repeat the test until the pieces butt together perfectly when one is flipped over.
- Adjust the miter gauge stop screw so the 90-degree crosscut setting can be obtained reliably at any time.

A similar method is used to check the 45-degree setting of the gauge:
- Turn the gauge to its 45-degree stop; crosscut a piece of wood at this angle, with a 2" face on the table.
- Flip one piece over and lay down both pieces on their wide faces to make a corner. Check the corner angle with a square: If it is exactly 90 degrees, the miter gauge was correctly set at 45 degrees. Again, any error in the gauge setting will be doubled in the corner.
- Adjust the gauge angle if necessary and repeat the test. Once the setting is correct, adjust the stop screw so the 45-degree position can be set reliably at any time.

Next, check the rip fence for alignment with the blade. Alignment must be checked with the fence locked; it is correct when the distance from the fence to the back of the blade is the same as the distance to the front of the blade. The fence must never angle toward the back of the blade. Since the miter slots have already been made parallel to the blade, measurements can be made in relation to them instead of to the blade. It may also be easier to measure the distance from the fence to the miter bar in the slot; a strip of thin material placed under the bar to raise it slightly will facilitate this **(3.24)**.

3.23 The corner angle will be exactly 90 degrees if the table-saw blade was set to exactly 45 degrees

3.24 Measuring the distance from the fence to the miter bar in the slot

4 The Bandsaw

4.1 In this photo and in 4.2, the bandsaw's covers and blade guards are removed to show the machine components. The machine must never be used with the covers or guards removed

A BANDSAW BLADE IS A TOOTHED steel ribbon that passes over tires on two or more pulley wheels, one of which is driven by a motor **(4.1)**. When the covers and guards are in place, the blade is exposed only at the cutting position. Other important components of the bandsaw are a flat table, a stiff support frame, a blade tension adjuster, a tracking adjuster, and blade guides.

An adjustable spring pushes the top wheel upward to apply tension to the blade, but even though it is taut, the blade can be deflected by thrust from a workpiece. Deflection is resisted by guides on each side of the blade and by thrust bearings behind it, as shown in **4.2**. This arrangement is duplicated above and below the table to keep the blade as straight as possible at the cutting position. The top guides and bearing are supported on a post that can be adjusted vertically to allow a workpiece to pass under them. The guides are usually metal blocks or ball bearings set a few thousandths of an inch from each side of the blade. A type of guide made from low-friction material can be positioned to touch the blade.

At the cutting position, the teeth move downward at high speed, thereby holding the workpiece down while cutting it. The bandsaw can crosscut, rip, cut curved shapes, resaw (cutting within the thickness of a board to make two thinner ones), and handle boards that are too thick for a table saw. Also, a bandsaw does all these tasks without the risk of kickback, so it is safer than many other machines. While it may not be absolutely essential, a bandsaw is very versatile and a worthwhile investment.

BANDSAW BLADES

Blades are obtainable with various tooth patterns, including straight-toothed, where the leading edge of each tooth is at 90 degrees to the blade; hook-toothed (like the one in **4.2**); with closely or widely spaced teeth; with no gaps between the teeth; or with a skip-tooth arrangement, in which every other tooth is missing. Except on special-purpose blades, the teeth are set (bent alternately

to left and right) to cut a kerf wide enough to allow the blade to cut curves.

Bandsaw blades also come in various widths. The narrower blades can follow tighter curves. Wide blades are less likely to deviate from a straight line when they are used for resawing.

I use a $\frac{3}{4}$" blade with three teeth per inch for resawing and a $\frac{1}{4}$" blade with four teeth per inch for most other work. Both are hook-tooth blades without the skip-tooth arrangement. These two blades cover most situations, including those that arise in this book's projects. On many machines, it may be necessary to use a $\frac{1}{2}$" blade in place of the $\frac{3}{4}$" one; check with the manufacturer to find the maximum-size blade that can be properly tensioned on your machine.

4.2 Above the table, a guidepost supports a thrust bearing behind the blade and a blade guide at each side. The post can be raised and lowered to provide clearance above the workpiece. There are similar guides and another thrust bearing below the table

MACHINE SIZE

Bandsaw size is the horizontal distance from the cutting position to the machine structure. A 12" bandsaw can reach to the center of a 2-foot-wide workpiece; an 18" machine can cut to the center of a 3-foot-wide board. The machine's size can limit workpiece length as well as width, because a long, narrow workpiece may be obstructed by the support post during a curved cut or during crosscutting. A useful size for the home workshop is 14", although in this case, bigger is better.

Another limitation on workpiece size is the maximum height setting of the guidepost. Small machines may not be able to accommodate very thick workpieces, and even with large machines, the guidepost limits the width of a board that can be resawn.

USING THE BANDSAW

Unlike rotating blades, a bandsaw blade does not pose a threat of kickback. However, if a workpiece is held above the bandsaw table when it touches the blade, it may be rammed down onto the table by the blade. The blade may be moving at more than 50 feet per second, so work should always be placed firmly on the table before it comes in contact with the blade. By keeping the guidepost as low as possible, you will make it less likely that in a moment's thoughtlessness you will hold the workpiece away from the table as you push it into the blade.

Operator contact with a bandsaw blade is, of course, just as dangerous as contact with a rotating blade, so similar precautions are necessary. All the covers and blade guards must be in place during the machine's operation, and a pushstick must be used to avoid bringing hands close to the blade. In particular, a pushstick should be used to help you complete through-cuts where your hands are close to the line of cut: for example, when you are completing a resawing operation. Always be aware that an unsuspected fault in the workpiece might cause it to suddenly accelerate into the blade while you are pushing it.

Before starting the machine, minimize the blade exposure by adjusting the guidepost so that the guides barely clear the top of the workpiece.

I do not try to make precise cuts with a bandsaw except when I am resawing a board. In general, I am content to cut at about $\frac{1}{16}$" from my marked line and then finish the job by other means. If you aim to cut very close to your line, you run a great risk of cutting into it: Remember, a workpiece may be ruined by an overly deep cut at any spot. Cutting at an adequate distance from your outline does more than provide a margin for error; it allows for sanding off tooth marks, which are generally a lot deeper than those made by circular blades.

When operating a bandsaw, a slow forward movement is the key to minimizing mistakes. Just accept the fact that bandsawing is a time-consuming procedure for which you have to be patient. If you cut slowly enough, you will have plenty of time to make corrections when the blade starts to crowd the line. When the blade gets too close to the line for comfort—and this will happen frequently—do not try to recover your margin while cutting; instead, back up a little and restart the cut with a fresh margin.

Always plan the sequence of your cuts before you begin. Make relief cuts first so that the blade never gets trapped in the kerf and so you do not have to back out from a long or curved cut. A numbered sequence of cuts for the shaped base of the Chest of Drawers project in Chapter 19 is

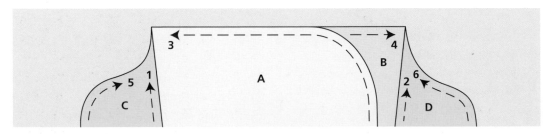

4.3 A numbered sequence of cuts for the shaped base of the Chest of Drawers project

shown in **4.3**. The blade must be backed out after cuts 1 and 2, and waste pieces can fall away in the sequence A, B, C, D after each of the other cuts.

While you are trying to maintain a constant margin in relation to your outline, you also must avoid exerting side thrust on the blade. Even though the guide blocks or bearings hold the blade in position above the workpiece and below the table, it is still possible to push the blade out of vertical alignment between the upper and lower pairs of guides. If this happens, the cut will not be square to the faces of your workpiece and the blade may break. This is more likely when using narrow blades, which deflect easily, and with thick workpieces, for which the distance between the upper and lower guides is greater.

GUIDING THE WORK

For most straight cuts, I do not use a bandsaw fence because I find that cutting freehand is just as accurate and less trouble. However, when I am resawing a wide board, I clamp a guide to the table to help keep the board parallel to the blade.

The guide is a tall piece of wood fixed to a base that can be clamped to the bandsaw table. First I clamp it just in front of the blade, almost touching the teeth; then I adjust the table tilt to make the guide exactly parallel to the blade. Next I move the guide a little farther from the blade to allow the blade to cut through the center of the workpiece when it is held against the guide. In **4.4**, preliminary cuts have been made with a table saw into each edge of the workpiece.

The guide edge is narrow in order to allow the workpiece to be pivoted around it. When it is correctly positioned, it will help you keep the workpiece parallel to the blade while you guide the cut.

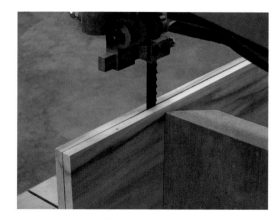

4.4 Resawing with the bandsaw

CHANGING BLADES

When you change a blade, you have to remove or reposition several parts of the machine. These include the top and bottom wheel covers, the blade tensioner, the tracking adjuster, the blade guides, blade thrust bearings, blade covers, and a pin that keeps the split halves of the saw table aligned with each other.

With the machine unplugged, remove the wheel covers and blade covers and then loosen the fixing screws of the guides and thrust bearings. Use a screwdriver, wrench, or Allen key as necessary. Push the guides and bearings clear of the blade, and then reduce the blade tension until the blade can be easily slipped off the wheels. Remove the table alignment pin, pull the blade off the wheels and clear of the guides, and guide it out through the table slot. Use gloves when handling the blade.

The blade needs to be stored safely. It could simply be hung from hooks on the wall, but it is better to fold it into loops as illustrated by photos **4.5** to **4.8**. To fold a blade, start by letting it hang from your hand, just touching the floor. Step on it lightly to keep it against the floor. Then put two twists into it and lower it toward the floor. As you lower the blade, it will fold

4.5 The first step in folding a bandsaw blade

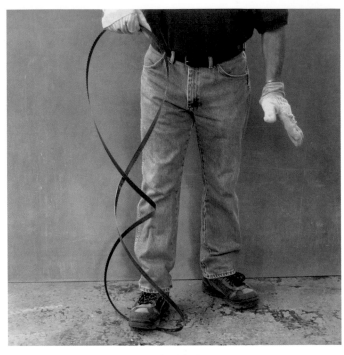

4.6 Putting two twists into the blade

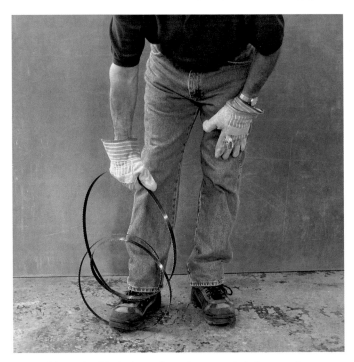

4.7 Folding the blade into three loops as it is lowered

4.8 The three loops are shaken until they are all the same size

itself into three loops. Hold the loops together and shake them until they are equal in size.

To install a new blade, hold it up by the machine with the teeth facing forward. If the teeth on the right-hand side of the loop (as seen from in front) are not pointing down, the blade needs to be turned inside out. Feed the right side of the loop through the table slot, with the back edge leading and the teeth pointing down, and then fit the blade over the wheels.

Turn the tension adjuster until the blade is held securely on the wheels, and then turn the wheels by hand until the blade takes a constant position on them. Be careful of the teeth while the blade is moving. Continue turning the wheels with one hand while turning the tracking adjuster with the other until the blade is running at the wheel tires' centers. Replace the blade covers.

Most bandsaws have a blade tension indicator showing where to set the tension adjuster for each size of blade. Cheap machines may have inaccurate indicators, and even on high-quality machines the tensioning spring may weaken so that the indicator is no longer reliable.

The Suffolk Machinery Corp., maker of Timber Wolf bandsaw blades, recommends the following test: running the machine and reducing the tension until the blade begins to flutter, then increasing the tension until the fluttering stops, and finally giving the tension adjuster another quarter turn. For a full description, see www.suffolkmachinery.com

After tensioning the blade, switch off and unplug the machine. Next, reposition and tighten the guide blocks and thrust bearings above and below the table. Set the thrust bearings to just clear the back of the blade so that the blade will touch them only when it is cutting. Fix the side guides to clear the blade by about the thickness of a dollar bill on each side (unless they are made of a material designed to touch the blade at all times).

Replace the table alignment pin. Last, plug in and start the machine, checking to see that it runs smoothly.

5 Routers

THE EASIEST WAY TO UNDERSTAND the router is by examining a typical router cutter, also known as a router bit.

The cutter shown in **5.1** has cutting edges on its sides and end. If it is driven by a rotary motor, it can bore a hole; if it is moved sideways as it rotates, it can cut a slot; if the sideways movement is suitably guided, the slot can become a perfect mortise or an opening of any shape. The corners of the slot or opening will have the same radius as the cutter.

Since the tool in **5.1** has a constant diameter, it will make straight-sided, flat-bottomed cuts, but consider the other cutters shown below.

The cutter in **5.2** can produce a round-bottomed groove; the one in **5.3** can cut a slot with angled sides (a dovetail slot); **5.4** shows a cutter for making a round edge; and the cutter in **5.5** would make an edge with a complex shape. These router bits are just a tiny sample of the variety available. With the appropriate bit, a router can be used to make any cutout, slot, channel, rabbet, or edge shape. With a suitable guide arrangement, a router can also be used for precision joinery.

A router comprises a high-speed motor, typically operating at 10,000 to 24,000 rpm, and a collet for holding a cutter, all in a housing that can be handheld or set into

5.1 A spiral router bit

5.2 Bit for producing a round-bottom groove

5.3 Dovetail bit

5.4 Bit for making a rounded edge

5.5 Roman Ogee bit

5.1   5.2   5.3   5.4   5.5

5.6 Shaping an edge

5.7 A shaped edge

5.8 Completed edge, with router and bit

a special table. The collet is like a drill chuck, but it grips the bit all around the shank instead of at just three positions.

When the router is handheld, the cutter is moved along a workpiece; when it is fixed in a router table, the workpiece is moved past the cutter. Photos **5.6** and **5.7** show a handheld router cutting a shaped edge, and photo **5.8** shows the completed edge, with the router and bit.

The next six photographs (**5.9** through **5.14**) show a small selection of router bits and the cuts they can make.

5.9 Router bit making a chamfered edge

5.10 Bit for making a round-bottomed cut (a "core box" bit)

5.11 Coving bit

5.12 "Keyhole" bit

5.13 Specialty edge-shaping bit

5.14 A spiral mortising bit and mortise

5.9

5.10

5.11

5.12

5.13

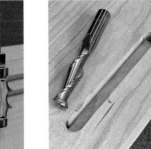

5.14

PLUNGE ROUTERS

Plunge routers incorporate a mechanism that allows the cutter to be lowered gradually into the workpiece and retracted up into the router again after a cut is made. Two identical plunge routers are shown in **5.15**: one with the cutter plunged below the base and the other with the cutter retracted.

The plunge mechanism is operated by pulling a locking lever while pushing the router body down or allowing it to rise under the mechanism's spring action. When the lever is released, the mechanism locks the router at its plunge depth. The router can be plunged in stages during a cutting operation, allowing successive cuts to be made instead of a single deep one. The lever can be controlled with a finger or thumb while the operator keeps a firm grip on the router handles (**5.16**).

Precise depth-of-cut settings are difficult to obtain solely by using the plunge mechanism, so plunge routers have an additional device to provide fine adjustment up or down. Fine adjusters are typically marked with 1/64" depth graduations. However, at least one model has an adjuster that is four times more finely graduated: Each marking represents a depth change of $\frac{1}{256}$", or about four-thousandths of an inch. When buying a router, it is important to check its fine-adjustment feature. The more precise the adjustment, the easier it is to set the depth each time the router is used. Ensure that the fine adjuster can make the final adjustment—if the system requires that the router must be plunged to an approximate depth and then plunged again after the fine-adjuster setting is changed, the tool will not be as convenient to use.

Plunge routers also have an adjustable depth stop, which serves two purposes. The stop prevents the plunging action from moving beyond a preset depth, and it allows for repeated plunging to exactly the same depth. To set the depth stop, first plunge the router to approximately the required depth of cut, and then release the plunge lever. Next, use the fine adjuster to increase or decrease the depth until it is exactly right. After the setting has been confirmed by a test cut, set the stop to prevent the router from plunging any deeper. Now you can raise the router from the plunged position and use it at any plunge level, down to the maximum set by the stop. In **5.17**, the depth stop is the rod at the left side of the router, fixed in position by the black thumbscrew. It is hitting the base of the router, preventing it from plunging deeper.

In **5.17**, note the stepped device directly below the depth stop. This is the depth stop turret, which is used to limit the plunge depth in small steps. When the turret is turned, it places different steps under the stop.

Many router applications do not require the cutting depth to be set to a high degree of accuracy. For example, a mortise that is supposed to be 1" deep will usually be just as satisfactory at $^{31}/_{32}$" or $1^{1}/_{32}$" because the tenon can be cut to suit the actual depth. For these applications, the depth stop provides a fast and easy way to set the cutting depth: The router is first placed on the work and then plunged until the cutter touches the surface; next, the depth stop is set to touch the router base and then raised by a distance that will allow the router to plunge to the required depth. Scale markings on the depth stop allow the adjustment to be made with an accuracy of about $^{1}/_{32}$" (**5.18**).

5.15 Two plunge routers: one plunged, one retracted

5.16 Using the plunge lever

5.17 Depth stop and depth-stop turret. The turret allows the cutting depth to be changed in preset stages

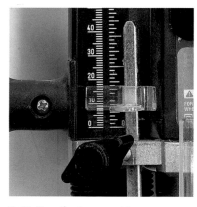

5.18 Depth-stop markings

ROUTER FEATURES

Not all routers have a plunge capability. Nonplunging routers cannot be used for cutting down into a surface to make stopped grooves and mortises, etc., although they can be used for shaping edges and for cuts that start at an edge. They have alternative depth-setting mechanisms that are easier to adjust than plunge routers, when mounted upside down in a router table. For this reason, many woodworkers have both types of router, but I find a plunge router adequate for all the handheld and router-table work that I do.

Many routers have a control that can vary the speed of the motor from around 10,000 rpm to 24,000 rpm or even more. The lower speeds are necessary when you are using large cutters that could develop dangerous centrifugal forces at the higher speeds. For small cutters (including most of the ones used for the projects in this book), the higher speeds are best.

Two other features are important in a router. The first is a spindle-locking device that allows the collet to be tightened with a single wrench; having to use two wrenches to install and remove cutters is an antiquated and annoying requirement. The second is a "soft-start" facility, that is, the router motor starts gradually and takes up to a second to reach full speed. Instant-start routers can jerk when they start.

GUIDING A ROUTER

The simplest guide is a straightedge clamped to the workpiece so that the router can be held against it while it is moved along. Photo **5.19** shows a router being moved along a straightedge guide, that is, along a fence. A stop block is clamped to the workpiece to limit travel and produce a groove of the required length. A straight cutter fixed in the router collet makes the groove.

5.19 Router with straightedge guide

If the straightedge is at just the right distance from the edge of the board, and a shaped cutter is used, the setup can be used to shape the edge of the board. However, a more convenient way to guide the router along an edge is to use a cutter that incorporates a pilot guide. A pilot guide can be a part of the shank of the cutter that bears against the edge of the board, as shown in **5.20**.

A similar router cutter with a ball-bearing pilot guide is shown in **5.21**; the advantage of this type of guide is reduced friction, and therefore reduced likelihood of burn marks where the guide touches the edge. These cutters are usually called bearing-guided router bits.

If a cutter is fitted with a guide bearing or a pilot, it can be made to follow a template fixed to the workpiece. The cutter will then reproduce the template shape on the workpiece, and any number of identical pieces can be made using the same template. In the next two photographs (**5.22** and **5.23**), a curved template made of MDF is attached to the underside of a workpiece. A bearing-guided cutter is shown running along the edge of the template, trimming the workpiece to the

5.20 Pilot-guided bit

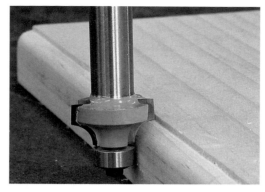

5.21 Bearing-guided bit

5.22 Bearing guided by template below workpiece

5.23 Alternate view of template and bearing-guided cutter

template shape. (This workpiece was first roughly cut to shape on a bandsaw in order to reduce the workload of the cutter.)

Templates can be attached by temporary means such as double-sided tape or hot-melt glue.

Another way of guiding a router is to fit a device to the router itself. One such device is an adjustable edge guide, as shown in **5.24**. The edge guide is pushed firmly to the edge of the work while the router is moved along. The bit then cuts at a fixed distance from the edge.

A guide bush is another guiding device that can be fitted to the router. It is fixed to the base and concentric with the cutter, as shown in **5.25**. It is used in conjunction with a jig that guides the bush, and in turn guides the router.

A dovetail jig is one very well-known example of a jig that guides a router via a bush. It has guide fingers that the bush fits into. With a dovetailing bit in the router, the jig makes precisely positioned dovetails, as shown in **5.26** and **5.27**.

CHOOSING A GUIDANCE METHOD

Apart from the dovetail jig application, none of the projects in this book involve using a guide bush to control a router. A guide bush can introduce inaccuracy into a router operation because it is difficult to obtain a perfect fit between bush and jig, and bushes do not always fit concentrically with the cutter. Therefore, I prefer to use other guidance systems whenever possible.

5.24 Adjustable edge guide fitted to a router

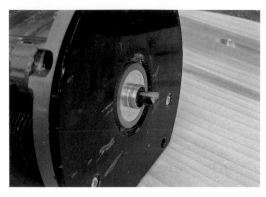

5.25 Guide bush and dovetail bit

5.26 A dovetail jig

5.27 Precisely made dovetails

When a router is used to shape only the upper or lower part of an edge's profile, the easiest guidance method will be provided by a bit with a bearing that runs against the part that remains uncut. The original edge should be straight and smooth because the bearing will follow any irregularities in it. When you need to shape all of an edge—to make it fully rounded, for example—this operation will cut away the part needed for the bearing to run on. The photographs of pilot-guided bits cutting into an edge show that an unchanged part of the edge is needed to guide the bearing. A temporary edge for the bearing to run on (i.e., a template) can be fixed flush with the edge.

You can use a straightedge guide to make straight cuts along the edge or at any dis-

tance from the edge provided that the guide can be securely fixed to the surface of the work and at just the right distance from the desired cut. You can determine the right position for the straightedge by clamping it to a piece of scrap material and using it to guide the router while you make a test cut. After making the test cut, you can measure the distance from the cut to the straightedge.

If the cut has to start and finish at precise positions, it can be controlled by end stops fixed to, or near, the straightedge. Whenever end stops are used, you can find their required positions by first placing them arbitrarily for a test cut into scrap material and then measuring the distances from the stops to the start and finish of the test cut.

Simple jigs can be made in the shop for specific purposes. A jig for making a slot of fixed length is shown in **5.28**.

The jig is used by clamping it to a workpiece, positioning its slot exactly where you require a slot in the workpiece. The router, fitted with a straight cutter, is pushed against the fence at the back of the jig and moved from side to side. The strips at either end of the jig determine the length of the slot in the workpiece; the cutter diameter determines the width.

ROUTER TABLES

Photo **5.29** shows a beading bit projecting through a piece of plywood screwed to the base of a router. In **5.30**, the plywood is clamped upside down to a bench, and a wooden fence is clamped to the plywood. The fence is notched at the center to provide clearance for the bit. This setup constitutes a practical router table.

A larger shop-made router table is shown in the next three photographs (**5.31**, **5.32**, and **5.33**). Here, too, it comprises a piece of plywood with a hole for the cutter and smaller holes for screws to support the router. The fence is fully adjustable and can be positioned accurately by slackening the clamps and tapping it in place. The support arrangements raise the table slightly higher than the bench to make room under it for the fence clamps. The whole apparatus can be dismantled when not in use.

Although commercially available router tables may offer more facilities and conveniences, they do not necessarily do a better job. A store-bought table might remove wood chips and provide for fine fence adjustment, but a dust mask, safety glasses, and a gentle touch are less expensive alternatives. An elaborate router table is not necessary to make any of the projects in

5.28 A simple slotting jig

5.29 Almost a router table

5.30 A small router table

this book; a simple, shop-made version can produce professional results equally well.

Making a Router Table

It is a good idea to have two shop-made router tables: one that measures about 24" × 36" for larger workpieces, and one that is about 15" × 15" for working on small items. The larger one will require a support

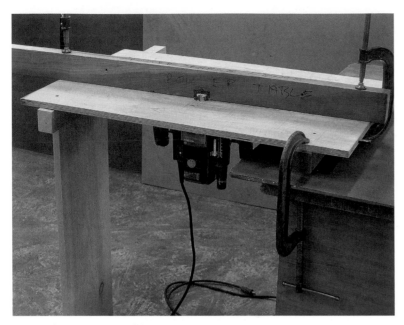

5.31 A larger router table

5.32 Fence and bit

5.33 Router table in use

stand at one end, as shown in **5.31**, but the small one can be conveniently suspended off the edge of the bench (**5.30**). Of course, a large router table can also handle small workpieces, but a small one is easier to set up when a large surface is not needed.

Your router comes equipped with holes through the base for screwing it into a router table. The first step in making a table, therefore, is to obtain some suitable flathead machine screws and nuts. The screws must be long enough to pass through the plywood and router base and still accommodate two nuts. (The second nut on each screw lessens the risk of nuts shaking loose.)

Use good-quality plywood (e.g., Baltic birch) for the tables. The large one should be ¾" thick, but the small one need only be ½". After cutting the plywood to size, bore a 1½"-diameter hole through the center of the large piece and a 1" hole in the small one. Center the router over each of these holes, and mark the plywood through the fixing holes in the router base. Drill clearance holes for the fixing screws at the marks, and countersink them so the screws will be sunk just below the top surface.

Make straight fences at least ¾" thick, 3" high, and about 2" longer than the tables. Cut 1"-wide by 1"-high notches at the fences' midlength to allow the fences to be centered over the router bits. The notches can be enlarged when necessary to accommodate larger bits. The advantages of making the fences rather tall are (1) helping to keep your fingers well clear of the cutter, and (2) making it easy to clamp shop-made guards to the fence. These guards can be pieces of wood of suitable size and shape that allow the workpiece to pass beneath them while protecting your fingers from the cutter.

Screw 2"-high battens to the underside of the large router table, about 2" from each end. The battens could be made from two thicknesses of plywood glued together. Cut a plywood support board 24" wide and long enough to reach the floor and hold the large table horizontal when one of the battens is resting on your workbench. Drill some screw holes into the support board so it can be screwed to one batten.

To set up the large table, install a cutter firmly in the router collet, and then screw the router to the underside of the table and plunge it to the approximate depth you require. One way to do this is to rest the table upside down on wood stand-off strips that let the router plunge down to the depth required. Turn the table and router over, screw the support board to one batten, and clamp the other batten to the bench. Make final cutter-height adjustments with the router's fine control.

The procedure for setting up the small table is similar; the difference is that its back edge can be clamped to the bench and the front edge left suspended.

USING A ROUTER

The projects in this book involve only a few of a router's myriad applications. Each application is fully described in the project pages, but an overview of the techniques, as given here, will give you added confidence. You should try out the techniques before using them on a project so there will be no surprises when you apply them to an actual workpiece.

Start by reading the manufacturer's manual: A router may not be the most dangerous tool in the workshop, but it has the potential to cause serious injury if not used in accordance with safety recommendations.

Prepare a test piece, at least 8" wide and 10" long, from scrap material or from the cheapest available hardwood. Flatten and plane it; then straighten and smooth the edges.

Any test piece or workpiece must be secured in place for routing. Often all that is needed is a friction mat; the weight of the router will hold the workpiece to the mat and the mat will hold it to the bench. Friction mats work well when the router is to be guided by the edge of the workpiece, but some form of clamping is necessary when guides must be fixed to the work. Friction mats are also useful when workpieces are being sanded, and are called sanding mats or router mats. A friction mat is not a safe method of securing the workpiece when large router cutters are being used.

For your first router procedure, an edge-shaping operation works well:

- Choose a bearing-guided edging bit, such as a beading bit or an ogee bit, and fix it securely in the collet while the router is unplugged. Use the router's plunge feature and fine adjuster to set the bit projection until it looks right for the desired edge shape.
- With your test piece on a friction mat or otherwise secured, place the rear part of the router base on the test piece, but keep the bit just clear of the front edge, as in **5.34**.

5.34 Preparing to shape an edge with a bearing-guided edging bit

- Hold the router firmly against the top surface. Then switch it on and move it onto the work until the guide bearing is in contact with the edge. Note that the bit begins to make a cut before the bearing touches the edge and then the horizontal depth of cut is limited by the bearing. Next, holding the router down on the workpiece, and applying slight pressure against the edge, move it from left to right along the edge for a couple of inches. Pull the router clear of the work, and then switch it off. When it stops, lay it on its side with the cutter facing away from you.
- Inspect the cut, and adjust the vertical depth of cut using the fine adjuster. Make another short cut and repeat the process until the depth is right. Finally, make a full-length pass with the router along the front edge.

The direction in which the router moves is significant. In the exercise above, you moved the cutter from left to right along the edge of the workpiece. If you had moved it from right to left, it would almost certainly have given you a different experience and yielded a different result.

As shown in **5.35**, the bit rotates clockwise when viewed from above. When the router is moved to the right, the cutting edge moves outward, through the wood to its right. (The wood to the left has already been cut away.)

The result of this action is an unbalanced force on the bit—there are no forces acting to the left of it because wood is being cut only on the right. Because the cutting edge is moving outward, through the wood, the resulting force on the bit pushes inward and helps to hold the router firmly against the work. At the same time, an opposing force resists the rightward movement of the router.

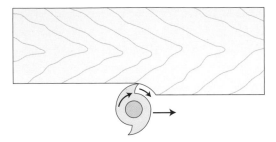

5.35 Cutter with clockwise rotation, traveling from left to right

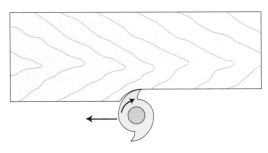

5.36 Cutter traveling from right to left

What happens if the router is moved to the left is shown in **5.36**. The wood to the right has already been cut away, so the cutting forces are all on the left. And, because of the bit's clockwise rotation, the router is being pushed away from the work and to the left.

The result of this leftward movement is that it becomes more difficult to hold the router against the edge, and the router tends to pull to the left. Because of this "self-feeding" tendency, when you make a cut in this direction, you may find yourself restraining the router rather than pushing it. A cut made in this way is known as a climb cut, because of the cutter's tendency to climb over the wood to the left. Moving a router in a "forward" direction (left to right) along an edge is safer because it will not tend to self-feed. Forward routing also produces a smoother, straighter cut because the router is more controlled and

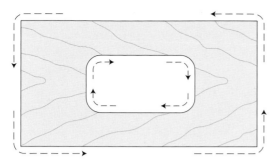

5.37 Forward directions of routing

because the cutter pulls itself against the edge instead of away from it.

Left to right is the forward direction of movement for a router when it is between the operator and the work, as it was for the cut described above. When the far edge of a board is being shaped, however, and the workpiece is between the operator and the router, the forward direction is from right to left. This rule is best remembered as working counterclockwise around the outside of a workpiece. That is, when the router reaches the back edge, it will be moving from your right to your left. Conversely, if you are working on the edges of an internal opening in the workpiece, the forward direction will be clockwise. These two situations are illustrated in **5.37**.

When routing around the outside of a board, it is best to rout the end grain first. If any tear-out occurs at the corners, it will be removed when the sides are routered.

When a router table is used, it is the workpiece and not the router that is moved. Work must always be moved from right to left on a router table, and never from left to right. Moving the workpiece from left to right would cause the cutter to throw it or pull it in the direction you are already pushing it, possibly dragging your fingers into the cutter.

For the next exercise, replace the bearing-guided bit with a mortising bit (a straight or spiral bit with cutting edges on its sides and bottom). Then try working with a fence:

- Clamp or screw a straightedge to your test piece at least 4" from the front edge. Also, fix stop blocks to it to limit the router travel to about 3".

- Place the router on the test piece and plunge it to the wood until the cutter touches the surface. Lock the plunge mechanism, and set the depth stop to allow a further plunge to about $\frac{1}{8}$" less than the thickness of the test piece.

- With the cutter retracted, place the router on the test piece. Start the router, and push it firmly against the fence and against one of the stop blocks; then plunge the cutter about $\frac{1}{8}$" into the surface. Move the router slowly along the fence until it reaches the other stop block, plunge it a further $\frac{1}{8}$" down, and move it back to the start position while pushing it toward the fence.

- Continue the process until you have cut a groove to the depth allowed by the depth stop. Then retract the cutter and switch off the router.

  Note: Unlike edge-shaping operations, where only one side of the cutter is making contact with the wood, the direction of travel for grooving or slotting operations is not important: It can go from right to left as well as from left to right. It is, however, essential to concentrate on keeping the router base firmly against the fence at all times.

Burning

The speed at which you move the router along will affect the smoothness of the cut surface. Moving the router slowly will produce the smoothest surface and reduce the risk of tear-out, but it will increase the risk of burning. Some woods are more susceptible than others to scorching or burning,

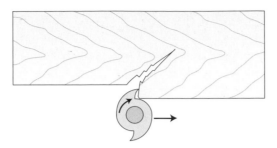

5.38 Cutter causing tear-out

and the resulting discoloration can go deep below the surface, making it difficult to remove by sanding. Prevention is much better than cure, and therefore you need to move the router at a speed that ensures adequate smoothness without burning.

It is a good idea to make the next-to-last cut just a few thousandths of an inch short of full depth. By doing so, any burning can be removed with a final, very light but fast cut. Another helpful approach is to use only very light downward pressure. If any burning occurs, an extra pass is made quickly, with increased pressure. This step may remove enough additional material to deal with the problem.

Tear-out

Tear-out can be a problem when edges are shaped with a router. It is most likely to occur when the angle of the grain to the edge is conducive to the cutter lifting the fibers. If a cutter is perfectly sharp, it will cut through the fibers rather than lift them. However, in the real world, some lifting force is always associated with a rotary cutter, and sometimes it can tear chunks of wood from the edge.

How grain orientation at the edge of a board can allow a cutter to lift and tear the fibers, instead of cutting them cleanly, is illustrated in **5.38**. (The router is moving along the edge from left to right, so material to the left has already been removed.)

Tear-out can be prevented by making an initial climb-cut to do most of the shaping. A final forward pass will remedy the unevenness the climb-cut produces. The reason that tear-out does not occur when you move the router in the "wrong" direction along the edge is that the bit is cutting into, not out of, the edge (**5.36**). Climb-cutting should never be done with large router bits because of the strong self-feeding forces that they exert. Unless the cutter is small, it is safer to reduce the risk of tear-out by making several shallow cuts and moving the router slowly forward. Climb-cutting also should not be used on end-grain edges—not even with small cutters—because it can leave end-grain fibers in a shattered condition.

USING A ROUTER TABLE

Many router operations can be performed either with a handheld router or on a router table. However, some applications are safer on the router table, and some cannot be done without it.

Only two items need to be adjusted on a router table: the cutter height (a function of the router, not the table) and the fence. You will see how precisely a simple clamped fence can be positioned by making a sliding dovetail joint, as follows:

- Reposition the straightedge on your test piece to guide the router across the grain. Fit a ½" dovetail cutter into the router and set the cutter projection to about ½". Cut a dovetail groove across the width of the test piece (**5.39**).

- Unplug the router and fix it in either the large or the small router table. Set up the table as described previously. Set the fine height adjuster to the middle of its range, and then plunge the router to obtain a cutter projection roughly equal to the depth of the slot in the test piece.

- Make a second test piece ¾" thick. Crosscut the ends square to the sides. Position the router table fence so that it almost entirely covers the cutter. The tips of the cutting edges should project from the cutout by no more than ¹⁄₁₆". Clamp the fence securely in place.

- Start the router, and then hold the test piece on-end and against the fence to the right of the cutter. Keeping your fingers higher than the cutter, move the test piece to the left and across the cutter about 2" (5.40). Switch off the router and inspect the test piece.

- Compare the height of the cut on the second test piece with the depth of the groove in the first one.

- The height of the cut must be the same as the groove depth, so increase or reduce the cutter height as necessary. Then make a short cut in the opposite face of the test piece. Repeat the adjustments and cuts until the height is correct. If you need to, renew the test piece by cutting off the ends. Remember that on a router table, the workpiece must always be moved from right to left past the cutter and must touch only the side of the cutter between you and the fence unless the entire cutter is to be in the workpiece (for example, to cut a groove).

- When the height of the cut is correct, make identical cuts in both faces at one end of the test piece. After doing so, compare the thickness of the dovetail with the width of the groove. If the dovetail is too thick, remove one of the fence clamps and slacken the other. Move the fence away from the cutter by gently tapping the free end. The second clamp should be slackened only enough to allow the fence to pivot when the free end is tapped. Tighten both clamps, start the router,

5.39 Cutting a dovetail groove

5.40 Cutting a sliding dovetail

5.41 Sliding dovetail joint

and pass both faces of the dovetail over the cutter again.

- When the dovetail is almost thin enough to fit in the groove, all subsequent fence adjustments must be very delicate. Make a short mark in pencil on the table against the fence at one end. Slacken the clamps just enough for the fence to be moved by tapping it, and then tap it until it clears the pencil mark. If the clamp pressure is right, you will be able to move the end of the fence by the thickness of a fine pencil line, and the movement at the center of the fence will be half of that.

- Continue the process until the dovetail has a sliding fit in the groove (5.41). Congratulations! The router table is now correctly set to cut accurate sliding dovetails in any number of workpieces of the same thickness as the test piece.

Part 4

Joinery

6 The Mortise-and-Tenon Joint

WHEN TWO PIECES OF WOOD ARE butted together at 90 degrees to each other, as in **6.1**, one piece presents end grain at the joint.

Because end grain makes for a poor gluing surface, a simple glue joint there would be weak. However, if the pieces are worked to form a projection (a tenon) on the end of one piece that fits into a slot (a mortise) in the other, as in **6.2**, a glue joint will be strong. The tenon and the mortise both present side-grain surfaces.

The piece with the tenon is commonly horizontal, and the mortised piece is vertical. If so, the horizontal piece is called a rail, and the vertical piece is a stile. Rail-and-stile construction is used for the front and back frames of the Chest of Drawers project in Chapter 19 (**19.2** and **19.3**), where horizontal rails are tenoned into the vertical posts (stiles). The End Table project in Chapter 21 also employs horizontal parts (the back and side aprons, and front rails) joined to stiles (the legs) by tenons glued into mortises.

In those examples, the parts are sufficiently narrow to avoid problems resulting from their crossed grain directions at the glue joint.

Frames with mortise-and-tenon corner joints can be used to hold wide components that must be allowed to shrink and expand. Examples are a frame-and-panel door and the frame-and-panel chest shown in **6.3**.

The frames in **6.3** do not change size, but the panels can expand and shrink in grooves in the frames. A grooved mortise-and-tenon frame, ready to hold a panel is depicted in **6.4**.

A traditional tenon is made with eight saw cuts. The four shoulders are cut first, and these cuts must be precise in order to avoid gaps where the rail meets the stile (**6.5**). Then the cheeks are cut accurately to ensure a snug fit with the mortise. However, there is an easier way to make the joint: This is the "floating-tenon" method illustrated by **6.6**.

A so-called floating tenon is made as a separate piece and then glued into a mortise in the end of a rail. Once glued, it is the same as a traditional tenon. The mortises are made with a router cutter, so they have rounded ends. It is a quick and easy task to round the tenon edges to match the mortises.

In making a floating tenon, the eight shoulder cuts are eliminated, and the tenons are quickly made to fit by using a planer. Then, when one joint fits well, so will all the joints because the tenons are all made with the same planer setting, and the mortises are all made by the same cutter. A

6.1 End-grain-to-side-grain contact

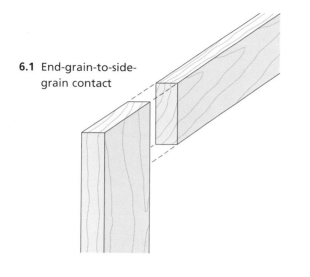

6.2 The side grain of the tenon will meet side grain in the mortise

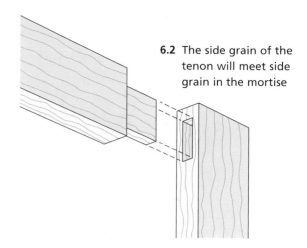

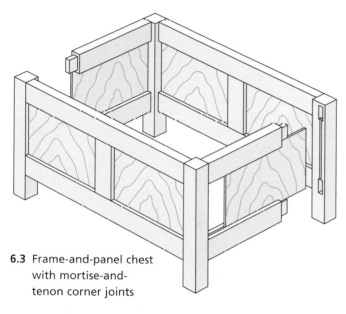

6.3 Frame-and-panel chest with mortise-and-tenon corner joints

6.4 A panel will be held in the grooves of this mortised-and-tenoned frame

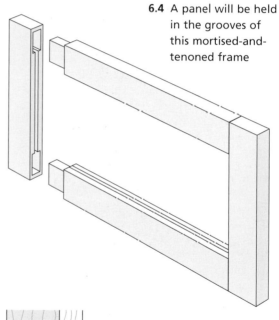

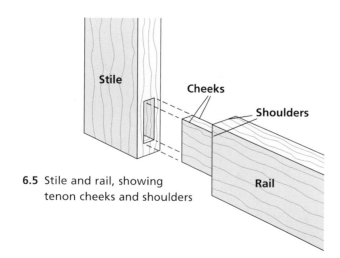

6.5 Stile and rail, showing tenon cheeks and shoulders

Stile

Cheeks

Shoulders

Rail

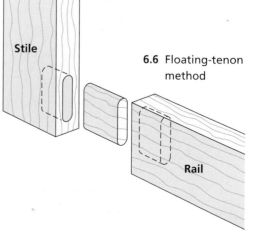

Stile

6.6 Floating-tenon method

Rail

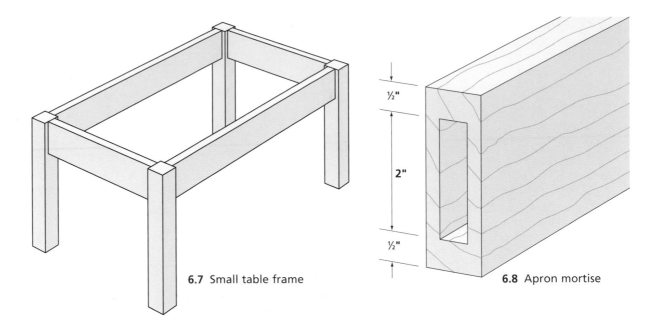

6.7 Small table frame

½"

2"

½"

6.8 Apron mortise

bonus of this method is that it saves expensive lumber because the rails can be shorter and the tenons can be made from scrap wood.

DESIGNING MORTISE-AND-TENON JOINTS

The best way to design mortise-and-tenon joints is by drawing them full-size on paper. Usually the mortises in the stiles and rails are made the same depth to avoid complicating the mortising procedure.

In most cases, tenons should be as large as possible provided that the correspondingly large mortises do not weaken the joint. As an example, consider the leg-to-apron joints at one corner of the small table frame shown in **6.7**.

If the aprons are 3" wide, the mortises could be 2" long, leaving ½" of wood at each end, as in **6.8**, or they might be 1½" long, leaving ¾" at each end.

If the aprons are ¾" thick, the mortise could be cut with either a ¼"- or ⅜"-diameter cutter. A ½"-diameter cutter would leave the walls only ⅛" thick, possibly strong enough for a small structure, but the best choice would be either the ¼" or the ⅜" cutter. Aim for balance between the strength of the mortise walls and the strength of the tenon.

You must decide how deep to make the mortises. The fact that each leg has two mortises cut into it will influence your choice. Whenever possible, it is best if the mortises do not run into each other **(6.9)**. This is because you may want to glue one of the aprons to the leg and let the glue harden before gluing on the other apron. If the mortises open into each other, the glue from the first assembly might be pushed into the second mortise where it will harden on the walls, thereby complicating the next step in assembling the legs and aprons.

If the job calls for longer tenons, the mortises can run into each other and the tenon ends can be chamfered at 45 degrees, as in **6.10**. In such circumstances, it is best to glue and assemble everything at the same time.

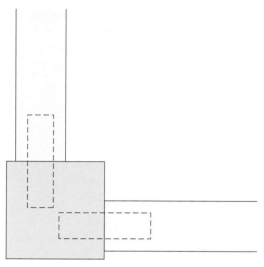

6.9 These mortises do not open into each other

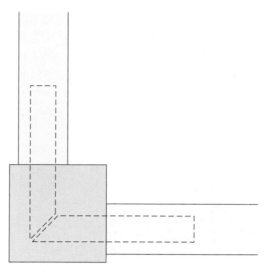

6.10 These mortises connect to each other, so the tenons can be chamfered to increase their length

Mortise Requirements

A floating tenon fixes two pieces of wood together with their relative positions determined by the mortises on each side of the joint. Often, outside faces must be flush with one another at the joint, as in the corners of door frames and face frames. For this to happen, both mortises must be the same distance from the outside faces. Sometimes a definite step at the joint is desired, as when the aprons of a table are set in from the legs (**6.7**, **6.9**, and **6.10**). If so, one mortise must be positioned farther from the outside face. In either case, the accuracy of the result depends on how precisely the mortises are set in from the outside faces. With a deliberate step at the joint, accuracy becomes less critical: A difference between steps of $^3/_{16}$" and $^7/_{32}$" is usually not noticeable.

When flush faces are required but the insets are slightly different, the result will be small steps at the joints, which can be easily sanded flush. However, it is sometimes necessary to make joints with double or triple mortises and tenons, as shown in

6.11. In these pieces, the spacing between mortises must be precisely the same each side of the joint. Precisely equal spacing sounds difficult to achieve, but there is a simple system that makes it easy. The system is described later in this chapter.

Other aspects of the mortises' position are less critical. If one of them is $^1/_{32}$" out of position along the length of a stile or leg, or if it is $^1/_{32}$" too shallow, you can compensate by reducing the width or length of the tenon.

6.11 Multiple mortises and tenons

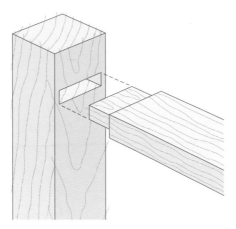

6.12 The stile mortise has mostly end grain

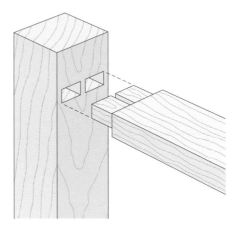

6.13 Multiple mortises increase the side grain gluing area in the stile

Multiple Tenons

A thin rail with a wide tenon is shown in **6.12**. With this arrangement, the corresponding stile mortise is nearly all end grain, and the glue bond will be weak.

A much better arrangement is to replace the large mortise and tenon with two or more small ones, thus providing more side-grain gluing surface, as in **6.13**. In the Chest of Drawers project in Chapter 19, the frame rails have triple mortises and tenons to produce maximum side-grain gluing area.

MORTISING JIGS

Jigs for mortising with a router are simple and easy to make and they produce accurate and consistent results. You need a surface to support the router, a fence to guide it, some end stops that limit its movement, and a means of holding the workpiece at the right distance from the fence. When these components are in place, any number of identical mortises can be made, and they will all be equally set in from the faces that had been oriented toward the fence.

The jig shown in **6.14** comprises a support surface with a fence and two side stops. It has a rectangular opening with a vertical support board below it. The fence is parallel to the vertical board.

In **6.15**, the jig is being used to cut a mortise into the edge of a workpiece that is clamped to the vertical support board. The fence keeps the router centered over the mortise; the side stops limit the length of the mortise, and the router's depth stop determines the depth of cut.

In **6.16** the jig is being used to cut a mortise in the end of the workpiece.

Mortises are cut by holding the router against the jig fence, plunging the cutter into the workpiece, and then moving the

6.14 A simple mortising jig

6.15 Using the simple jig to cut

6.16 Cutting a mortise into the end of a workpiece

router between the side stops. If the router is held in continuous contact with the fence, the width of the mortise will equal the cutter's diameter.

All mortises made with this setup will be identical and positioned at exactly the same distance from the faces clamped to the jig support board. These faces are the reference faces of the workpieces, because it is from them that the mortise insets are measured. The face of the jig support board is the reference face of the jig.

The simple jig can only make mortises of the same length and at the same distance from the reference faces; however, you can make the jig more versatile by making the fence and side stops adjustable. The improved jig described below will handle all the frame components for the Chest of Drawers, Bookcase, and End Table projects (Chapters 19, 20, and 21, respectively) as well as the components of many other pieces.

The improved jig is shown in **6.17** and **6.18**. It features a clamping block, B, fixed under a plywood support surface. W is a

workpiece clamped between the block and a clamping bar, A, by short pipe clamps. A support board (not visible in the photographs) is fixed to the back of clamping block B. The front face of the clamping block is the reference face of the jig.

On the top surface of the jig, an adjustable fence, C, can be fixed at any distance from the reference face by large wing nuts. The wood strip, D, keeps the front of the fence parallel to the reference face.

The fence guides the router at a constant distance from the reference face, B. When workpieces are clamped to B and the fence is set, the mortise insets will be the same for every piece. If the fence is moved, a second set of mortises can be cut at a distance from the first set, and this separation will be exactly the same for all pieces.

At each side of the opening in the jig top, slotted pieces of plywood attached by wing nuts act as adjustable side stops. Small pieces of plywood protruding from the back corners of the top support short pipe clamps.

6.17 The versatile mortising jig: The workpiece, W, is clamped to the fixed block, B, by the clamping bar, A, which is screwed to the front jaws of pipe clamps. The rear clamp jaws are screwed to B

6.18 Front view of the jig's top: The fence, C, and the slotted side stops are fixed at their required positions by wing nuts. The fence, C, is kept square to the opening by pushing it against the guide strip, D

The jaws of the pipe clamps are fixed to the clamping block and clamping bar with wood screws, which the jaws are drilled to accommodate. When the jig is not in use, the pipe clamps can be removed and put to general use.

One final feature must be mentioned: The clamp bar has a shallow rabbet cut into it at the center, as shown in **6.19**, that diverts pressure away from the tops of workpieces. Without it, pressure that could push the mortise wall inward and result in a mortise wider than the cutter diameter would be applied on the wall of a mortise as it was being cut. With the rabbet, the pressure is applied below the mortise.

Making the Jig

Materials

Jig top:
$\frac{1}{2}$" or $\frac{3}{4}$" plywood, 16" × 20" (1)

Side stops:
$\frac{1}{2}$" or $\frac{3}{4}$" plywood, 3" × 5" (2)

Fence:
$\frac{1}{2}$" or $\frac{3}{4}$" plywood, 6" × 8" (1)

Clamp supports:
$\frac{1}{2}$" or $\frac{3}{4}$" plywood, 2" × 5" (2)

Fence side blocks:
$\frac{1}{2}$" or $\frac{3}{4}$" plywood, $1\frac{1}{2}$" × $1\frac{1}{2}$" (2)

Fence guide:
$\frac{3}{4}$" × 2" × 7" plywood or hardwood (1)

Support stand:
$\frac{1}{2}$" or $\frac{3}{4}$" plywood, 10" × 10" (1)

Support stand base:
hardwood, $\frac{7}{8}$" × 2" × 14" (1)

Clamping block:
hardwood, $1\frac{1}{4}$" × $2\frac{1}{2}$" × 24" (1)

Clamp bar:
hardwood, $1\frac{3}{4}$" × $1\frac{3}{4}$" × 24" (1)

Carriage bolts:
$\frac{1}{2}$" diameter, 2" long, with wing nuts and washers (4)

Additional large washers:
2" diameter, $\frac{1}{2}$" hole (2)

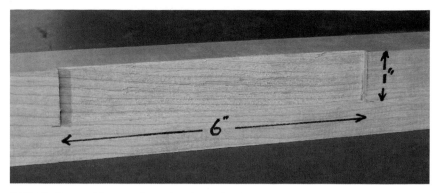

6.19 Shallow rabbet cut into the clamp bar's center

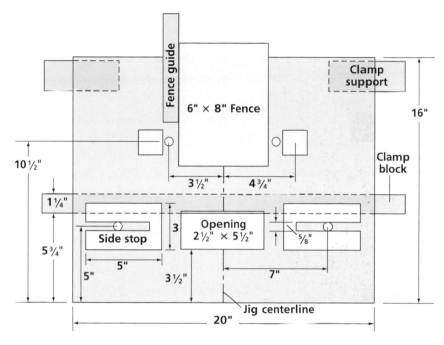

6.20 Jig diagram

The jig (**6.20**) uses about $20 worth of materials, excluding the pipe clamps, and can be made in less than three hours, as follows:

1. Cut a piece of $\frac{1}{2}$" plywood to 16" × 20" for the jig top. You can use $\frac{3}{4}$" plywood, but this will reduce the effective length of your router cutters by another $\frac{1}{4}$"—in some circumstances a significant loss. Square a centerline in ink across the plywood from front to back.

6.21 Checking the depth of the recess for the bolt head

2. On the back face, draw a pencil line parallel to the front edge and 5" from it. Mark the line at 7" each side of center. Drill into the back surface at these marked positions with a $1\frac{1}{4}$" Forstner bit to a depth sufficient to sink the dome of a carriage bolt head below the surface (**6.21**). Or, use a 1" Forstner bit and enlarge the recesses with a chisel to accommodate the carriage bolt heads.

   Drill all the way through at the centers of the recesses with a $\frac{5}{8}$" Forstner bit.

3. Turn the jig top right-way up again, and draw a line parallel to the front edge, $10\frac{1}{2}$" from it. Mark the line at $3\frac{1}{2}$" each side of center. Drill through at these marks with a $\frac{1}{2}$" Forstner bit.

4. Make the side stops, the fence, and the fence side blocks from $\frac{1}{2}$" or $\frac{3}{4}$"

plywood. Drill $\frac{5}{8}$" holes through the side stops 1" from one end, and then cut the slots with a bandsaw or handsaw (**6.22**).

5. Install the $\frac{1}{2}$" side-stop carriage bolts as follows:
   - Push the bolts through the holes in the jig top from underneath.
   - Place the side stops over the bolts and then attach the washers and wing nuts.
   - Tighten the wing nuts by hand to pull the bolts fully into the holes. Check that the bolt heads are below the surface.
   - Mix some 5-minute epoxy. Then turn the jig over and apply the epoxy around the bolt heads to fix them permanently in the holes. Keep the epoxy below the surface.

6. Screw the fence side blocks to the jig top, in line with the rear bolt holes and centered $4\frac{3}{4}$" to each side of the jig's centerline. Install the rear carriage bolts, place the jig fence between them, and then attach the large and small washers and the wing nuts. Tighten the wing nuts with pliers to force the bolt shanks into the plywood; slacken the nuts afterward.

7. Make a $2\frac{1}{2}$" × $5\frac{1}{2}$" opening on the centerline, set back $3\frac{1}{2}$" from the front edge, as follows:
   - Draw the opening on the jig top.

6.22 Side stops with holes drilled and one slot cut

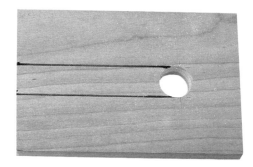

- Clamp the jig top to the bench, with the area of the opening protruding over the edge.
- Place a router with a $\frac{1}{2}$" mortising cutter on the marked opening, and plunge the cutter to touch the surface. Position it so that the cutter is just touching the back edge of the marked opening. Bring the fence up to the router base and clamp it in place with the wing nuts.
- Move the router until the cutter touches the left-hand side of the marked opening. Bring the left-hand side stop up to the router base, and clamp it with the wing nut. Move the cutter to the other side of the opening, and secure the other side stop.
- Make the fence parallel to the opening by adjusting it until the cutter touches the back edge of the opening at each side.
- Hold the router against the fence and one side stop. Switch it on, and plunge the cutter through the plywood. Move the router to the other side stop while holding it to the fence.
- Stop the router. Raise the cutter, and position it to touch the front edge of the opening. Adjust the fence to guide the router parallel to the opening so that the cutter touches the front edge at each side. Restart the router and cut along the front edge of the opening.
- Move the fence out of the way, and use the side stops to guide the router while cutting the sides of the opening (**6.23**). Don't worry if the opening is less than perfect.
8. Glue and screw on the 2" × 5" pipe clamp supports below the jig top,

6.23 Side stops limit the router travel while it is cutting the opening

close to the back edge and protruding 2" on each side.

9. Make a clamping block from hardwood. Its front face will be the jig reference face. Make it $1\frac{1}{4}$" thick, $2\frac{1}{2}$" wide, and 4" longer than the jig (i.e., 24" long). Joint and plane the faces square to each other. Fix it to the jig as follows:
- On the underside of the jig top, draw a line parallel to the front edge and $5\frac{3}{4}$" from it. It will be about $\frac{1}{4}$" forward of the back edge of the opening. Draw another line 7" from the front edge of the jig.
- Remove the side stops. Next, drill through the plywood with a $\frac{1}{8}$" drill midway between the two lines at five places along the length, including one close to the jig's centerline.
- Place the block between the lines; overhang the plywood by 2" at

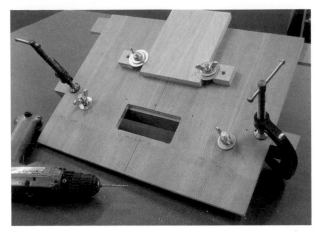

6.24 Drill into the block with a ⅛" drill through the ⅛" holes in the jig top

6.25 Jig on support stand

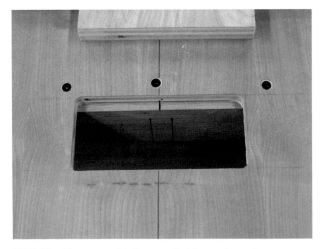

6.26 Marking a centerline on the top edge of the clamping block and vertical lines on the reference face

each end, and clamp it to the plywood in this position. Turn the jig over and drill through the ⅛" holes and into the block with the ⅛" drill (**6.24**).

- Unclamp the block, and enlarge the ⅛" holes in the plywood to ⁷⁄₃₂"; countersink them into the top surface enough for #8 flat head (FH) wood screws to fit flush with the surface. Slightly countersink the holes from underneath as well, to ensure that the block will fit tightly to the top without any interference from raised wood fibers.

- Spread some PVA glue on the top edge of the block, and screw it under the jig top with #8 FH screws.

10. Cut a 10" × 10" piece of plywood as a support stand for the jig. Screw and glue a ⅞" × 2" × 14" piece of hardwood to one edge, and then screw the opposite edge to the back of the clamping block. How the completed jig will be supported by the stand is shown in **6.25**.

11. Make a 1¾" × 1¾" × 24" hardwood clamp bar. Mark out a ⅛" × 1" × 6" rabbet at the center (**6.19**). Use a router with a ½" cutter to remove material from this area to a depth of ⅛". Guide the router freehand to within about ⅛" of the outline. Finish to the outline with a chisel and mallet.

12. Draw a center mark on the top edge of the clamping block where ¼" of it is visible in the opening. Also, draw vertical lines on the reference face at ⅜" to each side of center; stop these lines at least ½" from the top edge to avoid confusion with the center mark (**6.26**).

6.27 Drilling fixing holes through the clamp jaws

6.28 The clamp bar is screwed to the front clamp jaws

13. Drill $\frac{5}{32}$" holes through the jaws of both pipe clamps **(6.27)**.

14. Use the pipe clamps to hold the clamp bar against the reference face and touching the underside of the jig. Make sure the rabbet is uppermost, centered, and oriented toward the reference face. Fix the pipe clamp jaws to both items with #6 × $\frac{3}{4}$" wood screws **(6.28)**.

15. Clamp a flat piece of wood or plywood or MDF in the jig, sticking up higher than the fence, as in **6.29**. Bring the fence up to the material and clamp it with the wing nuts.

16. Cut a wood or plywood fence guide, about $\frac{3}{4}$" × 2" × 7", with straight edges. Drill and countersink two holes in it for #8 screws at 1" and 3" from one end. Position the guide against one side of the jig fence, just clear of the fence bolt washers, and clamp it to the fence **(6.30)**.

17. Screw the guide to the jig top, and remove the clamp. The guide will enable you to keep the fence parallel to the jig reference face at any distance from it.

6.29 Setting the fence parallel to the jig reference face

6.30 Clamping on the fence guide to the side of the jig fence

6.31 Parts marked ready for mortising

Using the Jig

Prepare parts for mortising by marking the midpoint of every mortise position. Extend the marks only to the edge that meets the reference face, which is usually the outside face.

On one workpiece, draw the outline of a mortise centered on one of those marks. Four center marks and one mortise outline are shown in **6.31**.

When the marking is done, set up the jig as follows:

- Take the part with the mortise outline and clamp it into the jig with the reference face against the jig's reference face and the center mark of the mortise at the jig's centerline.
- Fit the appropriate mortising cutter into a router, and place it on the jig exactly at one end of the mortise outline.
- Move the stop at that end of the jig up against the router base and tighten its wing nut. Move the cutter to the opposite end of the mortise, and set the other side stop.
- Position the cutter over the mortise outline near the center mark. Move the jig fence forward, to the router base. Hold the fence against the router base and against the fence guide. Tighten the fence's wing nuts.

Start the router and cut the mortise in shallow steps. Remove the workpiece and clamp one of the others to the reference face. Make sure the mortise's center mark is at the jig's centerline. Cut a mortise, and then repeat for all mortises of the same size and inset.

It is not necessary to draw mortise outlines on all the workpieces; all that is needed is to mark the centers of other mortises of the same size and of the same inset. When one of these marks aligns with the jig's center mark, the router will cut an accurate mortise in the right place. For mortises of different sizes or different insets, carry out a separate drawing and setup procedure.

MAKING AND GLUING TENONS

For making tenons, use any hardwood material available. Allow for some spare tenons and make generous allowances for losses in cutting. Cut the material to a width $\frac{1}{32}$" less than the mortise length. Pass it through the planer until it is nearly, but not quite, planed to the required thickness to fit the mortises.

When the tenon stock is almost thin enough to fit in the mortises, round over the edges to match the rounded ends of the mortises. You could use a suitable router cutter and a router table for this task, but a hand plane will be faster unless you have a lot of material to work on. The roundover does not have to be perfect; it need only allow the tenons to enter the mortises (6.32).

After rounding the edges of the stock, continue to plane it to thickness. Make very fine adjustments to the planer until the stock fits well in the mortises.

There is no such thing as a perfect fit, and some compromise is always necessary. On the one hand, you want the fit to be tight enough to produce pressure between the tenon and the mortise, because a good glue bond requires clamping pressure; however, if the tenon is very tight, all the glue will be scraped off as the tenon is inserted.

Individual tenons will feel much tighter than the tenon stock, which is easy to grip and push into the mortises. After the tenons are cut to length, they will be much more difficult to insert. Plane the stock

until it still has some resistance to insertion but can be pushed in easily. Tenons cut from it may need to be tapped in with a mallet, especially if PVA glue is used.

Before cutting tenons from the stock, check the depths of the mortises. Make the tenons about $\frac{1}{32}$" shorter than two mortise depths. The best setup for cutting tenons to length is a miter gauge, used in conjunction with a stop block fixed to the rip fence, as described under "Miter Gauges and Crosscut Sleds" in Chapter 3.

Sometimes it is better to make wide tenons in two pieces, if the tenons are thin. Thin material tends to cup across its width, so it is difficult to judge the tightness of fit, and it may be only the cupping that resists insertion. Perhaps it feels tight but there is little surface contact, and so the glue bond will be weak. By making the tenon in two pieces, cupping is minimized.

Strong glue bonds are more likely to result when glue is applied to both the tenon and the mortise. Unfortunately,

6.32 Rounded-over tenon stock

6.33 Mortise edges can be chamfered to reduce glue squeeze-out

gluing both parts is apt to result in squeeze-out when glue is scraped off the tenon during its insertion into the mortise. When the faces of the joint are flush, the excess glue can easily be removed by scraping it off before it hardens or by sanding it off afterward. When the faces are not flush, however, surface glue is much more difficult to remove, and it is better to minimize or prevent squeeze-out in the first place.

Excess glue in mortises will be pushed to the bottom, but excess glue on tenons will become squeeze-out. Where squeeze-out must be prevented, you should make small chamfers along the mortise edges to create a "pond area" to hold any glue that

is scraped from the tenon. If glue is applied only thinly to the tenons, the chamfers will prevent scraped-off glue from reaching the surface. The chamfers can be made quickly with a file or a card scraper (**6.33**).

When you are ready for glue-up, apply glue generously to a mortise and thinly to one-half of a tenon. Inexpensive ½" brushes, often sold in packs of a dozen or more, are convenient for applying glue. They can be made thinner and narrower with scissors when necessary. Insert the tenon into the mortise, apply glue to the matching mortise and the second half of the tenon, and then assemble and clamp together the parts.

The best way to learn about tenon tightness is to do some testing: Cut a series of mortises along the edge of a piece of scrap wood, and then plane some tenon stock to a very tight fit. Cut the stock into tenons that are about two inches longer than the mortise depth. Glue a tenon into the first mortise, with the assistance of a mallet. Sand the next tenon to a slightly looser fit and glue it into the next mortise. Make the third tenon even looser, and so on. Repeat the procedure with different types of glue. After forty-eight hours, break the tenons out of the mortises and inspect the surfaces. If no wood has been torn from either the tenons or the mortises, the glue bond was poor. The joints with the most surface damage reveal the best fit.

7 Dovetails

DOVETAIL JOINTS ARE INTERLOCKING wedges used to join the ends of parts at a right angle, across their widths. The basic dovetail joint is illustrated in **7.1** and **7.2**.

When dovetails are visible from two directions, as shown in **7.1** and **7.2**, they are called "through" dovetails. There is a variation **(7.3)** in which the sockets do not go through the full thickness of a board. These are called "stopped" or "half-blind" dovetails.

Because dovetailed parts are joined across their widths, grain directions do not conflict when the joint is glued. The joint can therefore be used for parts of any width. The fastest way to make them is with a router and jig.

Dovetails are especially useful for making drawers, where the wedging action of the tails and the strength of multiple glue bonds resist stresses when the drawer is pulled open. The Chest of Drawers in Chapter 19 has 90 dovetails and 90 sockets in the drawers plus another 80 of each in the carcass.

Half-blind dovetails are always used to join drawer fronts to drawer sides because they are hidden when the drawer is closed. Traditionally, drawer backs are joined to the sides with through-dovetails because through-dovetails are much easier to make by hand than half-blind ones. There is no reason why half-blind dovetails should not be used at the back of the drawer as well as at the front, so when the router and jig are set up to make half-blind dovetails for the fronts, you can make them for the backs at the same time.

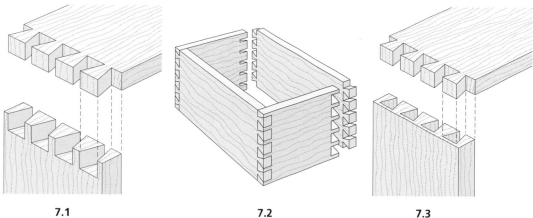

7.1 The through-dovetail joint

7.2 Dovetailed box

7.3 Half-blind dovetail joint

7.1   7.2   7.3

7.4 A router fitted with a dovetail cutter and guide bush

7.5 Workpieces clamped horizontally and vertically under the fingerplate

7.6 The vertical board is slightly offset from the horizontal board

DOVETAIL JIGS

There are many dovetailing jigs on the market, but some are only for making through-dovetails; others can be eliminated because of their sizes. The width limitations of most jigs are either 12" or 24", although 16" and 18" jigs are available. For the Chest of Drawers project, you need to be able to dovetail $14\frac{1}{2}$"-wide panels.

A further consideration when buying a jig is whether it can produce variable spacing between dovetails, or whether it allows only for constant spacing. The following procedures apply to typical fixed-spacing jigs with adjustable side stops. If you have a variable-spacing jig or one that has special features, you will need to refer to its instruction manual for additional setup procedures.

Setting up a jig can involve a great deal of adjustment before everything is right. Of all the procedures described in this book, setting up a dovetail jig may require the most practice—not to develop skills per se, but to keep in mind all the criteria for making perfect joints.

The fingerplate is the most fundamental part of any fixed-spacing dovetailing jig. It supports a router and has a series of slots along one edge, forming fingers. A guide bush fitted to the router base can move within the spaces between the fingers. Together the fingers and bush guide a dovetail-shaped cutter in the router.*

Photo **7.4** shows a router fitted with a dovetail cutter and guide bush.

Workpieces can be clamped horizontally or vertically under the fingerplate. Photos **7.5** and **7.6** show two boards clamped into these positions. Photo **7.7** shows the same boards after dovetails have been cut.

A few jigs use a special bearing-guided dovetail cutter that replaces the guide bush. As a result, replacement cutters may be available only from the jig manufacturer.

7.7 Tails have been cut in the vertical board, and sockets have been cut in the horizontal one

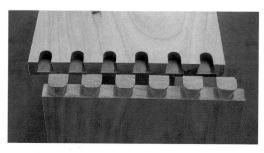

7.8 The dovetailed boards shown in their same relative positions out of the jig

7.9 Tails and sockets fitted together

7.10 Gap between fingerplate and socket board

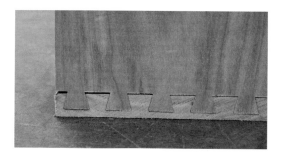

7.11 Shallow sockets produce gaps at base of tails

7.12 Gap between fingerplate and tail board

In **7.8**, the two boards are shown without the jig but in their same relative positions. The vertical board has tails formed on its end, while matching sockets have been cut into the horizontal board. The sockets are rounded at the back by the rotating cutter, and the fingerplate is shaped to produce matching rounding of the tails. Note that the tail board is offset from the socket board: This is how they are positioned in the jig.

When the tail board (the vertical piece in **7.8**) is inverted, the tails will fit into the sockets in the horizontal piece, as in **7.9**. The horizontal piece is sometimes called the pin board, but with half-blind dovetails it is more appropriate to call it the socket board.

An assembled dovetail joint will show gaps at the tops or bottoms of the tails unless the heights of the tails and sockets are exactly equal. It is important to understand how these gaps are caused.

If a socket board in the jig is not quite touching the fingerplate, as in **7.10**, the sockets will be shallow, producing gaps at the base of the tails (**7.11**).

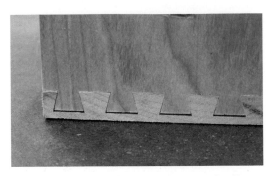

7.13 Short tails produce gaps at top of tails

7.14a A backer strip with its backboard

7.14b Strip and backboard placed at left-hand end of jig

If there is a gap between the tail board and the fingerplate, as in **7.12**, the tails will be short, producing gaps at the top of the tails (**7.13**).

Dovetail jigs allow the tails and sockets to be cut simultaneously. Having both pieces in the jig at the same time helps prevent the tails from chipping because the socket board is held tightly to the tail board. However, when the tail board is pushed up tight under the fingerplate, as it should be, it may flex the fingerplate slightly and produce a gap above the socket board.

Another problem arises because the socket board is positioned by pushing it firmly against the tail board. If the tail board is thin, it can be bent back, slightly away from the jig body. This will affect the rounding of the tails, and consequently the depth to which they can be inserted into the sockets.

Working on one piece at a time is preferable to cutting the tails and sockets together. This procedure will allow you to push the tail piece as hard against the fingerplate as you wish, without any effect on the socket board. Also, when you cut the socket board separately, you can clamp a thick board in front of it as an inflexible stop. You can prevent the tails from chipping by fixing a separate backer board under the fingerplate, against the tail board.

A separate backer board provides another advantage over cutting tails and sockets simultaneously: It can back up the full width of the tail board, whereas a socket board would leave one tail without backing because of the jig offset. The backer board will need to be renewed for each set of tails, which is best accomplished by making some strips about 1" wide. Since each strip will have two edges, it can be used to back up two sets of tails. Therefore, one strip is required for each tail board.

The backer strips will be too narrow to be clamped in the jig, but an added backboard can be clamped behind them to keep them in place. A backer strip with its backboard is shown in **7.14a**. The dovetail cutter will tend to move the strips to the right, but this can be prevented by installing a screw at the right-hand end of the backboard. The screw head stops the strip from moving to the right when it is at the left-hand end of the dovetail jig. At the right-hand end, either the jig itself may block rightward movement of the backer strips, or movement can be prevented by fixing a block to the end of the jig. The backboard can be flipped over at the right-hand end of the jig so that the screw is out of the way. The strip and backboard in place at the left-hand end of the jig are shown in **7.14b**.

JIG REQUIREMENTS

Perfect dovetails require an accurate setup. This will be easier to achieve if the jig has the following facilities:

- A fingerplate that is absolutely flat: If it is bowed, neither the tail board nor the socket board can make proper contact with it.
- Clamps that apply adequate pressure across the entire width of the workpieces. Clamps should be able to apply pressure at the center of the widest boards they are designed for; ideally, they should be able to clamp boards flat, even if the boards are slightly cupped.
- Easily adjusted side stops and fingerplate. Getting the offsets and the depth of tail insertion just right is a process of trial and error that takes time enough without the burden of clumsy adjustment facilities.
- The jig must be able to accept tail boards that are $\frac{3}{8}$" and $\frac{1}{2}$" thick and socket boards that are up to $\frac{7}{8}$" thick.

ROUTING TECHNIQUE

The most important habits to develop are to place the router on the fingerplate with the cutter clear of the workpiece before starting the router, and to pull the router clear of the entire setup before lifting it. It only takes one mistake to ruin the fingerplate.

Cut the sockets by moving the cutter straight into and out of the spaces in the fingerplate. Firm downward pressure on the router will help keep the fingerplate in contact with the socket board. Cutting the tails requires the same in-and-out movement, in addition to movement around the ends of the fingers.

It is best to start cutting the tails with a light, right-to-left cut along the back of the board. This will give the joint a clean inside edge. Next, move the cutter into the finger spaces to cut the tails, but take it slowly at the point where the cutter breaks through on the far side of the board; otherwise, you increase the risk of chipping. When you have cut all the tails, carefully move the router back around the ends of the fingers again, to make sure the tails are all equally rounded.

DOVETAIL CUTTERS

Carbide-tipped or solid carbide cutters are best. Sharpness is essential to avoid chipping, and tungsten carbide will stay sharp much longer than high-speed steel. Jig manuals commonly specify $\frac{1}{2}$" cutters, referring to the diameter at the widest part.

A shank diameter of $\frac{1}{2}$" is better than $\frac{1}{4}$". The jig manual will specify the guide bush diameter. The slope angle of the cutter is not critical, provided that it is between about 10 degrees and 14 degrees; however, the lower angles may be less likely to produce chipped tails because their corners will be less fragile.

DRAWER DOVETAILS

Drawer sides are tail boards; drawer fronts and backs are socket boards. The areas of uncut wood between sockets are known as pins. A well-made drawer front or back

7.15 Partial pins at the top edges of drawer fronts cover the tails

will feature partial pins at the top and bottom edges to cover the tails **(7.15)**.

The partial pins, usually called half-pins, should be approximately half as wide as a full pin. This requires that two conditions be met: The jig side stops must be adjusted to produce good bottom half-pins, and the widths of the drawer parts must be chosen to allow for good half-pins at the top edges.

DRAWER SIZES

Fixed-spacing dovetail jigs impose some restrictions on furniture design. For example, if the spacing between dovetails is always $\frac{7}{8}$", in order to produce exact half-pins at each end of a row of dovetails, the width of a drawer front could be 7" or $7\frac{7}{8}$" or $8\frac{3}{4}$" but not $7\frac{1}{2}$" or $8\frac{1}{4}$" or 9". In practice, the permissible sizing options are more flexible because the end pins need not be exactly half the width of a full pin.

An easy way to determine which drawer sizes are best for a particular dovetail jig is to cut a row of sockets with it along a side of a long test piece. The spacing between sockets on the edge will not change when the wood's moisture content changes, and the board can be kept as a permanent record. The spacing between sockets in the end of a test piece will change slightly with changes in MC. Use a square and a fine pencil point to draw lines exactly through the centers of each pin **(7.16)**.

The distances between any two pin centers on the test piece are the ideal drawer

7.16 A test board shows the best widths for drawer parts

depths for that jig because drawer fronts of these widths can have half-pins that are exactly half the width of a full pin.

When you have found the ideal drawer sizes for your jig, you can design the drawer openings for a piece of furniture. The opening for the single drawer of the End Table project in Chapter 21 is shown in **7.17**.

A drawer approximately 4" deep is appropriate for this end table, and the nearest ideal width for my dovetail jig is $4\frac{7}{32}$". The drawer opening has $\frac{3}{16}$"-thick beading fixed around it and is sized to accommodate the drawer plus two thicknesses of beading and an expansion gap above the drawer.

At the design stage, you will not know the required expansion gap, which will depend on the MC of the wood when the drawer is being made. The solution is to design for a gap of about 0.75 percent of the width of the drawer front, that is, the midpoint of an annual width change of up to 1.5 percent, as recommended in Chapter 1 (see "How Much Expansion?" in Chapter 1). When the drawer parts are being fitted to the opening, they can be trimmed to provide expansion gaps appropriate to their MC at that time; this will still leave adequate dovetail half-pins.

Three-quarters of one percent is approximately $\frac{1}{64}$" for every 2" of width, so it is about $\frac{1}{32}$" for the end table drawer. The required opening is therefore $4\frac{7}{32}$" + $\frac{3}{8}$" + $\frac{1}{32}$", which is $4\frac{5}{8}$" wide. Once you have calculated the opening, you will know where to position the rails, and hence where to put the mortises in the table legs. Similar calculations are shown in Chapter 19 for the Chest of Drawers project.

When constructing the drawer, refer to **Table 4** in Chapter 1 for the actual expansion gap to suit the MC of the wood. The drawer parts can then be cut to fit the opening and leave room for the gap.

7.17 Beaded drawer opening

This procedure will produce drawers with the proper expansion gaps and adequate half-pins.

SETTING UP THE DOVETAIL JIG

Getting all the adjustments right is an iterative process of testing, adjusting, and retesting. The items that have to be adjusted are (1) the router-cutter depth setting, which determines the tightness of fit of the tails and sockets; (2) the forward projection of the fingerplate, which determines the depth of insertion of the tails into the sockets; and (3) the jig side stops, which determine the distance from the bottom edges of the drawer parts to the first tails and sockets.

Each time a cutter is fitted into the router, you must adjust it to cut tails and sockets that have the right tightness of fit. The jig side stops and the fingerplate may also need to be adjusted at each setup. There are four side stops, so with a fingerplate adjustment at each end, and the cutter adjustment, you may need to make seven adjustments in

7.18 Check for gaps under the fingerplate

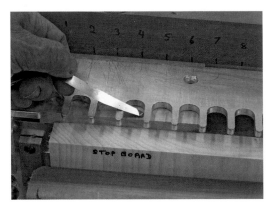

7.19 Check for gaps between the fingerplate and the socket board

7.20 To move the stop outward by a measured amount, clamp the socket board against the stop and then move the stop to allow a feeler gauge to be sandwiched between the stop and socket board

all—and each of these may need several trials with test pieces.

Make a tails test piece at least as thick as the actual tail boards, and a sockets test piece at least $\frac{1}{2}$" thick. Make both pieces at least 4" wide. Since the test pieces must be cut shorter after each test, it is wise to make them at least 10" long to begin with.

Make a stop board about 6" wide and at least $\frac{3}{4}$" thick for stiffness. It will need to be long enough to be clamped in the jig's front clamp.

If you are making drawers, prepare two backer strips for each one. Plane them all to the same size—at least $\frac{1}{2}$" thick, 1" wide, and an inch longer than the widest drawer side. The backer strips will be placed lengthwise under the fingerplate with one edge held tightly against a tail board. Make a wider board of the same thickness and length as the strips, or just a little thinner than the strips, to be clamped behind them under the fingerplate. Fix a screw near the end of the board, as shown in **7.14a**.

Begin the adjustments by installing the dovetail cutter and the guide bush in the router. Adjust the depth so the cutter will project below the fingerplate about $\frac{3}{8}$" or by the amount specified in the jig's manual. Next, clamp the tails test piece vertically in the front clamp at the left-hand end of the jig. The test piece must touch the side stop and the fingerplate. Use a 0.002" feeler gauge to check that there are no gaps between the fingerplate and the top of the test piece **(7.18)**.

Plug in the router and place it on the fingerplate, with the cutter clear of everything. Start the router and cut the tails. Stop the router and pull it clear of the jig before raising it. Remove the tails test piece.

Loosen the fingerplate and place the socket test piece under it at the left-hand end. Press down on the fingerplate and lock it. Place the stop board in the front clamp, about ⅜" below the fingerplate, so that the cutter will not cut into it deeply, and then clamp it tight. Now pull the socket test piece hard against the stop board and the jig top's left-hand side stop. Clamp the test piece, and check for gaps with the feeler gauge **(7.19)**. Place the router on the fingerplate and cut the sockets.

Remove the socket piece, and insert the tails into the sockets to check the tightness of fit. When the fit is right, you will be able to knock the tails in with the side of your fist and you will probably need to use a mallet to tap them apart again. It is better for them to be too tight than too loose, though if they are much too tight, splitting can occur. You can make the fit tighter by increasing the cutter projection and loosen it by reducing the cutter projection. Adjust the cutter projection by about 1/64" if necessary, and recut the tails and sockets after cutting off the first set at the table saw.

If the insertion depth is too shallow to allow you to properly test the tightness, adjust the fingerplate in toward the jig body and then recut the tails and sockets. Repeat until the tails can be inserted almost flush with the tops of the sockets. Do not try to get the insertion depth exactly right while you are working on the fit, and do not worry about the side-stop adjustments until both the fit and the insertion depth are correct: Concentrate on one thing at a time.

When you are satisfied with the fit, pay attention to the insertion depth. Move the fingerplate inward to increase the insertion or outward to reduce it. Aim to get the tails flush with, or less than five-thousandths of an inch above, the socket board. Work at one end of the jig until the depth is correct, and then correct it at the other end. If the fingerplate adjusting device is a screw, it is a good idea to calibrate it by using feeler gauges to estimate the change in insertion depth that results from one full turn.

Next, adjust the side stops at each end. There are three objectives here: (1) to make the bottom edges of the drawer parts exactly flush with each other when they are assembled, (2) to produce bottom pins that are about half the width of a full pin, and (3) to make the distance from the bottom tails and sockets to the bottom edges of the parts equal at both ends of the jig. The jig manual will probably describe how to set the stops initially, but final adjustments must be made by testing. Make the initial adjustments and then make test cuts in the socket test piece at one end of the jig.

If the half-pin that was against the stop is not approximately half the width of a full pin, the socket-board side stop must be adjusted. Select a feeler gauge of a thickness about equal to the adjustment the socket board will require. Adjust the stop by doing one of the following:

- To move the stop *outward* (and make the half-pin wider), clamp the test piece against the stop, loosen the stop and move it outward, insert the feeler gauge between the stop and the test piece **(7.20)**, tighten the stop against the gauge, and then remove the gauge and reclamp the test piece against the stop.
- To move the stop *inward,* first place the gauge against the stop **(7.21)**, clamp the test piece against the gauge, remove the gauge, move the stop in, and tighten it against the test piece.

When the half-pin's width is satisfactory, cut tails at the same end of the jig and insert them into the sockets. If the edges of the two pieces are not flush, the tail-board side stop will need to be adjusted. To

7.21 To allow the stop to be moved inward by a measured amount, place the gauge against the stop before pushing the socket board toward the stop

7.22 Find a feeler gauge equal in thickness to the step between the edges of the tail board and the socket board

7.23 Inside faces of the two socket pieces clamped together, with the sockets exactly aligned

7.24 The outside faces of the two tail pieces together, with the tails aligned

adjust the tail-board stop, select a feeler gauge as thick as the offset between the tail-board and socket-board edges, as illustrated in **7.22**.

Adjust the tail-board stop in or out, using the feeler gauge as you did previously for the socket-board stops.

When the side stop adjustments at one end of the jig are both correct, cut off the dovetailed ends of the test pieces at about 1" in length. Mark them "LH" or "RH", and save them.

Make test cuts at the other end of the jig. Here, the stops must produce not only

good half-pins and flush edges, but bottom tails and sockets that are set in from the edges by exactly the same amount as the ones at the first end. This way, when a groove for the drawer bottom is cut, it can be in the center of all the tails.

Cut sockets and tails at the second end of the jig, and place them against the pieces from the first end. Clamp the inside faces of the two socket pieces together, with the sockets exactly aligned **(7.23)**. If the edges of the pieces are not exactly flush, measure the discrepancy with feeler gauges and adjust the socket-board stop accordingly.

Place the outside faces of the two tail pieces together, with the tails aligned (7.24). If the edges of the pieces are not flush, adjust the tail-board stop.

Your goal should be to achieve edges to the tail and socket pieces that are flush when assembled, and to make any difference between the left and right end half-pins less than 0.010".

When placing the test pieces in the jig, always blow out any dust and debris that might prevent them from being held tightly to the side stops.

PROCEDURE FOR DOVETAILING DRAWERS

A dovetailed drawer has four sets of tails and four sets of sockets. Two of each must be cut at the left-hand end of the jig and two of each at the right-hand end. The faces and edges of each piece must be oriented correctly in the jig. You can take advantage of a simple routine that ensures that each piece goes to the right place, the right way up, and the right way around. The routine will also minimize clamp and fingerplate adjustments when you are making multiple drawers at the same time.

After you cut the drawer parts to size, sand their inside faces. Stand the parts on the bench in their correct relative positions with the front at 6 o'clock, the left side at 9 o'clock, the back at 12 o'clock, and the right side at 3 o'clock. Then lay them on their outside faces so their bottom edges form a hollow rectangle (7.25).

Mark the parts, as shown in 7.25 and 7.26. At the junction of the front and the left sides, mark the inside corners of both pieces with an L. Next mark R on the corners of the front and right side where they meet, mark L on the right side and back, and finally R on the adjacent corners of the back and left side. Check that the

7.25 The drawer parts are laid out with their outside faces down and their bottom edges forming a hollow rectangle. The drawer front is at the bottom of the photograph, the back is at the top, and the left and right sides are in their correct positions

7.26 Marking up the drawer parts to help position them correctly in the dovetail jig

arrangement is as shown in **7.25** and **7.26**, with LL, RR, LL, RR, at the inside corners of the rectangle, starting at the bottom left corner.

If you are making multiple drawers, lay out the others in the same fashion, on top of the first set of parts, and mark them in the same way.

Before dovetailing the drawer parts, make one last preparatory step. Because of the direction in which the dovetail bit rotates, chipping can sometimes occur at the tail-board edges that are to the right when clamped in the jig. Chipping on the right-hand edge of a dovetailed drawer side is shown in **7.27**.

Such chipping can be prevented by scoring these edges with a knife before dovetailing the drawer sides. The scoring must be exactly level with the bottoms of the tails and can be quickly done by holding one of the tail's test pieces against each appropriate edge and marking the edge with a knife, as shown in **7.28**. Then you can use the knife and a small square to score across the edge. The edges to be

scored are the tail-board edges opposite the L marks and the tail-board edges adjacent to the R marks.

The rules for positioning the drawer parts in the jig are as follows:
- The bottom edges always butt against the jig's side stops.
- The inside faces always face out from the jig.
- L and R denote which end of the jig each end of the parts goes to.
- The tail boards (drawer sides) always go vertically in the front clamp.
- The socket boards (drawer fronts and backs) always go horizontally under the top clamp.

When positioning the parts in the jig, remember to blow out any dust or chips.

The tails and sockets are cut in the following sequence:
1. Cut all the L ends of the drawer sides at the left-hand end of the jig.
2. Cut all the R ends of the drawer sides at the right-hand end of the jig.
3. Cut all the L ends of the drawer fronts at the left-hand end of the jig.
4. Cut all the R ends of the drawer fronts at the right-hand end of the jig.

7.27 Chipping of the right-hand edge of a drawer side

7.28 Marking the edges before scoring them

5. Cut all the L ends of the drawer backs at the left-hand end of the jig.
6. Cut all the R ends of the drawer backs at the right-hand end of the jig.

After all the jig and router adjustments have been made, prepare to dovetail the tail pieces (the drawer sides) by fixing a backer strip and backboard under the fingerplate at the left-hand end. Clamp the stop board into the front clamp, not quite touching the fingerplate, and push the backboard and backer strip firmly up to it. Clamp the backboard and remove the stop board. Then do the following:

- Clamp the L end of a tail board (a drawer side) into the front clamp, against the stop, at the left-hand end of the jig. The inside face must be facing out from the jig, and the L mark must be at top left.
- Check that there are no gaps between the tail board and the jig body or the backer strip.
- Use a 0.002" feeler gauge to check for gaps between the fingerplate and the tail board. If necessary, loosen the clamp and adjust the tail board.

- Check again that the L is showing at top left, and the edge is touching the stop.
- Cut the tails.
- Inspect the tails before removing the tail board from the clamp. Check to see that the backs of all tails have been equally rounded.
- Remove the tail board and flip the backer strip around so that its uncut face is to the front. Clamp the L end of the next tail board at the left-hand end of the jig. Repeat the above procedure until the tail board L-ends for all the drawers have been cut, using a fresh backer strip after every second set of tails.
- When all the tail board L-ends have been cut, move the backer strip and backboard to the right-hand end of the jig, after reversing the backboard to place the stop screw out of the way. Position them with the stop board as before, and clamp the backboard into position. Check that the backer strip cannot move toward the right. Remove the stop board.
- Cut the tails of all the R-ends of the tail boards at the right-hand end of the jig. Make the same checks before cutting: Ensure tight contact with the jig body at both edges of the boards, tight contact with the fingerplate, bottom edges hard against the stop, inside faces facing out from the jig, and R marks showing at the top right-hand corner. Repeat the two most important checks: R showing at top right and the R-edge touching the stop. Flip over or replace the backer strip each time.

When all the tails have been cut, remove the backer strip and backboard. Loosen the fingerplate and place a drawer front under it at the left-hand end, with the L-mark toward the left-hand stop and the inside face up. If the

7.29 Dovetailed drawer sides

L mark is obscured by the fingerplate, check to see that the R-mark is at the opposite end of the drawer front. Press down on the fingerplate and lock it into position.

- Clamp the stop board in the front clamp, about ⅜" below the fingerplate so that the router will not cut it deeply.
- Pull the drawer front hard against the stop board and the jig's side stop. Clamp it in place tightly.
- Check with the feeler gauge for gaps under the fingerplate. If necessary, adjust the fingerplate.
- Recheck to ensure that the L-mark is at the left front, the bottom edge of the socket board is against the left-hand side stop, and the end of the board is against the stop board. Cut the sockets.

- Repeat with the L-ends of the other fronts. If the fronts and backs have the same thickness, repeat with the L-ends of the backs also.
- Move the stop board to the right-hand end of the jig, and cut out the sockets on the R-ends of the fronts. Remember to check that no gaps are under the fingerplate, R is at front right, the bottom edge of the socket board is against the side stop, the end of the socket board is against the stop board, and inside faces are showing.
- After cutting sockets into all the drawer fronts, adjust the fingerplate height for the backs, if their thickness differs from the fronts. Cut the sockets into the drawer backs using the same procedure as for the fronts.

Part 5

Other Essential Tools and Aids

8 Essential Hand Tools

8.1 A 9" metal bench plane

8.2 Hand plane with blade assembly removed to show the frog

POWER TOOLS USUALLY GIVE BET-ter, faster, more accurate results than hand tools—and with much less effort. However, some jobs are so simple that they can be done with hand tools in less time than it would take to set up a machine. For example, making a small radius on an edge can sometimes be done with a hand plane and sandpaper in less time than it would take to fit and adjust a router bit. And then there are tasks for which no power tool is suited, such as removing hardened glue from an inside corner that can be easily accessed with a card scraper. For such occasions, you should become familiar with a few basic hand tools; otherwise, you will find yourself spending ten minutes setting up a machine for a job that could have been done in seconds by hand.

The hand tools you will need to use from time to time are a hand plane, a chisel, a handsaw, and a card scraper. Each of these tools is discussed below.

HAND PLANES

The most appropriate type of hand plane for occasional use is a metal bench plane. The 9"-long one shown in **8.1** is a good choice.

In **8.2**, the blade assembly has been removed to show an angled metal block, called the frog, screwed to the base. The frog supports the blade and is adjustable forward or backward. The frog is fixed in its adjusted position by two screws, which are visible in the photograph.

A steel plate—the cap iron—is held to the blade by a screw (8.3). The front end of this plate is curved so that when the plane is pushed forward, shavings are forced to curl away from the blade. The cap iron is sometimes called the chip breaker.

The blade and cap iron are held to the frog by a thicker plate, the lever cap. At the top of the lever cap is a lever that clamps all three parts (the blade, the chip breaker, and the lever cap itself) to the frog. The three items in place on the frog, with the lever in the clamped position, are shown in 8.4.

If the lever is raised, you can adjust the clamping pressure by turning the lever cap screw, which passes through the assembly and into the frog.

The frog has three functions:

1. It can be moved forward or backward to reduce or increase the gap between the cutting edge of the blade and the front edge of a slot in the bottom face, or sole, of the plane body (8.5). This slot is called the throat of the plane. Loosen the screws that fix the frog to the base of the plane to permit adjustment, and tighten them when the opening is correct. Every time the frog is adjusted, its front edge must be made parallel to the back edge of the slot.

2. The frog supports an adjustment lever that can pivot the blade from side to side to make its cutting edge either parallel to the sole, as in 8.5,

8.3 The cap iron and blade

8.4 Lever cap pressure-adjustment screw

8.5 The opening in front of the blade is controlled by the frog position

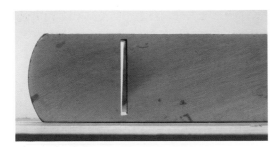

8.6 Blade angled

8.7 Depth-of-cut adjuster wheel

8.8 Planing with the grain

8.9 Grain reversal

or angled to it, as in **8.6**. When the blade is angled, it will cut deeper at one side.

3. An adjustment wheel at the back of the frog (**8.7**) controls how far the blade projects below the sole and sets the depth of cut.

Using a Hand Plane

Turn the blade adjustment wheel until the blade projects out roughly $\frac{1}{32}$" from the sole. Then sight along the sole from the front end and move the lever that tilts the blade. When the blade projects evenly out from the sole, turn the wheel back until the blade retracts and cannot cut. Using a piece of scrap wood as a test piece, turn the wheel to increase the blade projection until it begins to cut. Apply downward pressure on both handles for the forward stroke; release the pressure or lift the plane for the return stroke. With any luck, the plane will perform adequately and you will require little practice to get a feel for it.

The most fundamental rule for good planing is to cut "with the grain," that is, in the direction that pushes the grain down rather than lifting it. A workpiece from the side, with the grain rising from right to left, is shown in **8.8**. The plane is shown facing in the correct direction for planing when the grain is sloping like this.

Unfortunately, the slope of the grain in a typical workpiece is likely to reverse in places, as it does in the piece of wood shown in **8.9**.

The only way to plane this piece with the grain is to reverse the plane at each side of the transition area. In the transition area itself, it may be necessary to plane using a circular motion. With such an awkward grain pattern, the blade must be set to produce the thinnest shavings possible.

Fine Tuning

If the plane is adjusted as described, and its blade is sharp, its performance should be adequate for any hand-planing task this book's projects require. However, a hand plane's performance can usually be improved further by more detailed tuning. Start by removing the blade and cap-iron assembly, and then loosen the screw that holds them together. Position the cap iron $\frac{1}{16}$" from the blade edge. You can make this distance greater for heavy planing or smaller if you want to make thin shavings. Retighten the screw.

Check to see that the frog is tightened in place and that its front edge is parallel to the back edge of the throat. If necessary, loosen its fixing screws to make it parallel.

Seat the blade and cap-iron assembly against the frog, with the cap iron on top. Place the lever cap on the assembly, and clamp it with the lever. The lever should require firm pressure from your thumb to clamp the assembly to the frog. If necessary, raise the lever and adjust the lever cap screw to produce enough clamping pressure.

Turn the blade adjuster wheel until the cutting edge is approximately flush with the sole; then inspect the gap between the cutting edge and the front edge of the throat. If you wish to change the gap to suit heavier or lighter planing, remove the blade assembly and move the frog forward or backward by loosening its fixing screws and turning the adjuster screw that is below the blade adjuster wheel.

Using the tilt lever, set the blade parallel to the throat and then turn the blade adjuster counterclockwise to retract the blade to a noncutting position. When you begin planing, gradually turn the adjuster wheel clockwise until shavings are produced.

You can get optimum performance from your plane only through trial-and-error adjustments for each job. When planing wood that has difficult grain characteristics, the throat gap might need to be set to $\frac{1}{32}$" and the cap iron set to $\frac{1}{64}$" from the blade edge. With fine-grained woods, this arrangement can produce shavings that are about $\frac{1}{1,000}$" thick. If the wood grain will allow heavier cuts to be made without causing tear-out, you can increase the blade's projection and combine this with a throat gap of perhaps $\frac{1}{8}$", and a cap-iron setback of more than $\frac{1}{16}$".

For most planing jobs, you will probably compromise by choosing settings of around $\frac{1}{16}$" for the throat gap and $\frac{1}{32}$" for the cap-iron setback; if so, the only regular adjustments that you will make will be to the depth of cut.

Troubleshooting

If you are dissatisfied with the plane because it produces tear-out or because you cannot make it cut easily, further adjustments or modifications are necessary.

Sole Flatness

The bottom face (the sole) of the plane must contact the work at three places: at the front and back of the sole, and at the front of the throat. The front of the throat must hold down the wood to prevent tear-out ahead of the blade, and the front and back of the sole must support the plane at a constant angle to the work. These three areas must be in the same geometric plane.

As a rough-and-ready check of flatness, you can hold a steel rule on edge on the sole and hold it up to the light. No light should show under the rule at the three critical areas. For a more precise test, or to flatten the sole, you can rub it on a flat abrasive surface, such as a sheet of silicon carbide sandpaper taped to a 12" × 18" piece of quarter-inch plate glass with its edges ground smooth.

8.10 Hand plane throat area with frog removed

8.11 Frog aligned with chamfer

Flatten the sole with the blade in place and properly tensioned by the lever cap. Adjust the blade well back to keep it safe from the sandpaper. Start with coarse-grit paper, and rub the sole over it while keeping the sole flat to the paper and exerting pressure on both handles. Keep the paper wet, and check the surface of the sole after rubbing for a few seconds. It will be obvious which areas have been in contact with the abrasive. Continue the process until the front and back edges, as well as the area around the front of the throat, show a scratch pattern indicating that they are in the same geometric plane. Replace the silicon carbide paper with finer grades, up to 600-grit, and rub again to polish the important contact areas. When you are finished, remove the blade and wash everything with mineral spirits to remove any abrasive particles that would dull the blade.

If the sole is significantly "out-of-true," it will require a lot of work with the coarsest grade of sandpaper you can find. This situation is best handled at a machine shop, or, if the plane is new, by returning it for a replacement or refund.

In addition to flattening the sole, it is a good idea to chamfer its front and back edges with a file to minimize damage that can occur if they are accidentally rammed into part of a workpiece.

Throat Gap

The front edge of the throat can prevent tear-out only if it is close to the cutting edge of the blade. For most jobs, the front edge of the throat should lie no more than $\frac{1}{16}$" from the blade. It can be as much as $\frac{1}{8}$" for heavy planing, or as little as $\frac{1}{32}$" for fine planing. In principle, a smaller gap is better, but there is a limit: An overly small gap can become clogged with shavings.

The distance the blade projects affects the gap, so it should be set first. If the gap is not appropriate, it can be changed by moving the frog forwards or backwards. The blade must be removed to provide access to the frog's fixing screws. When these screws are loosened, a screw behind the frog can be turned to adjust the size of the gap. After each change, the frog's fixing screws must be tightened and the blade and lever cap replaced so that the gap can be checked.

Frog Seating

The throat area with the frog removed is shown in **8.10**. The back edge of the throat is chamfered at a 45-degree angle. When the blade is seated against the chamfer, it will be supported close to its cutting edge.

8.12 Underside of frog

In **8.11**, the frog is flush with the chamfer. Now the blade will be supported over most of its back surface. However, for other frog positions, the front part of the blade may be supported only by the frog. For good blade support in all situations, the angled face of the frog must be free of burrs. Eliminate burrs by gently removing any roughness with a smooth-cutting file. The chamfer at the back of the throat can also be smoothed if necessary. Any work on the chamfer must be minimal so as to avoid changing its angle. If you need to smooth the chamfer, it is safest to do it by sanding very gently with fine sandpaper wrapped over a steel rule.

The underside of the frog also has a chamfer (**8.12**), which slides along the seating area behind the throat. This chamfer, and the seating area, should be smoothed if necessary.

Cap Iron

The cap iron (chip breaker) is curved at its front end, as shown in **8.13** and **8.14**. Its function is to force shavings to curl upward. It complements the holding-down action of the front edge of the throat, which prevents tear-out.

When planing wood that is prone to tear-out, set the cap iron very close to the blade edge, as in **8.14**, and choose the smallest throat gap that will not become clogged.

To help the shavings to curl, the curved surface of the cap iron should be smooth. Its edge must contact the blade across its entire width; otherwise, shavings will be trapped underneath.

CHISELS

Your main use for a chisel is to clean out corners that power tools cannot reach. You will also use a chisel to carve the curved ends of the stile chamfers for the Bookcase or Chest of Drawers projects and to chop out the ends of stopped grooves. You could also use one to smooth the end grain of convex shapes (e.g., the plinth for the Chest of Drawers).

Two chisels, ¼" wide and ¾" or 1" wide, will suffice for general use. In addition, you should buy at least one very

8.13 The cap iron (chip breaker) is curved at its front end

8.14 Cap iron set close to cutting edge

8.15 Cutting with a chisel, at a marked line

8.16 Pressure on the bevel from the wood in front of it has forced the chisel into the wood behind the line

8.17 Removing waste after a vertical cut

8.18 Breaking out chips inside the perimeter of a mortise

8.19 Chiseling back to the line without bruising the wood

cheap chisel for removing glue before it dries, because a good chisel should never be used on wet glue. For occasional use, it doesn't really matter if the chisels have square edges or if they are the beveled type. The cheap glue chisels should not be sharp, but the others should be kept very sharp.

Chopping

Chopping refers to making rectangular slots or recesses. You will be working to pencil or marking-gauge lines and will want to cut exactly to the lines. To do so, begin by cutting at least $\frac{1}{16}$" away from the lines. The wood in front of the chisel will exert a backward force on the chisel bevel, so if you tried to start exactly at a line, you would find the chisel forced back behind it. In **8.15**, an attempt is being made to cut exactly at a marked line. How pressure on the bevel has forced the chisel back into the wood, behind the line, is shown in **8.16**.

When you are chopping out an area of wood, start with shallow vertical cuts at least $\frac{1}{16}$" inside the outline; then gently remove slivers from the area inside the cuts. In **8.17**, shallow vertical cuts have been chiseled at about $\frac{1}{16}$" from the marked outline. The chisel is shown removing a sliver of wood by cutting at an angle from the inside area toward the vertical cut.

Deepen the vertical cuts and remove more slivers to make a well-defined chopping area. Then make a series of vertical cuts across the grain within that area. After each cut, lever the chisel forward to break out a series of chips **(8.18)**. Keep the chisel vertical as you hit it with a mallet, and do not chop too deeply before clearing away the waste. Deepen the perimeter cuts and continue chopping out material inside the outline.

When you have reached the required depth, and there is no more than $\frac{1}{16}$" of wood in front of the lines, you will be able to cut at the lines without bruising the wood behind the chisel **(8.19)**.

Paring

Paring is pushing a chisel across a surface to make very shallow cuts, usually with the chisel held vertically. In **8.20** and **8.21**, a roughly cut curve is being pared smooth.

The chisel is being carefully controlled with the fingers of one hand while the other hand pushes it across the rough surface. Essentially, one hand holds back the chisel while the other pushes it forward. A smooth, solid surface under the workpiece

8.20 Paring a curve smooth

8.21 Taking very shallow paring cuts

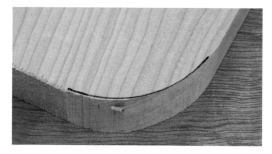

8.22 Partly pared end-grain surface

is necessary to prevent the bottom edge from chipping.

Very thin shavings are taken off each time until the surface is smooth. The secret lies in keeping the chisel vertical and starting each cut very close to the edge; if the chisel is sharp, this will not be difficult. Most of the curve pared smooth and a thin shaving just started on the remaining rough surface are shown in **8.22**.

8.23 Practicing shaping the ends of a chamfer

8.24 It is difficult to complete a concave shape with a flat chisel; the curve is best completed by sanding

8.25 Japanese-style handsaw

8.26 Close-up of teeth: 24 per inch

Carving

The only carving that is required for the projects in this book is to shape the concave ends of stile chamfers for the Chest of Drawers and Bookcase projects (**8.23** and **8.24**).

Very shallow cuts are needed for this task, so one hand must restrain the chisel to prevent it from shooting forward. Do not allow the back of the chisel to bruise the corner at the tip of the shape. Take note of the grain's slope, and change cutting direction as necessary to avoid tearout. With concave shapes like this, it is not possible to carve right to the line with a flat chisel; instead, the final shape can be produced by hand-sanding.

An alternative to controlling the chisel with both hands is to use a small wooden mallet. By holding the chisel with one hand and applying a series of light taps with a mallet, the chisel can be moved through the wood in very small guided increments. Guide the chisel edge close to the surface to cut thin chips or shavings. If the chisel starts to cut deeply, stop and remove the chip by cutting from the opposite direction.

HANDSAWS

I seldom use any handsaw other than the Japanese-style one shown in **8.25** and **8.26**. The blade is just over $\frac{1}{100}$" thick and is set into a brass rib for stiffness. It has 24 teeth per inch and will cut a kerf not much more than $\frac{1}{64}$" wide.

Unlike Western-style saws, this type cuts on the backstroke. A fine-toothed dovetail saw, which cuts on the forward stroke, would be a good alternative. The depth of cut either type can achieve is limited by the backing rib, but deep cuts with a handsaw are seldom necessary.

CARD SCRAPERS

A card scraper is a simple handheld sheet of thin, flexible steel. Its traditional use is for smoothing "wild grain" that would be prone to being torn out by even the sharpest and most finely set hand plane. The scraper can make shavings that are thinner than those made by any hand plane, and it can produce a very smooth surface on the most difficult woods.

As shown in **8.27**, a card scraper is flexed between the fingers and thumbs and held at an angle to the vertical. It can be angled forward and pushed, or backward and pulled. When properly sharpened, it will quickly produce a surprising volume of shavings. Scrapers are most often used on small areas or in places where power tools cannot reach.

A scraper needs periodic sharpening to renew its scraping edges. A scraping edge is a burr produced by applying pressure on the scraper with a piece of hard steel. The burr is almost too small to be seen without magnification, but it is very obvious to the touch. Burrs being raised by rubbing a hard steel tool on the scraper edge are shown in **8.28**. The tool in this photo is a purpose-made one, but alternatives such as the back of a chisel or the shank of a router bit could be used.

One of my main uses for a scraper is removing glue from inside corners. For this reason, I sharpen all four scraper edges. Since burrs are raised on both sides of each edge, this creates a total of eight burrs.

If an edge is even slightly rounded, it will be impossible to raise a burr, so the first step in sharpening an edge is to make it flat. This can be done with a file, but it is easier to use a belt sander. Clamp the scraper into a vise with a wide block of wood in front of it, just below the scraper edge. A scraper and wood block, clamped in a vise and being sanded, are shown in **8.29**.

8.27 A card scraper in use

8.28 Raising burrs by rubbing a hard steel tool on the scraper edge

8.29 Using a belt sander to flatten a scraper edge

8.30 Honing the scraper edge on a diamond sharpening stone

8.31 Honing the scraper faces on a medium-grit stone

8.32 Burnishing the faces

Note the pencil marks on the block in **8.29**. They will be sanded off evenly if the sander is held at 90 degrees to the scraper's sides. When they disappear, the scraper's edge will have been sanded flat and square to the sides. If you use this method, keep the sander moving along the edge; do not allow it to make the scraper so hot that the temper of the steel is affected.

The next step is to hone the scraper's edge, either on a sheet of wet-and-dry sandpaper taped to a flat surface or on a coarse sharpening stone (a diamond stone, shown in **8.30**, works best). Hold the scraper against a wood block. Use one index finger to press down on the block and the other to press down on the scraper. Keep the block and scraper perpendicular to the sanding surface but at an angle to the direction of movement to avoid making a groove in the sandpaper or stone. Check frequently to see that the block is not tilted. Inspect the edge with a magnifier to determine when the scratch pattern from the honing has replaced the marks left by the file or belt sander.

Repeat the honing procedure using a medium stone (around 700-grit). Again, use the magnifier to determine when the previous scratch pattern has been completely removed.

At this stage, the honing will have produced burrs in the scraper's edge. These are not the type of burrs we want, however, so remove them by honing the faces of the scraper. Lay the scraper on the medium-grit stone (**8.31**) and hold it absolutely flat while rubbing it over the stone. Be very careful not to allow the scraper to tilt, or you will produce a bevel and make it impossible to raise a scraping burr. Press down with your fingers all along the edge, and hone both faces until you can feel that all the burrs have been removed.

Clamp the scraper into a vise with about ½" sticking up. Since you are going to push down on the edge with a burnishing tool, it could be dangerous to have more of the scraper sticking up. Hold the burnisher horizontal, and stroke the edge forcefully (**8.28**). Feel each side of the edge to check that burrs have been created (you will be able to catch a fingernail on them).

Finally, with the scraper still in the vise, angle the burnisher about 3 degrees from horizontal. Make a few more strokes to turn down the burr on one side to form a hook. Repeat with the burnisher angled to the other side.

Although this procedure will raise usable burrs, an alternative method will produce better and longer-lasting ones. This method requires an extra stage after the edge and faces are honed: First flatten and hone the edge and the faces, as described above, then burnish the faces on each side, near to the edge, as illustrated in **8.32**.

The scraper must be placed on a flat hard surface. I use my table saw and hold the scraper in place with double-sided tape. Stroke the face of the scraper with the burnisher, using considerable force. Hold the burnisher's handle about two degrees lower than horizontal to concentrate pressure on the scraper's edge. Make about twenty strokes; then turn the scraper over and repeat on the other side. Depending on the hardness of the scraper, you may need to continue burnishing for a while. The harder the scraper steel, the longer the burr will last before it needs

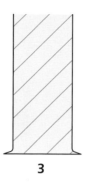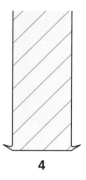

8.33 Stages in turning the burrs outward on the scraper edge using the longer method

renewing. The softer the steel, the easier it will be to raise burrs.

Complete the job by clamping the scraper into a vise with about ½" sticking up, as you would for burnishing using the simpler method. Your remaining objective is to turn the burrs outward, for which light burnishing pressure is adequate. Stroke the edge with the burnisher, and feel each side to ensure that the burrs have been turned. When you have pushed the burrs outward on each side, angle the burnisher to turn them down by about 3 degrees to form hooks.

The longer method just described transforms each edge through the stages shown schematically in the end views in **8.33**.

At stage 1 in **8.33**, the edge is made square; at stage 2, pressure has been applied on each face to squeeze out burrs that are parallel to the faces; at stage 3, the burrs have been pushed outward, perpendicular to the faces; and at stage 4, the burrs have been pushed back a few degrees to form hooks. The simpler method omits stage 2.

9 Drill Presses and Drills

A DRILL PRESS IS AN ESSENTIAL item in the workshop. The first choice you need to make is between a bench-mounted and a freestanding model. Freestanding drill presses are probably more versatile, but the decision really boils down to which type will most conveniently suit the available space.

Drill press sizes are defined by the diameter or width of the largest workpiece that can be centered under the chuck. For example, when the space between the chuck and the support column is 7", the drill press size will be quoted as 14". Although here bigger is better, a 14" drill press is quite adequate for most workshops.

Chuck capacity is important. You need one that can take a ½" drill bit; larger capacities are nice to have but are seldom needed.

Most drill presses have a variable-speed drive, which is important. Slow speeds are best for most drilling jobs, but higher speeds can be helpful when using drum sander attachments.

Keyless chucks offer an advantage but are not essential because this fast drill-changing facility is just a convenience. Also, the chuck key is not as likely to be mislaid as are those for handheld drills.

The maximum height between the chuck and the drill press table is an important

9.1 Twist drill bits

9.2 Forstner bits

consideration. My bench-mounted model has a maximum vertical clearance of 18", which has always been adequate.

Finally, a depth stop is an important feature on a drill press.

DRILL BITS

You will need two types of drill bits. The most frequently used are twist drills, like the ones shown in **9.1**.

Drill bits are made from high-speed steel and should be capable of drilling wood and metal. Quality is important because cheap drill bits tend to blunt quickly when they drill into metal. A full set comprises 29 bits, starting at $\frac{1}{16}$" diameter and going up to $\frac{1}{2}$" diameter in $\frac{1}{64}$" increments. Cheap bits may be too short for some jobs,

so buy the longer ones sold as jobber-length bits.

In addition to twist drills, you will need some Forstner bits, illustrated in **9.2**. They cut very clean flat-bottomed holes and come in sizes of $\frac{1}{4}$" diameter and upward. Small sets of Forstner bits sized from $\frac{1}{4}$" to 1" (in $\frac{1}{8}$" increments) will cover most situations, but bigger sizes are occasionally useful.

In addition to being able to cut very clean holes, Forstner bits are very stable during use. They can even drill overlapping holes without wandering off-center.

When using either twist drills or Forstners, it is important to first mark the center of the required hole with a pointed tool, such as a bradawl, to help position the drill at the start.

10 Measuring and Marking Tools

TOOLS THAT YOU USE TO MEASURE and mark could be seen as the most important tools in your workshop. And you do not need to spend a lot of money to buy very accurate ones: The difference in cost between a poor ruler and an excellent one is not much, and a dial gauge or micrometer that can measure to a thousandth of an inch can be bought for a modest amount.

MARKING GAUGE

When several pieces of wood have to be marked at exactly the same positions, a marking gauge is the best tool for the job. Even if there is a small error in the gauge setting, the marks will be in matching positions on every piece.

A modern-style marking gauge is shown in **10.1** and **10.2** It is a steel rod with a brass cheek that can be fixed at any distance from a small steel wheel with a cutting edge. The inside face of the wheel is

10.2 The marking wheel on the end of the gauge

tapered, so when it cuts a line on a workpiece, it pulls the cheek tight against the workpiece edge. This type of gauge is much easier to use accurately than traditional marking gauges. Variations on this style of gauge feature micro-adjustment facilities that are well worth a few extra dollars.

If you buy one without a micro-adjuster, choose one that has a large-headed fixing screw; small screw heads can be difficult to use accurately.

The cutting wheels will wear out, but not all suppliers carry replacements. You can encourage those who do by buying your gauge along with a spare wheel from them.

10.1 Marking gauge

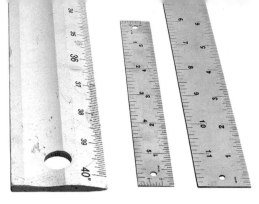

10.3 Steel rules with a bright satin finish

RULERS

A 12" steel rule will be your most frequently used measuring tool. Many rules are difficult to read because their markings are not distinct against the steel surface, and the problem only gets worse as the surface receives wear and tear. I find that rules with a bright satin finish, like the ones in **10.3**, are easiest to read.

Markings should begin and finish at the ends of the rule, that is, the rule should have an exact length. Graduations smaller than $\frac{1}{32}$" are not necessary. The best rules have machined edges and are guaranteed not to deviate from straightness by more than 0.001" per inch of length. This makes them able to double as straightedges.

Sometimes a 12" rule is too long to fit in the space you want to measure. For a small amount, you can buy a 6" rule of similar quality. One that is available (from www.leevalley.com) is graduated on its ends as well as its sides; the end markings are a great convenience when setting blade or bit heights.

You will occasionally need a longer rule, say 36", and it is a good idea to get one that can double as a straightedge. Aluminum rules are well-suited for this purpose if they are at least $\frac{1}{8}$" thick and their straightness is specified. For an even longer straightedge, which can be used to check the parallelism of jointer tables, 6-foot aluminum rules are widely available. Their straightness is unlikely to be specified, so check it by holding two of them edge to edge.

MEASURING CALIPERS

When the thickness of a workpiece is critical, you cannot depend solely on your planer's thickness indicator. Measuring calipers, as shown in **10.4**, will provide a much more accurate measurement of thickness. The one shown has a dial readout; traditional versions have a vernier scale that is just as easy to read (perhaps even easier) once you get used to it. Calipers are also available with digital readouts, as are versions with fractions and decimal markings on the same dial. Prices vary widely: I have found the cheap ones to be accurate but less durable than more expensive ones.

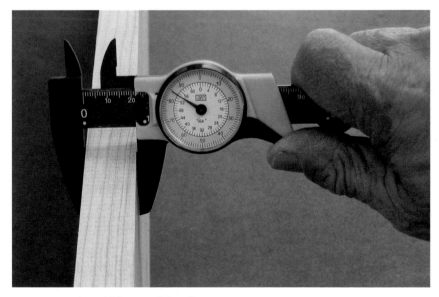

10.4 Measuring thickness with calipers

10.5 Dial gauge being used to measure movement of a table-saw fence

DIAL GAUGE

Gauges that can measure movement in thousandths of an inch are available for a modest amount. They have a spring-loaded rod that operates a dial pointer (**10.5**). The pointer makes a full revolution around the dial when the rod tip moves by $\frac{1}{10}$"; the dial has 100 divisions, so each division represents $\frac{1}{1,000}$" of tip movement. A tip movement of $\frac{1}{64}$" will move the pointer by almost 16 divisions, giving a very sensitive measurement. For a small investment, this device will allow you to move your table-saw fence with one-thousandth-inch accuracy.

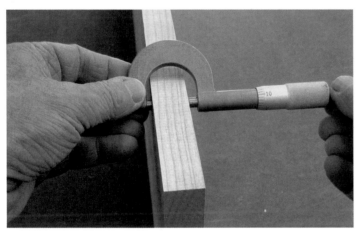

10.6 Micrometer

MICROMETER

A micrometer is another small but worthwhile investment (**10.6**). It will measure any thickness up to 1" with an accuracy of $\frac{1}{1,000}$". The main criterion when choosing one is whether its markings are easy to see. Micrometers with a digital readout are available but can be expensive; traditional-style micrometers can be obtained for a modest amount.

SQUARES

A reliable square is absolutely essential for quality woodworking. Engineer's squares, as illustrated in **10.7**, are the most suitable type. The eight-inch square shown is a practical size for most work, and the two-inch one will be a valuable addition for checking narrow edges.

Good-quality squares are guaranteed to deviate no more than $\frac{1}{1000}$" from squareness per inch of blade length. This deviation still allows a 10" square to have a $\frac{1}{100}$" error, so a square should be checked regularly to ensure that the error never exceeds this limit.

10.7 Engineer's squares: 8" and 2"

You can check the square by first using it to mark a line perpendicular to the edge of a piece of smooth material such as MDF (medium-density fiberboard). The edge must be straight and smooth, and the marking should be done with a knife (10.8). Then the square is flipped over so that if its stock was initially to the right of the line, it is now to the left, and vice versa. Any deviation between the blade of the square and the marked line will be double the error of the square. Perform this check immediately anytime the square has been dropped.

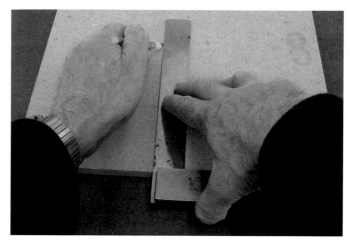

10.8 Checking a square by marking a line on smooth material

BAR GAUGE HEADS

When a box or a frame is glued together, it must be checked for squareness before the glue sets. The best way to do this is to compare the diagonals, that is, the distances between opposite corners.

Bar gauge heads are a cheap and convenient way to make a telescopic measuring stick for comparing diagonals. They comprise two separate components that allow two shop-made sticks to slide against each other until they fit between opposite corners of an assembly. On one of the heads, a screw holds the sticks together when they are fit snugly into the corners. Then the joined sticks are transferred to the other corners to compare the fit.

A set of bar gauge heads fitted to a pair of sticks is shown in **10.9** and **10.10**. More details on using them are provided in Chapter 14, "Square Assemblies."

10.9 Bar gauge heads fitted to a pair of sticks

10.10 Sticks can slide to fit between corners

11 Wood Screws

SCREWS ARE USEFUL FOR MAKING jigs and for holding together parts while glue is setting. They also provide some flexibility: They can lean one way or the other, their threads can stretch the wood fibers, and they can be allowed to move within oversized holes. When furniture parts have to be able to move a little, screws may be all that is needed.

Some aspects of selecting and using screws may not be obvious to the inexperienced woodworker. The following are some of the more significant points.

QUALITY

When a screw breaks off below the wood surface, it takes all the fun out of the day. Screws should not break if they are used properly, but the strength of screws sold by general hardware stores cannot always be relied on. Apart from the risk of breaking, if the material is soft, the driving slot or driving recess in the screw head will distort easily. Other quality-related concerns are the depth of the threads, which affects the holding power, and the way the recess in the head is formed, which affects the grip of the driver on the screw. The best way to avoid poor quality is to buy screws from a specialist supplier; one that I have used regularly is McFeely's Square Drive Screws (www.mcfeelys.com).

DRIVER RECESS

Screws from hardware stores usually have the Phillips-head style of screwdriver recess. These give the driver a better grip than a simple slot, but there is a still better alternative: the square-drive screw with a recess for a square-ended driver (11.1). The square recess and driver let you apply more torque to the screw before the driver slips out of the recess.

11.1 Square-drive screw, screwdriver, and driver

11.2 Washer head screw, flathead screw, and countersink bit

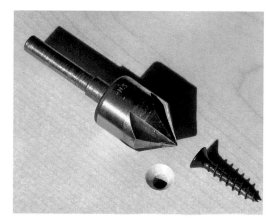

11.3 Countersink bit makes countersunk hole for flathead screw

HEAD STYLE

Most of the screws you use will be hidden from view, so the choice of head style is a matter of suitability for the job, not of appearance. The two styles that I use are flathead (FH) and washer head (WH) screws, both with square recesses.

Shown in **11.2** are a washer head screw, above the surface, and a flathead screw, flush with the surface.

Flathead screws have a conical taper below their flat top; they are intended to finish flush with, or below, the wood surface. The flathead screw needs a hole with a matching taper at the top. A hole like this is said to be countersunk, and the taper is made with a countersink bit like the ones shown in **11.2** and **11.3**.

Washer head screws have a large flat area under a domed head (**11.4**). Their heads usually finish above the wood surface, but could be set below it in bored-out recesses. They provide the benefits of a washer without the need to fit one.

Flathead screws will center themselves in the countersunk hole and do not allow for much lateral movement. If more freedom of movement is desirable, washer head screws should be used because they are able to move more freely within the drilled holes. If you require even more movement, use washer head screws in oversized or elongated holes, or in slots, and leave the screws loose enough for their heads to slide across the wood.

11.4 Washer head screws

SIZES

Screw diameters are represented by numbers: Higher numbers indicate larger diameters. The most frequently used sizes are 6, 8, and 10. Screw sizes are expressed by their diameter number and their length in inches; for example, a size 8 screw 1" in length would be written as #8 × 1".

Be aware that the length of a flathead screw is measured from end to end, while washer head screws are measured from the underside of the head. In both cases, the stated length is the depth to which the screw penetrates the wood.

USING WOOD SCREWS

A wood screw requires holes to be drilled in both pieces of wood being joined. The hole that the thread of the screw cuts into is the pilot hole. The pilot hole should be the same size as the "root," or "core," diameter of the screw, the part from which the threads extend outward. The hole in the other piece must be larger, to allow the shank and threads of the screw to pass through easily: This is the clearance hole. If it is meant for a flathead screw, the clearance hole must be countersunk.

Although you can estimate the necessary drill sizes for the two holes by holding drills up to the screw, a better way is to use the sizes recommended by the screw manufacturer.

After drilling at the screw positions, countersink the holes slightly where the two pieces come together. Countersinking removes any stray wood fibers caused by drilling and creates a recess to accommodate wood fibers that will be raised by the screw threads. The screwed pieces can then fit together tightly without interference.

Worse than having a screw break below the wood surface is having your drill bit break through to the outside. To avoid this, wrap some adhesive tape around the drill bit to show you when to stop drilling.

Part 6

Techniques for Perfect Results

12 Resawing

12.1 A pair of resawn boards and a piece of the board from which they were sawn

MANY PROJECTS INVOLVE MAKING thin panels such as ⅜"-thick bottoms for drawers or ¼"-thick panels for doors. Lumber thinner than 4/4 is not available, so the most economic way to obtain thin material is to saw through the thickness of available boards to make at least two thinner ones (**12.1**). You must do so very carefully to avoid losing too much thickness.

A table saw can be used for resawing pieces up to 6" in width; wider pieces can be resawn with a bandsaw. Alternatively, the table saw can make 3" cuts into each edge before you complete the job with a bandsaw or a handsaw.

Preserving thickness is the number one consideration when you need to make two ⅜" finished pieces from 4/4 lumber. Boards must be flattened and planed before resawing them. If they are not fairly flat to begin with, this process can easily remove ¼" of thickness. A 4/4 board would then be too thin for resawing into two ⅜"-thick pieces. The key is to start with lumber that is a generous four-quarters and not significantly warped.

Before cutting any boards into rough blanks for resawing, you should assess how warped the blanks are likely to be. To successfully convert a 4/4 blank into two ⅜"-thick finished pieces, you must flatten it and plane it to nearly ¹⁵⁄₁₆" thick before resawing. If the blanks wind up at $\frac{7}{8}$" after planing, they can still yield two pieces that are within $\frac{1}{64}$" of $\frac{3}{8}$" thickness.

Resawing may be the one table-saw operation best done without any guarding system in place. A guard over the workpiece would block the pushstick, and, since the first cut is not a through-cut, the standard splitter and kickback pawls must be removed. Shop-built guards could be devised, but they might increase the risk of kickback.

In lieu of a guard, an important safety measure you can take is to increase the height of the rip fence to make it a little higher than the tallest workpiece (12.2). This will make it easier to keep the workpiece vertical and to position a pushstick correctly while keeping your hands well above the blade. Before starting the table saw, check to see that the fence is not too high for easy use of the pushstick with every piece.

The pushstick itself presents choices: If it is thick, it can push both halves of a workpiece past the blade; if it is thin, it will allow the off-cut half to fall freely, like any off-cut. I reduce the pushstick thickness to push only on the fence side of the workpiece (see **3.10** in Chapter 3, which shows a pushstick for ripping narrow workpieces). When the fence-side piece is safely past the blade, I use the pushstick to make both pieces fall flat, away from the blade and fence (**12.3**).

Here is a summary of the procedure for resawing pieces up to 6" wide: (1) select suitable lumber; (2) cut blanks from it; (3) flatten and plane the blanks, leaving them as thick as possible; (4) resaw the boards,

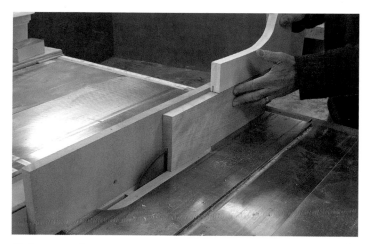

12.2 An auxilliary rip fence taller than the workpiece

12.3 Resawn pieces pushed clear of the blade

using a thin-kerf table-saw blade; (5) plane the resawn pieces to a smooth finish at $\frac{3}{8}$" thickness. More detailed procedures follow.

1. Choose 4/4 boards that are generous in thickness. Check them for cup, bow, and twist to determine if they will yield pieces that can be flattened and planed to $\frac{7}{8}$" or thicker. If you have a choice, pick boards that are mild grained rather than

highly figured or curly: You cannot afford any planer tear-out before or after resawing.

2. Cut your blanks. Three-inch and 4" widths are good for most applications. If the boards are very flat, you could cut them wider. If the boards have some warp, you may want to make blanks less than 3" wide—the wider they are, the easier it will be to make them into panels, but the more thickness they may lose.

3. Flatten and plane the blanks. Remove as little material as possible while making them all the same thickness. However, if one blank requires extra planing, do not plane all the others unnecessarily; instead, settle for getting only one ⅜" piece from that blank. After planing, joint the edges square to the faces.

4. Place an outfeed table behind the table saw and fit a thin-kerf blade.

5. Remove the standard table-saw guard, and fix a high auxiliary fence to the rip fence.

6. Set the fence for a cut exactly through the center of thickness of the pieces. Hold a piece to the fence and make a very short test cut—just a tiny nick at one end. Adjust the fence and make more tests until the cut is exactly centered.

7. Set the blade height to less than the width of any piece being cut so that the blade never emerges above a piece. For pieces less than 3" wide, the blade can be set to just above the midline so that two cuts will complete the resawing. For wider pieces, it is safer to make more than two cuts.

8. Mark an X on one face of each piece. This mark must always be oriented to the fence during cutting.

9. Use a pushstick to push the first piece into and past the blade. Keep the marked face toward the fence. Retrieve the piece (without reaching over the blade) and flip it end-to-end so that the next cut can be made with the opposite edge on the saw table but the marked face still toward the fence.

10. For wide pieces, increase the blade height in stages and make further cuts.

11. On the final cut, push the fence-side piece clear of the blade and allow it to fall flat, away from the fence, taking the off-cut half down with it. Stop the saw before retrieving the pieces. Repeat for the other pieces.

12. If your planer has bed rollers, fit an auxiliary bed over them (see "Planer Practicalities" in Chapter 2).

13. Set the planer to smooth the sawn faces in one pass rather than two. This setting will reduce the risk of tear-out by maximizing the roller pressure.

14. Plane the resawn faces. As the pieces leave the planer, pull them firmly upward to prevent snipe, as described in "Planer Practicalities" in Chapter 2.

If you are not going to use the finished pieces immediately, store them in plastic. Resawn stock is very prone to cupping because the moisture content (MC) of the resawn faces may be very different from the equilibrium moisture content (EMC) of the air; therefore, these faces may experience rapid loss or gain of moisture.

RESAWING WIDE PIECES

Pieces wider than 6" can be resawn entirely with a bandsaw if it has adequate cutting height. Even so, I prefer to first make 3" cuts into each edge at the table saw. A bandsaw blade can make a narrower kerf than any table-saw blade, but only if the cut is perfectly straight. A small deviation anywhere along the length of the cut can more than eliminate this apparent advantage. The preliminary table-saw cuts will leave less work for the bandsaw blade and make it easier to attain a straight cut. The wider the bandsaw blade, the easier it will be to cut straight: A $\frac{1}{2}$"-wide blade will be adequate for most jobs.

Clamp a vertical guide onto the bandsaw table, just in front of the blade and parallel to it. Place the guide at the distance required to center the blade in the kerf made by the table saw (4.4 in Chapter 4, "The Bandsaw"). Before cutting, check from behind that the blade is parallel to the guide and exactly centered in the kerf. Adjust the guide and the bandsaw table as necessary.

Cut very slowly so that you have time to correct for deviation and do not force the cut: The more pressure you put on the blade, the more likely it is to deviate from a straight and vertical cut. Keep the workpiece flat against the guide, and remember to use a pushstick for the last few inches in case the workpiece suddenly splits open.

12.4 You can use a handsaw to complete the cuts started with a table saw

If you do not own a suitable bandsaw, you can use a handsaw. None of the projects in this book require very wide resawn pieces, so if 3" cuts have been made into each edge at the table saw, hand-sawing through the remaining thickness will be easy **(12.4)**. Longer saws require less effort than short ones, but any saw that has a thin, stiff blade with no back stiffener, and teeth without too much set, can be used.

13 Making Wide Panels

TABLETOPS AND OTHER LARGE surfaces usually must be made from two or more boards glued together. You need to follow a careful procedure to produce panels that are attractive, strong, and flat. With a poor procedure, the panels may be distorted, like the one sketched in **13.1**.

Quite apart from its physical defects, the sketched panel is ugly—the grain patterns change abruptly at the junctions, making them obvious and producing unpleasing surface patterns.

The growth rings on the ends of the boards help us see why this panel is so unattractive: The slope or curvature of the rings is very different each side of the junctions, so edges with near-vertical growth

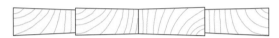

13.2 Quartersawn edges shrink more than the flatsawn ones

rings meet edges with almost horizontal ones. That is, wood with quartersawn characteristics is glued to wood with flatsawn characteristics. This arrangement produces another defect that cannot be shown in the drawing but might be obvious to anyone who touched the panel some time after it was made. In **13.2**, we can see why.

Because the characteristics of quartersawn and flatsawn lumber are different, the edges of the boards on each side of the junctions will not remain flush with each other. As soon as the MC of the wood changes, the quartersawn sides of the junctions will expand or shrink in thickness more than the flatsawn sides, resulting in a ridge at each junction. How the quartersawn edges shrink more than the flatsawn ones when the wood loses moisture is shown in **13.2**. (While quartersawn boards are more stable in width, flatsawn boards are more stable in thickness.)

Fortunately, the requirements for best appearance are compatible with those for good physical characteristics. If the boards

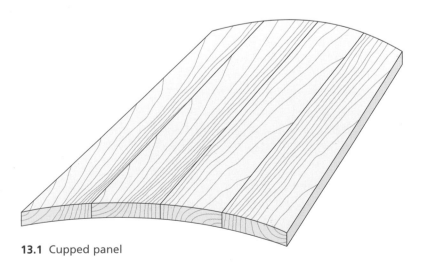

13.1 Cupped panel

are arranged so that the slope or curvature of their growth rings is similar on each side of the junctions, the patterns on the board faces will complement each other. By switching the boards around, turning them over if necessary, or flipping them end-to-end, they can be arranged so their junctions are almost invisible and the patterns of individual boards will merge (13.3). Then the tendencies toward expansion on either side of the junction will be similar, and the panel will not develop ridges.

There remains the question of flatness, which depends partly on how the board edges are jointed. If the edges are not made exactly square with the faces, the effects can accumulate across the boards, resulting in a cupped panel.

Cupping due to unsquare edges can be avoided if one edge of each board is jointed with the top face of the board against the jointer fence and its other edge is jointed with the bottom face to the fence. If jointing is done in a proper sequence, any deviation from squareness at an edge will be canceled out by an opposite deviation on the adjoining edge. The ends of boards that have out-of-square errors on their edges nullified by equal and opposite errors on adjacent edges are shown in **13.4**. (Note that the angles are exaggerated here: If the slope were as severe as this, the boards would slide out of alignment when glue and clamping pressure were applied.)

If you mark the boards' ends at one end of a panel after you have arranged them for the best layout, it will be easy to maintain the right sequence of faces to the fence. Boards arranged for a panel are shown in **13.5**. The ends showing in the photograph have been marked with horizontal lines by a lumber crayon.

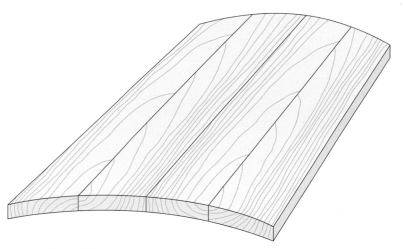

13.3 With careful arrangement, patterns of adjacent boards will complement each other

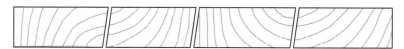

13.4 Exaggerated out-of-square errors

13.5 Boards arranged for a panel; the marked ends will be the leading ends when they are edge-jointed

13.6 Jointing the edges, leading with the marked ends

By making the marked ends lead when you joint every edge, as in **13.6**, you will maintain the right sequence, and any deviation from square will be reversed on the edges of adjacent boards.

You can check to see whether the boards will make a flat surface by clamping one of them on-edge in a vise and then balancing the others on top of it. A straightedge held against the boards will show how well the jointing sequence has worked.

HOW STRAIGHT IS STRAIGHT?

Sometimes the edges of two boards will not meet perfectly after being jointed. The question then arises as to what, if any, gaps can be allowed without compromising the strength of a glue bond.

The answer is that even the smallest gap can seriously reduce the strength of the bond. Normal woodworking glues have almost no strength unless pressure is applied between the glued surfaces—and where there is no contact, there can be no pressure. However, every pair of gluing edges need not be perfect, because small gaps may disappear under clamping pressure. The question then should be: How can you know whether relying on clamps to close a gap will produce a strong glue bond?

There are two points to bear in mind. One is that any force required to close a gap will remain in the wood after the glue has set and the clamps have been removed. This force will keep trying to break the bond and reopen the gap. The second factor is that if much of the clamping force is used for closing the gap, there may be little left to produce needed pressure.

You have to decide whether to carry on jointing or whether to close the gap by force. It is preferable to get the edges perfectly straight, but if there is little spare width in your boards, you should consider the other option. The decision is fairly easy: If you can close the gap with your hands, the glue bond will be fine; if it requires significant force from a clamp, check the jointer adjustments and rejoint the boards.

PROBLEMS WITH CLAMPS

Take a couple of boards, each about 6" wide, and then flatten them. Plane them to $\frac{3}{4}$" thickness, joint the edges square, put some glue on one edge, and push it against the other board. Press them both flush at the junction and clamp them together until the glue is set. You have made a glued panel.

Try it with half a dozen boards; you will find the experience to be rather different. Try it with boards that are only $\frac{1}{4}$" thick, and it will be dramatically different. Each type of panel has its own difficulties, and you must be prepared for them before glue meets wood.

The difficulties for which you must prepare may be due to the boards themselves (being bowed, for example) or the glue, which initially makes the boards slip out

13.7 Rear jaw of pipe clamp before tightening

13.8 Front jaw of pipe clamp before tightening

13.9 Rear jaw of pipe clamp after tightening

13.10 Front jaw of pipe clamp after tightening

of alignment and then develops a grip, or initial tack, that makes it difficult to get them back into alignment. In addition, the clamps' positions or characteristics can cause the panel to cup. You should be ready to correct for these problems, because while you try to cope with them, the glue will be rapidly setting.

Heavy-duty bar clamps are less likely than pipe clamps to cause problems, but you can buy several pipe clamps for the price of a good bar clamp. Pipe clamps will do an excellent job if you know how to use them, and a point in their favor is that they can be extended to any length by coupling sections of pipe together. The following procedures assume you are using pipe clamps. If you are fortunate enough to have good bar clamps, you will find the procedures even easier.

Ideally, you should apply clamping pressure evenly over the glued surfaces. If pressure is greatest near the bottom or top faces, the panel will have a tendency to cup upward or downward, respectively; the boards may even burst out of the clamps like a flexed pack of cards. If rigid bar clamps are used, the boards can be positioned so that the centerlines of the clamp screws align with the centers of thickness of the boards. This will usually produce a flat panel. However, when pipe clamps are used, placing the boards in line with the screws may not produce the desired result: The pipes may bend under stress and the clamp jaws may not be perpendicular to the pipes.

Photos **13.7** through **13.10** show the front and back jaws of a pipe clamp before and after being tightened. Initially they

13.11 A panel higher than the clamp screws will cup upward

13.12 Panel on support strips to raise it slightly higher than the clamp screws

lean inward, but when pressure is applied, they become more or less vertical. If the pipe bends under tension, the jaws will lean outward. This movement of the jaws as pressure is applied can distort the panel.

If the panel is higher than the clamp screws, it will probably cup upward, as in **13.11**. If it is in line with the screws, it may cup up or down. Cupping will be accompanied by weak glue bonds: With upward cupping, pressure is concentrated near the bottoms of the board edges; with downward cupping, only the tops of the boards have good contact pressure. If cupping is not corrected before the glue sets, it will usually be permanent.

I have found that the best way to work with pipe clamps is to force the panel to cup upward, if at all. This requires that the boards' center of thickness be placed slightly higher than the centerline of the clamp screw so that clamping pressure is initially greatest near the bottoms of the boards. When the panel is cupping upward, steps can be taken to correct it, whereas downward cupping is harder to correct.

When I am gluing thick boards, I place support strips under them to place the board centers about $\frac{1}{8}$" higher than the screws' centerlines (**13.12**).

The combination of support strips and a flat bench makes for a good gluing platform. Almost any material can be used for making the support strips. Chipboard is ideal because, if it inadvertently becomes glued to the boards, it will break away easily. The strips should be waxed to make removing glue from them easy, and they should be cleaned after each use. The panel will not lie flat if it is sitting on lumps of dried glue.

Another important preparation involves making some small wooden wedges, about 4" long, tapering from about $\frac{3}{4}$" to $\frac{1}{8}$" in thickness. Cut them to rough shape with a bandsaw, and smooth them with a hand plane.

Cauls between the clamp jaws and the boards will protect the boards' edges and distribute the clamping pressure. They should be about $\frac{1}{32}$" thinner than the boards so that they can be flush with, or below, the panel surface. If the outer boards are more than about 5" wide, cauls are not needed except to protect the edges.

THICK PANELS

A procedure for clamping up a panel that is at least $\frac{1}{2}$" thick is as follows:

- Using winding sticks, check to see that the bench is flat. Correct it if necessary.

- Place clamps on the bench at 10" intervals; the distance between the outside clamps should be about 2" less than the length of the panel.
- If you are using cauls, make them slightly thinner than the boards and at least 3" wide.
- Make support strips that are wide enough to raise the panel's center of thickness to about $\frac{1}{8}$" above the centerlines of the clamp screws. Make them at least as long as the width of the panel plus the widths of the cauls. Place a support strip by each clamp (13.13).
- Place the boards and cauls on the strips. Make sure that they line up at one end.

Make a dry run, as follows, to find any problems with the setup.
- Apply just enough pressure to an end clamp to hold the boards in position when they are pressed flush to each other. Then press the cauls flush with, or below, the boards.
- Increase the pressure and observe the effect on the caul or board nearest the rear clamp jaw. As you apply pressure, the jaw movement may lift the cauls and/or the boards off the support strips, as in 13.14.
- Slide support strips close to each side of the clamp, and knock the board and/or caul back down onto them. Usually it is the rear caul or board that rises, but check for rise at the front jaws as well.
- Knock the boards so they are flush with each other. For this task, use a hammer and a softwood block with smoothed ends (a heavy dead-blow, or "shockless," hammer will be best). You will need to place support strips under the boards close to where you hit them; otherwise, they may just flex but remain out of alignment.

- When the boards are flush, tighten the clamp a little more to ensure that nothing moves. Make sure that the cauls are seated on the strips and are flush with, or below, the top faces of the boards.
- Repeat at the next clamp position. Continue until every clamp is exerting some pressure. Knock down the cauls and/or boards whenever necessary; if the ends of the boards are difficult to make flush, they can be pressed flush with a C-clamp.

13.13 A support strip placed alongside each clamp

13.14 Movement of the jaws can lift a board off the support strips

13.15 Flattening a clamped panel by tapping wedges under the top clamps

- If you have to knock the boards flush between clamp positions, move the strips to give support near to each side of where you are hitting.
- When all the boards are flush, tighten each clamp fully. Check to see that the panel rests on the strips at every position.
- Place additional clamps over the boards, between the other clamps and high enough so that their screws' centers are above the panel's center of thickness. These clamps will apply most pressure to the top edges of the boards and should correct for much of the boards' upward cupping tendency.
- Use a straightedge at several positions to check for cupping in the panel. (The reason the cauls were kept flush with or below the boards was so they will not interfere with the straightedge.)
- Flatten the panel by tapping wedges under the top clamps to force the panel down at the high points (13.15).
- When the panel is no longer cupped, use winding strips to check for twist. If the panel is twisted, check to see that it is not raised above the support

strips at any position. The panel will be flat if the bench is flat, the panel is in contact with the support strips, and the strips are clean and in contact with the bench. Remember that if the panel has any cup or twist while the glue is setting, it is likely to be twisted or cupped when the clamps are removed.

- If the dry run is satisfactory, it is time to slacken all clamps and remove the top ones.

Do not expect the procedure to go quite as smoothly after the glue is applied as it did during the dry run. PVA is the best glue for the job, although it will develop grip ("initial tack") almost immediately when you apply pressure, making it more difficult to knock the boards flush with each other. This is when the heavy shock-less hammer becomes really valuable.

Glue up the panel as follows:

- Open the clamps to provide at least 1" separation between the two boards nearest to the rear jaws. Push the rear board (and caul) against the rear clamp jaws.
- Stand the second-farthest board on its front edge.
- Run a generous bead of glue (about $\frac{1}{8}$" wide for boards $\frac{3}{4}$" or $\frac{7}{8}$" thick) directly from a squeeze bottle onto the back edge of the board. Do not worry about using too much glue: PVA glue is cheap by the gallon, and dried glue can be removed easily with a belt sander.
- Lay down the glued board and push it hard against the farthest one until glue appears along the junction.
- Stand the next board on its front edge and repeat the procedure.
- When you have glued all the boards, tighten the first clamp just enough to squeeze out some glue.

13.16 A pair of panel restrainers, with their convex edges together

- Press the boards flush while in this position. If they will not stay flush, tighten the clamp a little more.
- Knock the boards down onto the support strips by the clamp jaws.
- Continue the procedure as you did for the dry run.
- When all the clamps under the panel are fully tightened, quickly scrape off most of the glue from the top surface. Apply top clamps and insert wedges under them where the straightedge indicates.
- Remove the support strips, and leave the panel in the clamps until the glue is set.

GLUING THIN PANELS

When several thin boards are clamped edge to edge, they will tend to first cup and then burst out of the clamps when pressure is applied. The tendency can be overcome by restrainers clamped across the thickness of the panel. The restrainers comprise pairs of wood strips, approximately $1" \times 1\frac{1}{2}"$ in section, and at least 6" longer than the panel width. The strips should be made of strong hardwood and jointed or hand-planed so that one face of each is slightly convex (**13.16**). They are clamped across the assembly using wood screws, with the convex faces inward. These faces should be taped and waxed so that they cannot become glued to the panel. The restrainers are not intended to keep the panel flat or to hold the boards flush; their purpose is to prevent the boards from bursting out of the clamps.

Arrange the boards so that the widest ones are to the outside. This will avoid the need for cauls, which can be difficult to use with thin boards. Proceed as follows:

- Lay out pipe clamps. A clamp spacing of up to 12" will be adequate at this stage.
- Place supports between the clamps to raise the panel to just above the centerline of the clamp screws.
- Place the jointed boards on the supports.
- Glue and clamp them, using the same procedure as for thick panels—but before applying pressure, fix restrainers across the panel. A clamped thin panel with restrainers is shown in **13.17**.

13.17 Thin panel controlled by restrainers and then clamped

13.18 A stack of thin panels for drawer bottoms

Notes:

1. Wedges are especially useful for thin panels. It may be necessary to push wedges underneath the panel—between it and the pipes.
2. It is better to leave a thin panel on the support strips until the glue is set; otherwise, it may distort at the wedge positions.
3. It is not necessary to tighten the clamps as much as for a thick panel. With narrow edges, you get the same pressure by applying less force.
4. Thin panels **(13.18)** are more likely to require the use of C-clamps at the ends because the boards have a greater tendency to cup or bow.
5. If boards resist being knocked flush in some places, try moving the support strips further apart, or even removing one.

VERY LARGE PANELS

Access to the underside of the panel is very desirable when you want to glue all boards for a large tabletop at the same time. This can be achieved by building a simple platform, as shown in **13.19**, in order to raise the clamps a few inches above the bench top. The platform comprises six components.

The platform's overall size should be about 4" longer and 6" wider than the panel you are making. Make the four bottom strips 6" high and the two cross-strips 3" wide. Make the outer bottom strips from two thicknesses of plywood, glued or screwed together to provide a stable base. Screw the cross-strips to the bottom strips to hold all the parts together. Check the assembly for twist.

When clamps and support strips are on the cross-strips, the space beneath the

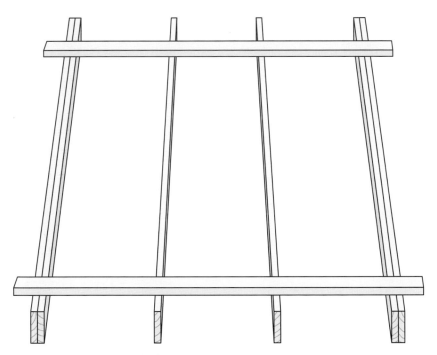

13.19 A clamp support platform

platform will allow you to insert wedges under a panel as well as over it. Prepare at least two wedges per clamp. If the panel is too wide for you to reach across, also prepare small pieces of material to support the top clamp bars on the panel at each side.

A WARNING

If the surrounding air is dry, boards can lose moisture very rapidly through their end grain. The ends try to shrink, but may be prevented from doing so by the wetter wood a few inches away. The resulting stress often causes splits in the boards' ends. The wider the board, the greater the stress can be, and a wide panel is just like a very wide board.

If your lumber was recently brought into the shop, and the shop RH is low, the MC of the lumber may be dropping rapidly. If so, before making panels you would be wise to wait for the lumber's MC to come more into balance with the shop RH. Otherwise, you may see splits develop in the ends of your panels; these splits may or may not occur at the glue lines.

If you are uncertain whether the MC of your lumber is in balance with the shop RH, cut some small pieces from the lumber and put them into a plastic bag together with a hygrometer (see "Measuring Moisture Content and Relative Humidity" in Chapter 1). If the RH in the bag is much higher than the shop RH, wait at least a few days before making the panels.

14 Square Assemblies

WHEN YOU GLUE TOGETHER A rectangular structure, you must check to see that it really is rectangular. An essential part of the assembly process is making sure that the corners are square while the glue is setting. If they are not, the structure will be forever out of square.

Checking for square is especially important when the structure is going to be matched with another rectangle. Examples are doors set into a cabinet, a frame for a rectangular mirror, and drawers in a chest.

An important example arises with the Chest of Drawers project, which is constructed as a large box glued to separately made frames. If either the frames or the box are out of square, problems will arise at every subsequent stage of construction.

For large structures, the best method of checking for square is to compare the lengths of the diagonals, which in a rectangle are equal. However, just because the diagonals are equal does not mean that the frame or box has 90-degree corners. A frame could have equal diagonals even if one side were shorter than the opposite side, as in **14.1**, where the top rail is shorter than the bottom one. This frame could never be pulled into square,

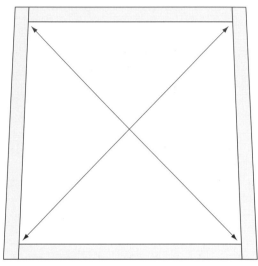

14.1 This frame is out of square but has equal diagonals

although it should still be pulled to an equal-diagonals condition, because that would be the best that could be made of the situation.

You can use a simple stick to compare diagonals. Place one end level with a corner, and mark the other end where it reaches the opposite corner. Move the stick to the other two corners to see if the second diagonal matches the first. Two

14.2 Sliding bar gauge

sticks are better for comparing internal corners: Make them longer than half the length of the diagonals, chamfer the ends to chisel edges, hold them in position in opposite corners, and mark where they overlap. Switch them to the other corners, and use the mark to show if this diagonal is longer or shorter. A more convenient way to use two sticks is to make them into a sliding bar gauge by joining them together by means of bar gauge heads **(14.2)**. These heads allow the sticks to be extended and retracted telescopically and then locked together at any length.

In principle, it is easy to equalize diagonals: Just squeeze the corners across the longer diagonal to make that diagonal shorter and the other one longer. Assemblies that are not clamped can often be brought into square simply by pushing on one corner of the long diagonal. Assemblies that are clamped, and therefore stiffer, may require an additional clamp across the corners of the long diagonal.

Often, however, the assembly clamps make it impossible to get another clamp across the corners. In these cases, angling the assembly clamps slightly in the direction of the long diagonal can create the effect of a diagonal clamp. For example, if the assembly is clamped across the top and bottom, and the long diagonal is the diagonal between the top right and bottom left corners, you may only need to shift the top ends of the clamps a little to the right and the bottom ends to the left.

Clamps can also make it difficult or impossible to get a bar gauge or a measuring stick into the assembly's corners. If so, it may be possible to clamp blocks at the corners so that measurements can be made between them, as in **14.3**.

14.3 Blocks clamped at a frame's corners make it easier to measure the frame's diagonals

15 Sanding

"FIRST DO NO HARM," IS A COMmand that could be hijacked from the Hippocratic Oath and applied to the sanding process. Clumsy sanding can spoil your work by creating hollows in what should be a flat surface or by leaving scratches and gouges. Often, these will not be noticed until a finish is applied—but then they will stand out like poster paint. Poor sanding can even make your joinery look amateurish by creating gaps at joints. For these reasons, this mundane process requires a little learning and a lot of care to ensure the success of your projects.

The reasons for sanding will change as you work. The initial objective may be to modify a part's shape or to make a glued panel flat. In both situations, coarse sandpaper and aggressive methods are appropriate. More often, the initial goal is to remove machining marks, in which case you will again be using relatively coarse sandpaper that works quickly and leaves scratches smaller than the marks it removes, thereby making the surface smoother with the least effort.

After any stage of sanding, the surface will be left with a pattern of scratches. The size of the scratches will depend on the size of the grit particles in the sandpaper, so further work with the same grade of sandpaper is a waste of time—your objective has now become to remove the new scratch pattern by sanding with a finer grade of sandpaper.

This sequence could continue indefinitely, with ever-finer sandpaper, but a point is quickly reached where any increase in smoothness would be undetectable.

SANDPAPER

The abrasive particles (the grit) in sandpaper can be made of many materials, but only three are commonly used in woodworking. Man-made aluminum oxide is the most common, and it is the best choice for general sanding. Garnet, which is naturally occurring aluminum oxide, is also widely used, although it tends to be less consistent in particle size and to lose its sharpness faster than the synthetic form. The third common material is silicon carbide, which is used to make sandpaper that is waterproof.

Waterproof ("wet-and-dry") sandpaper is made from silicon carbide grit on a waterproof backing paper. It is used to flatten or remove dust nibs from coats of dried finish, to prepare the finish for subsequent coats, or to produce a particular sheen. It can be lubricated using either water, thinner, or finish. The advantage of using it wet is that this reduces clogging and increases the sandpaper's useful life.

Sandpaper coarseness is graded on a scale that gives higher numbers to finer grits. The coarsest sandpaper you will use regularly will probably be 80-grit, and the finest for sanding many wood species will be 220-grit. Sandpapers up to and beyond 1200-grit are used for sanding finishes.

So far, so simple, but a complication arises because there are two grading systems in use: an American system, CAMI (the Coated Abrasives Manufacturers Institute), and a European system, FEPA (the Federation of European Producers of Abrasives). Both are in use in the United States, and fortunately, they are not too dissimilar. For grades up to 220-grit, the differences are small, but the systems diverge for grades finer than this. For example, 360-grit in the U.S. system is equivalent to about 600-grit European, and 600-grit U.S. is roughly the same as 1200-grit European. You can tell which system is being used because FEPA places the letter P before the number, e.g., P80, P120, P220, while the American system uses only the number.

Other characteristics of sandpaper that present choices are the weight of the paper, whether or not the grit is open-coat, and whether it is self-lubricating. But they are of secondary importance to choosing the right grades and knowing how to use them.

The thickness, and therefore the weight, of the backing paper is graded A, B, C, or D, the thinnest being A. Generally speaking, heavier paper is better, but thin paper can be folded more sharply for sanding into corners.

Open-coat paper has fewer grit particles per square inch, making it less prone to clogging. Sandpaper for woodworking is usually open-coat.

Self-lubricating sandpaper is coated with zinc stearate, which reduces clogging. If dust from stearated sandpaper is not thoroughly cleaned off, it can prevent polyurethane finish from properly adhering to a surface.

PRINCIPLES OF SANDING

If the surface is large enough to allow a power sander to be used, and it only has typical milling marks from jointer or planer blades, the best tool to begin sanding with is a random-orbit sander with a 120-grit sanding disc. In other situations (including those where it might be difficult to hold a sander flat), you may need to resort to hand-sanding with 80-grit sandpaper. On narrow surfaces, 120-grit will usually work fast enough, even when sanding by hand.

When sanding by hand or when using any sander that has a linear motion, it is important to sand in the direction of the grain, mainly because sanding across the grain will tear the surface, causing damage that is very visible and rough to the touch. Sandpaper scratches that are in line with the grain will cause less damage and will blend in better with the grain pattern. Sometimes you may need to sand across the grain; for example, when flattening a surface with a belt sander. In these cases, it is essential to finish by sanding in line with the grain to remove any across-the-grain scratches.

An equally important principle is to stick with the same grade of sandpaper until the only marks remaining on the surface are those made by this sandpaper. If you discover that the grade you are using is not effective enough, you can change to a coarser one, but do not change to a finer grit prematurely or the job will take much longer. Always remove sanding dust from

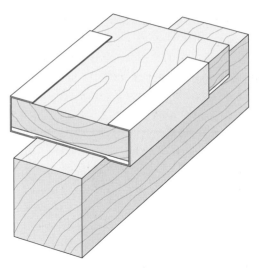

15.1 Sanding devices tend to sand deeper near the edges of a surface

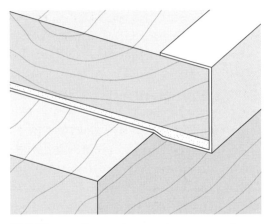

15.2 The sanding pad compresses unevenly where it overlaps an edge

15.3 A gap at the tenon shoulder has been caused by sanding the mortised face with a soft sanding block

the surface before switching to the next grit because dust from coarse grit sandpaper will continue to make coarse scratches.

To make scratches and other defects easier to see, set up a bright light at a low angle. Even a flashlight will help.

The grading system sequence is 80, 100, 120, 150, 180, 220, 240, 280, 320, 400, 500, 600, 800, 1000, 1200; it also continues below 80 and above 1200. Many experts say that switching to the next grade in the sequence will always result in the least work overall, but I find that a random-orbit sander works aggressively enough to allow me to start with 120-grit and then advance directly to 220-grit. However, if I were hand-sanding a large area, I might go from 80 to 120 to 150 to 220.

Because I work mainly with cherry, I usually stop sanding after using 220-grit, although I will go higher on important end-grain surfaces. Some species respond to sanding beyond 220-grit, but many show no significant improvement in feel or appearance, or if they do, the difference disappears when finish is applied.

An extremely important point to be aware of is that nearly all sanding devices—including hands, fingers, and cork-faced blocks—tend to sand more deeply near the edges of a surface. This is because the flexible material of the sanding pad (or your palm or fingers) compresses unevenly where it overlaps an edge, causing the sandpaper to curve over the edge, as illustrated by **15.1** and **15.2**.

This can result in some rounding or sloping of the surface near the edges. On many sanded parts, the effect is unnoticeable, but on a face that is mortised, such as a stile or leg, it can cause a gap where a mating rail or apron joins it. An edge that has been slightly beveled by sanding with a cushioned block, causing a gap where a mating rail butts against it, is shown in **15.3**.

The problem can usually be prevented by using very light pressure. However, it is safer to sand joinery faces with sandpaper glued directly to a flat hardwood block, with no cushioning. If you simply wrapped sandpaper around a block without gluing it, the sandpaper might still sag at the edges and cause rounding.

Whenever an unusually deep mark or scratch must be sanded out, you may be tempted to tilt the sander into the mark because holding the sander flat seems to be ineffective. The defect may be lower than the surrounding areas so that the sander cannot reach it. You must resist the temptation, because tilting will make a hollow in the surface. Shallow hollows may go unnoticed at the time, but will stand out when finish is applied or when the surface is seen from certain angles. Instead, sand the surrounding areas until they have been lowered—and then sand out the mark.

When every face of a project has been sanded, one more sanding job remains. It is crucial to sand any edge that can be touched because the feel of a sharp edge will spoil the impression of quality your work should project. Further, finishes will not adhere properly to sharp edges, and sharp edges are easily damaged. A few strokes with 120- or 220-grit sandpaper are all that is needed, but remember: Do not soften any edges that are required to mate with another component.

SANDING BY HAND

If you use a sanding block, the sandpaper sheets can be cut into four or six pieces depending on the block size by creasing them and then tearing them over the edge of a bench. If you are sanding without a block, it is usually convenient to fold these pieces into thirds **(15.4)**.

When you sand flat faces by hand, use a sanding block of some kind. Sanding without a block takes longer, applies uneven pressure, and makes it more difficult to maintain a flat surface. It is usually best to add some cushioning—such as a thin layer of cork—between the block and the sandpaper. Without this, the sandpaper will clog quickly and may cause deep scratches in the wood. Thin cushioning (up to $\frac{1}{8}$" thick) is best, and shop-made wood blocks are better than rubber or plastic ones because you can make sure they are flat.

You can make cushioned sanding blocks by gluing cork or stiff dressmaker's felt to flat wood blocks of any size. To ensure a flat surface, clamp another flat block against the outside face of the material while the glue dries. When sanding narrow surfaces, the block should be narrow; otherwise, it will wobble and cause sloping edges. Do not use cushioned blocks when you sand joinery faces.

In some situations, sanding is much easier with sandpaper that has been stiffened. A good way to stiffen sandpaper is to glue it to stiff dressmakers' felt with spray-on adhesive. (This felt is sold in sizes similar to sandpaper sheets.) If the sandpaper is glued to both sides of the felt, it becomes very stiff but can still be flexed to conform to curved surfaces. The high friction of the upper face makes it easy to grip. Small strips of felt-sandpaper "sandwiches" can be cut to suit the task; a pair of scissors should be kept only for this purpose because they will not be of much use for anything else.

POWER SANDERS

New and innovative sanders always find eager customers—woodworkers ready to invest in anything that promises to shorten the sanding process. I have bought

15.4 Folded sandpaper provides grip for fingers that push it

15.5 Sanding drum in drill press smoothes bandsawn curves; the circular cutout in the auxiliary drill press table allows the work to be kept flat and square to the drum

15.6 Sanding disc used in a table saw is fitted with a guard

most types of sander at one time or another, but I find that now I only use two of them—a handheld belt sander and a random-orbit sander. In addition, I occasionally use a couple of auxiliary devices: a sanding disc, which can quickly convert a table saw into a disc sander, and a sanding drum, which can convert a drill press into a drum sander.

Sanding drums, which cost upward of $5 each, fit into the chuck of your drill press and convert it immediately into a drum sander. They are widely available in sizes from $\frac{3}{4}$" to 3" diameter, and they provide valuable assistance in smoothing bandsawn curves **(15.5)**. Larger-diameter drums are available from a few suppliers.

When you use a drill-press sanding drum, fit an auxiliary table of plywood or particle board to the drill press. The table should have a hole cut out so that the bottom of the drum can be lower than the surface **(15.5)**. With this arrangement, the edges of a workpiece will be sanded at 90 degrees to the face that is on the table.

A table saw can be turned into a disc sander simply by replacing the blade with a sanding disc. Some blade manufacturers sell these.

The edge of a rotating sanding disc is dangerous, so fit it with a guarding arrangement like the one shown in **15.6**.

To make the guard, lower the saw blade below the table and clamp a suitable piece of wood or plywood to the rip fence. Move the fence so that the face of the wood or plywood is over the blade. Start up the saw and raise the blade to cut a recess in the face. Lower the blade again and move the fence one blade thickness toward it. Raise the blade once more to deepen the recess. Repeat until the recess is about $\frac{5}{16}$" deep.

Random-Orbit Sanders

A random-orbit sander has a complex, relatively slow motion. This motion (while not actually random) produces a scratch pattern that is much less noticeable than marks made by simple rotation. Also, the risk of gouging associated with high-speed rotation is eliminated.

The sander pads are made either for hook-and-loop sanding discs or for stick-on discs. Stick-on discs (also referred to as pressure sensitive, PSA, or preglued) are the cheapest, but glue from a previous disc may have to be cleaned off each time a replacement disc is fitted. With the hook-and-loop system, sanding discs can be removed and replaced instantly and repeatedly.

Random-orbit sanders will remove milling marks quickly with 120-grit sanding discs, in contrast to the coarser grits needed with less aggressive methods. Their aggressive action allows the next stage of sanding to be done by changing directly to 220-grit instead of working through one or more intermediate grades.

Use a random-orbit sander by moving it slowly over the surface, applying some downward pressure, and always keeping it flat. Replace the disc as soon as it loses its effectiveness.

On important surfaces such as tabletops, random-orbit sanding should be followed by hand-sanding in line with the grain.

Belt Sanders

Nothing beats a belt sander for smoothing glued up panels. No other handheld tool will remove surface glue and level boards as quickly as this one. On the other hand, no other sanding tool will inflict so much damage if your control lapses momentarily. If you allow it to tilt to its side, the edge of the belt will cut a groove; if you allow it to tilt backward, the rear roller will make a hollow. Nevertheless, it takes very little practice to become proficient in the use of a belt sander. Practice keeping the sander horizontal while lowering it onto the work. Never let it stay in one position; it must always be in motion.

When you buy a belt sander, buy a big one: A 4" × 24" belt is a lot more effective than a 3" × 21" belt, and a heavy sander exerts its own pressure. Also, it is easier to make surfaces flat with a large sander because it will straddle more of the bumps and hollows.

Your main use for a belt sander will be sanding glued panels. The 150-grit belts are good for this purpose. Coarser belts leave a hard-to-remove scratch pattern, and finer ones are unnecessary because it is better to switch to a random-orbit sander once the glue has been removed and the boards are sanded flush. It is worthwhile to keep one or two 80-grit, or even 40-grit, belts handy for occasional use.

When you sand glued panels, work with the sander at 45 degrees to the grain, first in one direction and then in the other, finally finishing with the grain. Changing directions like this gives fast results and is more likely to reduce thickness evenly across the panel than would sanding only with the grain. Place the panel on nonslip mats, and move the sander as far as it is comfortable for you to reach. You can move it in circles like a floor sander, or sand at 90 degrees to the grain to remove across-the-panel undulations; just make sure you finish in line with the grain to remove the cross-grain scratch pattern. Clean the belt frequently with a sanding belt-cleaner stick.

Before you discard a worn belt, reverse it on the sander. This will give it a new lease on life. Even if the belt has directional arrows on the inside, modern sanding belts can usually be used in either direction.

A final caveat: Two things that can cause the sander to tip and damage the work are letting the sander run over the cord and stepping on the cord. To prevent these mishaps, I run the power cord over my left arm (I am right-handed), and this helps to keep it out of the way.

16 Gluing

16.1 A cherry-to-walnut glue joint has been broken apart. Wood has been torn from both surfaces, but the glue bonds have not broken

IN MY SHOP, I USE THREE TYPES of glue. PVA glue and polyurethane glue cover almost all situations. The third type is epoxy glue, which is convenient on occasion.

PVA stands for polyvinyl acetate, which is the basis of the common white or yellow woodworking glues. Most of the white and yellow glues give similar results, although some are better for items that will be subjected to wet conditions. Polyurethane glues offer advantages when longer assembly times are required or when assembly is made difficult by friction in the joints. Epoxy glues are very strong and do not require clamping pressure; they are available in varieties that set in a few minutes and in varieties that set in several hours.

Choosing between the three glue types depends on the situation. Woodworkers develop an understanding of the bonding strengths they can obtain with different glues and under different circumstances. You can obtain the same understanding more quickly by experimenting. Make some edge-to-edge joints and some mortise-and-tenon joints from scrap wood; give the glue time to set fully, and then break the joints apart. You will soon get to know how glue behaves. Do these experiments during projects by always testing the bond strength of off-cuts from glued panels and by making extra joints from scrap wood when you are set up for mortising.

PVA

The power of PVA glue lies in its ability to bond molecularly with wood. A thick layer of PVA glue gives little strength. A strong bond between two pieces of wood occurs when a thin layer of glue sandwiched between them forms molecular bonds with both pieces. If the glue layer is thick, it can easily be broken, even though it may continue to adhere to both pieces. However, when two pieces of wood have been joined by a thin layer of glue and then broken apart, wood will be torn from the surfaces and will still adhere to the glue, as in **16.1**. The bond will be stronger than the wood.

The need for a thin layer does not mean that glue must be applied thinly. Glue should be applied generously. A thin and effective layer is obtained by applying enough pressure to push the wood surfaces very close together, forcing glue into the surfaces and squeezing out the excess.

PVA gluing procedure requires good surface preparation, an adequate application of glue, and pressure while the glue is setting. In addition, typical PVA glues should not be used at temperatures below 60° F, nor on wood that has a moisture content much above 12 percent. If the temperature is too low, PVA glue will become chalky as it dries instead of setting to form a strong bond.

Good surfaces for gluing are accurate, smooth, and fresh. Some woods exude oils onto their surfaces after they have been cut for a while. Gluing old surfaces is not a good idea in general, because even non-oily woods develop an oxidized layer that prevents glue from wetting or penetrating their surface. You can assess the freshness of a surface by placing a single drop of water on it. If the water immediately starts to spread and to sink in, the surface is not resistant to wetting. If it beads up, the surface should be recut.

In the context of gluing, accurate means that the surfaces come together without gaps. If they are flat, they must be precisely flat; if curved, the curvature of one must be the exact inverse of the curvature of the other.

It is not a good idea to make surfaces smooth by sanding because this might produce loose or frayed surface fibers that weaken the glue bond. A hand plane can produce a perfect surface for PVA glue if used skillfully. Otherwise, it may produce faceted surfaces that will not mate perfectly. A jointer or planer will produce excellent gluing surfaces provided that the work is not passed through them too quickly or too slowly. Moving the work too quickly produces scalloped surfaces that will only touch at the high spots; moving the work too slowly might burnish the surfaces and prevent glue from penetrating them.

Both mating surfaces should be thoroughly wetted by glue: Too much is better than too little. Restraint must be exercised when glue squeeze-out is undesirable, but even then, a cleanup job is preferable to "starved" joints.

After spreading PVA glue onto both surfaces, allow a minute or two for the surfaces to become properly wetted before applying pressure. When squeeze-out occurs, do not try to remove it immediately or you will spread it further. The glue will thicken into a gel in about 15 minutes, and then it can be easily removed without being spread. If it hardens on the surface, it can be removed with a chisel or scraper, but take care to avoid tearing the wood.

Sometimes ideal pressure cannot be applied while the glue is setting. For joints such as mortise-and-tenon or dovetail, the tightness of the fit determines the gluing pressure. Fortunately, these joints have mechanical strength independent of glue, which partly compensates for inadequate or excessive pressure on the glue. Simple edge-to-edge or face-to-face glue joints, of course, have no independent strength; if the glue fails, the pieces fall apart, so it is very important to get the pressure and other conditions right. Manufacturers' data sheets indicate an ideal pressure of around 200 pounds per square inch for good PVA glue bonds in hardwoods. Note that because PVA glue is not very strong in itself, it should not be used in loose joints.

You can clean brushes used to apply PVA glue by placing them in water immediately after use.

PVA is the least expensive of the three glues, and in many situations the most convenient. When the assembly is simple and clamping pressure can be applied easily, PVA is usually the best choice. It sets relatively quickly, and the clamps can be removed after an hour provided that the assembly is not stressed. Glued assemblies take many hours to reach full strength, so even after a couple of hours they should not be stressed severely.

Despite its long setting time, PVA glue will often hold two pieces of wood firmly after less than a minute. This effect is known as initial tack or initial grab, and while it is not even the beginning of a proper bond, it can be helpful in holding parts together while you apply clamps. However, it can be a nuisance when you are trying to align joints precisely.

This leads into the subject of "open time"—the time available for manipulating joints after the glue is applied. With most PVA glues, open time is only a few minutes. Therefore, you should always do a dry run before applying glue, to make sure an assembly goes together easily and correctly. In some situations, the more glue you apply, the longer the open time (up to a point), so using plenty of glue can be helpful. When very long open times are required, PVA glue is not the best choice.

POLYURETHANE

Although initial tack and short open times can offer advantages, they often cause serious problems. In such cases, you need the characteristics of polyurethane glues: open times of 30 minutes or more and a lubricating effect that makes joints easier to assemble. When you have a complicated assembly to be pulled together, polyurethane glue can make it feel as though the joints have been greased—and that you have all the time in the world. Although it is more expensive than PVA, and clamping times may be four hours or more, in the right circumstances polyurethane glue is a blessing. A disadvantage is that brushes used for applying it can be used only once.

The polyurethanes set by reacting with water. If the wood has a moisture content of more than 8 percent, this is all that is needed. If the wood is dryer, one surface must be wetted with water. It is safest to always wet one surface just to be sure. Apply a thin film of water with a brush or spray bottle. Then apply glue after the water has disappeared from the surface.

The glue should be applied to both surfaces. It will foam and increase in volume, so it is liable to produce more squeeze-out than PVA. Squeeze-out should not be removed until it is hard, when it can be removed relatively easily. Like PVA, this glue has little intrinsic strength and will not work with poorly made joints. Surfaces must be brought close together, and clamping pressure is necessary. Thin glue layers (called glue lines) are required, as with PVA glues.

Recommended clamping pressures are lower than for PVA: 50 pounds per square inch seems to be a typical recommendation. Also in contrast to PVA, sanding the surfaces with 20- or 40-grit sandpaper is sometimes recommended, though I use it successfully on smoothly machined tenons. The polyurethanes that I use are Excel One and Gorilla Glue, which have performed as well as PVA glue in my tests. Polyurethane glue is more expensive than PVA and requires longer clamping times, so there is no point in using it when PVA will do.

Fast-setting polyurethanes are available: One is Excel Xpress, marketed by Ambel Corporation (www.excelglue.com).

EPOXY

If you make a joint that is too loose to make a good bond using PVA or polyurethane glues, epoxy is the answer. Epoxy has great strength in itself, and will fill gaps where wood-to-wood contact is poor. It does not need clamping and is therefore useful where clamping would be difficult. Some varieties set in five minutes, and others have long open times and stay workable for hours. Disadvantages are that it is expensive compared with PVA and the polyurethanes, and it can be extremely messy if the assembly requires adjustment.

Epoxy is supplied as two separate fluids that must be mixed together immediately before use. The fluids are usually thick and require considerable stirring to mix properly. Setting begins when they are mixed, and for both fast and slow types, the setting time depends on temperature. Squeeze-out is difficult to remove because it is very messy when wet and very strong when hard; however, if it is left in place, it will increase the strength of a joint by forming a fillet of cement around it. The only clamping this glue needs is to prevent movement while the glue sets. No clamping is needed on horizontal surfaces.

Any clamping should be light so that the glue layer does not become too thin. You can apply the glue to one surface and rub both surfaces together to wet them. The rubbing pressure should be light so that not much glue is squeezed out. Squeeze-out can be controlled or prevented by applying glue to the center of a surface so that it barely reaches the edges when the parts are brought together.

For most jobs, you can apply the glue with a stick (if a brush is used, it will be for one time only). Epoxies have no initial tack, and surfaces with epoxy between them will slide across each other very easily until setting begins. The surfaces do not need to be smooth.

In general, the quick-setting epoxy glues are not as strong as the slow ones, but they are strong enough for fixing non-structural parts such as drawer stops. For structural joinery, use the stronger, slow-setting epoxies.

CLAMPING PRESSURE

PVA glues are best for gluing boards edge to edge, and for this, clamping pressure is critical. The ideal pressure for PVA glue joints is about 200 pounds per square inch. The question is how to achieve this.

Pipe clamps using $\frac{3}{4}$" black iron pipe can exert a force of just over 1,000 pounds when fully tightened. Pressure is force divided by surface area, so the 200 pounds per square inch that PVA glue manufacturers recommend can be produced by one pipe clamp for every 5 square inches of surface area. This would require a clamp to be placed every 7 inches for $\frac{3}{4}$" boards. In practice, a good glue bond can be obtained with fewer clamps than this—one every ten inches is enough to produce strong glued panels. On thinner boards, you could get the same pressure from fewer clamps, but it is better to keep the same clamp spacing and to tighten them less to obtain even distribution of pressure.

If the boards are narrow, pressure will be concentrated near the clamp positions and other areas will receive inadequate pressure. Pressure can be more evenly distributed by adding wide temporary boards, called cauls, between the clamps and the boards being glued. Cauls also protect the glued boards from being marred by the clamp jaws. If the outer glued boards are wider than about 4", clamping cauls are not necessary to spread the pressure, though they may still be necessary to prevent damage.

17 Sharpening Edged Tools

AN EDGE IS THE JUNCTION BETWEEN two surfaces. The smoother those surfaces are, the sharper the edge will be; and the sharper the edge, the longer it will stay sharp. All edges have irregularities at the microscopic level, and the larger ones break off sooner to leave the edge blunt. Smoother surfaces have smaller edge irregularities, which result in longer periods between sharpenings.

For ordinary chisels and bench planes, the end of the blade is beveled at about 30 degrees to the back face to produce an edge. The edge's sharpness depends equally on the smoothness of the bevel and of the back face. The bevel angle is a compromise: A smaller angle allows the blade to cut with less resistance, but it also makes the edge more fragile.

Often, the blade is beveled at two angles, as shown in **17.1**. One bevel is at about 25 degrees to the back and is produced by a grinding wheel. The other is at about 30 degrees to the back and is produced by honing on a sharpening stone.

The double-bevel system has the advantage of requiring only a small area to be resharpened. However, the advantage is limited because each time the edge is resharpened, the 30-degree area becomes larger and eventually the 25-degree bevel is lost. The 25-degree bevel can be restored with a grinding wheel, but this requires some skill. Grinding generates heat, which can destroy the temper of the steel.

Unless you are expert at using a grinding wheel, it is safer to continue working with only the 30-degree honed bevel once the 25-degree bevel has been worn away by many resharpenings. Each sharpening then takes a little longer, but it eliminates the risk to the blade—with modern sharpening methods, even a wide bevel can be smoothed quickly. If the edge becomes deeply nicked, or if you really want the advantage of a grinding bevel, you can always take the blade to a sharpening shop; it will be safer for the blade and less expensive than buying a grinder.

The cost of a good sharpening system can be significant. My system comprises a diamond-faced "stone" and two water-

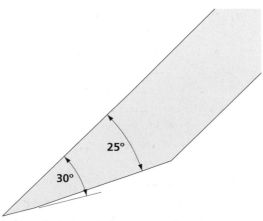

17.1 Blade beveled at two angles

stones; these plus a honing guide will cost from $150 to $200 (based on 2005 prices).

The diamond stone is graded at 350-grit. It is a steel plate with micron-sized diamonds embedded in the surface. The diamonds cut quickly to remove deep scratches from bevels or to flatten the backs of blades.

Resharpening does not usually require the diamond stone and can begin with a 700-grit waterstone. Waterstones are manufactured by binding fine abrasive particles into solid blocks that are typically around 1" thick, 3" wide, and 8" long. They are soaked in water before use. During use, a slurry is produced on the surface. It is this slurry that smoothes and polishes the blade.

For the final stage of sharpening, I use another waterstone. The action of waterstones is sufficiently aggressive to allow a step directly from the 700-grit stone to one graded at 8,000-grit or even higher. However, it is better to progress from the 700-grit waterstone to 3,000- and then 10,000-grit waterstones.

The coarser-grit waterstones can take a long time to become saturated, so it is best to keep them permanently in water. Very fine grit stones do not need to soak for so long, and are best stored dry and then immersed for a minute or two before each use.

The whole system is shown in **17.2**: The diamond stone is to the right on the bench, and the waterstones are on the white board. The board is a piece of melamine-faced chipboard that serves as a waterproof and easily cleaned sharpening station. Strips of wood fixed to the board hold the stones in place, and the board itself is clamped to the bench.

17.2 Sharpening stone setup with diamond stone, two waterstones, Nagura, honing guide, and containers

17.3 The setup can be stacked when not in use

The coarse waterstone is stored in water in a plastic container. The finishing stone also has its own water container, but it is stored on top of it, not in it; this stone is immersed in the container briefly before use.

Also shown in **17.2** is a small block of stone, called a Nagura, in front of the diamond stone. A Nagura is not essential, but it is very helpful for working up a slurry on the finishing stone.

When not in use, the system can be stacked as shown in **17.3** for easy storage.

A blade must be held at a constant angle while it is honed, and the easiest way

17.4 Using a honing guide to keep the blade at a constant angle

17.5 Using a 30-degree template to set the sharpening angle

17.6 Making a 30-degree template

to hold it so is by using a honing guide (**17.4**). Many woodworkers pride themselves on being able to maintain a constant angle without such aids, but I admit to needing the guide. I strongly recommend that you use one too, because if you do not keep the blade at a fixed angle, you will get a rounded bevel. Guides with a roller that runs on the stone are my favorite type; with these, the blade can be moved from coarser to finer stones without being readjusted in the guide.

The bevel should be honed at the same angle at every sharpening. If you increase the angle of the blade to the stone, you will get a multifaceted bevel; if you reduce it even slightly, you will add greatly to the work needed to produce a flat bevel. To ensure that you hone at the same angle every time, make a template to show when the blade is projecting from the honing guide by exactly the right distance to produce the required angle.

A blade fixed in a honing guide and held in a 30-degree template is shown in **17.5**. The edge just reaches the corner when one leg of the template touches the guide roller and the other leg is held to the blade. Adjust the blade projection until this position is achieved. If you do this every time you hone, the bevel will always be honed at the same angle.

The angle template consists of two strips of thin material glued together at their ends (**17.6**). Five-minute epoxy has been applied to the ends, and the strips are being held together by a spring clamp while they are adjusted to a 30-degree angle drawn on the bench edge. A 30-degree angle (30.07 degrees to be precise) is provided by a triangle with a base of 9½" and a height of 5½". After setting the angle, the clamp is left on while the epoxy hardens.

FLATTENING THE BACK

The first thing to do with a new blade is to flatten the back; without a flat back, the edge cannot be straight. Only the region near the edge needs to be made flat, which can be accomplished with a few minutes of rubbing on the diamond stone or on a waterstone of equivalent or coarser grit. Hold the blade flat on the stone and do not allow its back end to rise. Press down with your fingers close to the edge (**17.7**) and use short forward and backward strokes. You can use long side-to-side strokes for faster cutting, provided that you finish with fore-and-aft strokes to leave a scratch pattern perpendicular to the edge.

Continue until the scratch pattern runs the whole length of the edge, as shown in **17.8**. A watchmaker's eyeglass with about 3× magnification will help you to see when the sideways scratch pattern has been completely replaced by scratches that run perpendicular to the edge.

HONING

If the back of the blade is flat and the edge is not badly nicked, you can resharpen the edge with a couple of minutes' work on the waterstones. Start by clamping the sharpening station to the bench, and then place the coarse waterstone between its retaining strips. Place the finishing stone in its container of water.

Rub the back of the blade over the coarse waterstone. Hold it flat and work it on the stone as you did when you flattened it on the diamond stone. Sprinkle water on the stone as it begins to dry out. Continue until you have an even scratch pattern near the edge. Finish using strokes in line with the length of the blade to leave the scratch pattern perpendicular to the edge. Here, again, an eyeglass will help you to

17.7 Flattening the back of a blade

17.8 Perpendicular scratches should run the length of the edge

see when no further improvement can be obtained with this stone. The blade surface will be dull at this stage.

Next, place the finishing stone on the sharpening station and repeat the above procedure to produce a bright shine near the edge. If you have a Nagura, rub it on the stone to raise a slurry, which will enhance the stone's cutting action. Rub it over the entire surface to avoid creating a hollow.

Fix the blade in the honing guide, and use the angle template to set the blade projection for the 30-degree sharpening angle.

17.9 Honing the bevel

Rub the bevel over the coarse waterstone (**17.9**) until all imperfections have been removed and the bevel meets the back of the blade. When the bevel meets the blade's back surface, a burr will have formed along the back of the edge that you will be able to feel. This will tell you when to stop honing on the coarse stone and move on to the finishing stone. Work the bevel on the finishing stone until it is polished and bright. The burr on the back will disappear when the blade is sharp.

To make the bevel and the back perfectly flat, the stones must themselves be flat. Unfortunately, waterstones wear away relatively quickly, and after a few dozen sharpenings they will develop hollows. Maintaining waterstones involves occasionally restoring them to flatness. The coarse stone can be flattened by rubbing it over wet silicon carbide sandpaper on a flat surface, a procedure similar to flattening the sole of a hand plane. Use 120-grit paper to begin with, and finish with 220-grit. The finishing stone can be flattened by rubbing it with the flat, coarse stone.

A more convenient way to flatten waterstones is with a purpose-made flattening stone, and these are available at prices from $20 to around $100. The most comprehensive selection of stones and sharpening aids that I know of can be found in the Japan Woodworker catalog (www.japan woodworker.com).

18 Finishing

FURNITURE NEEDS PROTECTION against the grime and discoloration that can accumulate from handling and daily use. Lacquers and varnishes, which form a hard surface film, provide excellent protection, but they require either a dust-free workplace or facilities for spraying and fume extraction. These film finishes also require a degree of skill and experience to achieve perfect results. Another group of finishes, called wiping finishes, will provide adequate protection while enhancing the wood's natural beauty by bringing out its grain patterns and deepening its color. Wiping finishes are the main subject of this chapter because they do not demand previous experience or special facilities.

The first application of wiping finish soaks into the wood. It must then be wiped dry before any of it can harden on the surface. If you have never applied a finish to wood, you will be amazed by how the first coat brings out the wood's beauty. Wood finishers refer to this effect as "popping the grain"—an appropriate expression.

Subsequent applications can begin to build up a surface film, but it can never become thick because each application must be wiped off to leave no more than a microscopic layer. This requirement limits the protection that wiping finishes can provide against abrasion, and the gloss they can achieve. However, the limitations of wiping finishes are outweighed by their advantages: The finished surface still looks and feels like wood, the finish will last indefinitely in normal use, and if accidents happen, the finish can be restored by the same simple methods used to apply it in the first place. In comparison, when a film finish is damaged, it may require complete stripping and refinishing.

Wiping finishes are sold in various formulations. They can also be made in the workshop by mixing boiled linseed oil with polyurethane varnish and paint thinner. Since each coat is effectively wiped dry, it will not run, sag, or hold dust. It will bring out the beauty of wood more than thicker finishes do because it soaks into the surface ; also, the linseed oil in the shop-made mixture will produce an even richer color over time. No other finish produces more attractive results, and the wiping technique has the appeal of being very traditional.

SAFETY

Cloths or papers that are wet with wiping finish or any other oil-based finish can spontaneously combust. The drying process involves a reaction that produces heat. If the cloths or papers are spread out singly to dry, the heat will not build up to ignition temperature; if they are bunched, it may.

So-called boiled linseed oil is not, and must never be, boiled. The name refers to linseed oil that has drying agents added to it. Any attempt to boil it would be extremely dangerous.

PREPARING THE SURFACE

Before applying a finish, you must inspect every inch of all visible surfaces for scratches or dents. Scratches can usually be sanded out; dents can usually be ironed out.

A smoothing iron is an essential workshop tool. Provided that the wood has only been compressed, and not torn from the surface, an indentation can be restored to surface level by wetting it and applying heat. To repair a dent, apply a drop of water to it with your finger, let it soak in for a few seconds, and touch a hot iron to the dented area. Repeat the process until the wood has swollen back to its normal level. Complete the repair by sanding.

If the surface is nicked and wood has been lost, the hole must be filled. My preferred wood fillers are sticks of colored material that are melted into the hole using a hot knife. The material can then be sanded immediately. These fillers are made from colored shellac and resins. Rather than try to exactly match the wood, I use a color that resembles natural marks in it. For example, for cherry I use sticks the color of typical mineral streaks or pitch pockets.

The filler sticks are made from a hard, brittle material, not to be confused with wax sticks. To use them, heat a knife in a flame, and apply it to the end of the stick. Use a knife with an insulated handle. Transfer melted filler from the knife to the hole in the wood. Apply enough to overfill the hole, and then wait a few seconds for the filler to harden before sanding it flush.

WIPING FINISHES

Shop-made wiping finish is commonly made from equal parts of boiled linseed oil, polyurethane varnish, and mineral spirits (paint thinner). I prefer to use extra polyurethane, so my mix is 1:2:1.5, and the thinner still comprises one-third of the total.

The purpose of the thinner is to help the finish soak into the wood. The purpose of the oil is twofold: It gives some woods a richer color, either initially or over time, and it slows the drying of the polyurethane so there is no rush to wipe it dry.

The drying agents in the oil help it to harden in the presence of oxygen. (Raw linseed oil never hardens but will remain permanently soft or sticky.) Even with drying agents, boiled linseed oil by itself will dry slowly and will always be a little soft. Adding polyurethane speeds the drying process and increases hardness.

Note that shop-made finish is not suitable for the insides of chests and cabinets or for the insides of drawers. In an enclosed space, the linseed oil odor will persist for years and will taint anything stored within it. On outside surfaces, the smell dissipates quickly.

An ideal finish for inside faces—especially drawer parts—is shellac: One coat is all that is needed. It is best to treat it as a wiping finish and to wipe it off before it dries. Because it is very fast-drying, wiping must be done quickly. A few minutes after being wiped, it will be dry enough to sand. A few light strokes with fine sandpaper will produce a silky and clean-smelling surface.

In principle, opposite faces of wood should be coated identically so they will be equally affected by changes in humidity. Unequal coats of wiping finish on the insides and outsides of cabinets are unlikely to cause a problem because these finishes are not very effective in reducing the absorption of moisture. However, it is still essential that you apply balanced coats to tops and other parts that are not rigidly fixed.

When working with finishes, protect your hands with disposable gloves. Apply the oil-mix finish generously with a foam brush, and allow it a few minutes to soak in. Repeat the application on very absorbent areas, and then wipe off the finish with paper towels. Dry the surface thoroughly; if any areas are left wet, they can remain sticky for days. After wiping dry, run your hands over the surfaces to check for stickiness, and wipe again where necessary. Pay special attention to bottom edges where finish might collect. Spread the used towels out to dry, or put them in a proper fireproof container.

A second coat can be applied after 24 hours. At this stage, the surface can be smoothed further by rubbing in the second coat with 400-grit wet-and-dry sandpaper. After wet-sanding, wipe the second coat dry.

The sequence for finishing tops and similar parts is important. Upper or outside faces should receive the first application of finish, because if finish from the underside runs onto bare wood on the top face, it will color and seal patches of the surface, and these will stand out permanently.

The increase in sheen with each coat is minimal. One coat of polyurethane varnish will produce a thicker film than any number of coats of wiping finish. However, some proprietary wiping finishes will build up faster than the shop-made mixture.

BUILDING UP A SHEEN

You can increase the sheen of your finish and the protection it gives by applying one of the proprietary wiping finishes after the first oil-mix coat. One that I like is Minwax Wipe-On Poly. A very thin layer of it will flatten out to eliminate wiping marks. It dries slowly when thick, giving enough time for wiping it off to leave a thin but significant layer. When wiped to a thin layer, it will harden in a few hours, so two coats can be applied in one day. I use this finish only after an initial coat of the shop-made oil mix, which may emphasize the grain and deepen the wood's natural color.

Apply Wipe-On Poly as you did the oil mix, and then wet-sand the surface. Do not wipe it quite as dry as you would the oil mix. Instead, leave a smear of finish on the surface that is not thick enough to trap dust. After wiping off a coat, inspect the surface from a low angle. If necessary, wipe it again lightly with a paper towel for an even appearance. When each coat has fully hardened, you will be able to run your fingers over it without feeling any drag. Dry-sand each hardened coat very lightly with 400-grit sandpaper before recoating.

The sequence you use for building a sheen on tops is important. Place tops right-side up on supports to raise them a couple of inches above the bench. After coating and wiping the top face and the edges with Wipe-On Poly, wipe under the edges with dry paper towels to remove any finish that has run onto the bottom face. Rub firmly with towels to make sure the bottom face is completely dry.

When the first coat has hardened, turn the top over and coat the underside. Treat it as you did the top face. Since the first coat on the top is fully dry, you can vigorously rub below the edges to remove any wet finish. Before leaving the finish to dry, run your fingers below the edges to test for stickiness. If you feel any, wipe again.

When both faces have received one coat of Wipe-On Poly, the next coat can be applied to the bottom face while the top is upside down. Here again, thoroughly wipe dry any finish that runs onto the under surface. Then turn the top right-side up for another topside coat. No matter how many coats you apply, the final coat should be given to the top surface so that finish from the underside has no chance of running onto the final surface.

If you apply too many coats of Wipe-On Poly, they will begin to look like a film finish, and you will lose the hand-rubbed look. Unless you want a film-finish effect, do not apply more than two or three coats. While a thick film may be more protective, it will never acquire the character and patina that a close-to-the-wood finish will.

Part 7
Cabinetry Projects

19 Chest of Drawers Project

MAKING THE CHEST OF DRAWERS (19.1) involves most of the techniques described in the preceding chapters. It is a major project, but not a difficult one. Drawers are just boxes, and if you can make one, you can make five. The carcass is a bigger box, with frames glued to it at front and back. It sits on a base that is another frame, and it is covered by a top that consists mainly of a few boards glued edge to edge. The back is yet another frame, enclosing panels made by gluing more boards together. The chest is enhanced by beading fixed around the drawer openings, chamfers on the front corners, shapes cut into the front and sides of the base, and shaped top edges.

19.1 Chest of drawers—
approximate dimensions:
40"W x 43"H x 20"D

DESCRIPTION

How the main part of the chest is built as a dovetailed box to which front and back frames are added is shown in **19.2**. The box and the frames are constructed and assembled separately; then they are glued together to make a strong and rigid structure with openings for drawers.

The drawers are graduated in size—from about $8\frac{1}{2}$" for the depths of the two bottom ones to $6\frac{3}{4}$" for the twin top ones. After the frames are glued to the box, the drawer openings have $\frac{3}{16}$"-thick beading applied around them; therefore, the frame rails are positioned to accommodate the drawer fronts plus expansion gaps plus two thicknesses of beading.

Frame openings have been sized to suit drawers that are ideal widths for my dovetailing jig (see "Drawer Sizes" in Chapter 7, Dovetails). The widths are $6\frac{3}{4}$", $7\frac{19}{32}$", and $8\frac{7}{16}$". If the ideal drawer-front widths for your dovetail jig are different, you will have to follow a procedure similar to the one below to find equivalent measurements for the frames. In that case, the dimensions of your chest will vary slightly from the dimensions given here. A calculator that handles fractions will help when you do the calculations.

The openings have been designed to provide suitable expansion gaps above the drawers and to allow for $\frac{3}{16}$"-thick beading above and below the drawers. The average expansion gaps are 0.75 percent of the drawer heights (explained under "Drawer Sizes" in Chapter 7). It is roughly $\frac{1}{64}$" for every 2" of drawer height, so it is a little more or less than $\frac{1}{16}$" for each of the drawers of the chest.

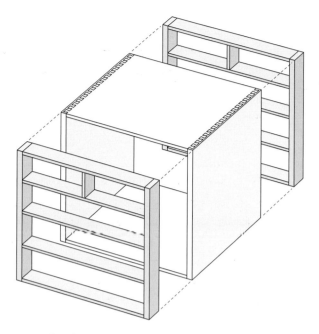

19.2 The chest is built as a dovetailed box with front and back frames added

The required openings to accommodate the drawers, plus expansion gaps, plus two thicknesses of $\frac{3}{16}$" beading, are as follows:

Top drawers:
$6\frac{3}{4}$" + $\frac{1}{16}$" + $\frac{3}{8}$" = $7\frac{3}{16}$"
Second drawers:
$7\frac{19}{32}$" + $\frac{1}{16}$" + $\frac{3}{8}$" = $8\frac{1}{32}$"
Third and fourth drawers:
$8\frac{7}{16}$" + $\frac{1}{16}$" + $\frac{3}{8}$" = $8\frac{7}{8}$"

These figures are used for calculating the frame rail positions shown in **19.3**.

The top and bottom frame rails are $\frac{7}{8}$" thick; the intermediate rails are $\frac{3}{4}$" thick. With these thicknesses, plus the openings, the bottom faces of the rails are at $9\frac{3}{4}$", $19\frac{3}{8}$", $28\frac{5}{32}$", and $36\frac{3}{32}$" from the bottoms of the stiles. The rail centers (and hence the centers of mortises in the stiles) are at $10\frac{1}{8}$", $19\frac{3}{4}$", and $28\frac{17}{32}$" from the stile bottoms. The stiles are $36\frac{31}{32}$" long.

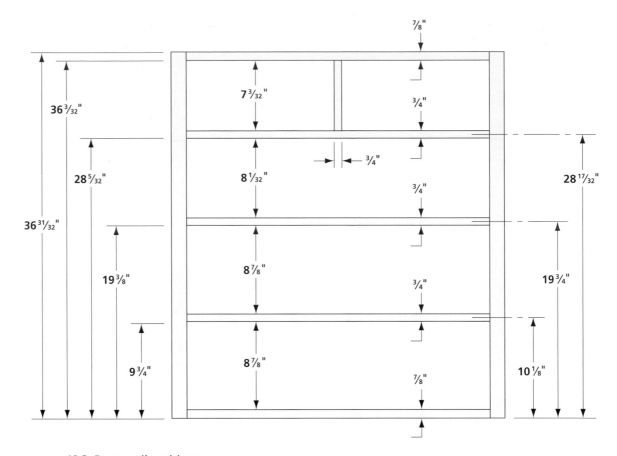

19.3 Frame rail positions

All the frame joints are mortise-and-tenon style. The gluing surfaces of the tenons are vertical in order to make side-grain to side-grain contact with the stile mortises. Since the rails are $\frac{3}{4}$" or $\frac{7}{8}$" thick, each tenon has only a small gluing area. To compensate, multiple tenons are used at each joint.

A top rail and an intermediate rail lying on a stile are shown in **19.4**. The intermediate rail has three tenons in the end, which will be glued into the matching triple mortises in the stile. The total gluing area of the three tenons equals that of a single 1"-wide one.

At the top and bottom of the stiles, the mortises cannot be effectively closed because the short end grain would be weak. Therefore, these mortises are left open and made larger to accommodate two strong $\frac{1}{2}$" tenons.

Multiple mortises, whether double or triple, must be made using a technique that ensures they are identically spaced on the rail and on the stile. The procedure described in Chapter 6, The Mortise-and-Tenon Joint, ensures identical spacing.

The grain of the chest sides runs from top to bottom, so the sides will expand and shrink from front to back while their height will remain constant. The drawer openings have unchanging heights and widths that are defined by the frames. Drawer side clearances can be made very small because the drawer fronts will not change in length.

The drawers slide on bearers fixed to the chest sides and to the front and back

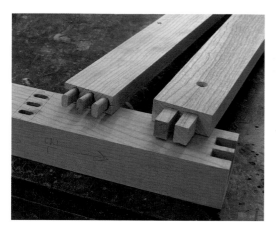

19.4 Top rail (two tenons) and intermediate rail (three tenons)

frames. Since the bearers are fixed lengthwise across the grain of the sides, the method for fixing them must allow the chest sides to expand and shrink. Drawer guides are glued to the bearers to keep the drawers to a straight in-and-out movement.

The case sits on a plinth whose outline does not change seasonally. Since the case expands and shrinks from front to back, it is fixed at the front of the plinth and allowed to move at the back.

The drawer openings are given extra visual impact by the beading that projects out all around. Cock beading, as it is called, enhances a piece's overall appearance and was traditionally fixed to drawer fronts, though furniture-makers soon began to fix it to the openings instead. Clamping it to drawer fronts is more awkward and requires a rabbet to be cut around the fronts to accommodate it. Also, a grain conflict occurs when the side grain of the beading is glued across the grain on the ends of the fronts. It is easier to apply the cock bead to the openings, but there is a trade-off because this method raises the bottom of the opening, which incurs extra work when the drawers are fitted.

The chest back is a light frame holding thin panels. There is no reason why the back could not simply consist of a piece of plywood, saving considerable work. However, I use only solid wood in my furniture.

Although the dovetailed box has a top, we will be adding a separate and more attractive top. The front and side edges of the top extend down over the chest front and sides to conceal any small gaps that might appear at the edges, and to avoid any need to fix a separate molding around the chest.

LUMBER SELECTION

Planning for economical cuts on a big project can drive you crazy. There are so many parts, and every board has its own special problems. Remember—you are making a luxury item, so getting the best appearance is more important than saving a few dollars.

Here are some requirements to consider when planning the cuts:

- Drawer fronts must have zero defects on their outside faces, and their grain patterns and color should be consistent. There are too many fronts for you to cut them all from one board, so you should select boards with similar color and figure. The two small drawer fronts at the top should be cut consecutively from one board so that their grain patterns are continuous.
- Drawer backs, sides, and bottoms can be made from a cheaper wood or from less desirable parts of the primary lumber.
- Quartersawn lumber is often used for drawer sides. It expands less and is less likely to warp than flatsawn boards. However, to benefit from quartersawn lumber's lower expansion, the drawer fronts would also need to be quartersawn, but then they would be rather plain. The risk of dovetailed drawer sides warping is small, and I have

PART	QTY	SIZE IN INCHES	REMARKS
Top and bottom rails	4	$\frac{7}{8}$" × $2\frac{1}{4}$" × $34\frac{1}{2}$"	See procedure for cutting to length
Intermediate rails	6	$\frac{3}{4}$" × $2\frac{1}{4}$" × $34\frac{1}{2}$"	See procedure for cutting to length
Top drawer dividers	2	$\frac{3}{4}$" × $2\frac{1}{4}$" × $6\frac{5}{16}$"	See procedure for cutting to length
Dovetailed box sides	2	$\frac{7}{8}$" × 14" × $36\frac{31}{32}$"	
Dovetailed box top/bottom	2	$\frac{3}{8}$" × 14" × $37\frac{1}{16}$"	
Drawer bearers	7	$\frac{3}{4}$" × $2\frac{1}{4}$" × $13\frac{1}{2}$"	
Bottom drawer bearers	2	$\frac{3}{4}$" × $1\frac{3}{4}$" × $13\frac{1}{2}$"	
Drawer side guides	10	$\frac{1}{2}$" × $1\frac{3}{8}$" × 13"	
Stiles	4	$1\frac{3}{4}$" × $2\frac{1}{4}$" × $36\frac{31}{32}$"	
Plinth front	1	$\frac{7}{8}$" × 5" × 39"	
Plinth sides	2	$\frac{7}{8}$" × 5" × 20"	
Plinth back	1	$\frac{7}{8}$" × 5" × $37\frac{1}{2}$"	Could be $\frac{3}{4}$" thick
Drawer front #1L & 1R	2	$\frac{7}{8}$" × $6\frac{3}{4}$" × $16\frac{1}{2}$"	
Drawer front #2	1	$\frac{7}{8}$" × $7\frac{19}{32}$" × $34\frac{1}{8}$"	
Drawer front #3 & 4	2	$\frac{7}{8}$" × $8\frac{7}{16}$" × $34\frac{1}{8}$"	
Drawer back #1L & 1R	2	$\frac{3}{4}$" × $6\frac{3}{4}$" × $16\frac{1}{2}$"	
Drawer back #2	1	$\frac{3}{4}$" × $7\frac{19}{32}$" × $34\frac{1}{8}$"	
Drawer back #3 & 4	2	$\frac{3}{4}$" × $8\frac{7}{16}$" × $34\frac{1}{8}$"	
Drawer sides #1L & 1R	4	$\frac{1}{2}$" × $6\frac{3}{4}$" × 17"	
Drawer sides #2	2	$\frac{1}{2}$" × $7\frac{19}{32}$" × 17"	
Drawer sides #3 & 4	4	$\frac{1}{2}$" × $8\frac{17}{16}$" × 17"	
Drawer bottoms #1L & 1R	2	$\frac{3}{8}$" × $17\frac{1}{2}$" × $15\frac{3}{4}$"	
Drawer bottoms #2, 3, 4	3	$\frac{3}{8}$" × $17\frac{1}{2}$" × $33\frac{3}{8}$"	
Chest top	1	$\frac{7}{8}$" × $21\frac{3}{16}$" × 40"	
Cockbeading	40 ft	$\frac{3}{16}$" × $\frac{15}{16}$" wide	
Bearer tenons	14	$\frac{1}{4}$" × $2\frac{1}{2}$" × $1\frac{9}{16}$"	
Rail tenons	44	$\frac{1}{4}$" × $\frac{17}{32}$" × $1\frac{1}{2}$"	
Top and bottom rail tenons	16	$\frac{1}{2}$" × $\frac{11}{16}$" × $1\frac{3}{4}$"	
Drawer stops	10	$\frac{11}{32}$" × 1" × 3"	See procedure to confirm thickness
Stiles for paneled back frame	2	$\frac{5}{8}$" × $2\frac{3}{4}$" × $36\frac{23}{32}$"	
Divider for paneled back frame	1	$\frac{5}{8}$" × $2\frac{3}{4}$" × $31\frac{7}{32}$"	
Rails for back support frame	2	$\frac{5}{8}$" × $2\frac{3}{4}$" × $30\frac{1}{2}$"	
Back frame panels	2	$\frac{1}{4}$" × $14\frac{5}{8}$" × $32\frac{1}{32}$"	

Table 5. Chest of Drawer Parts List

never known it to happen with well-made drawers. However, to increase your confidence with flatsawn lumber, you can make the sides and backs from narrow pieces glued together, with reversed ring curvatures on adjacent pieces (see "Furniture Stability" in Chapter 1). By gluing available pieces into wide panels and then cutting drawer parts from them, you can combine maximum utilization of your lumber with increased stability.

- The side panels of the dovetailed box must be perfect on their outside faces, whereas the top and bottom of the box will never be seen.
- The box sides will be glued to the frame stiles, so it is desirable to achieve a good grain pattern match at the junctions. Matching will be easier if the grain near the outside edges runs fairly straight. It can be difficult to find a match for a piece that has been cut through the center of curvature of the growth rings.
- The stiles for the front and back frames are cut from 8/4 lumber. Consider which faces of these need to be perfect: The front stiles will be visible on two faces, the back stiles on only one face.
- Frame rails should be straight-grained to reduce their risk of bowing and interfering with the drawers. They need only one perfect edge. Since the outside edges of boards are most likely to have straight grain and sapwood, the rails can be cut from the edges and flipped over to put the sapwood to the inside. The rest of the board will then be available for parts that must have no sapwood.
- It is best to cut unseen parts as they become required in the assembly so that you can utilize off-cuts, remainders, and sapwood as much as possible.

- The surface of the chest top, which covers the box top, must be defect-free.
- If the sides and front of the plinth are cut consecutively from a single board, you can make the grain continuous around the corners—as if the corners were folds.
- Material for the tops and bottoms of the dovetailed box will be obtained by resawing 4/4 lumber, each piece of which will yield two $\frac{3}{8}$" pieces. The same procedure applies to the back panels and the drawer bottoms.

In summary, these are the parts that are highly visible:

Drawer fronts (outside faces only)
Box sides (outside faces only)
Chest top (outside face and edges)
Front rails (outside edges only)
Stiles (two faces of front stiles, one face of back stiles)
Plinth front and sides (outside faces and top edges)

MILLWORK

Start by selecting boards to make the drawer fronts. It is important to match these properly while your stock is at its maximum level. If the boards are wide enough, begin by ripping strips from the edges for use as rails.

The rail strips must be wide enough to allow for a second rip to straighten the outside edge. Remember that when you cut lumber, you are making rough blanks that require a minimum of $\frac{1}{8}$" of extra width and $\frac{1}{2}$" of extra length after all the defects have been cut away. When you cut for the front rails, you must produce one edge that is free of sapwood.

Whether the drawer fronts are plain or figured is a matter of personal preference, but the degree of figure should be similar in all of them, as should the color. If you cannot judge the color from the surface of the rough boards, cut wafers from their ends and compare the cut surfaces. Cut the fronts for the two top drawers consecutively from a single board.

You will probably need to begin with full-length rip cuts from both edges of the boards to obtain suitable material for the rails. If the board edges are uneven, straighten them using one of the methods described under "Cutting Rough Lumber" in Chapter 3.

Crosscut and rip the boards as necessary to obtain rough blanks for the rails and drawer fronts. Always be careful to use appropriate methods for cutting rough lumber safely. Store the blanks on stickers until later in the project—do not flatten them at this stage.

Next, cut the pieces for the dovetailed box. The sides are nominally $\frac{7}{8}$" thick, but $\frac{3}{4}$" will do fine if you need to reduce them to this thickness during the flattening and thicknessing process. If you can achieve the full $\frac{7}{8}$", it will provide a little extra gluing surface for gluing the front and back frames to the box. You need fewer pieces for the top and bottom panels because each piece will be resawn into two. Make the pieces for the sides at least 3" wide and the pieces for resawing less than 6" wide. The blanks must have enough combined width to make the panels at least $\frac{1}{4}$" overwide, which might require more than 1" of total extra width before the edges are jointed. You will need to cut the pieces for resawing from fairly flat boards so that you can flatten them while removing the minimum of material. Remember that simply ripping boards into narrow strips reduces cupping and twist, while cutting to length reduces bow and twist.

After you have produced the rough blanks for the dovetailed box, turn your

attention to the frame rails. If you still need more rail material after cutting for the drawer fronts and box components, take it from the edges of wide boards. Take the opportunity to use wood that has sapwood on one edge. You will need more than 30 feet of material before cutting it into individual rails.

Cut the rails to rough length, and make at least two spares. Flatten one face of each piece, plane the pieces to $\frac{7}{8}$" thickness, and then set them aside on stickers and resume work on the dovetailed box. The longer they are left on stickers, the better.

DOVETAILED BOX

Before you cut the rails to final length, you must make the dovetailed box. The sequence of operations is as follows:
1. Flatten and plane the rough blanks.
2. Resaw the pieces for the top and bottom and plane them to $\frac{3}{8}$" thickness.
3. Make $\frac{3}{8}$"- and $\frac{7}{8}$"-thick panels.
4. Belt-sand the panels.
5. Joint one edge of each panel and rip to the finished width plus $\frac{1}{16}$".
6. Joint the ripped edges.
7. Square one end; then cut to length.
8. Make the dovetails.
9. Glue and assemble the box.

Start by flattening one face of each piece and then plane them all to thickness. Make the side blanks $\frac{7}{8}$" thick if you can. The blanks for the box's top and bottom must be as thick as possible because they will later be resawn.

Follow the procedures in Chapter 12, Resawing, to produce enough $\frac{3}{8}$"-thick pieces to make the top and bottom panels. If you are not going to glue up the resawn pieces immediately, put them in plastic—do not leave them exposed to the air for even a few hours.

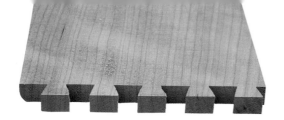

19.5 Tails test piece showing no rounding of the tails (fingerplate not adjusted)

19.6 Tails test piece with backs of tails rounded (fingerplate adjusted inward)

Glue up the ⅜" and ⅞" panels using the procedures detailed in Chapter 13 for thick and thin panels. Making the wooden restrainers is described under "Gluing Thin Panels" in Chapter 13.

Leave the panels clamped together until the glue has set, and then belt-sand them to remove all the glue marks and to make all the seams flush.

Decide which will be the inside faces; sand these with a random-orbit sander and a 120-grit disc, and then shellac them (see "Wiping Finishes" in Chapter 18). Wipe off the shellac before it dries. Sand it lightly when it is completely dry.

Mark the panels in pencil to show position and orientation: left and right sides, top and bottom, front edges, outside faces.

Joint one edge of each; rip them to nominal width plus ¼₆" (that is, to 14⁹⁄₁₆") and then joint the ripped edges lightly.

Fit a backer board to your miter gauge or crosscut sled to show an exact cutting line. Install a good crosscut blade. Make a test cut on a wide piece of material to check that the setup is cutting square, and then cut the panel ends square and to length. The lengths of the box's top and bottom are 37 ¼₆"; the lengths of the sides will be 36 ³¹⁄₃₂" if the drawer openings are to be 7 ³⁄₁₆", 8¼₃₂", and 8⅞". For other opening sizes, the side lengths must be calculated.

The box parts are now ready for dovetailing.

Dovetailing the Box

If you have not used the dovetail jig before, read Chapter 7, "Dovetails," and make a small drawer from scrap lumber as an exercise. You can make all the pieces for this about 4" wide and 6" long. Since the drawer is just an exercise piece, you can dispense with the backer board. A backer board is also not essential when you make the dovetailed box: The dovetails will never be seen, so a few chipped tails will not matter.

You can follow the system described under "Procedure for Dovetailing Drawers" in Chapter 7 by treating the box parts as drawer parts. The box sides will represent the drawer front and back because they will be the socket boards; the box top and bottom will be equivalent to drawer sides. Position the parts in a hollow rectangle as if you were about to dovetail a drawer; place them with their inside faces up, back edges facing inward like the bottom edges of drawer parts, box right side at 12 o'clock, box bottom at three o'clock, box left side at six o'clock, and box top at nine o'clock. Mark LL, RR, etc., on the inside corners of the pieces, starting with the front left corners of the rectangle, as you would if marking drawer parts.

Because the box top and bottom are only ⅜" thick, the fingerplate may have to be adjusted inward to allow the router cutter to round over the backs of the dovetails. The fingerplate must be readjusted outward again before cutting the sockets, or they will be too deep. Test pieces cut before and after the fingerplate has been adjusted inward are shown in **19.5** and **19.6**.

Make a tails test piece that is the same thickness as the box top and bottom, and

19.7 Excessive tails insertion due to unadjusted fingerplate

a sockets test piece that is at least ½" thick. Follow the instructions in Chapter 7 to achieve an acceptable tightness of fit between tails and sockets and to make the test pieces' edges flush when they are assembled. At this stage, do not worry about the depth of insertion or the width of the end pins. Since the box dimensions are not chosen to suit the dovetail spacing, there may not even be any end pins; this is of no consequence because the box edges will be glued to frame stiles.

When the cutter depth and the side stops are correctly set, adjust the fingerplate inward to produce rounded tails. Repeat the tests and adjustments until the cutter produces tails at both ends of the jig that have rounded, or partially rounded, backs. Do not recut the socket test piece.

Cut the tails of the box top and bottom. Position them in the jig as described in Chapter 7. Remember that the box top and bottom represent drawer sides.

After cutting the tails, adjust the fingerplate outward and make further cuts in the socket test piece after cutting off the first ones. If the fingerplate is not outward enough, the tails will insert too deeply, as shown in **19.7**. Repeat until the tails are flush with, or very slightly below, the ends of the pins when they are fully inserted.

When the fingerplate is correctly adjusted, cut the sockets in the box sides. Position them in the jig as if they were drawer fronts and backs.

Assembling the Box

The box sides will be glued to the stiles of front and back frames. These glue bonds are vital to the structural integrity of the chest. Jointed edges are required for a good glue bond, so before gluing the box parts together, check that the edges of the sides were jointed after they were ripped. If they were not, joint them now. Apply glue to the dovetails and sockets, and assemble the box. With so many dovetails, polyurethane glue is an obvious choice. Wet the tails lightly with water and then apply glue to each socket. When the surface water has disappeared from the tails, apply glue to them also, and assemble the box. Use pipe clamps and cauls to pull the joints together **(19.8)**.

Remove the clamps and then check the squareness of the box by comparing the diagonals **(19.9)**. Push the appropriate corners as necessary to make the diagonals equal. Leave the box until the glue has set, and then remove any squeeze-out from the inside corners.

FRAME COMPONENTS

While the dovetail glue is setting, check the flatness of your stickered rails. If any of them show significant bow, do not use them for front rails. Bowing of up to about ¹⁄₁₆" is acceptable in the back rails, but if any are worse than this, they should not be used. Select four straight ones to be the top and bottom rails. Plane the others to ¾" thickness. Select the eight best ¾" rails. Any spares can be used later for making bearers.

Joint the best edge of each rail square to the faces, and rip the other edges to a

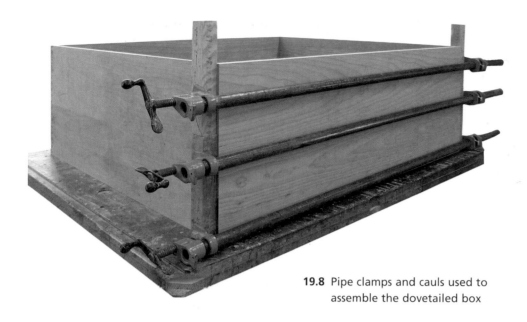

19.8 Pipe clamps and cauls used to assemble the dovetailed box

width of $2\frac{5}{16}$". All rails are now ready to be cut to length, which must be determined from the finished sizes of the dovetailed box and the frame stiles. You cannot cut the rails to length until the stiles are made, so make the stiles now.

Remember that the back stiles need only one defect-free face, while the front ones need two.

The $1\frac{3}{4}$" dimensions of the stiles will come from the thickness of 8/4 lumber, and the $2\frac{1}{4}$" dimensions from the width. If the lumber is significantly cupped, the ripped blanks will not be rectangular in section, and you will lose a lot of the width when jointing and planing the faces square. If cupping is a factor, rip the blanks to a generous $2\frac{1}{2}$" wide.

Make the stile blanks, and joint two adjacent faces of each stile square to each other. Fit an auxiliary planer bed and plane the opposite faces to make the stiles rectangular in section and exactly $1\frac{3}{4}$" thick by $2\frac{1}{4}$" wide. While the planer is set at $2\frac{1}{4}$", plane the ripped edges of the rails to make them the same width as the stiles.

Feed the rails carefully into the planer to keep their jointed edges flat on the bed.

The stiles must now be cut to exactly the length of the box sides. Use a crosscut sled with a backer board to cut one end of each stile square. Mark each squared end after you cut it. Lay down the dovetailed box on one of its sides and place a stile on the upper side. Position the squared end exactly flush

19.9 Checking the box for square

with the bottom end of the box side, and make a pencil mark on the other end of the stile where it meets the top of the box. Mark the other stiles in the same way.

The stiles must be cut exactly at the marked lines, so check that your crosscut blade is still cutting precisely at the edge of the backer board. Reposition the backer if necessary. Align the mark on each stile to this cutting line and cut the stiles to length. After cutting to length, sort them into front left, front right, back left, and back right, and then mark them as such. Designate stiles as if seen from the front, so that back left will be on your left when you are in front of the chest and facing it.

Now return to the rails and sort them for position: front top, front bottom, three front intermediates, back top, back bottom, and three back intermediates. Mark the designations on the best edges of the rails, which will be the outside edges. Adequate markings would be FT, FB, F1, F2, F3, BT, BB, B1, B2, and B3 (the front intermediate rails are F1 to F3 from the top down, the back intermediates are B1 to B3). In addition, mark arrows on the outside edges to show which will be the upper face of each rail.

You are now ready to cut the rails square and to length. Make cuts that are crisp, without any chipping or fraying at the front edges, because these edges will be the visible junctions of mortise-and-tenon joints. With this in mind, make all cuts with the outside edges facing the blade so they are cut cleanly and any chipping will occur at the inside edges. Start by cutting one end of each rail square. Mark these ends, and then determine the precise length the rails require as follows:

- Stand the box upright and clamp a $1\frac{3}{4}$" face of a stile to one side edge, with the outside faces of the box and the stile precisely flush. Take care not

to damage the edges of the box sides: These are gluing surfaces.

- Clamp a second stile against the inside face of the first one.
- Butt the squared end of a rail against the second stile, and mark the opposite end of the rail where it meets the other side of the box. This mark will show the length of a rail required for a frame to match the width of the box. However, it will be better to make the frame just a little wider so that it can be glued to the box with the stiles very slightly raised above the surface of the box sides. If it is not possible to assemble the frames absolutely flush with the box, sanding the stiles flush to the box will be easier than sanding the box flush to the stiles.
- Make a second mark on the outside edge of the rail just $\frac{1}{32}$" beyond the first mark.
- Place the rail on the crosscut sled. Fit a length stop to the sled fence, and adjust it so that the second mark on the rail is at the cutting line when the rail is butted to the stop.
- Cut each rail to length with its squared end against the stop and its outside edge to the blade.

The main frame components are now ready for mortising, but first you should make the two divider pieces to separate the top drawers. Their nominal lengths are $7\frac{3}{16}$", but at this stage you should make them $\frac{1}{8}$" longer so that they can be trimmed to final length after the frames are assembled.

FRAME JOINERY

Frame components are held together by double and triple tenons, as illustrated in **19.4**. Mortise outlines must be drawn on one workpiece and then used when setting the fence and side stops of the mortising jig.

Photo **19.10** shows a set of triple mortises drawn on a stile, with a line drawn from midlength of the mortises to the workpiece edge. Photo **19.11** shows the workpiece clamped to the jig reference face, with the centerline of the mortises aligned with the jig center mark.

The jig fence and side stops will be adjusted so that when the router is held to the fence, the cutter can move only within the outline of a mortise. Once the jig is set, identical mortises can be cut in any number of workpieces at exactly the same distance from the reference faces. Only the first workpiece needs to have the mortises drawn on it; subsequent pieces simply require a mark on the edge to show where the mortises are to be centered.

Marking Out

Start the marking procedure by very carefully measuring from the bottom end of a stile up along the $2\frac{1}{4}$" mortising face, and make a mark at the centers of each of the $\frac{1}{4}$" triple mortise positions, at the centers of the intermediate rail positions. For drawer openings of $7\frac{3}{16}$", $8\frac{1}{32}$", and $8\frac{7}{8}$", the rail centers are placed $10\frac{1}{8}$", $19\frac{3}{4}$", and $28\frac{17}{32}$" from the bottom. As explained earlier in this chapter, you may need different mortise positions to accommodate drawer sizes that are more suitable for your dovetail jig.

Use a small square to draw lines across the stile's mortising face at these marks. Make the lines short, to reach only to the reference faces (the front faces of front stiles or the back faces of back stiles). Do not extend the marks all the way across the mortising faces or onto the reference faces.

The other stiles should be marked the same way, and the positions must be identical on all of them. Clamp the first stile

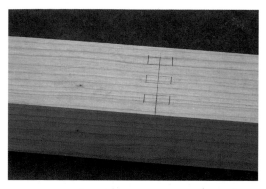

19.10 A set of triple mortises drawn on a stile

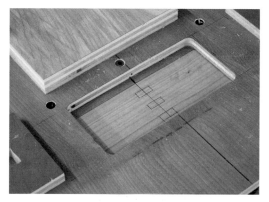

19.11 Aligning the mortises' centerline with the jig's center mark

against each of the others in turn with the bottom ends perfectly flush, and transfer the marks. Start the marks at the junction with each reference face; use a square to make marks about $\frac{1}{2}$" long on the mortising faces only.

After you mark the stiles, stand them upright, in their correct positions with the FR stile at front right, etc. Separate them enough to check that the marks are on the faces that will be joined by rails, and that they reach only to the front faces of the front stiles or the back faces of the back stiles.

The marks will ensure that mortises are cut at exactly the right positions. Now you need a way to align the intermediate rails so that matching mortises cut into their ends will be accurately positioned. The triple mortises must be centered in the thickness of the rails, so a mark at the center of each rail's thickness, as in **19.12**, is needed to align with the jig's center mark.

The best way to mark all the rail ends accurately is with a marking gauge set to half the rail thickness. Test the setting by marking from opposite faces; when the marks coincide, the gauge is set correctly. A wheel-type marking gauge is best, and the inside edge of any rail will provide space for repeated tests. Do not take the

19.12 At the ends of each intermediate rail, the centerline of the triple mortises is at the center of thickness of the rail. These rails can now be accurately positioned in the mortising jig

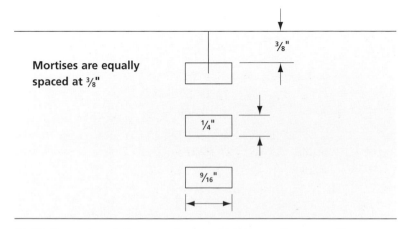

19.13 Dimensioned diagram of a set of triple mortises on a stile

gauge marks all the way to the reference faces because they would show on the outside after the joints are assembled. Stop the marks back from the edges and then continue them by using a pencil and a small square. Also use the gauge to mark the ends of the top drawer divider pieces.

Now draw one set of triple mortises centered on one of the marks on a stile, as shown in **19.10** and **19.13**. The ends can be drawn square, even though the cutter will produce a radius. The mortise outlines are $\frac{1}{4}$" × $\frac{9}{16}$", spaced $\frac{3}{8}$" apart and $\frac{3}{8}$" from the stile edges.

You should draw the $\frac{9}{16}$" mortise lengths accurately. The other dimensions can be less accurate—it does not matter if the first mortise in each set is $\frac{11}{32}$" from the edge, or if the mortises are not precisely $\frac{3}{8}$" apart. What matters is that they exactly match the positions of corresponding mortises in the rails. The correct use of the jig will ensure that this happens.

After you have drawn one set of $\frac{1}{4}$" triple mortises, draw a pair of $\frac{1}{2}$" double mortises at each end of a top rail on its upper face, as shown in **19.14a** and **19.14b**. The length of the mortises is $1\frac{3}{8}$". The ends can be drawn square even though they will be rounded by the mortising cutter.

Here, again, the drawings are merely an aid to setting the jig, and while it is a good idea to draw them as accurately as you can, errors of even $\frac{1}{16}$" would be of little consequence. Put a small X to mark the mortises nearest the reference face (**19.14a**).

You do not need to draw the remaining pairs of $\frac{1}{2}$" mortises, but you should mark their positions to eliminate the risk of mortising the wrong faces by mistake. You need only sketch a pair of mortises very crudely at each position and put an X by the one nearest the reference face (the outside edges of the rails, the front faces of the front stiles, and the back faces of the back stiles). A lumber crayon is suitable for this. Sketch the mortises on the upper faces of the top rails, the lower faces of the bottom rails, and the end faces of the stiles. Completed markings for the $\frac{1}{2}$" mortises are shown in **19.15**.

Double-check all your markings, making sure that the mortise drawings are on the faces into which you want to cut mortises. Check that the $\frac{1}{4}$" mortise centerlines reach the reference faces and only the reference faces. Also check that the $\frac{1}{2}$" mortises sketched on the stile ends are open on the faces that have the $\frac{1}{4}$" triple mortises.

Mortising

If you have not already made the mortising jig, as described in Chapter 6, make it now and clamp it to the front of the bench.

Take the top rail with the $\frac{1}{2}$" mortises drawn on it and clamp the rail horizontally into the jig with the marked mortises up and one end of the rail exactly at the jig's center mark; the rail's reference face should be against the jig reference face **(19.16)**.

Fit a $\frac{1}{2}$" spiral cutter in the router, and center it on one of the mortise outlines. Hold the jig fence against the fence guide, bring it up to the router base, and clamp it in place.

Set the side stops for the $\frac{1}{2}$" mortises. These mortises are not marked with a centerline because they are open-ended; it is the ends of the rails that align with the jig center mark. Position the $\frac{1}{2}$" cutter at the closed end of a mortise, and clamp the appropriate end stop in position against the router base. Unclamp the rail and slide it toward the other end of the jig; keep the same face toward the jig reference face, and clamp it with its other end at the jig's center mark. Position the cutter at the closed end of a mortise, and clamp the other end stop in position.

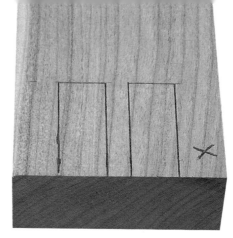

19.14a A pair of $\frac{1}{2}$" double mortises drawn on the a top rail's upper face or a bottom rail's lower face

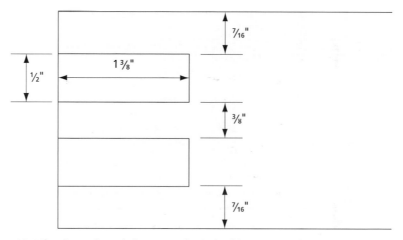

19.14b Dimensioned diagram of $\frac{1}{2}$" double mortises for the ends of top and bottom rails

Plunge the cutter so that it touches the rail surface. Set the depth stop to allow a cut $\frac{11}{16}$" deep.

Start the router and cut a mortise in stages. Push the router firmly against the fence while moving it slowly from side to side. After the mortise is cut, slacken the rail clamps and slide the rail to align its other end with the jig's center marks. Tighten the clamps and cut a mortise in that end of the rail.

Cut one mortise at each end of the other top rail and both bottom rails. Use the X marks to ensure that the mortising faces

19.15 Completed markings for the ½" double mortises

19.16 The top rail with ½" mortises drawn on it fixed in the jig

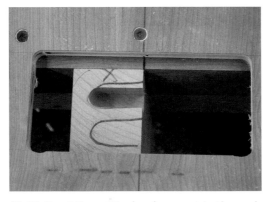

19.17 One ½" mortise has been cut in the end of this stile fixed vertically in the jig

are uppermost and the reference faces are toward the jig's reference face. After you have cut one mortise at each end of each rail, do not move the fence.

Place a stile vertically in the jig, and clamp it with its mortising face level with the jig's center mark. The open ends of the sketched ½" mortises are in the mortising face. Check that the X is toward the jig reference face.

Start the router and hold it firmly against the fence while you cut a mortise in the end of the stile (**19.17**).

Reverse the stile, and clamp it in the jig with the mortising face at the center mark, but this time with the stile to the other side of center. Check that the jig and stile reference faces are together, and cut a mortise in this end. Repeat the procedure with the other three stiles. After cutting each mortise, clear the sawdust away from the fence and side stops.

When one ½" mortise has been cut into both ends of every stile and every top and bottom rail, reset the fence for the second ½" mortise position, using the accurately drawn mortise pair on the top rail. Cut a second ½" mortise at each end of every stile and top and bottom rail (**19.18**).

Change to a ¼" spiral cutter, and set the jig for one of the ¼" mortise positions. Clamp the stile with the triple-mortise drawing into the jig horizontally, with the mortise centerline aligned with the jig's center mark (**19.11**). Place the cutter at the right-hand end of a mortise outline, and set the right-hand side stop. Move the cutter to the left-hand end of the mortise, and set the other side stop. Place the cutter centrally over the mortise outline, and fix the fence against the router base and the fence side guide.

Set the router depth stop for a ¾"-deep cut, start the router, and cut the mortise in stages. Keep the router firmly against the fence. Slacken the clamps, and slide the stile along to the next mortising position. Cut another mortise. Repeat this procedure at every marked position on all the stiles. Remember to keep the fence and side stops free from debris.

Clamp an intermediate rail vertically in the jig with the centerline on its end aligned with the jig's center mark (19.19). Cut a mortise in the end of the rail (19.20), and then reverse the rail and cut one in the other end. Repeat this procedure for the other intermediate rails.

Check to see that one $\frac{1}{4}$" mortise has been cut at every mortising centerline in all the stiles and intermediate rails, and then use the stile with the mortise drawing to reset the fence for the second mortise position. Cut a second mortise at every centerline in the stiles and rails; then reset the fence again and complete the triple mortises.

The only mortises you still need to cut are those for fixing a drawer divider between the top rail and the first intermediate rail of each frame. Two $\frac{1}{4}$" mortises must be cut into the ends of the top drawer dividers and through the rails at midlength. The divider mortises are the same length as the triple mortises ($\frac{9}{16}$") but must be deeper so as to go completely through the rails, and cut deep enough into the dividers to allow for trimming the dividers to fit. Double mortises in the ends of the dividers and at the centers of rails are shown in 19.21. The dividers are $\frac{1}{8}$" longer than needed, and they will be trimmed to final length and fixed after the frames are assembled.

Mark the upper faces of the top rails and first intermediate rails of both frames at exactly midlength with short lines. Start the lines at the reference edges. Draw one pair of mortises on the top surface of one rail. The layout and the short centerline are shown in 19.22. The mortises are at the

19.18 Completed $\frac{1}{2}$" double mortises in the stiles and the top and bottom rails

19.19 An intermediate rail clamped vertically into the jig

19.20 A mortise cut into the end of an intermediate rail

19.21 Double ¼" mortises in the ends of the top drawer dividers and at the centers of a top rail and a first intermediate rail

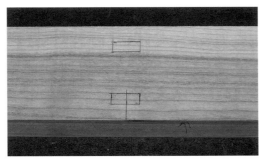

19.22 A pair of ¼" mortises for the top drawer dividers drawn onto the top surface of a rail

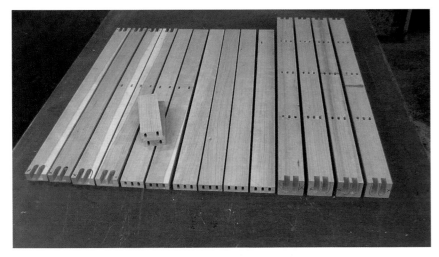

19.23 The frame mortising completed

same distances from the edges as the outside mortises of the triple mortises.

Clamp the rail into the jig with the reference mark aligned with the jig's center mark. Set the fence for one of the mortises, and set the router depth stop for a $^{15}/_{16}$" depth of cut. Cut a through-mortise in the rail. Cut mortises at this position in the other three rails, and then cut a mortise to a depth of $^{15}/_{16}$" in each end of both dividers at the same fence setting. Reset the fence for the second mortise position, and cut the second mortise in the four rails and two dividers.

After completing the mortising (**19.23**), sand the mortised faces of the stiles to remove any material that is sticking up from the mortises. Use sandpaper glued to a hardwood block, and sand only enough to remove the fuzz. These are joinery faces, so there must be absolutely no rounding or beveling of the edges.

With the frame mortising completed, a few things remain to be done before the frames are assembled. Tenons must be made, and provision must be made for installing the drawer bearers, the chest top, and the back.

DRAWER BEARERS

The bearers are screwed to the chest sides at their centers and tenoned into the intermediate frame rails at their ends (except for the bottom bearers, which will be dealt with separately). The tenons are glued into shallow grooves in the rails but are left unglued in the bearer grooves to allow the chest sides to expand and contract without opposition from the bearers. When the chest sides expand or contract, the tenons move farther into or out of the bearer grooves.

A tenon fitted into grooves in a rail and in one end of a bearer is shown in **19.24**.

Make nine bearers, $\frac{3}{4}$" $\times$ $2\frac{1}{4}$" $\times$ $13\frac{1}{2}$", using any spare rail material plus suitable off-cuts and fresh lumber as necessary. Mark one face of each as the upper face.

Rail and Bearer Grooves

You have to cut $\frac{5}{16}$"-deep grooves in the inside edges of the intermediate rails, and 1"-deep grooves in the ends of the bearers. The easiest way to do this is with a $\frac{1}{4}$" dado cutter in the table saw. Alternatively, you can make two cuts from a standard blade with $\frac{1}{8}$"-thick teeth. Before using either method, some safety measures are necessary.

First, you should make a special push-stick for cutting the deep grooves in the bearers (19.25). This will allow you to apply pressure toward the fence while you push the bearers over the blade.

Make the pushstick 5" wide, 8" long, and at least 1" thick. Use the table saw to cut a rabbet $\frac{5}{8}$" deep and $1\frac{1}{4}$" wide in one end and one side (19.25). Screw and glue a handle about $2\frac{1}{2}$" wide and 5" long to the face that is not rabbeted. For comfort, round over the corners and edges of the handle. An alternative to rabbeting a 1"-thick piece is to fix a $\frac{5}{8}$" $\times$ $3\frac{3}{4}$" $\times$ $6\frac{3}{4}$" piece to a $\frac{5}{8}$" $\times$ 5" $\times$ 8" piece.

Second, because standard table-saw fences are too low for working safely with a narrow piece on-end, you should increase the fence height by screwing a 5"-wide board to it.

Third, since the standard blade guard must be removed, you should use other means to reduce the hazards of working with an unguarded blade. A strip of wood $1\frac{1}{2}$" high clamped across the saw table $\frac{1}{2}$" from the blade will reduce the risk to your fingers when you pass the rails over the blade, which will be only $\frac{5}{16}$" high. The strip will be low enough to let you hold the rail firmly to the fence as you push it

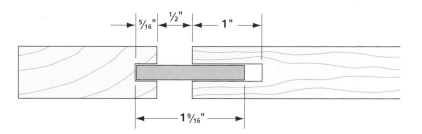

19.24 Dimensioned diagram of a tenon fitted into grooves in a rail and in one end of a bearer

19.25 A special pushstick for use when cutting deep grooves into the bearers

over the blade. You will need to modify this arrangement when you groove the bearers, because it is too close to the blade to allow a pushstick to pass through and because the blade will be much higher. So for the bearers, use a guard that is at least 3" high, and clamp it just far enough from the blade to allow the pushstick and bearer to pass.

You must make the grooves in the inside edges of the rails. As a safeguard against mistakes, draw a freehand line in pencil or lumber crayon along the inside edges, and make sure that these edges go down on the saw table. You must make the cuts in the

19.26 A rail being grooved

19.27 Cutting a groove in the end of a bearer

rails and bearers while their upper faces are pushed toward the fence, so make sure that the upper faces are clearly marked.

Only the intermediate rails are to be grooved—not the top or bottom rails.

Remove the standard saw guard and install a $\frac{1}{4}$" dado blade. Adjust the fence and blade height for a cut $\frac{5}{16}$" deep at $\frac{1}{4}$" from the fence. Make test cuts in scrap wood, and make any necessary adjustments. Fix the $1\frac{1}{2}$"-high guard strip in position.

Start the table saw and pass the inside edge of a rail over the blade. Push its upper face firmly against the fence while keeping your hands above the guard strip. A rail being grooved is shown in **19.26**.

Repeat with the other intermediate rails; then switch off and remove the guard strip. Do not move the fence.

Increase the blade height to 1", and clamp the 3" guard about $1\frac{3}{4}$" from the fence. Cut a groove in the end of a bearer: Use the pushstick to keep its upper face toward the fence as you move it over the blade; keep your other hand on the upper end of the bearer to maintain downward pressure **(19.27)**.

Reverse the bearer and cut a groove in the other end, with the upper face still against the fence. Repeat with the other bearers. If you used a dado cutter, the grooves are now completed.

If you are using a blade with $\frac{1}{8}$" teeth, you must repeat the procedure after you move the fence $\frac{1}{8}$" farther from the blade. The upper faces of every piece must always be toward the fence. You may find that after the second series of cuts thin slivers of material are left uncut in the grooves. In this case, simply move the fence again $\frac{1}{16}$" back toward the blade, and repeat the procedure once more to clean out the grooves.

ARRANGEMENTS FOR A CHEST BACK

Provision for a chest back should be made before the back frame is assembled. The type of back should be chosen now so that you can take appropriate action.

The simplest, cheapest, and by far the most quickly made back is a piece of $\frac{1}{4}$" plywood over the back frame. If the back is not going to be seen, nothing is wrong with this option, but you may feel, as I do, that the chest deserves something better. Then the best choice will be a light frame-and-panel back.

No special preparations are necessary for a thin plywood back, but a frame-and-panel back should be set into the back frame of the chest. To allow for this, you must make the back intermediate rails of the chest narrower. Do so before assembling the back frame of the carcass. The back rails are initially made the same width as the front ones only to avoid introducing complications into the mortising procedure.

A frame-and-panel back about to be fitted into the back frame of the chest is shown in **19.28**. The back intermediate rails of the chest have been reduced in width, and the edges of the paneled frame have been rabbeted. With this arrangement, the back can be set into the chest, and the rabbeted

edges screwed to the outside faces of the chest stiles and top and bottom rails.

Preparations for a Frame-and-Panel Back

Set the table-saw fence to $1\frac{15}{16}$" from a rip blade and then, with their inside edges against the fence, rip $\frac{5}{16}$" from the outside edges of each of the three intermediate back rails.

SCREW HOLES FOR THE TOP

Before assembling the frames, the final operation on the rails is to drill holes in the top rails for screws to fix the chest top when it is made. Seasonal expansion of the top will be from front to back—the same direction as that of the chest sides—so it is not essential to allow for this. However, the amounts of expansion may not be exactly the same, so it is a good idea to make the screw holes a little oversized to accommodate any differences.

Drill $\frac{1}{4}$"-diameter holes centered in the width of each top rail at 2" from each end and 5" each side of center. Countersink the holes in the undersides of the rails for #8 flathead screws.

At this time, drill and countersink $\frac{1}{4}$" holes in the top of the dovetailed box—one at each end of the top, midway between the front and back edges, at 1" from the inside faces of the side panels. These holes also will be used for fixing the chest top.

PREPARATIONS FOR FRAME ASSEMBLY

You are about to assemble a pair of large complex frames, each of which involves gluing 26 tenons into 52 mortises. The frames must be clamped square, and each of the drawer openings formed by the

19.28 A rabbeted frame-and-panel back

19.29 Clamping pressure can be centralized by using a caul with a length of dowel glued to it

19.30 Thick cauls with beveled backs are another way to centralize clamping pressure

19.31 Cauls with shallow grooves cut into their faces will direct the clamping pressure to the edges

frames must be perfectly rectangular. The bottom rails must be exactly flush with the ends of the stiles so that the bottoms of the frames can make perfect contact with a plinth. With so much gluing and tenon insertion and adjustment, the success of the operation depends on making careful preparations, using the right glue, and having all necessary facilities in place.

Careful preparation for assembly will guarantee perfect results. The first step is to provide suitable clamping cauls to protect the stiles and produce evenly distributed clamping pressure. Pipe clamps will be laid over and under the frames.

Because the clamp jaws are not very deep, the pressure at the clamp positions will tend to be concentrated at either the top or bottom edges of the stiles, depending on whether the clamps are over or under the frame. To correct this tendency, you can fix a length of dowel to each caul with hot-melt glue or fast epoxy (**19.29**) to provide centered contact points for the clamp jaws.

Alternatively, if the cauls are thick, you could bevel the backs as shown in **19.30**. Thick cauls could also have shallow grooves cut into their front faces, as in **19.31**, to ensure that clamping pressure is greatest where the stile-to-rail junctions are visible.

The mortise center marks on the stile mortising faces will help you to position the intermediate rails if lines are drawn $\frac{3}{8}$" each side of them. The rails will be correctly positioned when they are centered exactly between these lines. Measure $\frac{3}{8}$" very carefully on each side of the marks, and use a square to draw lines across the mortised faces.

Some small pads, about $1\frac{1}{2}$" square, are needed to prevent the front or back faces of the stiles from being marred by contact with the clamp pipes. These could be $\frac{1}{4}$"- or $\frac{3}{8}$"-thick Masonite, MDF, or wood. You should make four per clamp.

After you have glued up the frame, the most reliable way to check for squareness is to compare the lengths of the diagonals, but the clamps will be in the way and will prevent direct measurements between opposite corners (**19.32**). You can solve this problem by clamping a small block of wood at each corner so that the line of the corner is extended upward; you can then measure between the blocks. In **19.33**, a bar gauge is measuring between the corners of two blocks, and these corners are exactly in line with the inside corners of the frame. You should prepare four blocks, about $\frac{7}{8}$" $\times$ $\frac{7}{8}$" $\times$ $2\frac{1}{2}$", with the ends cut square to the sides.

An important device you should prepare is a forked piece of wood with which to twist the rails slightly (if necessary) to make them parallel to the pairs of lines across the stiles at each mortise position. The fork should be $\frac{3}{4}$" $\times$ $2\frac{1}{2}$" $\times$ 10" with a $\frac{7}{8}$" $\times$ 2" slot cut into one end (**19.34**).

Tenons

Each frame requires eighteen $\frac{1}{4}$" tenons and eight $\frac{1}{2}$" tenons. Eight additional $\frac{1}{4}$" tenons will be required later for the top drawer dividers. The $\frac{1}{4}$" tenons should be $\frac{17}{32}$" wide to allow a little adjustment of the rail positions, and the $\frac{1}{2}$" tenons should be a little wider than the depth of the mortises so they are above the surface when glued in place.

To make the $\frac{1}{4}$" tenons, first flatten some scrap hardwood and plane or resaw it to slightly more than $\frac{1}{4}$" thickness. Rip it into strips $\frac{17}{32}$" wide. The combined lengths of the strips should be at least seven feet.

With an auxiliary table fitted to the planer, reduce the thickness of the strips until they are almost thin enough to enter the mortises; then chamfer or round over the corners (see "Making and Gluing

19.32 Clamped frame

19.33 Using squaring blocks in conjunction with a sliding bar gauge

19.34 A forked piece of wood for aligning the frame rails

Tenons" in Chapter 6). Using only one of the strips, make very small adjustments to the planer and reduce the thickness until it is an easy, but rubbing, fit in the mortises. If planer snipe has reduced the thickness at the ends, cut a strip in half and test the cut ends. When the fit is right, run the other strips through the planer at that setting. Reserve at least 15" of tenon stock for making $1\frac{1}{2}$"-long tenons for the top drawer dividers. Also, cut one piece about 3" long, and sand it to make it a very loose fit in the mortises. Chop the remainder of the strips into pieces that are $\frac{1}{16}$" shorter than the combined depths of two mortises—about $1\frac{7}{16}$".

Follow a similar procedure to make the $\frac{1}{2}$" tenons, except for the rounding over. Do not make them too tight, or they may cause splitting when they are inserted into the open-sided mortises. Make them about $\frac{3}{4}$" wide so that they will be above the surface, and cut them to $2\frac{1}{4}$" lengths.

FRAME ASSEMBLY

Check that you have carried out all the preliminary work:

- Back intermediate rails have been ripped to $1\frac{15}{16}$" wide.
- Four squaring blocks have been made.
- Wooden fork has been made.
- Three inches of tenon stock have been sanded to a very loose fit.
- Lines have been squared across the stile mortising faces $\frac{3}{8}$" to each side of the mortise centers.
- Twenty-four pads of thin material have been made.

In addition to the above, check that the following items are to hand:

- Four 6" C-clamps
- Five pipe clamps that can span the frames and cauls

- Cauls
- Mallet
- 12" steel rule
- Bar gauge

You need to work without hurrying. Polyurethane glue will give you ample time as well as lubricating the tenons to make insertion and adjustment easy. Use an inexpensive $\frac{1}{2}$" glue brush and trim the bristles so that it will fit easily into the $\frac{1}{4}$" mortises without spreading glue on the outside.

Begin the assembly procedure by placing the components of one frame on the bench in their correct positions and with their outside faces up, as in **19.35**.

Dampen the tenons for that frame, and while the surfaces are drying, apply polyurethane glue to the $\frac{1}{4}$" and $\frac{1}{2}$" mortises in the rails. Apply glue to one end of each tenon, and insert the glued ends into the glued mortises **(19.36)**. Tap them fully home with a mallet.

Take the long piece of $\frac{1}{4}$" tenon material that was sanded to a loose fit, and insert it into one of the $\frac{1}{4}$" stile mortises. Mark the depth of the mortise on the tenon piece, and then insert it into all the other stile mortises in turn. If any mortises are shallower, mark the tenon piece to show the depth of the shallowest one. Use the shallowest mark to check that none of the tenons in the rails is too long. Shorten any that are.

Apply glue to the stile mortises and to the protruding ends of the tenons, and then assemble the frame:

- Place one stile on the bench, with its mortised face up, and insert the rail tenons into it. Make sure that "up" faces are up and outside faces are outside.
- Place the other stile over the top and pull it down to insert the tenons. It may be helpful to place a pipe clamp

over the assembly at one end, and clamp it to the bench. This will prevent the tenons at that end from pivoting out of the mortises as the stile is pulled down onto subsequent tenons. A second clamp farther along will help as tenon insertion progresses **(19.37)**.

- When all the tenons are at least partially inserted, remove the frame from the bench and place two pipe clamps on the bench. Lay them along the bench rather than across it. Position the clamps 36" apart: the approximate distance between the top and bottom rails. Place the frame on the clamps, with the outside faces up, and slip thin pads between the stiles and the clamp pipes to protect the inside faces of the stiles.

- Place the cauls between the clamp jaws and the stiles. Slip pads under the cauls if necessary to raise them level with the stiles. Tighten the clamps until the tenons are almost fully inserted. Place three more clamps over the frame, and place more thin pads under them where they rest on the stiles. Tighten all the clamps to fully assemble the frame and close all the gaps.

- Loosen the bottom clamp, and tap the bottom rail flush with the ends of the stiles; then retighten the clamp. Repeat for the top rail.

- Slacken all the clamps except the bottom one, and tap the intermediate rails into alignment with the lines marked across the stiles. Use the wooden fork to make the rail ends parallel to the lines.

- Starting at the bottom, measure the drawer openings at each side. If necessary, tap the rails to make the openings the correct sizes and equal at each side. Do not move the bottom rail: It must stay flush with the ends of the stiles. Adjust the position of the top rail, if

19.35 The frame components prior to assembly

19.36 Tenons are first glued into the ends of the rails

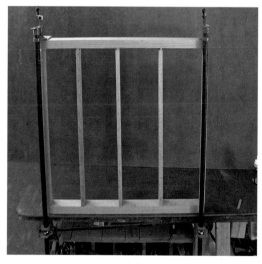

19.37 Pipe clamps can help to get the rail tenons started into the stile mortises

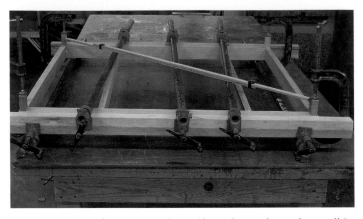

19.38 A clamped frame. Two clamps have been skewed to pull in the long diagonal of the frame (top right to bottom left in the photograph). A bar gauge is measuring the distance between blocks clamped at the corners

FRAMES-TO-BOX ASSEMBLY

The glue bonds between the frame stiles and the box sides will be very strong because the gluing area at each stile is more than 30 square inches—equal to that of ten $1\frac{1}{2}$"-wide tenons glued into 1"-deep mortises. You do not need to glue the top and bottom of the box to the frame.

During the assembly procedure, adjusting the position of parts is simple. Ideally, the frame stiles should be flush with or very slightly proud of the box side surfaces, and perfectly flush with the box bottom. Any small differences between the heights of the stiles and box will then be at the top only, thereby avoiding complications when the chest is later fitted to its plinth. Small irregularities at the top will be less troublesome. It will be easier to make the bottoms flush if everything is upside down during assembly.

To keep the top of the assembly at a convenient height, you must support it on a surface that is lower than a normal bench. An ideal assembly platform would be about 20" high and could be improvised from a piece of plywood on blocks; otherwise, the floor will have to do.

Both of the frames can be glued and clamped at the same time with PVA glue.

Preliminaries

The front or back edges of the box's top or bottom may protrude beyond the sides because of small errors in jig side-stop settings when the box was dovetailed. If so, these edges must be cut back with a hand plane. Otherwise, they will prevent contact between the box sides and the frame stiles. During this operation, take great care to avoid removing any wood from the box sides, because these have been jointed and are ready for gluing. Make some pencil marks on these gluing surfaces where they meet the box's top and bottom.

necessary, to make the top drawer openings at each side the same. Aim to get any discrepancies down to less than $\frac{1}{32}$". Keep the rail ends parallel to the lines.

- When every drawer opening is equal on both sides, tighten all the clamps fully, but first move the outer clamps at least $\frac{1}{2}$" away from the top and bottom rails to give clearance for clamping on the squaring blocks. Clamp a squaring block to each corner, as in **19.33**, and check the frame for square. Angle some or all of the clamps as necessary to make the frame diagonals equal **(19.38)**.
- Finally, check for twist by placing winding sticks across the stiles at the tops and bottoms of the frame. Make sure the cauls are not holding the winding sticks above the stiles.

Repeat the assembly procedure for the other frame.

When the glue is set, remove any squeeze-out from inside corners with a sharp chisel. Also, remove glue from the corners of the rail grooves, where it would interfere with the bearer tenons.

Stop planing near them as soon as any of the pencil marks begin to be erased.

Check the top and bottom edges of the box with a straightedge, and then plane them until the straightedge can touch both sides of the box without rocking. After every couple of strokes of the plane, check with the straightedge, using a flashlight to find gaps and high spots underneath it. Plane away from the sides and toward the center of the box so that you avoid damaging the gluing surfaces.

Although the box's top and bottom edges are not gluing surfaces, you should avoid planing them too much, as this will cause gaps between the box and the frames. When the straightedge can touch both sides at the top and bottom, place the frames on the box and check to see that the stiles make perfect contact with the box sides. If necessary, carry out a similar planing procedure on the top and bottom rails of the frames. Remove any dried glue on the side edges with a card scraper.

To make it easier to ensure that their bottoms are flush, the box and frames are going to be assembled upside down. The bottoms of the stiles and the box sides will be uppermost and must be assembled absolutely flush with each other. The easiest way to make them flush and keep them that way is by tapping wedges under the parts that are too low. Make four wooden wedges about 6" long that taper in thickness from 1" to $\frac{1}{2}$". To allow the wedges to be inserted, some clearance under the assembly will be necessary, so prepare two strips of material $\frac{3}{4}$" thick and at least 20" long for the box and frames to sit on.

You will need at least eight pipe clamps for the assembly, and four clamping cauls to protect the stiles. The cauls should be at least $\frac{3}{4}$" thick by 1" wide and as long as the stiles. It is a good idea to fix a small piece of wood to each caul, at the same height on

each one, to act as supports for a clamp. Make the pieces about $\frac{3}{4}$" square and long enough to project about $1\frac{1}{2}$" horizontally beyond the stiles. The support pieces will enable you to fix the first clamp to each side without having to support it while you position it. The supports will also allow these clamps to be loose enough to allow adjustment of the frames without falling off. Place the cauls within reach at the assembly position. Also, have some masking tape ready to be used to hold everything together while clamps are being applied.

A clamped box and a view of a caul with a clamp support block are shown in **19.39** and **19.40**. Note that the assembly is raised off the table by pieces of plywood underneath.

The assembly procedure will be simple. However, you must work quickly, so be sure to have some glue in a squeeze bottle to apply directly to the stiles.

Full Assembly

Make a dry run of the assembly procedure before you apply any glue. Place the box upside down on the assembly bench, and then place the two strips of wood under it to raise it by $\frac{3}{4}$". Put the frames in position, also upside down, on the strips and against the box. Use pieces of masking tape to hold the frames and box together at the top (really the bottom) and to stop the frames from falling over. Position cauls against the stiles, and use tape again, if necessary, to keep them upright.

Apply one clamp at each side and tighten them only very lightly. Tap wedges under the box or frames until the bottoms of the stiles are exactly flush with the bottoms of the sides (remember: everything is upside down, so the bottoms are at the top). Adjust the frames horizontally either until they are flush with the box at both sides or until the overlaps are equal on

19.39 Front and back frames glued and clamped to the dovetailed box

19.40 One clamp is supported on wood blocks screwed to the cauls; this allows you to tighten the clamp without holding it, after which you will have both hands free to apply the other clamps

each side; then tighten the single clamp on each side and add the remaining clamps.

When you are satisfied that you will be able to manage the assembly process, remove the clamps and place a frame on a bench with the inside surfaces up. Run a light pencil line down the gluing faces of each stile in the middle of the gluing area, at about $7/16$" from the outside edge. Run a $3/16$"-diameter bead of glue straight from the squeeze bottle down the stiles following the pencil lines. This generous application of glue will extend the time available for positioning the frame to the box. Place the frame in position on the support strips, and press it against the box to spread the glue. Use tape to keep it in position.

Glue the second frame also, and place it back in position with tape to hold it.

Replace the cauls and a single clamp at each side. Apply very light pressure with the clamps; then make the frames and box flush at their bottoms (which are still uppermost) as before. Use wedges for assistance where necessary. When everything is aligned as well as possible, tighten the clamps just a little more, and then realign anything that moved as a result of the tightening. Replace all the other clamps, and tighten each one only a little to avoid changing the alignment between the frames and box. When all the clamps are in place, tighten them progressively and fully.

Scrape off the glue from the outside faces so that you can see the glue lines. Reposition or add clamps to close any gaps.

Before leaving the assembly for the glue to set, remove the wedges, and make a final check that outside faces are outside, the box and both frames are upside down, and the front frame is at the front of the box.

This procedure will produce a lot of squeeze-out at the inside corners. Give this time to gel and then remove it before it hardens, using a blunt chisel and then a sharp scraper.

Drawer Dividers

When the glue has set, you can remove the clamps from the assembled carcass and cut the central dividers to precise lengths to create the twin top-drawer openings.

In case any of the rails are bowed, cut the dividers to match the openings by the stiles. Hold a divider near one stile with its bottom end resting on the lower rail and its top end against the top rail. Mark the divider where it touches the top rail, and then repeat this procedure near the stile at the opposite end of the opening. The two marks should coincide; if they do not, make a third mark midway between them. Carry out the same procedure for the second divider. Cut the dividers to length. Use a backer board to show the cutting line on the crosscut sled or miter gauge.

Cut eight tenons, each $1\frac{1}{2}$" long, from the $\frac{1}{4}$" tenon stock. Apply polyurethane glue to the mortises in the dividers and the rails, and push the dividers into position. Apply glue to the tenons, and tap them through the rail mortises and into the dividers. Tap the tenons below the surface, wipe off any squeeze-out, and then clamp the top and second rails with short pipe clamps (19.41). Sand the rails to remove any glue after it has set.

LEVELING THE CARCASS TOP AND BOTTOM

Place the carcass upside down on the floor with a protective mat underneath. Push it up against a bench to keep it stable. Use a straightedge to see how flat the perimeter of the bottom is. When it is fitted, the outermost region of the bottom will be in contact with the plinth. This region is about $\frac{5}{16}$" wide, and it must be flat to avoid gaps between carcass and base. The flatness of the area farther from the edges is of no consequence.

Draw a pencil line around the perimeter of the bottom about $\frac{1}{8}$" from the edges. Use a hand plane to make the tenons and dovetails flush with the bottom. Stop planing before the pencil lines disappear. Plane inward from the ends to avoid chipping the side edges.

When the tenons and dovetails are made level, check the perimeter with a straightedge. If it is not flat, use a belt sander to lower the high areas. Use pencil lines as a guide to avoid sanding the low areas. Only the areas close to the perimeter will make contact with the plinth; the whole inner area can be sanded with impunity, so start sanding there, in the safe area, and move outward to the high spots. Stop sanding before the pencil lines are removed. Keep checking with the straightedge until the perimeter is flat all around.

Turn the carcass upright, and flatten the top by the same methods. Flatness here is less critical because the overlapping chest top will hide small irregularities.

LEVELING THE CARCASS SIDES

Sand the stiles and box sides flush with a belt sander. Use a straightedge frequently to check that you are keeping the sides flat. Be very careful not to let the sander slip off or tilt over the ends or sides. You can sand across the grain and at 45 degrees to the grain, so long as you finish by sanding with the grain to remove all cross-grain scratches.

19.41 Short pipe clamps applied across the top and second rails

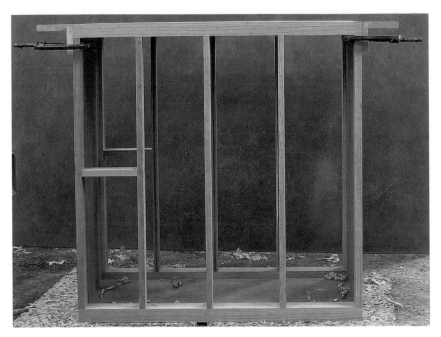

19.42 L-brackets clamped to the ends of the chest

19.43 L-brackets provide a fixing surface for stop blocks

19.44 Chamfer lines drawn on the front stiles

FRONT STILE CHAMFERS

The decorative chamfers on the front corners of the chest are about $\frac{3}{4}$" wide and end in curves at $\frac{3}{4}$" from the stile ends. Although it would have been easiest to chamfer the stiles on a router table before the front frame was assembled, doing so would have cut away the clamping surfaces needed for assembling the frame.

With the carcass assembled, the easiest method of chamfering the front stiles is still by using a router. The guide bearing of a 45-degree chamfering bit can run along the front face of a stile while a router is supported on the carcass side. Stop blocks must be fixed to the carcass so that the chamfers stop short of the stile ends. The blocks have to be positioned beyond the ends of the stiles and therefore require supports that extend beyond the carcass. Wood or plywood L-brackets clamped to the ends of the chest, as in **19.42** and **19.43**, provide a fixing surface for stop blocks. The stop blocks should project forward of the stiles, as in **19.43**, so the router base touches them before the bit touches the stiles.

If you do not have a suitable chamfering bit, you can use a jigsaw and a hand plane. See "Jigsaw Method" on page 196. If neither a jigsaw nor a chamfering bit is available, you could use a hand plane to remove most of the material, and finish with a chisel and sander as described for the other methods.

Whichever method you use, the first step is to draw the chamfers on the front stiles. Start by drawing lines down the front and side faces of the stiles, $\frac{9}{16}$" from the outside corners. Mark the edges $\frac{3}{4}$" from the top and bottom ends, and draw curves from these marks to meet each of the lines at about $1\frac{1}{2}$" from the ends (**19.44**). Remember that only the front stiles are chamfered.

Router Method

To prepare for chamfering with a router, you must determine two things: the correct depth setting for the bearing-guided 45-degree chamfering bit, and the correct positioning of stop blocks to prevent the bit from cutting beyond the marks on the stiles. The depth setting is easily found by making cuts of increasing depth on a test piece; the same test piece will show you where to fix the stop blocks.

Take a piece of scrap wood with one straight edge, and draw a line $9/16$" from the edge. Clamp it to the bench with the edge projecting out so that the bearing of the chamfer bit will clear the bench. Clamp pieces of wood to the test piece to limit the travel of the router. Make the distance between them at least 2" more than the diameter of the router base. Set the bit depth for a shallow cut, and chamfer the edge of the test piece over the distance allowed by the stops. Gradually increase the depth setting until the chamfer reaches the drawn line (**19.45**). Measure the distance from each stop to the start of the chamfer at each end. (They may be different if the cutter and router base are not exactly concentric.)

Lay the chest on its side so that you have the opposite side as a bearing surface for the router. At the right-hand end at the chamfer, use a chisel to cut the tip of the curve (**19.46**). This will prevent tear-out at the start of the router cut.

Fix end stops $1/8$" closer to the curve tips than indicated by the test cut; this will stop the router bit just short of the chisel cuts. Place the router against each stop, and check to see that the cutter will be stopped before the marked limits of the chamfer. Switch on the router and, starting at the right-hand end, make a controlled climb-cut from right to left; then make a finish pass from left to right.

Remove the stops; then complete the curves with a chisel and sandpaper. You will see that the ends of the chamfer are not the same on both faces of the stile. On the vertical face, the ends need to be shaped with a chisel to make them conform to the drawn curves. This process is not difficult, but you may want to practice on the test piece first. Often, the most controlled way to do this type of carving is to move the chisel by tapping it lightly and rapidly with a small mallet. Keep in mind two things: first, you need a sharp chisel, and second, you must not cut too deeply—leave a little wood to be sanded.

19.45 Test piece used to determine positions for stop blocks

19.46 A chisel cut at the tip of the chamfer prevents tear-out

Sand the chamfers to 120- and 220-grit using sandpaper and a sanding block. At the chiseled ends, use sandpaper wrapped around a piece of $\frac{1}{2}$" dowel, and sand in the direction of the grain while rotating the dowel (**19.47** and **19.48**).

With the chest on its side, sand the upper side to 120- and 220-grit with a random-orbit sander.

Turn the chest over and repeat the procedures on its other side.

19.47 Sanding the chamfer end with a wrapped dowel

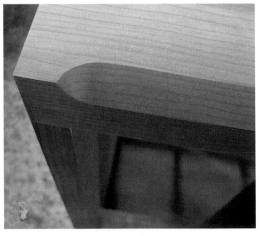

19.48 Completed chamfer

Jigsaw Method

This method works only if you can set the base plate of your jigsaw to an angle of 45 degrees to the blade. The jigsaw base plate rests on the side of the carcass, like the router, but must be guided by hand so that the blade cuts to within about $\frac{1}{16}$" of the lines drawn on the stiles. Try your cut first on a test piece that is at least 2" wide and 1" thick. Clamp the test piece at the edge of a bench and draw a chamfer on it. Before cutting with the jigsaw, make a chisel cut into the curves at each end to prevent the wood from splitting when the jigsaw blade approaches the ends. If the base plate is exactly at 45 degrees, and if you keep it flat on the test piece, the blade will cut to the same depth on both faces.

The sawn surface will not be smooth, but it can be finished smoothly with a hand plane and sander. The curves will need to be made entirely with a chisel and sandpaper. When you are confident that you can keep the cut $\frac{1}{16}$" from the lines, cut the stile chamfers as follows:

- Make a short cut into each end with a chisel in order to avoid tear-out from the saw blade.
- Saw to within $\frac{1}{16}$" of the lines; stop when the blade reaches the curves.
- Chisel the curves to within $\frac{1}{32}$" of the lines. The chisel must be sharp.
- Hand-plane the straight sections to within $\frac{1}{32}$" of the lines.
- Sand the straight sections with a 5" random-orbit sander and a 120-grit disc.
- Sand partway into the curves with the sander, but do not tilt the sander.
- Sand with a narrow hardwood block and 120-grit paper to flatten the surface, which will tend to be rounded by the random-orbit sander.

- Finish the curves with 120- and 220-grit sandpaper wrapped around a piece of $\frac{1}{2}$" dowel.
- Finish the straight sections with the sanding block and 220-grit paper.

SANDING THE FRAMES

When the chamfers are made, the front and back of the chest can be finish-sanded with a random-orbit sander. Start by laying the chest on its back and sanding the front frame. This will be easier if you have a low bench or platform to raise the chest off the ground by about 20".

Use a 5" random-orbit sander with a 120-grit disc to sand the rails and stiles and to make them flush where they join. The sander requires a special technique to be used because it is very easy for the edge of the disc to gouge the corners of the junctions between the rails and the stiles as well as the junctions of rails and the top drawer divider. This happens because either the disc edge is not perfectly flat, or else you may inadvertently tilt the sander.

The solution is never to sand into a junction. As the sander approaches a junction, lift it up and place it down onto the junction; then sand away from it (19.49). Do this repeatedly—place it down on the junctions, and then move it away from them. Repeat the process with a 220-grit sanding disc.

COCK BEADING

Although cock beading is a simple detail, it has a powerful effect on the appearance of the chest front. Cock beading consists of strips of wood $\frac{3}{16}$" thick and $\frac{15}{16}$" wide glued to the insides of the drawer openings. The strips are mitered at the corners and project out $\frac{1}{8}$" from

the face of the chest (19.50). They could be made a little less than $\frac{15}{16}$" wide, but no wider, or they would interfere with the fixing of drawer stops.

The projecting edges are rounded to a $\frac{3}{32}$" radius on a router table before the strips are cut to length and fixed in place.

Beading or roundover bits that produce a full roundover of $\frac{3}{16}$" in diameter are not common in tool catalogs. Two online sources for them are: www.routerbits.com and www.grizzly.com

19.49 To prevent gouging, lower the sander onto the rail-stile junctions and then sand away from them

19.50 Close-up of applied cock beading

Making Beading

I make cock-beading strips by jointing and planing a board to $^{15}\!/_{16}$" thickness and then ripping strips from the edges. A good procedure is to joint both edges of the board, rip a strip from each edge, and joint the edges of the board again, and so on until the board is too narrow to be jointed safely. If your saw blade leaves a reasonably smooth surface, you can rip to $^{3}\!/_{16}$" and use the ripped face as the gluing surface.

If you prefer to use a planer for final thicknessing, rip strips to nearly $^{1}\!/_{4}$" thickness and plane them to $^{3}\!/_{16}$" with an auxiliary bed installed in the planer. In this method, you will have to make longer strips to allow for planer snipe at the ends.

After thicknessing the beading, round over one edge on a router table. The roundover bit must be adjusted to the precise height for rounding, and the router table fence must be adjusted to allow for full rounding of the edge without significantly narrowing the strips.

When you adjust the bit and fence settings, concentrate first on the bit height until it produces a perfectly rounded edge. Next, adjust the fence. When the fence is correctly adjusted, the rounded strip will not be reduced in width by more than $^{1}\!/_{64}$".

After you have rounded the beading, sand the best face of each strip to 120-grit with a random-orbit sander, and lightly sand the rounded edges by hand with 120-grit sandpaper.

Fitting the Beading

The strips must be mitered to meet at the corners of the drawer openings. There is only one sensible way to make the miters, and that is by sanding them. Use a sanding disc or belt on a fixed machine such as a disc sander, a belt sander, or a sanding disc for a table saw. If your handheld belt sander has a rectangular body, you might

be able to clamp it on its side to the bench. Whichever device you use, you will also need a fence positioned at 45 degrees to the sanding surface. A miniature belt sander with an angled table and fence is shown in **19.51**. A sanding disc in a table saw with a miter gauge set to 45 degrees is shown in **19.52**. In the table-saw setup, note the clamped wood block stopping the miter gauge from moving backward.

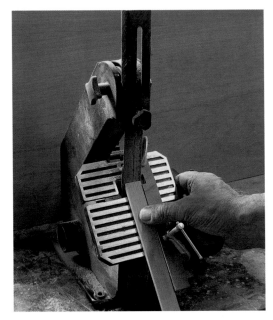

19.51 Miniature belt sander with an angled fence used to miter a piece of cock beading

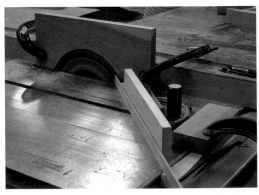

19.52 Sanding disc in a table saw with miter gauge set to 45 degrees

Cut and fit the long pieces first. Select a beading strip, and decide which face you want to show. Cut off any planer snipe from one end, and miter that end with your sander and the angled fence. The good face goes toward the fence and is the shortest one after mitering; the gluing face is the longest.

Place the mitered end at one side of a drawer opening. Mark the other end of the strip at the other side of the opening. Since the good face will be placed against the fence, make the mark on the gluing face so that it is visible when the strip is being mitered. Cut the strip straight across at about $\frac{1}{16}$" beyond the mark. A fine-toothed Japanese-style handsaw will cut the strip quickly and easily.

Miter the second end with the good face to the fence, but stop before the mark is sanded off. Try the strip for fit. It will probably be too long, so sand one of the miters a little more. It is difficult to assess how much you are sanding, so make a pencil mark very close to the end to help your assessment. You should aim to remove no more than $\frac{1}{64}$" each time. Continue until the strip fits snugly in the opening. Do not make the fit so tight that the strip bows by more than about $\frac{1}{4}$" when fitted.

After fitting all the horizontal strips, mark them on their gluing faces so that you know where they fit, and then remove them. Cut and fit the vertical pieces without the horizontal strips in position. Aim to make them fit in easily, without any end play.

When all the vertical pieces are fitted, replace the horizontals by springing them into place. If any are really tight and require significant force to hold them flat against the rails, sand the miters a fraction more. Be careful—this is when the lightest touch on the sander makes a big difference to the fit.

Gluing on the Beading

Before gluing the cock beading in place, sand the mitered ends lightly by hand to remove fuzz. Then make a gauge to help position the strips with their rounded edges protruding exactly $\frac{1}{8}$" from the frame. The gauge in use is shown in **19.53**. The gauge's dimensions are shown in **19.54**.

19.53 A gauge sets the cock beading projection to exactly $\frac{1}{8}$" from the frame

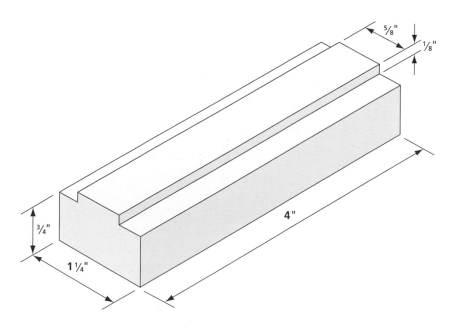

19.54 Dimensioned diagram of cock-bead gauge

19.55 Gluing on the beading strips

The gauge is $1\frac{1}{4}$" wide by 4" long with $\frac{1}{8}$" rabbets cut into one face. You can make the gauge either by cutting $\frac{1}{8}$" $\times$ $\frac{5}{16}$" rabbets with the table saw or by gluing a $\frac{1}{8}$" $\times$ $\frac{5}{8}$" strip to the center of the block. The gauge is used in conjunction with a mallet.

Small spring clamps that open to 2" are the best clamping devices for holding the strips in place after they are glued. You will be using PVA glue, and it will be all right to remove the clamps after 30 minutes for use on the next set of beading strips. However, since it is best to simultaneously glue all the strips for a complete opening, it would be better to have at least 16 clamps (**19.55**).

Place two battens under the chest to raise it up by about 1" to allow clamps to be applied to the bottom rail.

Take one of the vertical strips and apply a very thin line of PVA glue to the underside. To prevent squeeze-out, cover the opening of a glue squeeze bottle with three or four layers of masking tape and then use a $\frac{1}{16}$" drill to make a hole through the tape that will pass only a thin bead of glue. Apply the glue closer to the back edge than to the front to further reduce the risk of squeeze-out at the front.

First glue the short vertical strips for an opening and place them in position; then glue the horizontal strips for that opening and spring them into place. Adjust the positioning of the strips with the gauge and a mallet until they all project exactly $\frac{1}{8}$" from the rails and stiles. Get the beading height right at the corners first, and then clamp the strips at their centers while using the gauge to obtain the correct projection there. Apply the remaining clamps.

If you have enough clamps, repeat the procedure at another drawer opening that is not adjacent to the first one so that you do not have to remove any of the first set of clamps. Otherwise, wait at least 30 minutes before removing the clamps from the first opening. In any case, inspect for squeeze-out before it hardens, and scrape it off using the back of a cheap $\frac{1}{2}$" chisel. If any of the spring clamps prevent the removal of squeeze-out, put them on the inside of the rails.

When the glue has set, sand the beading at the mitered corners to make them flush. A useful tool for this job is a narrow strip cut from sandpaper glued to both sides of a piece of stiff felt (see Chapter 15, "Sanding").

DRAWER BEARERS, LINERS, GUIDES, AND KICKERS

The bearers for all the drawers except the bottom drawer will be supported at each end by tenons, which will place them level with the rails. You will need to glue bearer liners—wood strips of approximately $\frac{3}{16}$" thickness—onto the bearers to bring the bearing surfaces to the same height as the cock beading.

The bearers will also be supported and fixed by screwing their centers to the chest sides. Drill a screw hole into the edge of each bearer, at midlength, through the width to the opposite edge. This hole must then be counterbored to allow the head of a 1¾" FH woodscrew to be sunk 1¹⁄₁₆" below the surface. When the screw is inserted, the point will protrude ⁹⁄₁₆".

The bottom drawer bearers are constructed differently. They will be approximately ⅝" thick and will be fixed to the floor of the chest, that is, to the bottom of the dovetailed box.

The underside of each bearer acts as a "kicker" that prevents the drawer below it from tipping down at the front when it is pulled forward. These surfaces also need added ³⁄₁₆"-thick strips to bring them level with the cock beading on the undersides of the rails. Since the top drawers have no bearers above them to act as kickers, a separate kicker has to be fixed to the underside of the box's top—a single central kicker serving both top drawers.

Bearer Screw Holes

The most satisfactory way to drill and counterbore the screw holes is by using a drill press.

Start by fitting a ⅜" drill bit in the chuck, and set the depth stop so that the point of the drill is stopped ¹⁵⁄₁₆" above the drill table.

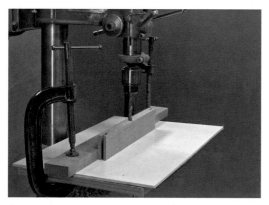

19.56 A fence fixed to the drill press table keeps the drawer bearers centered under the drill bit

Clamp a fence to the drill table ⅜" behind the drilling center (**19.56**).

Mark the fence at 6¾" each side of the drill. When a bearer is placed between these marks, the drill will be midway along the bearer. Hold a bearer against the fence with its ends aligned with the marks, and drill into its edge as deeply as the depth stop allows. Repeat for all bearers. This will produce blind holes with V-shaped bottoms corresponding to the drill point.

Remove the fence, and fix a ³⁄₁₆" drill bit in the chuck protruding at least 2⅜" from it. Adjust the drill press table to 2½" below the point of the bit, and change the depth stop to allow the drill to reach the table. Start the drill press: Hold a bearer up to the bit so that the bit enters the ⅜" hole and centers itself on the V at the bottom of the hole. Maintain contact between the bit point and the V, and lower the drill and the bearer onto the table to make a through-hole centered within the ⅜" hole.

Check to see that a 1¾" FH screw protrudes between ½" and ⅝" when fully inserted into the ⅜" hole. Repeat for the other bearers. Fit a countersink bit in the drill press, and countersink the entry and exit holes very slightly.

Bearer Tenons

Make 14 tenons that are ¼" thick, 2½" wide, and 1⁹⁄₁₆" long. They should fit tightly within the rail grooves, but not so tight that you cannot push them into the deep bearer grooves. Their extra width helps to ensure a good glue bond in the shallow grooves of the rails. Glue the tenons into the rail grooves at each end of the front and back rails with PVA glue. Also, glue a tenon into the centers of the front and back top ¾" rails.

Fixing the Bearers and Top Kicker

When the tenon glue has set, push all the grooved bearers except for the top center bearer onto the tenons at each end of the rails; adjust their positions so that the tenons are equally inserted at front and back. Remember that the bearers have their faces marked to show which face must be uppermost. If the fit is tight, some paraffin wax on the tenons will help, but do not wax the center back tenon. When the bearers are correctly positioned, fix them to the chest sides with $\#8 \times 1\frac{3}{4}$" FH screws.

Apply some polyurethane glue to the rear tenon for the center top bearer and into one groove of the center bearer. Push the glued groove over the glued bearer, but leave the front groove and tenon unglued. Make sure that this bearer is centered and that the tenon has at least $\frac{1}{4}$" expansion space in its front groove.

The bottom bearers still have to be made. They will be screwed to the chest floor and should be just thick enough to be level with the bottom rail cock bead. Make two pieces for the bearers, $\frac{3}{4}$" $\times 1\frac{3}{4}$" $\times 13\frac{1}{2}$", and place them on the chest floor at each side. Place a long straightedge on one of these pieces and extend it over the bottom cock bead. Use feeler gauges to measure the gap between the straightedge and the cock bead, which will probably be roughly 0.060". You must reduce the bearer's thickness until this gap just disappears.

Run the bearer through the planer, taking very light cuts. After each pass, place it on the chest floor and check the clearance under the straightedge. Continue until the clearance is between zero and 0.005", which sounds more difficult than it is. Repeat for the other bottom bearer.

Now lay the chest on its back and drill two screw holes into the bottom on each side for fixing the bottom bearers. Use a $\frac{1}{4}$" drill bit and position the holes 6" from the front and back of the chest and $1\frac{3}{4}$" from the outside faces of the sides. Position the bearers against the chest sides, equidistant from the front and back, and then fix them from below with either $\#8 \times \frac{3}{4}$" washer head screws or round head screws with washers. The $\frac{1}{4}$" holes will allow some movement of the screws to accommodate expansion over the 7" between them.

While the chest is on its back, drill two $\frac{1}{4}$" holes through the top. Center them between the left and right ends of the chest and at $7\frac{1}{2}$" from the front and back so they are spaced about 4" apart. These holes are for the central top kicker, and flat head screws must be used since the chest top will be fitted over them. Flat head screws do not allow for much movement; thus, they are placed only 4" apart. Countersink the holes from the outside, and then make and fix a $\frac{21}{32}$" $\times 2\frac{1}{4}$" $\times 13\frac{1}{2}$" central top kicker with $\#8 \times \frac{3}{4}$" FH screws.

Place the chest upright again.

Drawer Guides

Strips of wood glued to the bearers constrain the drawers to a straight in-and-out movement. These guide strips must be level with the vertical cock beading on each side of the openings, and they must be parallel to the chest sides.

Make 10 hardwood strips, $\frac{1}{2}$" $\times 1\frac{3}{8}$" $\times$ 13", and slightly bevel or round over one end edge of each. The rounding or beveling will make inserting the drawers easier. A guide fixed on a bearer is shown in **19.57**; the front vertical edge of the guide is rounded.

When the guides have glue on them, they will be difficult to clamp precisely in position. Because precision in positioning the guides is essential, the best glue for the job is epoxy, as it does not require clamping pressure. Fast or slow epoxies are equally suitable, but if you choose the slow glue you must leave the chest for several hours while it sets.

To position a guide, lay a thin straightedge on a bearer; extend the straightedge over the front and back rails so that it touches the front vertical cock bead. Cut a short piece of spare cock beading, and place it between the straightedge and the back stile to make the straightedge parallel to the chest side (19.58).

Apply a thin line of epoxy to the bottom ½" face of a guide, nearer to the back face to avoid squeeze-out at the front. Place the guide on the bearer and behind the straightedge. Pull the guide against the straightedge while you hold the straightedge against the cock beading at the front and back. Slide the guide back and forth a little to spread glue onto the bearer. Do not use so much pressure that it squeezes out. Avoid gluing either the guide or the bearer to the chest side.

Check that the guide does not overhang either end of the bearer, and then carefully remove the straightedge without shifting the guide. Fix the other guides in the same way.

When fixing the center top guides, place the cock-beading material against the back drawer divider.

Bearer Liners

In principle, the grooves in the rails and bearers are all exactly the same distance from the upper faces, so the tenons should make the rail and bearer faces exactly level. The thickness of the liners needed to make the bearing surfaces level with the cock bead would therefore all be the same—that is, the same thickness as the cock bead. In practice, this will almost never be the case: Working with wood is not like machining metal, and discrepancies of a few thousandths of an inch are likely to accumulate.

These discrepancies must be accommodated by thicknessing each liner individually so as to bring each bearing surface to the level of the corresponding cock bead. To achieve this, plane one or more pieces of 13"-long lumber, with a total width of about 10", to ¾" thickness. Joint the edges of the material, and then fit a zero-clearance insert in the table saw, and rip a ¼" strip from each edge. You will have to remove the blade guard, so fit alternative safety measures such as the one shown in **3.9** in Chapter 3, under "Guarding Arrangements," for making narrow rip cuts. Use a smooth-cutting blade. Joint

19.57 A drawer guide glued to a bearer

19.58 To position a guide, lay a straightedge across the front cock bead and a piece of cock-beading strip at the back stile

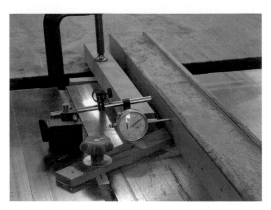

19.59 Setup for reducing the thickness of strips on a table saw using the rip fence, dial gauge, and featherboard. The clamped block is an improvised blade guard

the edges of the material again, and repeat the procedure until the material is too narrow to be jointed safely. This will produce more than enough strips to make the liners and the kickers. Do not move the table-saw fence after ripping the strips.

Place a strip on a bearer, with its jointed face up. Place a straightedge on the strip, extending over the cock bead. Use feeler gauges to measure the clearance under the straightedge at the beading: That is how much the thickness of the strip must be reduced.

The table-saw fence is already set to produce the existing thickness. Therefore, it must be moved closer to the blade by exactly the measured clearance. It is possible to set a table-saw fence to within a thousandth of an inch by using a dial gauge. The setup is shown in **19.59**.

To reduce the thickness of a strip, proceed as follows:

- Replace the guarding arrangement with a guard block higher than the blade. Position it to allow a pushstick to be used **(19.59)**.
- Place a dial gauge with a magnetic base and adjustable arm on the saw table just in front of the blade, with the measuring tip horizontal and touching the fence.
- Set the dial ring to zero.
- Unlock the fence and tap it gently toward the blade so that the dial gauge reading increases slightly. Lock the fence and note how much the gauge has increased from zero.
- Repeat the procedure until the dial shows that the fence has moved toward the blade by the required amount when the fence is locked.
- Remove the dial gauge and, at this fence setting, rip a strip with its jointed face toward the fence. Replace it on the bearer, and use the straightedge and feeler gauges again to check that the strip is level with the cock bead. A gap of up to 0.005" above the cock bead is acceptable. However, if the strip is lower than the cock bead, save that strip for use as a kicker and cut another bearer liner after moving the fence away from the blade by the necessary amount.
- When the liner is the right thickness, place it on the opposite bearer and check with the straightedge. If it is level with the cock bead on that side as well, cut the next liner with the fence at the same setting. Otherwise, adjust the fence as needed, using the dial gauge as before.

Glue the first liner to its bearer with PVA glue, and clamp it with spring clamps. Always glue the ripped faces so that the jointed faces are uppermost. Use each liner to determine the fence setting for the next one before you glue it.

Kickers

After the bearer liners are fixed, the remaining strips can be thicknessed and glued to the undersides of the bearers.

This will bring the underside surfaces low enough to stop the drawers from tipping up at the back and down at the front as they are pulled forward. The strips do not have to be exactly level with the cock bead, but they must not be any lower or they will reduce the expansion space for the drawers. They can be level with the cock bead or up to 0.010" above it. Only one kicker per drawer is necessary.

When the glue for the liners has set, remove the clamps, and hold a $\frac{1}{4}$" strip against the underside of a bearer. Use the straightedge and feeler gauges to estimate how much thinner the strip needs to be. Set the table-saw fence by using the dial gauge, as you did before, and rip the strip. Recheck with the straightedge. If the clearance is all right, glue the strip to the bearer. Make sure that it does not overhang either end of the bearer. Repeat for the other drawer openings until you have fixed one kicker for every drawer except the twin top drawers.

For the top drawers, you can fix a single central kicker directly to the top of the box. Make this kicker $2\frac{1}{4}$" wide and 13" long, and plane it until it is just thick enough to be level with the top cock beading when held against the top of the box. Fix it with #8 × $\frac{3}{4}$" FH screws through the holes previously drilled in the top.

THE PLINTH

Without a base of some sort, the bottom drawer would be inconveniently low. The plinth provides 5 inches of extra height (19.60). As well as being decorative, it has to be strong to survive the severe stresses that can occur if the chest is moved by dragging or pushing. It is a frame that does not expand or shrink, except in height; it must therefore be fixed to the chest in a way that allows the chest sides to expand and shrink.

The plinth's mortise-and-tenon joinery is shown in **19.61**. At the front corners, the mortises are cut at 45 degrees to the faces of the parts. The tenons are short, and the glue bonds are weak because most of the mortise surfaces are end-grain.

All four corners are strengthened by special reinforcing pieces that solve an old problem. Traditionally, plinths or bracket feet have been strengthened by gluing wood blocks to their inside corners. However, because the grain direction of the blocks has to be vertical to provide side-grain gluing surfaces, a conflict occurs with the horizontal grain of the feet or

19.60 The plinth

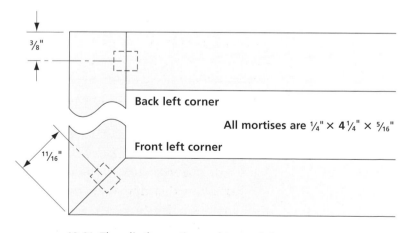

19.61 The plinth mortise-and-tenon joinery

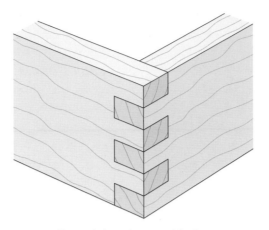

19.62 A finger-jointed corner block

plinth that sometimes causes splitting—as can be seen in many old pieces. Multiple short blocks can be used instead of single long ones (short pieces will not cause splitting), but the procedure is more awkward and there remains a second problem.

The second problem is that clamping pressure is necessary for a good glue bond, and it is almost impossible to apply pressure at both sides of a corner. You can clamp a block hard against one side but not both. Epoxy glue would get around this difficulty, but applying it to several blocks at each corner is very messy, and holding them in place would still be quite a task.

A corner strengthener* developed at North Carolina State University solves the problem. It is intended for reinforcing the corners of chair seats, but I see no reason why it cannot be used for other types of corner. The strengthener comprises two finger-jointed pieces, as shown in **19.62**. The grain of both pieces is horizontal, which avoids the crossed-grain situation. Also, it can pivot at the fingers to allow each half to be clamped or screwed to its

side of the corner. The fingers are glued together, and the strengtheners are glued into the corners to reinforce them.

The regular mortising jig cannot handle the plinth's mortises, but two very simple jigs to deal with them can be made from plywood in about two hours. Once they are made, mortising takes just a few minutes, and the jigs can be used for many other mitered joints.

Before assembling the plinth, you must decide what method of clamping you are going to use. The back corners can be held together by a pipe clamp, but special clamping is needed for the mitered front corners.

A band clamp around the plinth can produce good results. This is a long strap of strong woven material or flexible steel with a ratchet mechanism. It will encircle the whole plinth and ratchet the pieces tightly together. Two narrow band clamps would be better than a single wide one. They are not expensive, but they have some drawbacks, the most important one being that they do not allow you to adjust individual corners.

I prefer to use C-clamps, in conjunction with shop-made 45-degree blocks, as shown in **19.63** and **19.89**.

At each mitered corner, one block is clamped to the front and another to the side. An 8" C-clamp is then clamped across the blocks to close the corner. Each corner is clamped individually, and the positions of the blocks and the large C-clamp can be adjusted to achieve tight 90-degree corners. Four blocks are required for the plinth. Each pair of blocks uses one 8" clamp and two 4" or 6" clamps. The back corners are closed with pipe clamps.

Described in Willard R. Furniture Construction, 4th ed., Raleigh, NC: North Carolina State University Dept. of Industrial Engineering; 1982.

The stages of making the plinth are the following:

1. Make blanks for the front, back, and sides.
2. Miter both ends of the front and one end of each side.
3. Cut the sides and back to final lengths.
4. Make simple mortising jigs (if not previously made).
5. Cut the mortises.
6. Cut out the shapes in the front and sides.
7. Unless you are using band clamps, make four miter-clamping blocks.
8. Assemble and clamp plinth.
9. Cut a decorative bead along the top edges of the front and sides.
10. Make and fix corner strengtheners.
11. Glue fixing strips to the top inside edges of plinth's front and back.
12. Sand the plinth.
13. Fix the plinth to the chest.

Making the Blanks

By consecutively cutting pieces for the left side, the front, and then the right side of the plinth from one board, the grain pattern can be made continuous around the front corners (19.64). However, this involves extra work. Also, unless you have a very flat 4/4 board, you will have to use 5/4 lumber to produce pieces with the necessary thickness.

If you decide to make the plinth without the complication of matching the grain at the corners, start by measuring the width and depth of the bottom of the chest. Cut a 5 ½"-wide blank from 4/4 lumber. Make it 2" longer than the side-to-side measurement of the chest. Cut blanks for the sides, each 5 ½" wide and 1 ¼" longer than the front-to-back dimensions. Use lumber that is flat enough to finish close to ⅞" thickness when flattened and planed.

Flatten and plane the blanks as close as possible to ⅞" thickness. Joint their top edges. Rip the pieces on the table saw with their top edges toward the fence to ensure they are parallel sided and all the same width. Keep them as wide as possible: the extra width will allow you to remove any chipping that occurs on the top edges during mitering.

If you decided to use the grain-matching procedure for the front corners, start by cutting a 5 ½" wide by 80" long blank. Use 4/4 lumber that is flat enough to be face-jointed as one piece without

19.63 Two mitered test pieces held by shop-made miter clamping blocks. This method of clamping requires three C-clamps and two miter clamping blocks for each mitered corner

19.64 Continuous grain pattern around plinth corners

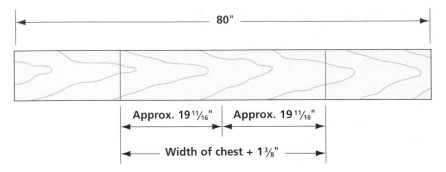

19.65 Marking a board to obtain continuous grain patterns at the plinth corners

losing more than $\frac{1}{16}$" of thickness. If you do not have a flat 4/4 board, you will have to use 5/4 lumber.

Significant changes in grain pattern can take place over a half-inch of length or an eighth of an inch of thickness. For a continuous grain pattern, no planing should be done after the parts are cut from the 80" piece, and minimum length should be lost to saw kerfs when the parts are cut and mitered.

Joint the outside face of the board to make it completely flat. Plane the inside face to $\frac{7}{8}$" thickness if possible, or $\frac{13}{16}$" if $\frac{7}{8}$" is not achievable.

Joint the top edge, and rip the other edge parallel to it. Mark the board to show the plinth's left side, front, and right side sequentially. Make the front piece exactly $1\frac{3}{8}$" longer than the front of the carcass. It will be approximately $39\frac{3}{8}$", but you should find the exact length you need by measuring the chest width. Divide the required length by two, and mark this distance from each side of the board center **(19.65)**.

Crosscut the piece carefully to leave the front as marked and the two sides each about 20" long. Mark the outside faces of each piece with an "up" arrow to indicate the top edges. Mark the sides "left" and "right."

Whichever of the above procedures you used, the parts are now ready for mitering.

Mitering

Pieces of this width can be mitered by laying them flat on the table saw, tilting the blade to 45 degrees, and pushing them into the blade with the miter gauge. First you must make sure that your setup is accurate.

Start by making two test pieces about $\frac{7}{8}$" × 5" × 9". Joint one edge of each and mark these as the top edges; rip the bottom edges parallel to them. Mark one face of each as the outside face. Stand them together on their bottom edges as though they were the front left-hand corner of the plinth. Mark an L near the left-hand end of the front piece and an R near the right-hand end of the piece that represents the left-hand side of the plinth.

Check that the miter gauge bar is a good fit in the table slots. If necessary, dimple the sides of the bar with a center punch to remove any play (see "Adjusting the Table-Saw" in Chapter 3). Use the slot away from the direction of tilt: the right-hand slot for left-tilting blades or the left-hand slot for right-tilting blades.

Make a wooden fence about 24" long for the miter gauge, low enough to be used with the blade guard when the blade is tilted. Fix it to reach about an inch beyond the tilted blade.

Raise the blade to its maximum height. Tilt it to 45 degrees.

Start the saw, and push the miter gauge forward to cut off the end of the fence. This establishes an exact cutting line **(19.66)**.

The tilt of the blade to the left or right will determine the position of the work during mitering. For left-tilting blades, proceed as follows:

• Place the front test piece on the saw table with its outside face up and its bottom edge toward the miter gauge fence. Start the saw, and make a miter cut at the end marked L. Stop as soon as the cut is complete but before the test

19.66 An extended miter gauge fence establishes an exact cutting line for mitering the plinth

Place one piece on a flat surface with its outside face down, and push the other piece against it to bring the mitered faces firmly together, as shown in **19.67**. Check the corner carefully with a square; it should be exactly 90 degrees. If the corner does not make an exact 90-degree angle, the blade is not at 45 degrees to the saw table. If necessary, adjust the blade angle and repeat the cuts.

Stand the test pieces on their edges on a flat surface, and bring the mitered ends together **(19.68)**. If there is a gap at the top or bottom of the corner, the miter fence is not at 90 degrees to the table slot. If necessary, adjust the miter gauge angle and repeat the cuts.

piece reaches the back teeth. Switch off the saw and wait for the blade to stop. Stopping the cut before the work reaches the back teeth of the blade reduces the risk of marring the cut.

- Place the left-side test piece on the table, outside face up, top edge to the fence, and make a cut at the end marked R.

For right-tilting blades:

- Place the front test piece on the saw table with its outside face up and its top edge toward the miter gauge fence. Start the saw, and make a miter cut at the end marked L. Stop as soon as the cut is complete but before the test piece reaches the back teeth. Switch off the saw and wait for the blade to stop. Stopping the cut before the work reaches the back teeth of the blade reduces the risk of marring the cut.
- Place the left-side test piece on the table, outside face up, bottom edge to the fence, and make a cut at the end marked R.

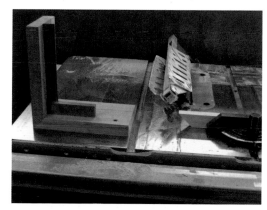

19.67 Checking the accuracy of the blade tilt angle

19.68 Checking the accuracy of the miter gauge fence setting

When the setup is correct, mark the plinth front for cutting as follows:

- Place the front against the chest carcass, with the outside face up and the top edge toward the chest. Position it to overhang the chest equally at each end. Mark the position of the chest sides on its outside face at each end.
- Measure $\frac{9}{16}$" further toward the ends from these marks, and mark these positions also. Square a line across the outside face at each of the outer marks, and measure the distance between these lines. It should be $1\frac{1}{8}$" more than the width of the carcass, or approximately $39\frac{1}{8}$".
- Mark an L near the left-hand end of the front piece and an R at the right-hand end.
- Take the left-side piece of the plinth, and square a line across its outside face less than $\frac{1}{16}$" from the right-hand, or front, end. Mark this end with an R.
- Square a line across the outside face of the right-side piece, less than $\frac{1}{16}$" from its left-hand (front) end. Mark an L at this end.

Miter the marked ends using one of the following procedures.

For left-tilting blades:
- Place the front piece on the saw table, outside face up, bottom edge toward the miter gauge fence.
- Carefully align the line drawn on its left-hand end with the cutting line of the blade, which is shown by the cut end of the fence.
- Start the saw, and push the miter gauge forward. Stop as soon as the cut is complete but before the workpiece reaches the back teeth of the blade Do not push the workpiece past the blade. Switch off the saw and remove the front when the blade stops.

- Rotate the front end-for-end and cut the right-hand end, outside face up, top edge toward the fence. Do not push the workpiece past the blade. Stop it before it reaches the back teeth. Switch off the saw and remove the front when the blade has stopped.
- Place the left-side piece on the saw table, outside face up, top edge toward the fence, and miter its right-hand end at the squared line. Stop as soon as the cut is complete.
- Miter the left-hand end of the right-side piece, outside face up, bottom edge toward the fence. Stop as soon as the cut is complete.

For right-tilting blades:
- Place the front piece on the saw table, outside face up, top edge toward the miter gauge fence.
- Carefully align the line drawn on its left-hand end with the cutting line of the blade, which is shown by the cut end of the fence.
- Start the saw, and push the miter gauge forward. Stop as soon as the cut is complete but before the workpiece reaches the back teeth of the blade. Do not push the workpiece past the blade. Switch off the saw and remove the front when the blade stops.
- Rotate the front end-for-end and cut the right-hand end, outside face up, bottom edge toward the fence. Do not push the workpiece past the blade. Stop it before it reaches the back teeth. Switch off the saw and remove the front when the blade has stopped.
- Place the left-side piece on the saw table, outside face up, bottom edge toward the fence, and miter its right-hand end at the squared line. Stop as soon as the cut is complete.

- Miter the left-hand end of the right-side piece, outside face up, top edge toward the fence. Stop as soon as the cut is complete.

Restore the table-saw blade to vertical.

Add $\frac{9}{16}$" to the front-to-back measurement of the chest to find the required length of the sides (about $19\frac{9}{16}$") if no allowance is made for expansion. It is best to allow for about $\frac{1}{8}$" expansion in the chest sides from winter to summer so that the chest never overhangs the back of the plinth by very much. If the chest is being made in a low-humidity season, add a further $\frac{1}{8}$" to the length of the plinth sides so that they total about $19\frac{11}{16}$" long. Mark this length on the plinth sides measured from the tip of each mitered end. Cut the sides to length with a crosscut sled or miter gauge.

Measure the inside length of the plinth front, that is, the distance along the inside face between the miters (about $37\frac{3}{8}$"). Make a back for the plinth $\frac{3}{4}$" to $\frac{7}{8}$" thick, $5\frac{1}{4}$" wide, and as long as the inside length of the front.

Very lightly joint the top edges of the front and sides again, to remove any chipping that has occurred at the miters. Fit a zero-clearance throat plate to the table saw, and rip the bottom edges of all four pieces to make them 5" wide.

Jigs for Corner Mortises

Each jig comprises two pieces of plywood plus a hardwood fence and side stops. The pair of jigs can be made in less than two hours. The two pieces of the jig for the front corner mortises are joined at 45 degrees, while the pieces of the jig for the back corner mortises are joined at 90 degrees **(19.69)**.

To make the jigs, cut four 7" × 10" pieces and two 9" × 14" pieces from good-quality $\frac{1}{2}$" plywood. Glue two 7" × 10" pieces face

19.69 Jigs for the front and back corner mortises

19.70 Jig bases

to face to make a thick base for the 45-degree jig, and then glue together the other two 7" × 10" pieces to make the 90-degree jig base. Use flathead screws instead of clamps so that you can work on the glued pieces immediately. Position the screws about $1\frac{1}{2}$" from the edges, and make sure they are flush with or below the surface. After screwing the pieces together, rip the long edges flush and parallel to each other; then crosscut the short edges square to the long ones. (It does not matter that this step will reduce the dimensions slightly.) Mark one of the glued bases "45-degree base" and the other "90-degree base." Mark the 9" × 14" pieces "45-degree face" and "90-degree face."

Tilt the table-saw blade to 45 degrees and cut one 7" edge of the 45-degree jig base at this angle. Use a miter gauge, and check first that the blade will not contact any of the screws. The two bases at this stage are shown in **19.70**.

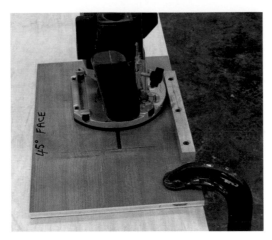

19.71 Cutting a slot in a face board

Glue and screw a $\frac{3}{4}$" × $\frac{3}{4}$" × 8" hardwood strip on the 45-degree jig face board. Make it flush with a 14" edge. Do the same for the 90-degree jig face board. Position the strips centrally: They are the jig fences.

Clamp a face board to the bench with some scrap material under it to protect the bench. Position the clamp near one end to allow a router to be placed against the fence. Draw lines along the board that are parallel to the 9" edges and about $2\frac{1}{2}$" each side of center. Fit a $\frac{1}{4}$" mortising bit into a router, place the router against the

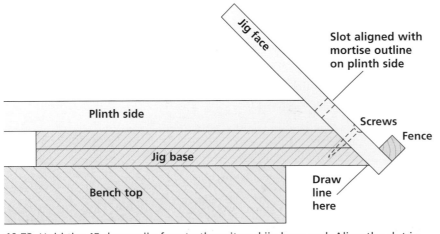

19.72 Hold the 45-degree jig face to the mitered jig base end. Align the slot in the face with the mortise marked on the mitered end of the plinth side.

fence, start it, and plunge the cutter through the board (**19.71**). Hold the router firmly to the fence, and move it from side to side to cut a slot about 5" long between the lines on the board. Mark the slot at the center and at $2\frac{1}{8}$" each side of center. Carry out the same procedure to cut a slot in the other face board.

Draw a $\frac{1}{4}$"-wide mortise on the mitered end face of a plinth side, centered $\frac{11}{16}$" from the outside edge of the miter (see the joinery drawing **19.61**). Make the mortise parallel to the faces by using a marking gauge set first to $\frac{9}{16}$" and then to $\frac{13}{16}$". Mark from the "sharp" edge of the miter. Stop the mortise outline $\frac{3}{8}$" from each end of the mitered face; that is, make it $4\frac{1}{4}$" long.

Draw a $\frac{1}{4}$" mortise on one end face of the plinth back, also stopping $\frac{3}{8}$" from each end but centered $\frac{3}{8}$" from the outside face. Set the marking gauge to $\frac{1}{4}$" and then to $\frac{1}{2}$" and mark from the outside face.

Darken both pairs of gauge lines with pencil. Draw lines across both mortises at the center, $2\frac{1}{2}$" from the edges.

Take the plinth side with the marked mortise on its mitered face; place its outside face against the shorter face of the 45-degree jig base and make the mitered surfaces flush with each other. Clamp the arrangement like this to the bench so that it projects about 2" over the edge.

Hold the 45-degree jig face against the mitered surfaces, and align the slot with the marked mortise. While the slot is aligned with the mortise, draw a line on the back of the jig face where the underside of the base meets it (**19.72**).

Remove the jig face, and drill four screw holes through it at suitable positions for screwing it to the mitered face of the jig base. Use the line on the underside as a guide to these positions. Countersink the holes and then replace the face over the base and plinth side. Realign the slot with the mortise, and fix the face piece and base together with a single screw. If necessary, adjust the positioning with a mallet to keep the mortise aligned perfectly with the slot in the face piece. Insert the other screws.

Remove the screws and apply PVA glue to the 45-degree face of the jig base; then fix the pieces together again lightly with two screws. Readjust the positioning by tapping with a mallet. Tighten the two screws and then replace all screws tightly. Remove the plinth side and wipe off any glue that may be on it; also, check the jig for squeeze-out. The 45-degree jig is now almost completed, except for the side stops, which limit the mortise length.

Clamp the base of the jig to the bench, and place the router on the jig face and against the fence. Move the router until the cutter reaches one of the end marks at $2\frac{1}{8}$" from the center; then mark the position of the router base on the jig face at that side. Move the cutter to the other $2\frac{1}{8}$" line, and mark where the router base is on the jig at that side. Remove the router, and fix $\frac{3}{4}$" $\times$ $\frac{3}{4}$" $\times$ 2" strips of wood at the router base marks to act as side stops.

Finally, fit a $\frac{1}{2}$" bit into the router, and enlarge the slot to improve visibility. The fence and end stops will guide the router while you do this. Square a line across the bottom-inside face of the new slot at the center. The 45-degree jig is now ready for use.

Clamp the outside face of the plinth back to the 90-degree jig base with the marked end of the plinth back flush to a 7" edge of the base. Fix the clamped pieces vertically in a vise, with the jig base farthest from the bench, and check again that their ends are perfectly flush (19.73).

Place the 90-degree jig face piece horizontally on the ends of the vertical pieces, with the fence uppermost and on the base side of the arrangement (19.74).

Align the slot with the marked mortise, and mark the face piece with suitable positions for four screw holes for fixing it to the end of the base. Remove the face piece, and then drill and countersink the holes.

Replace the face piece on the vertical pieces, and position the slot over the mortise outline again. Insert screws into the holes and tap them to mark their positions on the end of the jig base. Remove the jig face and predrill the end of the base for the screws.

19.73 Fix the plinth back in a vise and clamp the 90-degree jig base to it, with ends flush to each other

19.74 Put the 90-degree jig face piece horizontally on the ends of the pieces in the vise

19.75 The completed 90-degree jig clamped to the plinth back

19.76 Mortises cut into the mitered front ends of the plinth front and sides, and into the inside faces at the rear ends of the plinth sides

19.77 A mitered end marked for alignment in the mortising jig

19.78 The mitered end of a plinth side is clamped in the jig ready for mortising

Apply glue to the end face of the jig base. Screw the face piece to it with two screws. If you need to shift the face piece to perfectly align the slot with the mortise outline, tap it with a mallet before the glue sets. Further tighten the two screws. Insert and tighten the remaining screws, and then remove the assembly from the vise and unclamp the jig from the plinth back.

Clean off any glue from the jig and the plinth back, and then clamp the jig in the vise without the plinth back. Fix side stops to the face piece: First, fit a $\frac{1}{4}$" bit in the router and place it at each of the $2\frac{1}{8}$" end marks in turn, mark the positions of the router base on the jig face each time, and fix stops at these positions.

Enlarge the slot in the jig face with a $\frac{1}{2}$" router bit. Mark the new slot at the center. The completed jig with the plinth back is shown in **19.75**.

Cutting the Corner Mortises

Mortises for the rear corners of the plinth must be cut in the end faces of the plinth back and into the inside faces of the plinth sides **(19.76)**. It would be easy to do the reverse by mistake, so the best way to start the procedure is to mark these mortise positions. Rough-marking with a lumber crayon is adequate to prevent mistakes. At the front corners, the mortises will be cut into the mitered faces, and the jig almost eliminates the possibility of errors.

The only accurate marking-out required is for the midlengths of the mortises. On the four mitered faces, draw a line across, $2\frac{1}{2}$" from the top edge **(19.77)**.

On each end face of the plinth back, draw a line across, $2\frac{1}{2}$" from the top. At the back end of each of the plinth sides, make a mark $2\frac{1}{2}$" down on the inside face.

To mortise the miters, place a side or front in the 45-degree jig, outside face down, and push the mitered end tightly into the 45-degree corner of the jig. Align the center mark on the mitered face with the jig's center mark, and clamp the arrangement to the bench, as shown in **19.78**.

Fit a $\frac{1}{4}$" mortising bit in the router, plunge it to touch the mitered surface, and set the router depth stop for a $\frac{5}{16}$"-deep cut. Start the router, and cut the mortise while holding the router firmly against the fence. Repeat for the other three miters.

After mortising the miters, place a plinth side on the bench with its outside face down and its back end protruding slightly over the edge of the bench. Place the 90-degree jig on it, with the mortise center aligned with the jig's center mark. Clamp the arrangement to the bench **(19.79)**. With the router set as before, cut a $\frac{5}{16}$"-deep mortise. Repeat for the other plinth side.

Clamp the plinth back vertically into the bench vise with its outside face away from the bench and at least 11" of it above the vise. Place the 90-degree jig on the end of the plinth back with the jig base against the outside face, and align the mortise's center mark with the jig's center mark. Clamp the jig to the back as in **19.80**, and while you hold the router firmly to the fence, cut a $\frac{5}{16}$"-deep mortise. Repeat for the other end.

Shaping the Parts

A bandsaw with a narrow blade is the ideal tool for cutting out the shapes, although a jigsaw with a narrow fine-cutting blade can be used.

It is best to first make templates for the shapes out of Masonite or thin MDF. If you make one template for a long front foot and another for a short side foot, you can be sure of drawing identical shapes at each

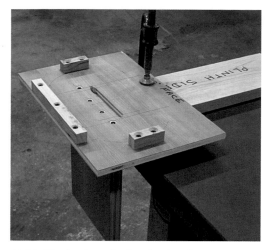

19.79 The back end of a plinth side is clamped in the 90-degree jig ready for mortising

19.80 The plinth back is fixed in the bench vise with its outside face away from the bench. The 90-degree jig is clamped to the outside face of the plinth back, and the jig center mark is aligned with the mortise center mark on the end of the plinth back

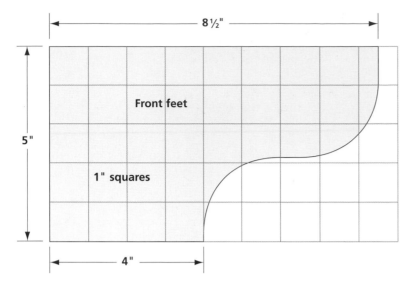

19.81 Front feet template pattern

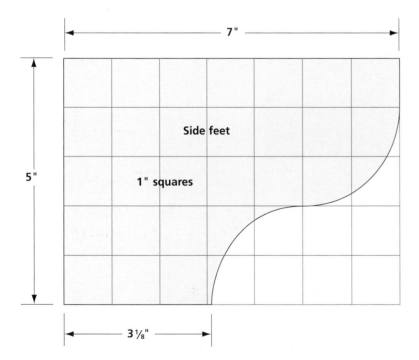

19.82 Side feet template pattern

end of the front and sides. This way, you can get the shapes right before transferring them to the plinth. The thin material can be shaped and smoothed very quickly. A 1" grid drawn on the template material will help you to resize the shapes from the patterns in **19.81** and **19.82**.

After cutting the templates, smooth the curves with a 3" sanding drum in a drill press or drum sander.

Draw around the templates onto the plinth front and sides, and then draw a horizontal line between each pair of feet $1\frac{3}{8}$" below the top edge, as in **19.83**. If you are going to use a bandsaw smaller than 18", it will be best to draw the feet on both faces. Erase the short vertical part of each foot between the horizontal line and the top edge.

Fit a $\frac{1}{4}$" blade into the bandsaw or use a narrow fine-tooth blade in a jigsaw, and cut out the shapes. Start by making straight cuts at each end, from the bottom edge into the junction of the foot and horizontal line. Then pull back and reenter to make the other cuts from the bottom edge so that the waste material falls away when you meet the first cuts (shown in **4.3** in Chapter 4, "The Bandsaw"). Do not cut closer to the lines than $\frac{1}{16}$", and do not use a fence when cutting the straight section; just cut freehand.

After cutting the shapes, sand the sawn edges using the 3" sanding drum. At the drill press, fit a plywood or chipboard auxiliary table with a $3\frac{1}{2}$"-diameter hole so that the end of the drum can be below the surface (**19.84**). The $3\frac{1}{2}$" hole can be roughly cut with a jigsaw.

You can sand the straight sections with the drum, but practice on some scrap first. The drum will not be able to sand into the corners, of course. Take care to stop far enough from the corners to prevent the drum from touching at two places simultaneously.

The best way to clean out the corners is by paring them with a sharp chisel and then finishing the job with sandpaper folded over a scraper blade or steel rule. A fine rasp would be an alternative to the chisel, but move it only from the front faces toward the back so you avoid chipping the outside edges. Keep $\frac{1}{8}$" away from the corners with the sandpaper so as not to make a groove with the folded edge.

After shaping the front and sides, make straight cuts in the plinth back to form short rectangular feet at each end (**19.85**). Make vertical cuts $\frac{3}{4}$" deep into the bottom edge 4" from each end, and then make the long horizontal cut between them (**19.85**). This relief cut will help to stabilize the chest if it is on an uneven floor.

Miter Clamping Blocks

You will need four miter clamping blocks—two for each front corner. Each block comprises two components screwed and glued together. One piece is $\frac{3}{4}$" × 5" × 9", and the second is $1\frac{3}{4}$" × 3" × 5" with a 45-degree angled cut made at one side. The blocks are illustrated in **19.86**, **19.87**, and **19.88**.

Drill and countersink two screw holes in the 5" × 9" pieces; then glue and screw them to the angled blocks. Sandpaper glued to the clamping faces will help them grip the plinth.

Plinth Assembly

Make four $\frac{1}{4}$" × $3\frac{3}{4}$" × $\frac{5}{8}$" tenons (you can use a number of narrower tenons to make up the $3\frac{3}{4}$" width). Remember that $\frac{5}{8}$" is the length of the tenons, so their grain direction is from mortise to mortise. Do not make the tenons too tight; just make them an easy fit. After you cut the first tenon to length, try it in all the mortises to check that it is not too long for them to close fully. Cut the other tenons after you confirm the length. Insert the tenons and

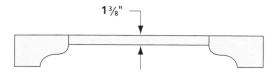

19.83 Horizontal line drawn from the left foot to the right foot at $1\frac{3}{8}$" below the top edge of the plinth

19.84 Drill press sanding drum for smoothing the sawn shapes

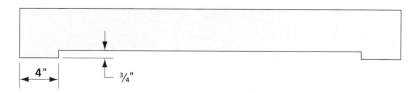

19.85 Straight cuts in the plinth back improve stability on uneven floors

dry-assemble the plinth; check that it all goes together without any problems.

Dampen the tenons, and then apply polyurethane glue to all the mortises. Apply glue to the ends of the tenons, and insert them into a mortise at each corner. Glue the other ends of the tenons and push the joints together.

If you are using miter clamping blocks, place them about $\frac{1}{4}$" from the front corners, and clamp them to the plinth sides and

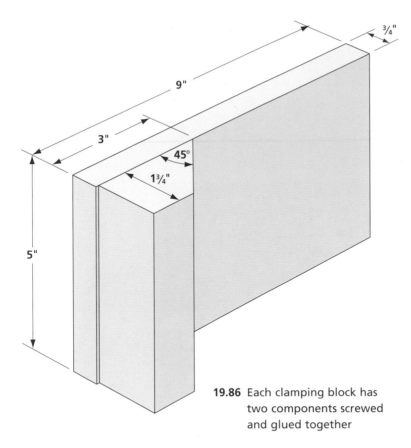

19.86 Each clamping block has two components screwed and glued together

19.87 Miter clamping block, showing the angled face for a C-clamp

19.88 Miter clamping block, showing its clamping face with sandpaper glued to it for increased friction

front. Clamp the plinth sides to the back with two pipe clamps plus clamping cauls. Close the front miters by applying 8" C-clamps across the angled faces of the blocks. The clamped plinth is shown in **19.89**.

Check that the top edges are flush at each corner. If necessary, slacken the clamps and tap the edges flush using a mallet and block.

The clamping blocks can be shifted as needed to close the miters tightly at the front. Or the 8" C-clamps can be moved slightly closer to or further from the plinth, usually the best way to achieve the desired result. Raise or lower the 8" C-clamps to close the miters more tightly at the top or bottom. Two 8" C-clamps at each front corner are ideal but seldom necessary.

Check for squareness by comparing the diagonals. When the diagonals are equal, leave everything until the glue has set.

If you are using band clamps, follow the maker's instructions. Do not tighten them excessively or they may cut into or bruise the corners. Two narrow bands will give you more control than a wide single band, but they are more likely to cut into the wood. If the plinth does not clamp up square, you may need to add a pipe clamp across two opposite corners. Here, too, you must take care to avoid damaging the corners. Check that the top edges are flush at each corner.

Decorative Beading

A bearing-guided beading bit and a bead cut along the top edges of the plinth are shown in **19.90**. The bead radius is $\frac{1}{4}$", and the vertical and horizontal steps (called quirks) are both about $\frac{1}{8}$" wide. Only the front and sides of the plinth are beaded, not the back.

19.89 Clamped plinth assembly

19.90 Beaded plinth edge and a bearing-guided beading bit

The bead could be cut in two ways: by running the router along the top edges with the bearing running against the faces, or with the router on the faces and the bearing on the edges. I always run the router on the top edges because the depth of cut is vertically adjustable, which enables me to ensure that the top quirk is a full $\frac{1}{8}$" high. The other quirk is not adjustable and may be rather shallow, but it is the vertical quirk that seems most important for giving the bead definition.

The plinth edges are too narrow to provide an adequate support surface for the router; therefore, you will need to fix some wood strips to the inside faces, flush with the top edges, to provide surfaces at least $1\frac{1}{2}$" wide. The strips can be temporarily fixed with double-sided tape or hot-melt glue.

Fit the $\frac{1}{4}$"-radius bearing-guided beading bit in the router, and then make

some test cuts on scrap. Adjust the depth of cut to make the top quirk $\frac{1}{8}$" deep. When the setting is correct, cut the bead on the plinth front and sides. Do not cut a bead along the back! I always make an initial climb-cut (right to left) before finishing with a forward cut—this would be a bad time to get tear-out!

Corner Strengtheners

The finger-jointed corner strengtheners are made by using a simple attachment to the miter gauge. Before making the attachment, cut a test piece about $\frac{3}{4}$" × 3" × 10" from scrap wood.

The individual pieces of the corner strengtheners are $\frac{3}{4}$" × $4\frac{3}{4}$" × 2". It would be dangerous to cut finger slots in pieces that are 2" long, so make a stock piece $\frac{3}{4}$" thick, $4\frac{3}{4}$" wide, and at least 20" long.

Make the attachment as follows:

- Mill two pieces of wood about $\frac{3}{4}$" thick and 5" wide. Make one of them 2" longer than the miter gauge fence, and the other one long enough to project at least 1" beyond the table saw blade and 1" beyond the opposite end of the miter gauge fence.
- Cut a $\frac{1}{4}$"-wide open-ended slot about 2" long into each end of the shorter piece at midwidth.
- Screw the shorter piece to the miter gauge fence, and then fix the longer piece to the front of it by screws through the slots. Position the long piece to project about 1" beyond the blade. Fix the screws near the left-hand ends of the slots **(19.91)**.
- Fit a $\frac{3}{8}$" dado cutter in the table saw and raise it to $\frac{3}{4}$" high.
- Start the table saw, and push the miter gauge forward to cut a $\frac{3}{8}$" × $\frac{3}{4}$" slot through the front piece of wood.
- Make a $\frac{3}{8}$" × $\frac{3}{4}$" × 2" wooden peg that is an easy, but not loose, fit in the

19.91 Rear view of the finger joint jig fixed to the miter gauge

19.92 Cutting a second slot in the test piece

19.93 Use the test piece to position the stock board for its first cut at one end

slot. Glue or screw it into the slot with about 1" jutting out at the front. Fast epoxy is convenient for this.

- Loosen the screws holding the front fence, and slide the fence ¾" to the right so that the peg is ⅜" from the cutter.
- Take the test piece and hold it on end against the front fence of the jig, with one edge against the peg. Cut a slot in the end of the test piece.
- Fit the test piece slot over the peg so that the test piece is moved ¾" along the fence **(19.92)**.
- Cut another slot, and fit that one over the peg. Continue until no more of the test piece can be cut.
- Reverse the test piece, and cut slots in its other end.
- Cut off about 1¼" of the test piece from each end, and fit the "fingers" together. If the fingers will not fit together, the front fence, along with the peg, must be moved very slightly back toward its initial position. If the fingers fit loosely, the fence must be moved farther outward.
- Make an adjustment if necessary, and cut new fingers in both ends. Repeat the process until the fingers fit together snugly. If the test pieces become too short, make new ones to avoid having to place your own fingers too close to the cutter.

Unlike the test pieces, the strengtheners must be assembled flush at the edges, which requires one-half of each strengthener to start with a slot instead of a finger. To achieve this, place the first slot of the test piece over the peg, with its first finger to the left of the peg. Place the 20" stock piece against the test piece finger and cut a slot **(19.93)**.

Remove the test piece and continue cutting slots in that end of the stock piece.

Cut fingers into the other end of the stock piece without using the test piece finger. One end of the stock will now start with a finger and the other end with a slot.

Using another saw (a miter saw, radial arm saw, bandsaw, jigsaw, or, as a last resort, a handsaw), cut a 2" piece off each end. Immediately after cutting, assemble the pieces as an L-shaped joint. Repeat the procedure until you have four corner strengtheners.

Mark positions for two screw holes on the inside face of every piece so that there are four holes per corner. Drill clearance holes for #8 FH screws at these marks, and countersink them in the inside faces. Four completed blocks are shown in **19.94**; note that they do not have to be works of art.

Apply polyurethane glue to the fingers and reassemble the joints. Apply glue to their outside faces and to the inside corners of the plinth. Place the corner blocks level with the plinth bottom, and screw them into the corners with #8 × 1¼" FH screws (**19.95**). You can reclaim the screws after the glue has set.

Fixing Strips

The last step in building the plinth is to make and fit the front and back strips for fixing it to the chest. The strips are shown in **19.96**.

Both strips are 1" × 1⅜" × 33" pieces of hardwood, each fixed by gluing a 1⅜" face to the inside faces of the plinth front and plinth back. They are positioned flush with the top edges of the plinth.

Holes in one strip and slots in the other are made to accommodate screws that fix the plinth to the bottom rails of the chest. The front strip has the holes and the back one has the slots; this arrangement will

19.94 Four completed corner-strengthener blocks

19.95 A corner block screwed and glued into a plinth corner

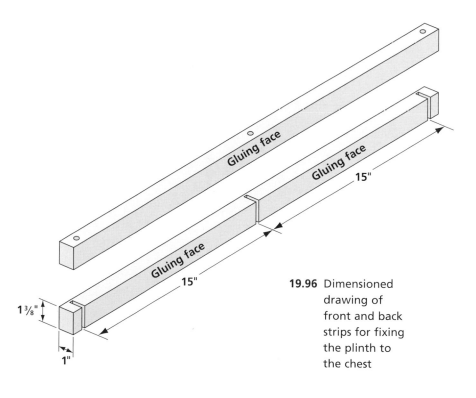

19.96 Dimensioned drawing of front and back strips for fixing the plinth to the chest

keep the chest and plinth in register at the front while allowing seasonal movement of the chest sides at the back.

After milling the strips, make three $\frac{7}{8}$"-deep slots in a $1\frac{3}{8}$" face of the rear strip—at the center and 15" to each side of center. The slots must be wide enough for #10 screws and could be made by a $\frac{1}{4}$" dado cutter or with two cuts of a standard $\frac{1}{8}$" blade. Use a miter gauge, and set the cutter to $\frac{7}{8}$" high. The slots will come to within $\frac{1}{8}$" of cutting through the strip.

Make clearance holes for #10 screws in the 1" face of the front strip. Make the holes at the center and at 15" each side of center.

Glue the strips to the inside faces of the plinth. Position them flush with the top edge or just $\frac{1}{32}$" below it to ensure that the plinth will fit tightly against the chest rails. Note that the $1\frac{3}{8}$" face with the open fronts of the slots is the gluing face for the rear strip. Either $1\frac{3}{8}$" face of the front strip can be the gluing face. Use C-clamps if you have enough of them; otherwise, drill holes in the $1\frac{3}{8}$" faces of the strips, and use screws for fixing them; reclaim the screws after the glue has set.

Sanding the Plinth

Sand the top edges carefully with sandpaper wrapped around a block; then sand the bead, including the quirks, with narrow strips of sandpaper. Because all these surfaces are narrow, there is no need to go finer than 120-grit.

Turn the plinth upside down and remove all sharpness from the bottom edges, on the inside as well as the outside. Anyone who has to lift the chest from the bottom will appreciate this. To reduce the risk of chipping, sand a small chamfer about $\frac{1}{8}$" wide on all edges that will touch the floor.

Sand the front, back, and sides with a random-orbit sander using 120- and 220-grit discs. Finally, because sharp edges

are vulnerable to damage, remove the extreme sharpness from the front corners with a couple of light strokes with 220-grit sandpaper.

Fixing the Plinth

Before fixing the plinth, hand-sand the chest sides with sandpaper and a cushioned block. Work in the direction of the grain to remove the random-orbit scratch pattern.

The plinth should be fixed with about $\frac{1}{4}$" of the flat top edge showing at the front and sides. The back of the plinth will be mostly under the chest. Two people are needed to move the chest during the fixing procedure.

Turn the chest upside down and place the plinth (also upside down) on the bottom. If any gaps are visible between the chest and the plinth that you think will not be closed by the fixing screws, flatten the chest bottom with a belt sander (refer to "Leveling the Carcass Top and Bottom" earlier in this chapter). When the plinth and chest fit closely, fix the plinth as follows:

- Carefully position the plinth upside down on the inverted chest, making sure it overhangs the front and sides equally.
- C-clamp the plinth to the bottom rails, keeping the clamps clear of the fixing holes.
- Tap #10 × 2" washer head or round head screws into the front fixing holes to mark their positions on the front rail. Scratch the outlines of the back fixing slots onto the back rail with a bradawl or similar tool.
- Remove the clamps and plinth. Predrill $\frac{5}{8}$" deep for #10 screws into the undersides of the bottom rails at the front screw positions and at the midpoints of the rear slot marks.
- Fix the plinth to the chest with #10 × 2" washer head screws or round head screws with washers.

THE TOP

The top is a $\frac{7}{8}$"-thick glued panel with its thickness increased to $1\frac{1}{4}$" at the front and side edges. When it is fitted to the chest, it extends 1" over the front and each side **(19.97)**. A drawing of the edge cross-section is shown in **19.98**.

Making and shaping these thick edges involves more work than do simpler edge treatments. However, this treatment gives the edge a profile that is distinctive and in keeping with the style of the chest. It also provides a lip to hide any gaps that might appear beneath the top of the chest.

The edges are made thicker by gluing $\frac{3}{8}$"-thick strips of wood to the underside. The top, upside down, with the strips glued to it ready for shaping is shown in **19.99**.

The grain directions of the wood strips and the top must be parallel to avoid conflict when their moisture contents change. To achieve this, the end strips have very short grain; they are 20" wide but only $\frac{1}{2}$" long; the front strip is $\frac{1}{2}$" wide and 40" long.

After you have glued on the strips, you will use a circular saw guided by a straightedge to shape the edges. This requires a circular saw with an adjustable base plate that will allow the blade to cut at angles other than 90 degrees. The position of the straightedge and the required base-plate angle are determined beforehand by trial and error with a test piece.

After doing the initial shaping with the circular saw, you will hand-sand the edges to their final shape.

Making the Top

Lumber for the top needs to be defect-free on one face and at the ends. The rough boards should be reasonably flat so that they can finish at or near $\frac{7}{8}$" thickness. Ideally, the top and edging strips would be made from a single board to ensure good color matching.

19.97 The chest top in position

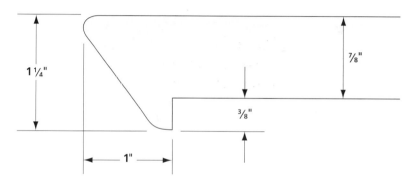

19.98 Dimensioned sectional drawing of top edge

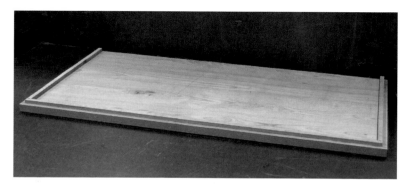

19.99 The top, upside down, with strips glued to it ready for shaping

Start by cutting pieces 41" long, and make a panel $\frac{7}{8}$" thick and at least 21" wide. If you are making everything from a single board, first cut a strip about 1" wide and 48" long to use as the front edge thickener.

Belt-sand the panel. Then joint the front edge and rip the back edge parallel to it at about 20$\frac{3}{4}$" in width. Place it on the chest, overhanging it at the front by 1" and at each side by roughly equal amounts. Make sure that the overhang is the same all along the front. Mark the outline of the carcass on the underside in pencil.

Remove the top and use a circular saw with a straightedge guide to cut the ends to 1" beyond the carcass outlines. Determine where to put the straightedge by making a test cut on some scrap material: (1) clamp the straightedge to the material at about 2" from the edge, (2) make a cut with the saw base plate against the straightedge, and (3) measure the distance from the cut to the straightedge.

When you have cut the top to length, rip its back edge on the table saw to a width that will overhang the back top rail of the chest by $\frac{3}{16}$" and the front edge by 1".

Making the Edge Thickeners

Make a strip $\frac{3}{8}$" × $\frac{1}{2}$" × 41" for adding thickness to the front edge. Because planer snipe must be cut off, it will need to be a few inches longer before it is planed.

Make two end strips, $\frac{3}{8}$" × 21" × $\frac{1}{2}$", with grain running in the direction of the $\frac{1}{2}$" dimension. These pieces will be planed across the grain, and they should initially be made wider than 21" to allow planer snipe to be cut off. They must be made by gluing several pieces side by side to obtain the width. It can be difficult to glue together short, thin strips, so make a thicker strip as described below. Make it 2" long, and then cut it into $\frac{1}{2}$"-long strips. Some short pieces glued together are shown

in **19.100**. One way to keep a strip like this flat while it is clamped is shown in **19.101**.

Make the end strips by flattening and planing a piece of 4/4 lumber and then jointing its side edges. Cut enough 2"-long pieces from it to give the required width. Allow for planer snipe by making the width at least 25". Glue the pieces together as in **19.100** and **19.101**. Use light clamping pressure to minimize cupping.

When the glue is set, joint one end-grain edge of the piece to make it straight. Remove hardened glue from one face and then run the strip through the planer; plane across the grain until you reduce it to $\frac{3}{8}$" thickness. Cut two $\frac{1}{2}$"-long strips from it.

19.100 Gluing short pieces together to make strips for thickening the side edges of the top

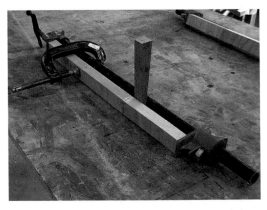

19.101 Keeping a side edging strip flat while the glue is setting

Fixing the Edge Thickeners

When the strips are glued to the top, they must be clamped every few inches to produce perfect contact at all positions. Spring clamps are ideal for this job, although C-clamps can be used if you protect the top with clamping cauls or a pad under each clamp. For the long front strip, you will need at least a dozen clamps.

Glue the front strip first. Fix it exactly at the outside of the marked outline on the underside of the top. Remove squeeze-out from the inside edge when the glue has gelled.

Fix the side strips in a similar way, but leave a full $\frac{1}{32}$" between the strips and the lines to provide clearance for the chest sides. Before gluing the side strips, check that their ends will butt precisely against the front strip. If necessary, cut their ends at a slight angle by crosscutting them on the table saw, with the blade tilted by about 1 degree. Repeat with different blade angles until the strips butt perfectly to the front strip. Restore the table-saw blade to 90 degrees.

Before leaving the glue to set, check that there is still a full $\frac{1}{32}$" clearance between each side strip and the lines.

The top with an end strip clamped in place is shown in **19.102**.

Initial Shaping

Diagram **19.103** shows how the edge profile will be shaped from the square edge and the thickener strips. Diagram **19.104** shows the first stage toward achieving this by cutting the edge and strip at an angle. For this step, use a circular saw with a base plate that can be set at an angle to the blade.

The required angle is about 38 degrees from vertical. Angle adjustment markings on circular-saw base plates are usually only a guide, so the correct setting must be found by making trial cuts on a test

19.102 The top with an end-thickener strip under clamps

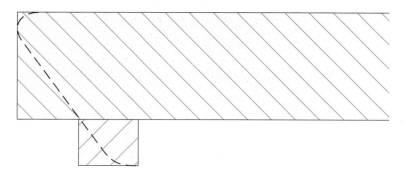

19.103 How the thickened edges will be shaped

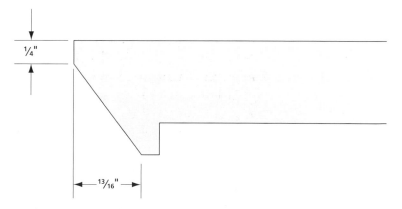

19.104 First stage of shaping by cutting at an angle

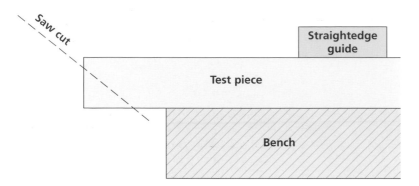

19.105 Test piece and straightedge clamped to bench ready for angled saw cut

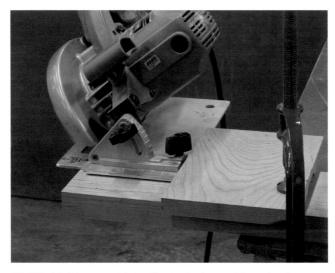

19.106 Making a cut into the test piece with a circular saw guided by the straightedge

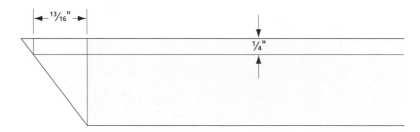

19.107 Draw lines to check angle of cut

piece. The trial cuts will also determine the correct positioning for a straightedge saw guide.

Measure the thickness of the top plus the edging, and plane some material to that thickness for use as a test piece. Make it at least 4" wide and as long as necessary for safe jointing and planing—a piece 10" long would be adequate. Cut the ends square to the edges, and then draw a line on one side edge ¼" from the top face. Set the base plate of the circular saw to 38 degrees from normal.

Place the test piece on the bench with an end projecting over the edge, and place a straightedge on it as a guide for the saw. Position the straightedge far enough from the projecting end to allow the circular saw to cut through the test piece. The tilt of the base plate will determine the edge of the base plate that must run against the straightedge.

Use a square to make the straightedge parallel to the end of the test piece, and then clamp the straightedge and test piece together to the bench **(19.105)**. Draw a line across the top of the test piece to record the position of the straightedge.

Hold the base plate against the straightedge, and cut through the test piece **(19.106)**.

Use a square to draw two lines: one down the side edge from the top surface to where the cut meets the horizontal line, and another to where the cut meets the bottom face **(19.107)**.

Measure the distance between these two lines. If it is ¹³⁄₁₆", the angle of the cut is correct. If it is less than ¹³⁄₁₆", increase the base plate angle; if it is more than ¹³⁄₁₆", decrease the angle. Move the straightedge, and make repeated test cuts until the angle is correct. Chop the end square before making each angled cut, and mark the position of the straightedge each time.

When the angle is correct, measure from the straightedge to where the angled cut meets the $\frac{1}{4}$" line (the distance A in **19.108**). This is the distance from the end to where you will clamp the straightedge for the next test cut.

Cut the end of the test piece square again. Then square a line across the top face at the measured position for the straightedge (distance A from the end). Clamp the straightedge at the line and make another angled cut.

If the second cut meets the horizontal line at exactly the end of the test piece, as in **19.109**, the straightedge position was correct. If not, cut the end square again and repeat the test with the straightedge a little nearer to or further from the end. Continue making test cuts until you find the straightedge position that leaves $\frac{1}{4}$" of the squared end uncut by the angled blade.

Place the chest top right-way-up with an end projecting beyond the bench. Using the measurement you found from the test piece, clamp on a guide and make the angled cut (**19.110**). Make another cut at the other end and then at the front.

Final Shaping and Sanding

Final shaping is a procedure I have not been able to delegate to a power tool: It remains a time-consuming job that has to be done by hand. The objective is to sand the angled edges of the top to a slight concavity. A 0.010" hollow will create the desired shape; any more than this would spoil the appearance.

Make a sanding block by milling a piece of wood to $1\frac{1}{4}$" $\times$ 2" $\times$ 10". With a hand plane and sandpaper, make one of the $1\frac{1}{4}$" $\times$ 10" faces very slightly convex—just a $\frac{1}{8}$" depth of curvature is needed. Glue a strip of felt to this face with spray adhesive, and then glue very coarse sandpaper to the felt. I use strips cut from a 36-grit

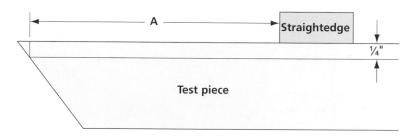

19.108 Measure the distance A

19.109 The end of the test piece after being cut when the straightedge saw guide is in the right position

19.110 Making an angled cut into an edge of the top with the saw guide at the measured position

19.111 Inverted chest top with sanding block ready for sanding the edges

19.112 Light showing under a straightedge indicates that sanding has made the edge concave

sanding belt. Bevel the edges of the opposite face of the block to make the grip comfortable. The sanding block and the upside-down top before the edges are made concave by sanding are shown in **19.111**.

Making long strokes with both hands on the block, sand the angled faces of the edges. Rotate the block a little during the stroke, and sand the angled face to a shallow concave curve. After about 100 strokes, hold the edge of a steel rule across the sanded face, as in **19.112**, and check for a gap under it. If you can push a 0.010" feeler gauge under the rule at the center of the curve, you are done with the coarse-grit sanding.

When all the edges have been sanded with the coarse sandpaper, repeat the procedure with 80-grit paper glued to the block; finally, finish with 120- and 220-grit papers. When you are using 120- and 220-grit paper, it is easier to dispense with the block and use felt strips with sandpaper glued to them. Glue sandpaper to both faces of the felt, and cut strips to the width of the edges. The finer grits should not require nearly so many strokes because they have to remove only the scratches made by coarser grits.

Using the coarsest grit, you might take 30 minutes or more to sand to 0.010" concavity on all edges. You may need another hour to work through the three finer grits.

After sanding the angled faces to 220-grit, shape the tops and bottoms of the edges, as shown in **19.98**. You can do this very quickly with either a random-orbit sander or a flat sanding block and 80-grit sandpaper. Follow this step by sanding with felt strips with 120- and then 220-grit sandpaper glued to both sides.

Finish the process with 220-grit sandpaper molded over the profile with your fingers.

Sand the top surface using a random-orbit sander with 120- and 220-grit discs.

Round over the top-front corners by hand enough to make them smooth to the touch. Finish by hand-sanding the top surface in the direction of the grain with 220-grit sandpaper and a cushioned block.

This much hand-sanding is a job for the morning, when you are fresh and energetic. It is a good upper-body workout, so when it is finished, take the rest of the day off and go fishing!

Fixing the Top

Place the top on the chest with the front lip touching the front top rail. Use paper or card spacers to obtain equal clearance at each side between the side lips and the chest sides. Clamp the top to the top rails, and mark the fixing screw positions by inserting a screw in each screw hole in the top rails and the box's top and giving it a tap.

Remove the top, and using a $\frac{1}{8}$" drill, predrill it for screws at the marked positions to a depth of $\frac{1}{2}$".

The top is now ready for fixing, but do not fix it until after the finish is applied. To fix the top, use #8 × $1\frac{1}{2}$" FH screws through the rails and #8 × 1" washer head screws through the box's top.

DRAWERS

Drawer bottoms are wide, so when they are made of solid wood, expansion and contraction can be very significant. Unless the woodworker provides for it, expansion of a bottom could even break the drawer joints. For this reason, bottoms are made so they can expand from front to back, and so the grain direction is from side to side.

A solid wood bottom is held in grooves in the drawer front and sides, and it passes below the drawer back. It is glued into the front groove, and all expansion and contraction takes place at the back. (A bottom extending beyond the back with a screw providing support can be seen in **19.128**.) The bottom is slotted so that the screw does not impede movement.

Dovetailing is the only form of joinery that makes sense for drawers; its advantages far outweigh any savings of time offered by other methods. While it may take a little while to get a dovetailing jig properly adjusted, the subsequent dovetailing of multiple drawers is a quick and reliable process. Drawers that have been dovetailed correctly can be assembled easily, in-square and free of twist.

Overview

The drawer fronts comprise most of what we see when looking at the chest of drawers. Therefore, lumber for them should be selected for the way the fronts will look as a group.

The backs, sides, and bottoms can be obtained in three ways: (1) from secondary and cheaper species of lumber, (2) from the same species as the fronts but with less regard to appearance, or (3) by gluing up off-cuts into wide panels and then cutting from these.

You can prepare rough blanks for the parts from the selected material at any time, but once they are flattened, work on the drawers should not be delayed. A long delay between flattening the parts and final assembly will increase the risk of cupping, which could make dovetailing and assembly more difficult.

As soon as possible after being jointed and planed, the fronts, sides, and backs are cut to fit their respective openings in the chest. Accurate cutting to width is essential to provide the right expansion gaps. You need to cut to length accurately to provide equal side gaps for all the fronts. Accuracy is ensured by using feeler gauges and a dial gauge to assist in setting the table-saw rip fence and the crosscut length stop.

Calculate the expansion gaps for each drawer front. The calculations are based on the width and moisture content of each front, so a realistic estimate of MC is necessary. This estimate is obtained either by measuring it with a moisture meter or by knowing the relative humidity to which the lumber is acclimated.

When the fronts, backs, and sides have been cut to fit the openings, they are almost ready for dovetailing, but first, their inside faces should be sanded and given a coat of shellac.

The procedure for dovetailing is detailed in Chapter 7, "Dovetails." After the drawer parts have been dovetailed, you still need to do two things before assembling them: You have to cut grooves in the front and sides to accommodate the drawer bottoms, and you have to cut the backs so that the bottoms can pass under them.

When the parts are ready to assemble, apply polyurethane glue, use pipe clamps to squeeze the tails fully into the sockets, and then remove the clamps. Check the assembly for squareness, and leave it until the glue is set.

Clean the hardened glue from the dovetails and the drawer sides with a belt sander, and test the drawers for fit in the openings. Use the belt sander again on the sides to create the required side clearances.

Make sure the bottom edges of the drawer sides sit flat on the bearers. If necessary, shave the bottom edges with a hand plane until full contact is obtained between them and the bearers at each side.

After you fit the drawers satisfactorily to their openings, do some final sanding and apply a coat of shellac to all unfinished surfaces except for the front.

Top Gaps

To size the drawer parts in order to leave an adequate top gap, you must first gauge their MC or the RH to which they are acclimated and then use **Table 1** and **Table 3** in Chapter 1 to determine their future expansion. Possible ways to determine these include the following:

- Use a pin-type or contactless moisture meter to measure the MC of boards before cutting them for drawer parts.
- Use a contactless meter on cut parts.
- Estimate the MC of the lumber from the RH in which it has been stored. This would require that the RH has

19.113 Planed drawer parts are stored in plastic to maintain their moisture content

been constant for several weeks and that the lumber has been stickered.

- When cutting rough blanks for the parts, cut a few small wafers from the boards (not from near the ends) and put them in a plastic bag with a hygrometer. Note the hygrometer reading when it is steady.

Find the appropriate top gap for each size of drawer from **Table 4** in Chapter 1.

Cutting for Drawer Parts

Choose the lumber for the fronts first, which must be defect-free on one face. The twin top fronts should be cut consecutively from one board so that the grain is continuous from one to the other. All the fronts should be similar in pattern and color. Cut rough blanks for the fronts, but do not flatten and plane them at this stage.

Cut rough blanks for the sides and backs, or glue up some panels of suitable length. Panels made from narrow strips (e.g., 2" wide with pith sides and bark sides alternating) are excellent for drawer parts because they are more stable. They also allow for the most economical use of wood. Make them in widths that will provide multiple parts. Cut the glued panels into blanks for the sides and backs.

When you are ready to make the drawers, flatten the blanks and plane them to thickness: $\frac{7}{8}$" for the fronts, $\frac{3}{4}$" for the backs, and $\frac{1}{2}$" for the sides. Store the planed parts in large plastic bags, or wrap them in plastic sheeting (19.113) to keep their MC constant.

Cutting to Width

Sort the planed parts into drawer sets, and mark the outside faces to show what component each piece is and which drawer it belongs to. Mark an arrow on each outside face to show which way is up. Mark an additional arrow on the sides to show which is the front end.

Joint the top edge of every piece.

All parts must now be ripped to widths that will provide the necessary top clearances. Precise adjustments to the rip fence setting are needed to create these gaps. You can use a dial gauge to measure the adjustments, just as you did when making the bearer liners.

If any drawer openings are not perfectly parallel, despite the care you took in the frame assembly, make the gaps correct at the widest places. Planing or sanding the fronts after the drawers are completed will even out the gaps.

Smooth cutting is important so that saw marks can be sanded off without significantly increasing the gaps. A thin-kerf blade is unlikely to produce a smooth cut. Since it has only to shave the edge, your crosscut blade might make the smoothest cut.

Cut the parts to width as follows:

- Hold a drawer side at its opening with its jointed edge against the upper rail. Mark the lower edge for a snug fit. Repeat at different positions along the opening to find the widest place.
- Set the rip fence to cut the piece about $\frac{1}{32}$" wider than the widest part of the opening. Rip the lower edge of the drawer side. Leave the fence locked at that position.
- Place the side at the opening again. Estimate the fence adjustment needed for a snug fit; adjust the fence, and then rip the side again. Repeat until the side just fits in the opening. Use feeler gauges to measure the top gap, if any.
- Subtract the measured gap from the required gap: This is how much the rip fence must now be moved.
- Use a dial gauge to help you move the fence toward the blade by the required amount.
- Rip the side again, and check the new top gap. If it is within 0.005" of the target, rip the other three parts of the drawer at this fence setting.
- Repeat all the above steps for the other drawers.

Cutting to Length

Each front must be sized to its individual opening because the drawer openings may be different lengths owing to variations such as cock-bead thickness and fitting. At this stage, the objective is to make the fronts a snug fit lengthwise with no side clearance. The backs will be cut 0.010" shorter than the fronts to make the drawers slightly narrower at the back.

Cut the fronts and backs to length as follows:

- Cut one end of each front and back square to the edges. Use a good crosscut blade, and keep the outside faces uppermost when cutting so they will be cut cleanly. Mark the squared ends.
- Fit a screw-adjustment length stop to the crosscut sled.
- Place the squared end of a front in its opening, and mark the opposite end for a snug fit. Set the adjustable stop to cut the front about 0.010" longer than the mark.

- Place the squared end against the stop, and cut the other end.
- Place the front in its opening again, and estimate how much shorter it needs to be to ensure a snug fit. Adjust the stop screw by that amount and cut again.
- Check the fit, and cut again until the front fits snugly in the opening.
- Cut the drawer back with the same stop setting, but place a 0.010" feeler gauge between the stop and the back so the back will be cut 0.010" shorter.
- Repeat the procedure for the fronts and backs of the other drawers.

After completing this procedure, cut one end of each drawer side square to the edges, and then cut the opposite ends to a length of 17".

Sanding and Finishing the Parts

After cutting the parts to size, remove all the milling marks from the inside faces with a random-orbit sander and a 120-grit disc. Take care when you sand near the ends because any sanding hollows you produce may appear as gaps in the dovetails. Keep the sander flat, and stop sanding as soon as the milling marks have disappeared.

Give the sanded surfaces a coat of shellac. Wipe off the shellac while it is wet, and then allow the surfaces to dry. When they are dry, sand them lightly with 220-grit paper by hand or with a random-orbit sander.

The parts are now ready for dovetailing. Return them to storage in plastic while you set up the dovetailing jig.

Dovetailing

Proceed as detailed in Chapter 7, "Dovetails." When all the dovetails have been cut, store the parts in plastic again if you are not ready to proceed to the next stage.

Grooves for Drawer Bottoms

Grooves in the sides and front of each drawer accommodate the drawer bottom. The drawer backs are cut to allow the bottoms to slide under them. The grooves are $\frac{1}{4}$" wide, positioned exactly at the center of the bottom dovetails so that the ends of the grooves will not be visible. The easiest way to cut the grooves is with a $\frac{1}{4}$" dado cutter in the table saw, although you could cut them with two or more passes with a normal crosscutting blade.

Start by drawing a $\frac{1}{4}$"-wide by $\frac{3}{16}$"-deep groove on the end face of a bottom tail of one of the drawer sides. Draw it at the inside face of the piece (19.114).

Fit a $\frac{1}{4}$" dado cutter or a $\frac{1}{8}$" crosscut blade in the table saw, and set the blade height to $\frac{3}{16}$". Use scrap wood as a test piece to check the setting. Place the marked drawer side on the saw table with its inside face down and its bottom edge toward the fence. Adjust the fence so that either the dado blade will cut the groove exactly as drawn or a $\frac{1}{8}$" crosscut blade will cut half of the marked groove. Make a test cut on the scrap piece; then hold it against the end of the drawer side to check that the groove will be in the center of the

19.114 Groove outline drawn on the bottom tail of a drawer side

bottom dovetail. If necessary, adjust the fence and test again.

Draw a pencil line on each piece approximately where the grooves are needed. These marks will help ensure that you do not cut the grooves in the wrong faces or near the top edges instead of near the bottom edges. Cut grooves into all the inside faces of the sides. As you place each piece on the table saw, check that the inside face is down and the pencil line and the L and R marks are going toward the fence.

To cut the maximum depth of groove in the fronts that will not show when the drawers are assembled, increase the blade height to $\frac{1}{32}$" less than the depth of the sockets—that is, to approximately $\frac{11}{32}$". Cut a groove in the test piece, and then hold it against the end of a drawer front to confirm that the groove will not quite reach the bottoms of the sockets. Cut grooves into the inside faces of the fronts and backs.

If you are using a standard blade, adjust the fence so that the blade will now cut the other half of the groove; repeat the two previous cuts to complete the grooves. Remember to change the blade height for sides and fronts.

Final Work before Assembly

You must cut off the bottom part of each drawer back so that the drawer bottoms can slide under them. The grooves in the backs were cut only to make it easier to set the table-saw fence at the right distance from the top edges. Replace the dado cutter with a rip blade, and cut off the bottom edges of the drawer backs so they are level with the tops of the grooves.

One step remains to be done before you assemble the drawers. That is to chamfer the back ends of the drawer sides where the bottom dovetail is below the drawer back (**19.115**).

19.115 Chamfer the back ends of the drawer sides

This chamfer is not essential, but the sides look better with it. Draw a short line on each drawer side; start the line at the top of the groove on the end of the bottom dovetail, and finish it on the bottom edge at $1\frac{1}{4}$" from the end of the rear dovetail. Double-check that you have drawn the lines on the back ends, not the front ends. Use a handsaw to cut to within $\frac{1}{16}$" of the lines on the waste side, and finish with a hand plane.

Assembly

Prepare for assembly by getting out two pipe clamps, two clamping cauls at least 9" long, a small glue brush trimmed to about $\frac{3}{8}$" in width, polyurethane glue in a shallow container, and some water with a small piece of cloth or a foam brush.

Place a set of drawer parts on the bench with their inside faces up. Dampen the sides of the tails with water, and then apply glue sparingly to the sides of the sockets. When the water has disappeared from the surface of the tails, apply glue to their side surfaces also. There would be no point in gluing the bottoms of the sockets or the backs of the tails because they do not make contact side grain to side grain.

When every socket and tail has been glued, push the tails partway into the sockets, and set the drawer on the bench.

Place a caul against the front dovetails at each side, and then squeeze them into the sockets with the pipe clamps, as shown by **19.116**. The tails should be assembled flush with or just above the sockets.

Remove the clamps and cauls, and use them to squeeze the back dovetails in; then unclamp the drawer.

19.116 Squeezing the dovetails into the sockets using cauls and pipe clamps

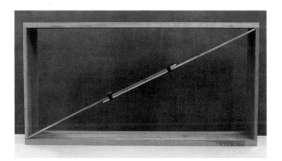

19.117 Checking the drawer for square before leaving the glue to set

19.118 Drawer hangs from battens screwed to bench

The tails should be flush with or just above the sockets. They should not be inserted below the ends of the socket boards.

Stand the drawer on its front or back and check it for square (**19.117**). Push on the appropriate corners to make the diagonals equal, and then leave the drawer until the glue is set.

Repeat the assembly procedure with the other drawers.

Sanding the Drawer Sides

When the glue has set, the drawers are ready to be cleaned up and fitted to the drawer openings. To do this, you need a convenient way to support the drawers. The best way is to clamp or screw to the bench three battens that project over the edge by about 10". They should be spaced so that a drawer front can be hung on the outer two and a drawer side can be hung on two more closely spaced ones (**19.118**).

Traditionally, a hand plane is used to skim drawer sides and the ends of dovetail sockets to fit a drawer in its opening with very small side clearances. Hand planes can be very controllable and accurate, but some tearing can occur if the drawer sides have difficult grain. I find that hand-planing a whole set of drawers is hard work and that it usually leaves patches that require significant sanding. Instead of a hand plane, I use a belt sander with an 80-grit belt.

To sand the drawer sides flush to the front and to remove glue stains from the end grain of the sockets, the belt sander must move over the ends of the drawer sides. If you allow the sander to tilt over the ends, you will create ugly side gaps between the front and the drawer opening. Even if you do not tilt the sander, you could still produce uneven side gaps.

The solution to these problems is to clamp an auxiliary end-grain surface flush

19.119

19.120

19.121

19.119 Clamping a block to the drawer front

19.120 The block's jointed end-grain surface is flush with one end of the drawer front, allowing a belt sander to be used without risk of undercutting the front

19.121 Check progress frequently with a straightedge

with the end of the drawer front so that the sander cannot tilt and the "edge effect" is transferred to the auxiliary surface. With this contrivance, you can also sand off controlled amounts by positioning the auxiliary surface slightly below the surface you are sanding.

For an auxiliary surface, I recommend a block of wood about 2" thick and slightly wider than the widest drawer front, that is, about 9½" wide. Make it at least 8" long for easy clamping, and joint its end-grain surfaces flat: Set the jointer for a light cut, and sand a small chamfer at the trailing edge to prevent splitting.

Clamp the block to the drawer front as shown in **19.119** and **19.120**, with the jointed end-grain surface exactly flush with one end of the front. This is easy if you apply the clamps lightly, tap the block into position with a mallet, and then tighten the clamps. Use clamp pads to protect the inside face of the drawer front.

Make pencil marks on the jointed face of the block so that you will know how the sanding is progressing. You can now sand the drawer side without any danger of rounding or undercutting the end of the drawer front.

Hang the drawer and clamped block from the battens, and belt-sand the drawer side. Use the pencil marks as an indicator of your progress, and stop when they are sanded off. The glue stains should disappear from the end grain of the dovetails.

Sand the rest of the drawer side and the rear dovetails.

Use a straightedge to check that you have kept the side flat. You should not have any high spots between the dovetails at each end (**19.121**). You should not be able to rock the straightedge when you place it along the length of the drawer: It should rest on the dovetails at each end. Repeat the procedure for the second side; then try the drawer in the drawer opening.

You will have cut the front to a close fit, so any high spots in the sides will prevent the drawer from going in. If it will not go in, do not immediately sand the sides again; other factors are involved, and you need to carefully inspect the work to find the causes of the tightness. There are many possible causes: Kickers may be too low, top or bottom edges of the drawer sides may not be flush with the edges of the front or back, side guides may be wrongly positioned, or bearer liners may be too thick. Use a straightedge to check the relationships of the kickers, bearer liners, and side guides to the opening.

If the drawer sides are too tight against the drawer guides, even though the guides are correctly positioned, clamp the end-grain block to the back of the drawer, 0.015" below the end. Sand off another 0.015" from the drawer side near the back, but not near the front. Try the drawer again, and then sand closer to the front if you need to.

When the drawer will go all the way in, shine a light under it from behind and check to see how the sides sit on the bearers. The side edges should be in full contact with the bearers on both sides, and no gap should show below the drawer front.

If you have to remove material from the bottom edges of the sides to allow the drawer to sit lower or more level, identify exactly how much to remove and from where. If one side is high, determine where that side edge is touching the bearer, and estimate how much to remove. Any gap under the front at that side will give you a clue, but be conservative and remove incremental amounts each time. If no gap is visible under the front, the drawer may be tilted down at the front and you will need to take material off the back regions of the side edges to allow the drawer to tilt up a little. Similarly, removing material from a region of one side edge may correct a forward or backward tilt on the other side.

Before taking action, check to see that the drawer front is not hitting the rail below it. It may be the bottom edge of the front that needs attention. If it does, deal with it before touching the side edges. Think twice before removing any material from the front because you will not be able to put it back.

If material has to be removed from the front or side edges, a hand plane is the best choice for the job. The narrow edges will be easy to plane, and only a little planing will be required. However, you may not have much confidence in your ability to plane accurately while maintaining a straight edge. In this case, you can use a similar device to the auxiliary surface you used to help you sand the sides flat.

A flat board with jointed edges can be clamped to the drawer sides or to the front, and set below the edges by the amount that you want to remove (19.122). The drawer will have to overhang the bench because of the clamps, so you may need to clamp it to the bench. If you want to remove material from only one end of an edge, position the board flush with the edge at the other end. The thicker the board is, the better.

Be very careful when you plane the side edges at or near their front ends. Always plane away from the front to avoid running the nose of the plane into it.

Next, measure the front side gaps with feeler gauges. Aim for a side gap of 0.025" when the front is pushed to the opposite side. If the gap is less than this, sand one side again, but this time with the block clamped below the dovetails by the amount needed to produce a 0.025" gap. If the gap is tapered, mark the corner of the drawer front where the most sanding is needed (19.123) and clamp the block lower at this corner by the appropriate amount. Use feeler gauges to help position the block. For example, if the gap is 0.025" at the bottom and only 0.017" at the top, use a 0.008" feeler gauge to position the block lower at the corner where the gap is small.

Once the drawer is installed, move it from side to side by reaching inside and pushing on each inside face in turn. The drawer should move so it completely closes the front side gap at each side of the opening. This test will show that there are no high spots or bulges in the sides that might cause the drawer to jam in times of high humidity. The drawer sides and the guides will expand and contract a little in thickness.

Make sure that it is not just the drawer front that has some sideward movement—the drawer sides must also have some side clearance. Do not worry if the drawer does not slide smoothly—some surfaces are

19.122 One way to ensure you plane or sand off the right amount

19.123 Mark the corner of the drawer front that needs the most sanding

rough and dry at this stage, and the bearers may be covered with a layer of dust.

Transfer the drawer designation marks (1L, 1R, 2, 3, 4) to an inside face where they will be permanent. I put these marks on the inside face of the front, below the groove.

Repeat the above procedures for the other drawers. Joint the end grain of the auxiliary block flat for each one.

Finishing Touches

When the drawers have been fitted, you can final-sand them, except for the outside faces of the fronts, and apply some shellac to the sanded faces. As a part of final sanding, I remove all sharpness from the

back outside corners to eliminate any possibility of these jamming against the drawer guides. It would be a disaster if the front corners were rounded by mistake, so I recommend that you make a point of starting to sand by placing the drawer on the bench, with its front down, and slightly rounding the back corners with a random-orbit sander and 120-grit disc. Next, continue sanding the sides with the same disc to remove the belt sander's marks. Be very careful when you sand the front dovetails: You do not want to increase the side gaps, so it is best if you barely allow the sander to touch the dovetails. Sand the backs to remove milling marks.

Sand the top and bottom edges with the random-orbit sander. Do not remove enough material to affect the top gaps; sand just enough to make everything feel smooth. After you have used the random-orbit sander, use sandpaper to soften all sharp edges except the outside edges of the fronts.

Check for glue squeeze-out at the inside corners, and remove any that you find. Give all unfinished surfaces (except for the front face) a wipe-on, wipe-off coat of shellac, and sand this lightly when it is dry. Do not worry if some shellac gets onto the front face, which has still to be sanded.

Remove all dust from the bearers and place the drawers in the chest. They should now be sliding freely, and will slide even more freely later, when the runners are waxed.

Drawer Pulls

The size of the drawer pulls should be correct in relation to the size of the drawer fronts. The right size gives the finished piece a balanced appearance. The positioning of the pulls on each size of front is important for the same reason. On wider fronts, the pulls should be placed farther

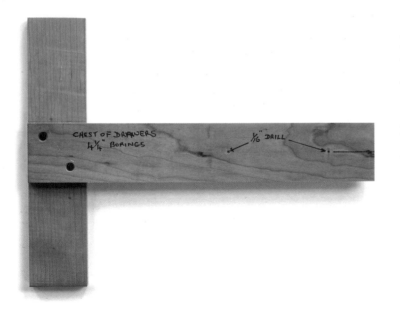

19.124 T-square drilling guide

If you are not using these particular pulls and positions, you will have to insert all the drawers into the chest in order to judge the best pull positions.

You could rely on careful marking and drilling to precisely position the holes, but I recommend making a simple drilling guide as a safeguard against getting any holes out of alignment. The guide is a wooden T-square with $\frac{1}{16}$" holes drilled through it at the appropriate distances from the crosspiece **(19.124)**. For pulls with $4\frac{1}{4}$" borings, these distances are $6\frac{1}{16}$" and $10\frac{5}{16}$". The centerline of the holes is marked on the end of the guide.

An advantage of the guide is that you can test it on a piece of scrap wood to confirm that the hole spacing is correct. To use it on the drawers, draw horizontal lines on the fronts at the appropriate distances down from the top edges. Clamp the guide to a drawer front, with the hole centers on the horizontal line and the crosspiece against the drawer end. Drill through the guide holes with a $\frac{1}{16}$" drill bit. For drawers with two pulls, switch the guide to the other end of the front and drill through again. When you drill the top drawer fronts, make sure the guide is against the outside ends, that is, the left end of the left drawer front and the right end of the right drawer front.

In $\frac{7}{8}$"-thick drawer fronts, the threaded posts of the H-10 pulls extend about $\frac{1}{4}$" beyond the holes. Other pulls may have longer or shorter posts. The question arises whether to leave the posts long or to cut them and sink the fixing nuts below the surface. If you decide to sink the nuts, the next step is to counterbore the $\frac{1}{16}$" holes on the inside to a depth of about $\frac{3}{16}$", at a diameter that will accommodate the appropriate socket wrench. The point of a Forstner bit will center accurately in the $\frac{1}{16}$" hole. After you finish counterboring, enlarge the $\frac{1}{16}$" holes to accept the posts.

from the top edges, although exactly how far from those edges they should be is a matter of personal preference.

The pulls that I normally use are shown in the photo of the chest. Details of these pulls and their positioning are as follows:

- Drawer pulls are item H-10A, $4\frac{1}{4}$" boring, from Horton Brasses Inc. (www. horton-brasses.com). "Boring" means the distance between fixing holes. The A in H-10A stands for antique finish.

- In the chest as shown, the first post hole for each pull is drilled $6\frac{1}{16}$" from the end of the drawer front. This is so that the pulls are all vertically aligned with the single pull on each top drawer.

- The holes are centered at the following distances down from the top edges of the drawer fronts:

Top drawers	$2\frac{7}{8}$"
Level 2 drawer	$3\frac{1}{4}$"
Level 3 drawer	$3\frac{5}{8}$"
Level 4 drawer	$3\frac{5}{8}$"

Because the counterbored holes would be large ($\frac{5}{8}$" or more), I prefer to leave the nuts on the surface, as they are in many antique chests. If the nuts and post ends are smooth, this will not cause any problems. If you choose this option, you can make the holes in the drilling guide large enough for the posts and omit the $\frac{1}{16}$" drilling.

Drawer Bottoms

The bottoms are made as glued panels from resawn lumber. Making the bottoms involves several steps: (1) The panels must be cut accurately to size, (2) the front and side edges must be chamfered to fit the drawer grooves, (3) screw slots must be made near the back edges, and (4) after the bottoms have been sanded and finished, the front edges must be glued into the front drawer grooves.

The grain direction of drawer bottoms should always be parallel to the drawer fronts so that seasonal expansion and contraction can take place below the back. Provide support at the back by screwing the bottom to the drawer back. This entails making screw slots, rather than holes, to allow for movement. The bottoms are glued into the front grooves to stop them from pulling out when they shrink.

The $\frac{3}{8}$"-thick bottoms are made to fit into the $\frac{1}{4}$" drawer grooves by chamfering their front and side edges. The best way to decide on an appropriate chamfer angle is to make full-scale drawings similar to **19.125**.

The top drawing in **19.125** shows a chamfer fitting fully into the deeper grooves in the drawer front. Although the side grooves are shallower, the same chamfer angle produces an acceptable fit. The angle is about 4 degrees, the chamfer is about $1\frac{1}{2}$" long, and the edges are just over $\frac{3}{16}$" thick. Lower angles would result in long chamfers, and steeper ones would leave a thinner edge.

Making the Bottoms

Measure the distance from the bottom of a front groove to the outside face of the drawer back. Add $\frac{1}{4}$" to this measurement to obtain the required width of the drawer bottom. Then, at the back of the drawer where the side grooves are accessible to a ruler, measure the distance between the bottoms of the grooves. Subtract $\frac{1}{16}$" from this measurement to obtain the length of the bottom allowing for $\frac{1}{32}$" clearance each side. Repeat the measurements for each drawer.

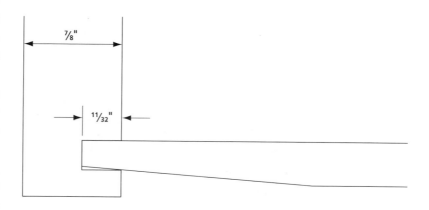

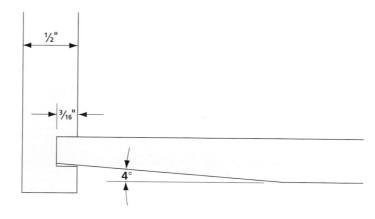

19.125 Full-scale drawings help you choose an appropriate chamfer angle

Choose the lumber for the bottoms; keep the resawing requirement in mind, but aim to use the least desirable boards, or parts of boards, and any suitable pieces from the off-cuts pile. Although appearance is of secondary importance, everything must, of course, be free from significant defects.

Make the panels. Allow an extra inch in length and enough width to accommodate all the edge jointing that making panels involves.

After making the panels, smooth them with a belt sander and then assign them to individual drawers. Joint one side-grain edge of each, and rip them to their widths. Chop them all square at one end, and then cut them to final length. Mark the best face of each one as the upper face, and indicate the front edge.

Chamfering the Bottoms

Make a test piece at least ⅜" thick and about 4" wide by 6" long.

Remove the table-saw guard, and fit a zero-clearance insert and a rip blade. Set the blade to 2" high and 4 degrees from vertical. Then clamp a board or block across the saw table, about ½" from the off-cut side of the blade, as a safeguard against touching the blade (**19.126**).

Add a tall auxiliary fence to the rip fence, and position it about ⁷⁄₃₂" from the blade. Start the saw and cut the test piece. Hold the piece on edge and against the fence. Check the fit of the chamfer in the grooves. It should just reach the bottom of the front grooves. If necessary, adjust the fence and chop off about 1" of the test piece, repeating the tests until the fit is right. Stop the saw after each cut to remove off-cuts from between the fence and the guard board.

The fit should not be loose at this stage, because the chamfers will be thinner after they are sanded. However, the fit should not be so tight as to create a major sanding job.

If you have difficulty making fine adjustments to the fence, you can use a dial gauge (as you did when you were thicknessing the bearer liners and cutting the drawer parts to width). Although the front face of the fence is obstructed, the gauge can be placed against its back.

When the setup is correct, start the table saw. Take a drawer bottom, and chamfer one of its ends with the upper face toward the fence, holding it as flat as you can. If the guard board is high enough to protect your fingers, you can keep the drawer

19.126 This guard block is part of the setup for chamfering drawer bottoms safely. When the rip fence is also in position, there will be little chance of the operator touching the blade

19.127 Chamfering a drawer bottom using the high guard block for protection

bottom flat and against the fence with the spread fingers and thumb of one hand as you push it along with the other hand (19.127). Chamfer the other end and then the front. Do not chamfer the back edge.

When all the drawer bottoms have been chamfered, return the blade to vertical.

Fitting the Bottoms

Sand the chamfers with a random-orbit sander. Remove any burn marks, and disguise any unevenness by rounding over the boundary between the chamfer and the horizontal surface. Check that the chamfers will fit all the way into the bottom of the front grooves. Continue to sand any that are too tight. Number the rear edges to mark which drawers they fit. Sand the entire upper and lower surfaces to remove belt-sander scratches, and give them a wipe-on, wipe-off coat of shellac. Try to avoid getting shellac on the front edges, which are gluing surfaces. Sand the drawer bottoms lightly when the shellac is dry.

Screw Slots

The screw slots could be made either with a single cut at the table saw by using a miter gauge and a $\frac{1}{4}$"-thick blade or with two cuts and a $\frac{1}{8}$" blade. However, with slots like this, the screw heads would be exposed under the drawer bottoms and could scratch the cock beading when the drawers are installed or removed. Avoid this problem by cutting a recess around the slot to sink the screw head below the surface of the drawer bottom, as in 19.128.

You can make recessed slots with a very simple router jig. The jig clamped to a drawer bottom is shown in 19.129.

The slotting jig can be made in about 15 minutes from $\frac{1}{2}$" or $\frac{3}{4}$" plywood as follows.

Cut a piece of plywood 8" by 12", and screw and glue two strips parallel to the 8"

19.128 A recessed screw slot in the drawer bottom

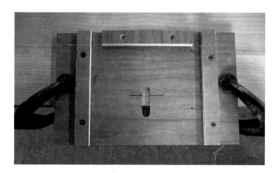

19.129 Jig clamped to a drawer bottom ready for making a recessed slot

ends to guide your router in a straight line from front to back. These are the side strips shown in 19.129.

Screw and glue another strip close to the back edge to act as a stop. Next, clamp the jig to the bench with something under it to protect the bench. Fit a $\frac{1}{2}$" spiral cutter into your router, and place the router on the jig, against the stop. Start the router, plunge the cutter through the plywood, and move the router back from the stop to cut a slot at least $1\frac{1}{2}$" long. Remove the router, unclamp the jig, and mark a line to each side of the slot about $\frac{1}{2}$" from the forward end of the slot to complete your slotting jig.

To use the jig, first mark the undersides of the drawer bottoms at the screw positions. (The two small drawer bottoms each have a single central screw; the others have a screw 11" from each end.) Hold a square to the back edges of the drawer bottoms at these positions, and draw lines about 1" long.

Measure the distance from the bottom of a front groove to the drawer back's center of thickness. Transfer this measurement to the lines drawn on the bottoms to determine the centers of the screw slots.

Double-check that you have made the marks on the undersides of the drawer bottoms in every case. Place a bottom, underside up, at the edge of the bench. You are going to cut through it, so put something under it to protect the bench. Place the slotting jig over it, and center the jig lines over the slot center. Clamp the jig and bottom together to the bench, as in **19.129**.

Place a router with a $\frac{1}{2}$" spiral cutter on the jig. Set the depth stop for a $\frac{3}{16}$"-deep cut into the drawer bottom. Start the router, and make a plunge cut starting at the edge and finishing when the router hits the strip. This cuts a rabbet for a screw head.

When you have cut rabbets at every screw position, change to a $\frac{1}{4}$" spiral cutter and position the jig accurately over a rabbet. Set the depth stop for a cut that will go through the drawer bottom and into the material beneath it. Move the router very slowly at the start of the cut to prevent tear-out at the edge.

Remove the rough edges from the slot (**19.130**).

19.130 Fuzzy edges need sanding

Fixing the Bottoms

Glue the drawer bottoms into the front grooves of their respective drawers as follows:

- Apply some polyurethane glue along the bottom of a front groove.
- Sand the front edge of the drawer bottom to remove any shellac.
- Slide a bottom into the grooves. Use pipe clamps to force it against the bottom of the front groove. Use a caul or pads to protect the drawer front.
- Predrill into the drawer back to accommodate screws; then fix the bottom with #8 × $\frac{3}{4}$" washer head screws and remove the clamps (**19.128**).
- When the glue has set, loosen the screws slightly to allow the bottom to expand or shrink.

DRAWER STOPS

When the drawers are closed, their fronts hit blocks that are glued to the front rails. These blocks keep the closed fronts flush with the face of the chest and $\frac{1}{8}$" behind the cock bead.

Only a narrow range of thickness for the stops is possible: They must be thick enough to protrude above the cock bead but thin enough so the drawer bottoms clear them. The optimum thickness resulting from my dovetail sizes is about $\frac{11}{32}$". You will need to determine the best stop thickness by measuring the clearance below your drawer bottoms.

A simple jig is used to position the stops.

Use epoxy glue in order to avoid problems with clamping.

Make two stops per drawer that are 1" wide by 3" long. This size is larger than strictly necessary, but the extra area allows the glue to be kept back from the edges so there is no squeeze-out.

Make the positioning jig shown in **19.131**, which should be about 3" long.

When the jig and the stops are ready, mix up some epoxy (fast- or slow-setting) and apply it to the underside of a stop. Keep it well back from the edges so it does not squeeze out. Place the stop on a drawer rail, just behind the cock bead and about 1" from the end of the rail. Hold the positioning jig against the front of the cock bead, and pull the stop to the jig **(19.132)**. Move the stop side-to-side a little to spread the glue, but not enough to cause squeeze-out. Leave it in place while you fix the other stops.

THE CHEST BACK, OPTION 1: PLYWOOD

A strong plywood back panel is often used to make a construction more rigid, but this chest is so strongly built that the back is really just for keeping out dust.

If you opt for a plywood back, use $\frac{1}{4}$" plywood and cut it to overlap the top and bottom rails and the stiles by $\frac{3}{4}$". Sand the back's edges smooth, and then drill and countersink holes for #6 × $\frac{3}{4}$" FH screws at about 9" intervals, $\frac{3}{8}$" from the edges.

If you planned for a plywood back but now wish to use a frame-and-panel back, it is not too late to change your plan. The width of the intermediate rails must be reduced to permit a frame-and-panel back to be inset. If you did not do this before the chest was assembled, you can do it now as follows:

- Use a router and a bearing-guided rabbeting bit that has a cutting width of $\frac{3}{4}$" or more.
- Clamp a wide strip of wood to one of the intermediate back rails, flush with the rail surface, to act as a support surface for the router. The strip must be approximately the same length as the rails.

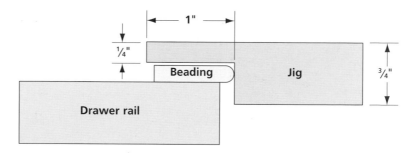

19.131 Diagram of drawer stop positioning jig. The stop will be glued onto the drawer rail behind the jig and the beading

19.132 Pull the drawer stop toward the positioning jig

- Set the depth of cut to $\frac{5}{16}$". Start the router, and cut away the edge of the rail. Start and stop the cut just before the cutter reaches the stiles at each end of the rail.
- Use a chisel to finish the cut where the rail meets the stiles.
- Repeat for the other three intermediate back rails.

THE CHEST BACK, OPTION 2: FRAME-AND-PANEL

Like the plywood option, the frame-and-panel back is just a means of keeping out dust, so light construction is appropriate.

The frame parts are joined with mortises and tenons. A central vertical frame

19.133 The paneled chest back in place

member divides the frame into two (**19.133**). The inside edges of the frame parts are grooved to hold two $\frac{1}{4}$"-thick panels. The frame has a $\frac{5}{16}$" × $\frac{3}{4}$" rabbet cut all around the outside edge to allow it to be set into the chest.

Diagram **19.134** shows the positions of the mortises. The top drawing shows a rail-to-stile corner junction, and the bottom one shows a junction between the center divider and a rail.

Diagram **19.135** shows a rail end indicating the mortise, the groove, and the rabbet. The rabbet is cut after the frame is assembled.

The frame is made from two vertical stiles, two horizontal rails, and one center divider. All are $\frac{5}{8}$" thick and $2\frac{3}{4}$" wide. Their lengths are determined as follows:

- Measure the distance between the top and bottom rails of the chest. Add $1\frac{1}{2}$" to this measurement, to give you the required length for the stiles of the paneled frame. It will be approximately $36\frac{23}{32}$".

- The central vertical divider is $5\frac{1}{2}$" shorter than the stiles—about $31\frac{7}{32}$".
- Measure the distance between the chest stiles. Subtract 4" to get the length of the paneled frame rails, which is nominally $30\frac{1}{2}$".

Frame Joinery

Mill the frame parts and cut them to size. Place them on the bench in their correct relative positions. Mark their outside faces with those positions: L and R on the stiles, T for top and B for bottom on the rails, and an up arrow on the center divider.

Mark the outside edges of the rails and stiles. Then set a marking gauge to $1\frac{1}{2}$" and mark the mortise centers from the ends of the stiles and the outside edges of the top and bottom rails.

Mark the centers of the mortises for the center divider on the ends of the divider at midwidth and on the rails at midlength. Draw the center marks to reach only the outside faces.

The mortises should all be $\frac{3}{8}$" wide, $1\frac{1}{4}$" long, and 1" deep, centered in the thickness of the wood. Draw one mortise reasonably accurately at one of the positions to guide you in setting up the mortising jig. Clamp this piece into the mortising jig with its outside face to the jig reference face and the center of the mortise aligned with the jig's center mark. Fit a $\frac{3}{8}$" mortising bit into a router and then position the bit on the mortise outline. Set the jig fence and side stops in the usual way, and set the router depth stop for a 1"-deep cut.

Cut all the mortises, making sure that the outside faces of the parts are always toward the jig fence.

Make some $\frac{3}{8}$" × $1\frac{1}{4}$" × 2" tenons. Do not make them fit too tightly—the mortise walls are quite thin. Using PVA glue, glue them into the end mortises of the rails and the central divider, not into the center mortises of the top and bottom rails. Clean off the squeeze-out before it hardens.

Panel Grooves

The grooves should be made $\frac{1}{4}$" wide × $\frac{1}{2}$" deep and run the full length of the rails and stiles. The procedure for making them is similar to that for grooving the drawer rails for the chest. To avoid mistakes, you should run a pencil or crayon line along the edges that are to be grooved—that is, the inside edges of the rails and stiles, and both edges of the center divider.

Cut the grooves as you did for the drawer rails of the main chest frames, but set the fence to center the grooves in the $\frac{5}{8}$" thickness of the rails. Set the blade height to $\frac{1}{2}$". Keep the outside faces of the parts to the fence.

Panels

Dry-assemble the frame, and measure the width and height of the two "windows." Make two $\frac{1}{4}$"-thick panels with widths and lengths at least $\frac{3}{4}$" more than the window measurements.

Belt-sand the panels, and then cut them to fit into the frame grooves. Allow $\frac{1}{8}$" expansion room in each side groove and $\frac{1}{8}$" clearance in the top grooves when they are fully inserted into the bottom grooves.

Test the fit of the panels in the grooves. If necessary, sand their edges more to make them an easy, but not loose, fit.

Assembly

Sand the inside edges of the frame parts with a block and sandpaper. Remember to avoid rounding the mortised areas.

When the tenon glue is set, dry-assemble the central divider to the rails, insert the panels into the rail grooves, and assemble the stiles to the rails. Check that

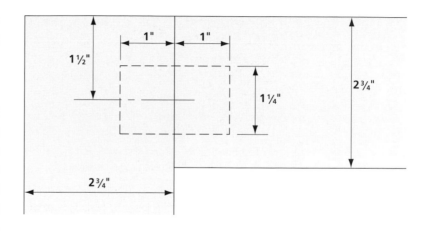

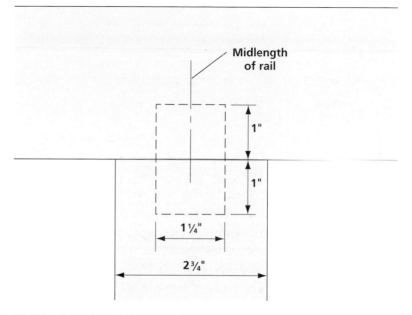

19.134 Dimensioned diagram of chest back mortises

the dimensions of each subframe allow $\frac{1}{8}$" at each side for the panels to expand. Disassemble the frame. If necessary, reduce the panel widths to allow for the proper amount of expansion.

Give the panels one coat of the finish you plan to use for the chest. This will prevent unfinished edges from appearing during dry seasons, when the panels shrink.

Apply polyurethane glue to all mortises and tenons, and assemble the rails to the central divider. Slide the panels into the rail and divider grooves. Fit the stiles onto the

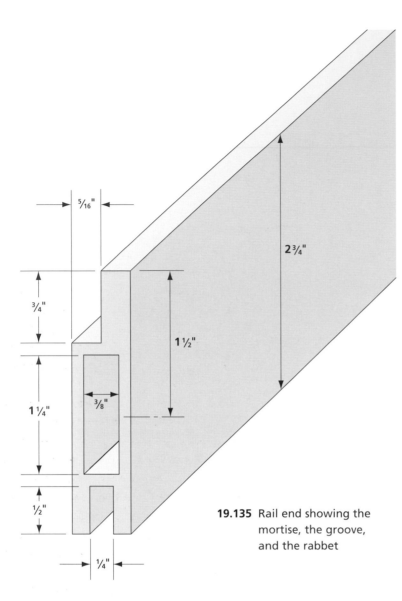

5/16"

2 3/4"

3/4"

1 1/2"

1 1/4"

3/8"

1/2"

1/4"

19.135 Rail end showing the mortise, the groove, and the rabbet

rail tenons. Place the frame on the support strips you used for making glued panels. Apply two pipe clamps across the stiles, and one across the top and bottom rails.

When the glue has set, sand the faces and outside edges of the rails and stiles. Sand off sharpness from all edges that can be touched.

Edge Rabbets

Draw lines on the inside face of the frame 3/4" from the perimeter. Fit a 1/2" mortising bit into the router, and set the depth of cut to 5/16". Clamp a straightedge across the frame to guide the router for making a cut along one of the lines. (Find the position for the straightedge by making a test cut in scrap wood and measuring the distance from the cut to the straightedge.)

Cut a 1/2"-wide groove along the rail or stile by guiding the router along the straightedge.

Repeat for the other three edges of the frame.

Bring the guide 3/8" closer to the edge. Make another cut to convert the groove into a rabbet (**19.136**).

Fixing the Frame

Drill the frame for #8 screws at 3/8" from the edges. Position the holes near the corners and halfway along each rail and stile. Screw the back to the chest with #8 × 1" FH screws.

19.136 A second cut with the router converts the groove into a rabbet

20 Bookcase Project

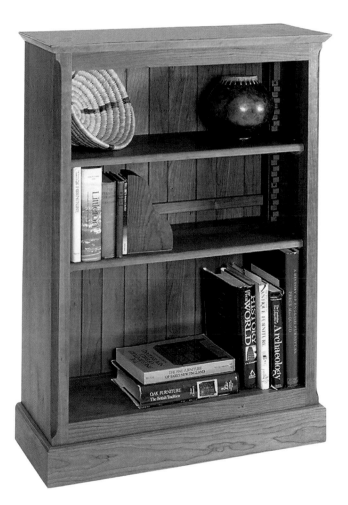

20.1 Bookcase: 32"W x 44"H x 13"D

STRENGTH AND RIGIDITY ARE THE first considerations when designing bookcases. The shelves must be stiff enough to carry heavy books without bending, and the carcass must be able to support the fully loaded shelves. The way the bookcase in this project is constructed is shown in **20.1** and **20.2**.

The inner part of the carcass is a dovetailed box, which is glued to mortised-and-tenoned front and back frames. Because open-fronted pieces such as this have no intermediate rails, the top and bottom frame rails are L-shaped in section to add stiffness to the frames.

Two views of an L-rail are shown in **20.3** and **20.4**. How it is made from two pieces glued together is shown in **20.5**. The vertical sides of the L are 2" high; the horizontal dimension is $2\frac{1}{4}$". Two tenons in each end of the horizontal piece and one in each end of the vertical piece fit into matching mortises in the frame stiles. The joinery procedure uses the shop-made mortising jig detailed in Chapter 6, "The Mortise-and-Tenon Joint."

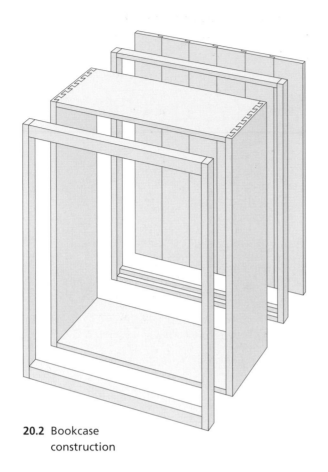

20.2 Bookcase construction

20.3 L-rail with mortises

20.4 L-rail with tenons to fit into frame stile mortises

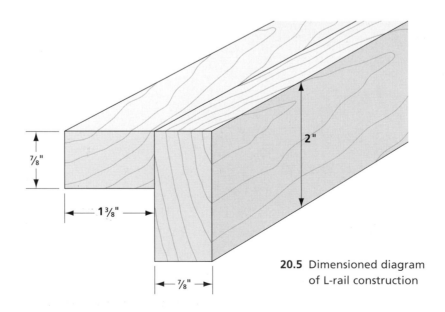

$\frac{7}{8}$"

$1\frac{3}{8}$"

$\frac{7}{8}$"

2"

20.5 Dimensioned diagram of L-rail construction

The top L-rails are oriented with their 2" faces to the outside and their $2\frac{1}{4}$" faces at the top, as seen in **20.5**. The bottom rails are inverted so that the floor of the bookcase can sit on a support inside the L, while the 2" faces remain to the outside (**20.6**).

A decorative top for the bookcase covers the dovetailed box and the frames, and the bookcase itself is seated on a plinth base.

Open-fronted pieces demand extra care when selecting lumber because more surfaces are seen; they also provide an incentive to make a back that is attractive. The back for this piece has overlapping vertical boards that add visual interest and allow for seasonal expansion.

The back frame has a thin cross-rail at midheight to provide a fixing point for the boards. The cross-rail is visible in **20.1**.

made to fit into the notches between the front and back standards at each side of the bookcase (**20.7**). The shelves rest on these.

You will make three shelves and a floor for the bookcase by gluing together narrow strips of wood. By making them from narrow strips, you reduce the risk of warping. This step is necessary because the floor and shelves are not fixed to anything that would hold them flat.

To make the $\frac{3}{8}$"-thick overlapping backboards (sometimes called shiplap boards), you will resaw 4/4 lumber. Then with the table saw, you will cut rabbets $\frac{3}{16}$" deep and $\frac{3}{8}$" wide on the edges of the resawn boards on opposite faces. After cutting them to length and sanding them, you will screw them to the back of the bookcase with the rabbets overlapping by $\frac{1}{4}$".

SUMMARY OF PROCEDURES

Your starting point is to make the dovetailed box and the front and back frames. You will be using the same methods as for the Chest of Drawers project, except for an extra step of gluing together the two parts of each L-rail. After the box and frames are made, they are glued together to form the carcass of the bookcase. The carcass is then sanded, and decorative chamfers are routered along the outside corners of the front stiles.

Next, you will make the plinth and top. The procedure for making the plinth is the same as for the chest of drawers, except that the front and sides are not shaped. The top is similar to the chest of drawers top, but the lip is only $\frac{1}{8}$" thick.

You will make vertical supports (standards) for the shelves. The standards have notches that make the shelf heights adjustable in $1\frac{1}{4}$" steps. The standards do not support the shelves directly; instead, short wooden pieces (two per shelf) are

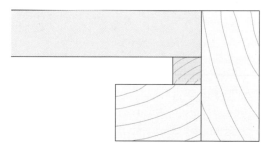

20.6 The floor fits inside the bottom L-rails

20.7 Shelf standards are notched to accept wooden shelf supports at any level

PART	QTY	SIZE IN INCHES	REMARKS
Dovetailed box sides	2	$\frac{7}{8}$" × $7\frac{1}{2}$" × 39"	
Dovetailed box top/bottom	2	$\frac{1}{2}$" × $7\frac{1}{2}$" × 29"	
Face frame stiles	4	$1\frac{3}{4}$" × $2\frac{1}{4}$" × 39"	
L-rails, part A	4	$\frac{7}{8}$" × 2" × $26\frac{5}{8}$"	See procedure for sizing rails
L-rails, part B	4	$\frac{7}{8}$" × $1\frac{3}{8}$" × $26\frac{5}{8}$"	See procedure for sizing rails
Center back rail	1	$\frac{3}{4}$" × $1\frac{1}{4}$" × $26\frac{5}{8}$"	See procedure for sizing rails
Bookcase top	1	$\frac{7}{8}$" × $12\frac{7}{8}$" × $31\frac{3}{4}$"	
Plinth front	1	$\frac{7}{8}$" × 4" × $31\frac{3}{16}$"	See procedure before cutting
Plinth sides	2	$\frac{7}{8}$" × 4" × $12\frac{9}{16}$"	See procedure before cutting
Plinth back	1	$\frac{3}{4}$" × 4" × $29\frac{1}{2}$"	See procedure before cutting
Shelves	3	$\frac{3}{4}$" × $11\frac{1}{8}$" × $28\frac{1}{4}$"	
Floor	1	$\frac{3}{4}$" × $10\frac{1}{4}$" × $28\frac{1}{4}$"	
Corner-strengthener parts	8	$\frac{3}{4}$" × $3\frac{3}{4}$" × 2"	
Board for shelf standards	1	1" × $4\frac{1}{2}$" × $36\frac{3}{8}$"	Cut into $\frac{3}{4}$" strips when notched
Shelf support pieces	6	$\frac{19}{32}$" × $1\frac{1}{4}$" × 10"	
Shiplap boards	—	$\frac{3}{8}$" thick	See procedure for quantity and sizes

Table 6. Bookcase Parts List

DOVETAILED BOX

Choose the lumber for the sides carefully because it will be visible inside and out. The bottom of the box will be covered by the floor and, unless you are making a tall bookcase, the underside of the box top will not be seen.

The box top and bottom are $\frac{1}{2}$" thick rather than $\frac{3}{8}$", as in the chest of drawers. The added thickness provides extra stiffness to the open-fronted box.

Read through the procedures detailed in Chapter 19 for making the dovetailed box. Make the box parts, with top and bottom $\frac{1}{2}$" thick. Because they are thicker, make them directly from 4/4 lumber without resawing it.

Mark the box parts as though they were for a drawer, and then dovetail them as described in Chapter 7. The additional fingerplate adjustments required for the chest of drawers' dovetailed box are not necessary here, because this box top and bottom are $\frac{1}{2}$" thick.

After dovetailing the box, sand the inside faces of the side panels to 120-grit with a random-orbit sander.

Glue and clamp the box as described for the chest of drawers.

FRONT AND BACK FRAME COMPONENTS

Make four stiles using lumber that will be defect-free on the following faces:

- For the front stiles: front face and both side faces.
- For the back stiles: both side faces.

Note that, as in all the projects, left and right are as seen from the front of the piece.

The front faces of the back stiles will be covered by the shelf standards, as will the back faces of the front stiles.

Using the procedure described under "Frame Components" in Chapter 19, cut the stiles to lengths that match the dovetailed box.

Mill the center back rail, but leave it with at least $\frac{1}{2}$" extra length.

Make the L-rail components $\frac{1}{8}$" wider and at least $\frac{1}{2}$" longer than their final sizes. You need four pieces $\frac{7}{8}$" $\times$ $2\frac{1}{8}$" $\times$ $27\frac{1}{8}$" and four pieces $\frac{7}{8}$" $\times$ $1\frac{1}{2}$" $\times$ $27\frac{1}{8}$". Choose lumber that will give a perfect face and edge on each $2\frac{1}{8}$"-wide component of the front rails. Label each individual component and mark the outside faces of the front $2\frac{1}{8}$"-wide pieces.

Glue the two parts of each rail together. For convenience, clamp up all eight parts as a group:

- Apply PVA glue to one edge of each $1\frac{1}{2}$"-wide piece, and press it to the wide face of a $2\frac{1}{8}$"-wide piece; place the rail on a flat surface with the widest part of the L down, and clamp across all four L-rails lightly with three pipe clamps **(20.8)**.
- Use a hammer and a block of wood to knock all the components down onto the flat surface so the faces and edges are flush where they join. It is all right if they are out of flush by up to $\frac{1}{32}$" because they are going to be jointed

again along the glue line after the glue is set.

- Tighten the clamps a little more, and then turn the whole assembly over and fix additional clamps over the other side. Remove the clamps from underneath, and place these over the top also **(20.9)**.
- Flip the assembly back over, and remove the squeeze-out from the inside corners after the glue has gelled.
- After the glue has set, lightly joint the widest face of each L-rail to make the two components flush at their junction. Hold the $2\frac{1}{8}$" faces to the jointer fence to maintain squareness. Pass the jointed rails through the planer to reduce their dimensions to 2" $\times$ $2\frac{1}{4}$".

20.8 The first stage in clamping the glued L-rails

20.9 Turn the clamped L-rails over and fix more clamps to the other side

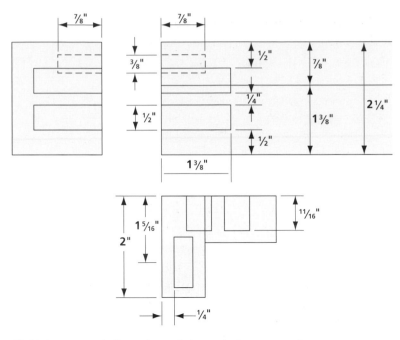

20.10 Layout and dimensions of the main frame mortises

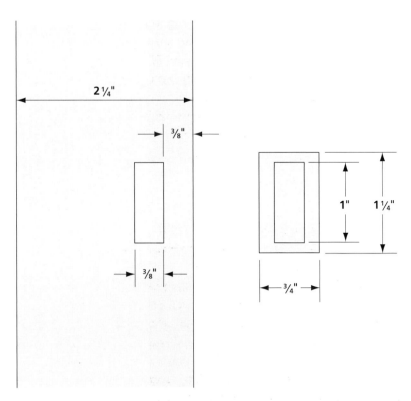

20.11 Mortises in ends of cross-rail and at midlength of back stiles

- Use a card scraper to remove glue stains and milling marks from the inside faces and corners. Sand the inside faces and the $\frac{7}{8}$"-wide edges.
- Cut square an end of each L-rail and the end of the center back rail.
- Now cut all rails to length. Use the procedure described in "Frame Components" in Chapter 19 to match the rail lengths to the dovetailed box dimensions and stile thicknesses.

SCREW HOLES FOR TOP

Drill clearance holes through the upper ($2\frac{1}{4}$") faces of the top rails for #8 flathead (FH) screws. Position the holes $1\frac{1}{4}$" from the outside faces at 2" from each end and at the center. Countersink the holes for the screw heads.

Also drill and countersink $\frac{1}{4}$" holes in the top of the dovetailed box. Drill one at each end of the top, midway between the front and back edges and 1" from the inside faces of the side panels.

JOINERY

The frame joinery is all mortise-and-tenon. It is simpler than for the chest of drawers because there are no triple mortises. The extra mortise for each L-rail is made using the standard procedure.

Review the marking and mortising procedure in Chapter 6.

The layout and dimensions of the double $\frac{1}{2}$" mortises and the single $\frac{3}{8}$" mortises in the L-rails and stiles are shown in **20.10**. The $\frac{3}{8}$" mortises in the end of the cross-rail and at midlength of the back stiles are shown in **20.11**.

Marking Out

Sort the frame components, and mark them for position and orientation. For

20.12 A short line on the end face of an L-rail marks the midlength of the ⅜" mortise

example, mark FR, FL, BR, or BL on the stiles to designate them front right, etc., with arrows to indicate which ends are the tops. Mark on the reference faces, that is, the front faces of the front stiles and the back faces of the back stiles. Use left and right as seen from the front. Mark "up" arrows on the reference (outside) faces of the L-rails and the center back rail.

Set a marking gauge to 1 5/16", and mark a short line on the end faces of each L-rail at this distance from the 2¼" faces. These marks define the midlengths of the ⅜" mortises. Keep the gauge marks clear of the edges, and use a square and pencil to extend them to the 2" faces, but not onto the 2" faces **(20.12)**.

With the same gauge setting, mark the centers of the corresponding mortises in the stiles: L face of FR stile, R face of FL stile, R face of BL stile, and L face of BR stile—all as seen from the front of the bookcase. Keep the gauge marks away from the edges, but extend them in pencil to the back or front outside faces as appropriate. Again, do not draw them onto the outside faces. Draw an accurate ⅜" × 1" mortise centered on one of these marks and set in ¼" from the outside face of a stile.

Mark the midlengths of the back stiles on their 2¼" inside faces, and extend these

marks to the back faces. Mark the end faces of the center back rail at ⅝" from the top edge. Extend this mark to reach the back face of the rail. Draw an accurate ⅜" × 1" mortise on one of the back stiles. The mortise must be centered on the mark and set in ⅜" from the back face **(20.11)**. Draw a similar mortise on one end of the center back rail set in 3/16" from the back face. The different insets will result in the back rail being set in 3/16" from the stile, which is required for fixing the shiplap backboards.

On the 2¼" face of one L-rail, draw as accurately as you can a pair of ½" × 1⅜" double mortises. Position them ½" from each edge and separated by ¼", as shown in the joinery drawings. Draw another pair at the opposite end of the rail. Put an X at each end against the mortises nearest the reference face of the rail (the 2" face), as for the one shown in **19.14a** in Chapter 19.

Use a pencil or a lumber crayon to sketch all the mortises on the rails and stiles at their approximate positions **(19.15** in Chapter 19). This step is simply to reduce the risk of error when you use the mortising jig, so very rough sketches will be appropriate. Mark an X near the reference face of the rail or stile at every double-mortise position.

Mortising

Follow the routine procedure for using the mortising jig: (1) Start with a component that has a mortise accurately drawn on it; (2) place the reference face of the component against the jig reference face; (3) clamp it with the mortise centerline at the jig's center mark; (4) center the router on the mortise drawing; (5) fix the jig fence parallel to the jig reference face and against the router base; (6) set the jig side stops and the cutter depth stop; (7) cut the mortise; and (8) repeat for the other mortises with the same inset.

Always check to see that the X is toward the fence. Before changing any jig settings, check that all the appropriate mortises have been cut at the existing settings.

Clamp the L-rails vertically into the jig to cut the $\frac{3}{8}$" × 1" × $\frac{7}{8}$" mortises in their ends. Cut the corresponding mortises in the stiles with the stiles held horizontally in the jig.

Cut the center mortise in the back stiles with the stiles horizontal in the jig. Cut the corresponding mortises in the center back rails with the rails held vertical in the jig.

Cut the double $\frac{1}{2}$" × $1\frac{3}{8}$" × $\frac{11}{16}$" mortises in the L-rails with the rails horizontal in the jig. Cut the $\frac{1}{2}$" mortises in the stiles with the stiles vertical.

Tenons

Use the procedure described under "Making and Gluing Tenons" in Chapter 6 to make sixteen $\frac{1}{2}$" × $\frac{3}{4}$" × $2\frac{1}{4}$" tenons and ten $\frac{3}{8}$" × $\frac{15}{16}$" × $1\frac{3}{4}$" tenons.

Before cutting the tenons to length, measure the depths of the mortises, and make the tenons short enough to avoid hitting the bottom in the mortises. The $\frac{3}{4}$" dimension of the twin $\frac{1}{2}$" tenons will allow you to sand or plane them flush with the rails after assembly. Note that the $\frac{1}{2}$" tenons do not extend to the radius at the end of each mortise.

The $\frac{15}{16}$" widths of the $\frac{3}{8}$" tenons will allow the top and bottom rails to be adjusted to make them flush with the ends of the stiles.

RABBETS FOR BACK FRAME

The overlapping boards of the back will fit into rabbets in the back faces of the stiles and L-rails of the back frame. The rabbets are $\frac{3}{16}$" deep by $\frac{5}{8}$" wide (**20.13**) and are very simple to make on the table saw before assembling the frame.

20.13 Rabbeted back frame

With a pencil or lumber crayon, draw a line on the back faces of the back stiles and L-rails to indicate roughly where the rabbets will be. Place the stiles and L-rails of the back frame near the table saw, but keep the front frame components somewhere else to avoid rabbeting them by mistake.

The following procedure produces full-length rabbets in the stiles. Stopped rabbets would be more appropriate, but it is safer to rabbet the stiles this way and then stop the rabbets by gluing small pieces of wood at each end after the frame is assembled. The stile rabbet in **20.13** has been stopped by this method.

Rabbet the back frame parts as follows:
- Set the table-saw blade height to $\frac{5}{8}$", and set the rip fence to $\frac{3}{16}$" from the outside faces of the teeth. The fence will be about $\frac{1}{16}$" from the blade. Check the settings with a piece of scrap wood.
- Pass the bottom edge of the top rail over the blade while you hold its back face to the fence.
- Pass the top edge of the bottom rail over the blade; hold its back face to the fence.
- Pass the inside $2\frac{1}{4}$" face of each back stile over the blade while you hold the $1\frac{3}{4}$" back face to the fence.

- Set the blade height to $\frac{3}{16}$" and the fence to $1\frac{1}{8}$" from the inside (nearest) faces of the teeth.
- Pass the back face of each stile over the blade while you hold its outside face to the fence. The outside faces are the right face of the right stile and the left face of the left stile, all as viewed from the front of the bookcase. This step will complete the stile rabbets.
- Set the fence to $1\frac{3}{8}$" from the blade, and pass the top rail over the blade with its 2"-wide back face down and its top face against the fence.
- Complete the rabbeting process by passing the back face of the bottom rail over the blade while you hold its bottom face against the fence.

CENTER BACK RAIL

After mortising the center back rail, round over its top and bottom inside edges with a $\frac{3}{8}$"-radius round-over cutter in the router. Sand the inside faces to 220-grit.

ASSEMBLING THE FRAME

Sand the $2\frac{1}{4}$" inside faces of the stiles—not the $1\frac{3}{4}$" gluing surfaces. Use sandpaper glued to a wood block when sanding near the mortises. Also sand the center back rail.

Lay out the necessary tools for assembly: polyurethane glue, glue brush, small protective pads of thin MDF or similar material, water for dampening the tenons, two pipe clamps for the front frame, and three pipe clamps for the back frame.

Assemble the frames:

- Place the components of the back frame on the bench in their approximate assembled positions.
- Wet the tenons slightly.
- Apply glue to all mortises in the rails and stiles.

- Apply glue to one end of all tenons and insert them into the rail mortises. Apply glue to the other ends of the tenons.
- Turn one of the stiles so that its mortised face is up. Then take the rails and push the glued tenons as far as possible into the stile mortises.
- Place the other stile over the assembly and pull it down to partially insert the other tenons.
- Check to see that up faces are up and outside faces are outside.
- Lay the frame down with the outside faces up.
- Tap the $\frac{1}{2}$" tenons further into the mortises, and then place a clamp over the frame at each mortised position.
- Slip protective pads between the clamp jaws and the stiles and under the clamp pipes.
- Tighten the clamps to pull the tenons fully in.
- Slacken the clamps enough to allow the top and bottom rails to be tapped flush with the ends of the stiles.
- Move the clamp pipes at each end clear of the frame so the jaws apply pressure through the center of the $2\frac{1}{4}$" stile faces (**20.14**). Tighten all clamps fully.
- Check for squareness with a bar gauge. Angle the clamps if necessary to equalize the diagonals (**19.38** under "Frame Assembly" in Chapter 19).

20.14 The back frame in clamps

Because the center rail is in the way, you may find it easiest to turn the assembly over to use the bar gauge.

- Check for twist with winding sticks on the rails at each end; if necessary, slacken a clamp and adjust the height of one corner.

Assembling the front frame is slightly simpler because there is no center rail.

After the glue has set, remove squeeze-out from the inside corners with a sharp chisel.

STOPPING THE BACK STILE RABBETS

Make some small pieces of wood: $\frac{1}{4}$" thick and slightly longer than the spaces they will fill. Try to find pieces that approximately match the grain of the stiles. Glue and clamp them into the spaces; make them fit tightly, flush with the ends of the stiles (**20.15**). When the glue has set, plane

20.15 Stop the rabbets by gluing and clamping small pieces of wood into them; sand the pieces flush when the glue has set

and sand them flush with the surface. Use a sharp chisel to chop the inside ends flush with the rails.

FRAMES-TO-BOX ASSEMBLY

Follow the procedure described in "Frames-to-Box" Assembly in Chapter 19.

Work after Assembly

The procedures are the same here as for the Chest of Drawers project, which describes them fully. The stages are as follows: (1) level the carcass top and bottom; (2) level the carcass sides; (3) cut the front stile chamfers with a router and a chisel; and (4) sand the carcass sides and front.

PLINTH BASE

In **20.1**, the bookcase is shown with a base with a plain front and sides—unlike the chest of drawers, which has a plinth shaped to suggest bracket feet. Although you could shape the bookcase base, a plain base seems more appropriate for a library piece. Follow the procedures for making the chest of drawers' base in Chapter 19, but omit the shaping process if you prefer to leave the base plain. Even for a plain base, it is still a good idea to make the $\frac{3}{4}$"-deep straight cut in the back piece.

Since the bookcase plinth is only 4" high, while the chest of drawers plinth is 5" high, you must make two other modifications to the procedures in Chapter 19:

1. The router movement on the plinth mortising jigs must be reduced by $\frac{1}{2}$" on either side. This can be accomplished simply by sticking a piece of $\frac{1}{2}$"-wide wood to each side stop with double-sided tape.
2. The corner strengtheners must be $3\frac{3}{4}$" wide, not $4\frac{3}{4}$" like those for the chest of drawers.

THE TOP

Make the top as a $\frac{7}{8}$"-thick glued-up panel large enough to overhang the bookcase front and both sides by at least $1\frac{1}{4}$": that is, make it at least $13\frac{1}{4}$" wide and $32\frac{1}{2}$" long. After belt-sanding the panel, joint the back edge and then place it on the bookcase, flush with the back edge and overhanging each end about equally. Draw the outline of the carcass on the underside in pencil.

The edges of the top must have strips of $\frac{1}{4}$"-thick wood glued to them, as illustrated by stage 1 in **20.16**. The thickened edges must then be cut at an angle (stage 2) and then sanded to the final shape shown at stage 3.

Make a front edging strip $\frac{1}{4}$" thick by $\frac{3}{8}$" wide and a little longer than the panel.

Make two $\frac{1}{4}$"-thick side edging strips, wider than the panel but only $\frac{3}{8}$" long. The grain will run parallel with the $\frac{3}{8}$" dimension. It will probably be easiest to first make a strip similar to those shown in **19.100** and **19.101** in the Chest of Drawers project, and then to cut it into two side strips.

Read the procedure in Chapter 19 for gluing on the edging strips to the chest of drawers top; then, at the pencil line, glue a $\frac{3}{8}$" face of the front strip to the underside of the panel for the bookcase top.

Glue a side strip to the underside at each end about $\frac{1}{32}$" outside the pencil lines to produce $\frac{1}{16}$" total side clearance when the top is fixed to the carcass. The top with edging strips glued to the underside is shown in **20.17**.

Shape the edges in three stages: (1) cut the front and side edges square to the top surface at exactly 1" from the inside faces of the strips; (2) cut these edges at an angle to leave them ready for final shaping; and (3) sand the edges to final shape.

The vertical and angled cuts must be made at precise distances from the inside

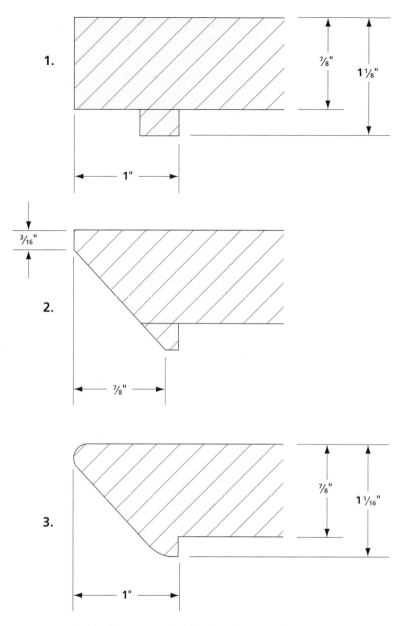

20.16 Three stages in shaping the top edges

20.17 The top with edging strips glued to the underside

edges of the thickener strips. The first step is to mark the top surface with the outline of those edges. Using a square, mark lines with pencil from the inside edges of the strips to the ends and front and back edges of the panel. Next, connect the marks with lines across the top of the panel to transfer the strip positions onto the top surface. Draw a second set of lines exactly 1" outward from the first one.

A top marked with these two sets of lines is shown in **20.18**. The outer lines mark the final perimeter of the top.

20.18 Two sets of lines mark the top; the outer ones denote the final perimeter

20.19 Straightedge saw guide clamped to test piece; a line is drawn on the test piece side at ³⁄₁₆" below the top face

Now cut the top to final size along the outer lines. Cut the ends first and then the front edge with a circular saw guided by a straightedge. Find the right position for the straightedge by making a test cut on scrap wood while the base plate of the saw is guided by a straightedge. Measure the distance from the cut to the straightedge.

When you have cut the top to final size, you must find the correct saw base-plate angle and straightedge guide position for making the angled cuts. The procedure is similar to that used to make the chest of drawers top:

- Make a test piece about 4" wide and 10" long, the same thickness as the top plus the edging strip ($1\frac{1}{8}$").
- Cut the ends of the test piece square. Draw a horizontal line on one side edge $\frac{3}{16}$" from the top face. The line on a test piece clamped to the bench is shown in **20.19**.
- Set the base plate of the circular saw to 42 degrees.
- Clamp the test piece to the bench so that it projects over the edge by at least 2" (**20.19**). Across it, clamp a straightedge square to the sides and far enough from the front end to allow the circular saw to cut through the test piece. Draw a pencil line on the test piece to record the position of the straightedge.
- Cut through the test piece while you hold the base plate of the saw against the straightedge.
- Using a square, draw a line down the side edge of the test piece from the top surface to where the cut meets the bottom face. Draw another line to where the cut meets the horizontal line (**20.20**).
- Measure the distance between these two vertical lines. If it is less than

$\frac{7}{8}$", increase the base-plate angle by 1 degree; if it is more than $\frac{7}{8}$", decrease the angle by 1 degree.

- Cut at least $\frac{3}{8}$" off the end of the test piece, and clamp it to the bench with the straightedge clamped at the same distance from the end as before. Draw a line at the front of the straightedge to record its position.
- Make another angled cut, draw new vertical lines on the side edge, and then measure between them. Repeat the above procedure until the distance between the lines is $\frac{7}{8}$".

When the angle is correct, find where to clamp the straightedge to produce the right edge thickness:

- Measure the distance from the tip of the cut end to the straightedge position.
- Subtract $\frac{3}{16}$" from that measurement. This is the distance from the end where the straightedge must be clamped for the next test cut.
- Cut off the tip again, and then square a line across the top face at the position calculated for the straightedge. Clamp the straightedge at this line and make another angled cut.
- Repeat if necessary with the straightedge a little closer to or further from the end until you find the position that leaves $\frac{3}{16}$" of the squared end uncut by the angled blade, as shown in 20.21.

When you have found the right settings, use the same setup to cut the front and side edges of the top:

- Fix a guide for the saw at the required distance from one end of the top. Make an angled cut at this end.
- Repeat at the other end and then at the front edge to give the edges the profile shown in 20.22. Do not cut the back edge.

20.20 Draw two vertical lines from where the angled cut meets the horizontal line and the bottom face; measure the distance between these lines

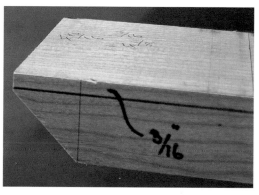

20.21 The saw guide is correctly placed when $\frac{3}{16}$" of the squared end is left uncut by the angled blade

20.22 The edges of the top after the angled saw cuts are made

20.23 Shelf support pieces

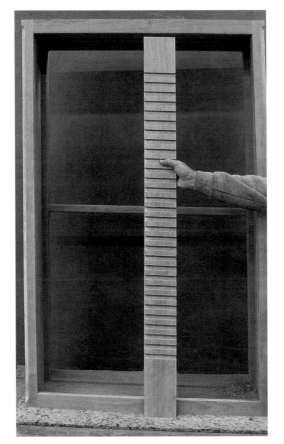

20.24 Cut notches across a wide board

Reduce the thickness of the edging strips to ³⁄₁₆" either with a block and coarse sandpaper or by careful use of a random-orbit sander.

Use the procedure described under "Final Shaping and Sanding" in Chapter 19 to sand the edges to the desired shape.

Predrill the top for the fixing screws following the procedure under "Fixing the Top" in Chapter 19.

SHELF SUPPORTS

The vertical standards are notched at 1¼" intervals to provide for adjustable shelves. However, the shelves are not supported directly by the standards but by small horizontal strips of wood that fit into the notches. These notched standards and their small support strips are shown in **20.7** and **20.23**.

Notching the standards is similar to making finger joints. As with finger joints, small discrepancies in the intervals between notches can add up, causing progressive differences in the positions of the notches on a set of standards. The solution is to cut notches across a wide board and then to rip it into individual standards (**20.24** and **20.25**).

Make a ⅞" × 4½" × 37" board with the ends cut square. Notch it as follows:

• Fit a ⅝" dado blade into the table saw and set the blade height to ⅜".

• Check that the miter gauge is cutting square with the fence, and then fit a new wood fence to the gauge that extends beyond the dado blade.

• Cut a ⅝" slot across the face of the board at about 8" from one end. Push the miter gauge forward far enough for the dado blade to cut a slot in the new fence.

- Fix a $\frac{3}{8}$" × $\frac{5}{8}$" × 6" peg in the fence slot to extend at least $4\frac{1}{2}$" at the front. Make the peg an easy fit in the slot in the $4\frac{1}{2}$" board. Fix it in the fence slot with a screw and/or some glue.
- Remove the fence from the miter gauge, and reposition it $1\frac{1}{4}$" to the right of its original position so that the peg is $\frac{5}{8}$" beyond the dado blade.
- Fit the slot in the board over the peg. Cut a second slot separated from the first one by $\frac{5}{8}$".

Continue the process until you have a series of regularly spaced slots reaching to about 5" from the other end of the board.

Make four standards from the board:
- Sand the notched face of the board with a random-orbit sander and a 120-grit disc.
- Sand the sharp edges of the notches to soften them by making one pass across each edge with the sander tilted.
- Rip the notched board to make four $\frac{7}{8}$"-wide shelf standards, jointing the board edges before each rip. Plane the ripped edges to reduce each standard to $\frac{3}{4}$" in width.
- Sand the planed and jointed side edges using a random-orbit sander and 120-grit disc.
- Sand the side edges of the teeth to soften them.
- Soften the four sharp corners of each tooth by giving each one a light dab with the sander.
- Drill and countersink the standards to fit #6 FH screws in the first, middle, and last notches.

For each shelf, make two pieces of wood $\frac{19}{32}$" × $1\frac{1}{4}$" × 10". Cut $\frac{3}{4}$" × $1\frac{3}{4}$" notches in each end, as shown in **20.26**.

20.25 Rip the notched board to make individual shelf standards

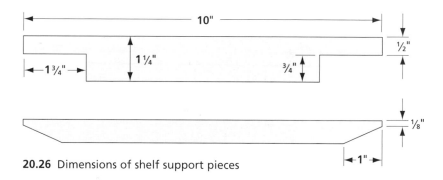

20.26 Dimensions of shelf support pieces

The safest way to do this is with a bandsaw or handsaw.

Shape the ends as shown in the drawing using a bandsaw and then a hand plane. Sand the pieces with a random-orbit sander and 120-grit disc. Soften the edges by hand with sandpaper.

SHELVES AND FLOOR

Make two strips of wood approximately $\frac{3}{8}$" × $\frac{3}{4}$" × 30", and screw or glue them to the bottom rails of the carcass $\frac{3}{4}$" below the top edges. The strips will support a $\frac{3}{4}$"-thick floor flush with the rail edges.

Make the shelves and the floor by gluing together narrow strips of wood, about 2" to 3" wide. Reverse the growth-ring curvature of every second strip (see "Furniture Stability" in Chapter 1) to ensure that the free-floating shelves and the loosely fixed floor will stay flat. You will need to use lumber that is defect-free on both faces so that you have flexibility when orienting the strips. Follow the procedures in Chapter 13, Making Wide Panels, and then smooth each panel with a belt sander.

Rip the floor panel to fit between the front and back bottom rails, making it approximately $10\frac{1}{4}$" wide. Rip the shelves to a width $\frac{3}{4}$" less than the distance from the rabbets in the back stiles to the front faces of the front stiles: That will be approximately $10\frac{13}{16}$".

Cut one end of the floor and the shelves square to their side edges; then cut the other ends to a length $\frac{1}{16}$" less than the distance between the bookcase sides. Use a sliding bar gauge to measure this distance.

Carefully measure how far the stiles intrude into the floor area. Mark these areas on the floor using a square. These areas must be cut out, the safest methods for which are with a bandsaw or with a fine-cutting handsaw.

Alternatively, you could make straighter, cleaner cuts with a table saw. If you use the table saw, you need to take special precautions because the blade guard has to be removed for this operation and the blade has to be raised to maximum height. One possible arrangement is shown in **20.27** and **20.28**.

The miter gauge arrangement shown in **20.27** and **20.28** has a high fence and a baseboard fitted with a tall piece of wood that is parallel to the blade, offering protection from it. A gap between the fence and the tall piece of wood allows workpieces set on edge to be held to the fence. The edge of the baseboard shows exactly where a workpiece will be cut.

A stop block clamped to the table limits the miter gauge's travel, and another block on the back of the fence guards the blade when it emerges from the fence. You could still touch the blade, but this arrangement greatly reduces the risk.

After notching the floor around the stiles, check to see how it fits in the bookcase. Drive a couple of screws into the corners to make it easy to lift out the floor again. (The screw holes will be covered by the shelf standards when they are fitted.)

When the floor is in place, screw the shelf standards to the stiles with #6 × 1" FH screws. The longer unnotched ends will rest on the floor. Clamp the standards flush with the sides of the stiles while you fix them.

Next, notch the shelves to fit around the stiles and shelf standards. If you use the table saw for this step, you must finish the deeper cuts either by hand or with a bandsaw because a 10" table-saw blade cannot be raised quite high enough.

Remove the shelves, standards, and floor. Round over the front top edges of the shelves with a router fitted with a $\frac{3}{8}$"-radius round-over bit. Sand the shelves and the floor to 220-grit.

THE BOOKCASE BACK

Vertical boards with overlapping rabbets have an attractive appearance in the back of open-fronted pieces; also, they offer a good way to deal with expansion and shrinkage.

For the bookcase, several $\frac{3}{8}$"-thick boards of random widths are rabbeted on opposite edges and faces so they can overlap, as shown in **20.29**.

One edge of each board is fixed by screws; the other edge is held by the next board overlapping it. Expansion is allowed for by making the overlap narrower than the rabbets. The last board is fixed by screws at both edges. Provided that the two last screws are no more than 3" apart, any expansion of the wood between them will not be a problem.

To construct the back, choose lumber of 3" to 5" widths that is flat enough to be resawn and planed to $\frac{3}{8}$" thickness. One face of all resawn pieces will be visible from the front of the bookcase, so the lumber must be capable of yielding two $\frac{3}{8}$" pieces, each of which has one good face. Not only does the number of pieces needed depend on their widths, but the overlaps lose $\frac{1}{4}$" of width per piece and the two end boards overlap the stiles by $\frac{1}{2}$" each.

Cut the 4/4 lumber $\frac{1}{2}$" longer than final length and in random widths between 3" and 5". Cut enough to make $\frac{3}{8}$" boards with a total width at least 6" wider than the back opening.

Flatten and plane the blanks, preserving as much of their thickness as possible. Joint one edge of each, and rip the opposite edges to make the blanks parallel-sided. Lightly joint the ripped edges; then resaw the blanks and plane the sawn faces.

The widths of individual boards may not be entirely suitable to match the opening, even though their total width is adequate. The last board to be fixed may have to be made very narrow. To see how the widths will work out, check the width of the opening between the back stiles, add 1" to allow for $\frac{1}{2}$" overlap on each side, and then add $\frac{1}{4}$" for every board

20.27 This miter gauge setup offers protection from the table-saw blade when making deep cuts into a board held vertical against the fence

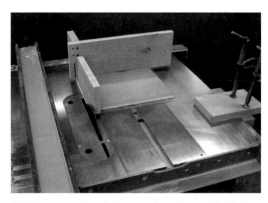

20.28 A stop block clamped to the table limits the miter gauge's travel

20.29 Boards that are $\frac{3}{8}$" thick are rabbeted on opposite edges and faces so they can overlap and allow for expansion

that will be used. This is the required total width of the boards. If eight boards are used for the 32"-wide bookcase, their total width should be $26\frac{5}{8}$" + 1" + 2", which equals $29\frac{5}{8}$".

Lay down the boards side by side, and mark the left- and right-hand ones. Starting from the left-hand board, measure out the total required width and see how wide the right-hand board must be if it is the last one to be fixed.

If the right-hand board will need to be narrow (say, less than $2\frac{1}{2}$"), reduce the widths of one or two others just enough to allow a reasonable width for the right-hand one. Do not cut the right-hand board to width at this time.

If more $\frac{3}{8}$" boards are needed, make them now.

Cut one end of every board square with the sides, and mark these ends. Then place the squared end of one piece against the chest back, resting in the bottom rabbet. Mark the other end for about $\frac{1}{32}$" clearance in the top rabbet. Set up a length stop on a crosscut sled or miter gauge, and cut every piece to this length.

Choose the best face of each board and mark it as the inside face; also, draw an up arrow to designate the top end of each one.

The boards need to be fixed at three points to keep them flat. Stand a board in position in the rabbets and mark where a screw hole is required to fix it to the center back rail. Square a line across the board's back face at this level, and then square lines across it at $\frac{5}{16}$" from each end. Drill clearance holes for #6 FH screws at 1" from the left-hand edge at these three levels. Drill these holes into every board with the drill press set as follows:

- Fix an auxiliary table of plywood, particle board, or wood to the metal drill-press table.
- Fit a $\frac{5}{32}$" drill bit into the chuck.

- To locate the boards for drilling, fix a fence along the auxiliary table 1" behind the drill center. The fence should be long enough to extend from at least 6" left of the drill center to at least 22" to the right of the center. A small chamfer on the bottom edge of the fence will help prevent sawdust from getting between the fence and the boards.
- Fix a stop block to either the fence or the table, $\frac{5}{16}$" to the right of the drill center. A chamfer on the bottom edge of this will also be helpful.
- Place a board on the drill table, back face up, top end to the stop block, and left-hand edge to the fence. Drill the top screw hole **(20.30)**.
- Flip the board over end for end so that its bottom end is against the stop, its inside face is up, and its left-hand edge is still to the fence. Drill a hole at that end.
- Repeat for all other boards.
- Remove the stop block and place the marked slat on the table, top end to the right, with the intermediate screw position centered exactly under the drill bit. Clamp the stop block to the fence so that it touches the right-hand end of the board. Drill the third hole in each slat with the top ends to the right and the back faces up.
- Replace the drill bit with a countersink bit. Remove the stop block.
- If the drill press has a depth stop, set it to countersink the holes to a suitable depth for #6 FH screws, and then countersink every hole. If it has no depth stop, try to countersink every hole to the same depth. Make sure that you are countersinking into the outside (back) faces.
- Leave the countersink bit and the fence in position while you cut rabbets into the boards.

Fit a zero-clearance insert to the table saw. Set the blade height to $\frac{3}{16}$" and the fence to $\frac{3}{8}$" from the outside of the blade teeth (that is, to $\frac{3}{8}$" from the side of the teeth farthest from the fence). Check these settings on a test piece. The cut should be $\frac{3}{16}$" deep and should extend only to $\frac{3}{8}$" from the edge of the test piece.

Take the two boards marked left and right and set them aside for the moment. They must be dealt with differently from the others because they are the end boards.

Start the table saw. Pass one of the ordinary boards over the blade with its outside face up, its bottom end leading, and its left-hand edge (the edge 1" from the holes) to the fence. Flip over the board and pass it over the blade again. This time the inside face will be up and the right-hand edge will be to the fence, and the bottom end still leading. Repeat for all the other boards except for the ones you set aside.

Take the set-aside right-hand board and pass it over the blade with its outside face up, its left-hand edge to the fence, and the bottom end leading. Do not turn it over or make a second cut. Set it aside again.

Take the left-hand set-aside board and pass it over the blade with its inside face up, right-hand edge to the fence, and bottom end leading. Do not turn it over for a second cut. Set it aside again.

Now set the blade to cut $\frac{3}{8}$" deep and the fence to $\frac{3}{16}$" from the near side of the teeth. Check these settings on a test piece. Fix a featherboard just before the blade to hold the boards against the fence when you stand them on edge. Set the featherboard about $\frac{1}{4}$" from the fence. This is very important if any of the boards are bowed or cupped. Pass each board (except for the set-aside ones) over the blade with its outside face to the fence and its left-hand edge down, bottom end leading, to complete the rabbet in the inside face and

20.30 Drilling the top screw hole in the back boards

to leave $\frac{3}{16}$" of thickness in the outside edge. After completing each inside face rabbet, flip over the board and complete the rabbet in the outside face with the inside face to the fence, bottom end still leading. On every pass, the previous $\frac{3}{16}$"-deep cut must be facing the blade at the bottom edge of the board.

When all the ordinary boards are done, take the set-aside ones and complete the single rabbet in one edge of each. Keep the inside face of the left-hand board to the fence and the outside face of the right-hand board to the fence, bottom end leading on both, and the $\frac{3}{16}$"-deep cut showing on both.

Sand the boards to 220-grit with a random-orbit sander. As a finishing touch, sand a small bevel on the top outside edges with a sanding block and 80-grit paper.

The boards are now ready to be screwed to the back of the chest in shiplap fashion. To help achieve regular spacing, make a gauge from a $\frac{1}{8}$"-thick strip of wood that is just a few inches long for positioning the boards with the rabbets overlapping by $\frac{1}{4}$".

Take the board marked as the left-hand end, and rest its bottom end in the bottom rail rabbet. Place the $\frac{1}{8}$" gauge between the board and the inside edge of the left stile rabbet. With the board held in this position and set firmly against the gauge, install the bottom screw, then the top screw, and, lastly, the middle screw. Place the second board in position by using the gauge to maintain a $\frac{1}{8}$" expansion gap between it and the first board; hold it hard against the gauge, and install the bottom screw. Move the gauge to the top end, and install the top screw and then the middle screw. Continue fixing the boards, using the spacer to position them. Stop when only one more is required.

Rip the right-hand edge of the right-hand end board to produce $\frac{1}{8}$" expansion gaps on each side when it is fitted. Make a second set of screw holes 1" from the right-hand edge. Square a line across the back, through the center of each existing hole; position each line under the countersink bit that is still in the drill press; and make the countersinks. Drill through with the $\frac{5}{32}$" bit. Screw the board in position to complete the back.

21 End Table or Bedside Table Project

THIS ATTRACTIVE SIDE TABLE CAN be made in two versions (21.1). If you intend to place it at the end of a sofa, the front-to-back depth should be 26". If you want to use it for a bedside table, a more appropriate depth is 17".

Making the table involves mortise-and-tenon joinery, dovetailing, glued-up panels, and a drawer. However, it is a relatively simple project and can be completed quickly.

How the table base is constructed is shown in 21.2 and 21.3. Two wide side aprons, a wide back apron, and two front rails are tenoned into four legs. Stretchers and substretchers near the bottoms of the legs add stiffness and strength as well as provide a framework to which to fix the shelf. The grain direction of the side aprons and stretchers runs from the front to the back of the table, and the grain of the back apron, front rails, and sub-stretchers runs from side to side. The footprint of the base is therefore stable because there is no seasonal side-to-side or front-to-back expansion or shrinkage. The drawer opening formed by the front rails and legs also has constant dimensions.

In the assembly procedure, two side frames (each comprising two legs, a side apron, and a stretcher) are glued together first (as seen in 21.30). The side frames are then joined together by the back apron, the front rails, and the substretchers (21.3).

The table includes several other parts: a top, a shelf, cock beading around the drawer opening, facilities for fixing the top and shelf, supports and guides for the drawer, and the five parts of the drawer.

21.1 End table: 21"W x 25"H x 26"D
Bedside table: 21"W x 25"H x 17"D

21.2 Table base construction

21.3 Table base assembled

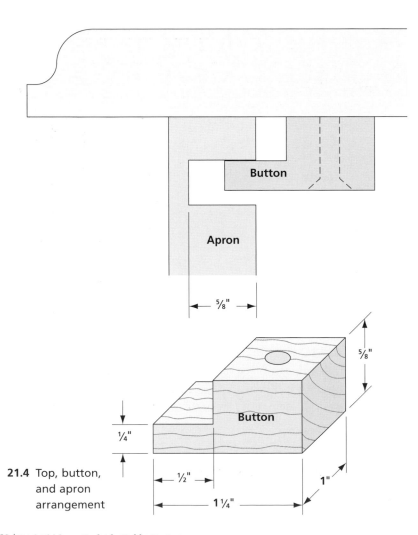

Button

Apron

5/8"

5/8"

Button

1/4"

1/2"

1"

1 1/4"

21.4 Top, button, and apron arrangement

The top, the shelf, and the drawer bottom are made by gluing narrow pieces together to achieve the required widths. Since the shelf and drawer bottom are only ⅜" thick, they are made from resawn 4/4 lumber.

Edge treatments are simple: The shelf edges are rounded, and the top has a routered Roman ogee edge.

The drawer construction is the same as for the Chest of Drawers project. However, the grain direction of the side aprons allows the drawer bearers to be glued to them without allowing for any expansion.

The grain directions of the top and shelf go from the front to the back of the table, so their seasonal movement will be from side to side. This movement is allowed for by the way they are fixed to the carcass. Slots are cut into the inside faces of the side aprons, and wood "buttons" are inserted into these and fixed to the top. When the top expands or contracts, the buttons move further into or out of the slots (**21.4**). A similar arrangement is made at the back apron, but here a button is glued into a central slot so that the top remains centered and expands equally at each side. The button positions are shown in **21.5**. At the front, the top is fixed by a screw through the center of the top rail.

The shelf is too thin for buttons to be screwed to it, so small blocks of wood are glued to the underside to solve this problem. The bottoms of the blocks are level with the bottoms of the substretchers, so thin pieces of wood screwed to the blocks can hold the shelf to the substretchers and allow seasonal movement. These arrangements are shown in **21.6** to **21.8**.

The shelf does not extend between the front legs or between the back legs, so the legs will not interfere with sideways expansion. Seasonal expansion will be similar to that of the top.

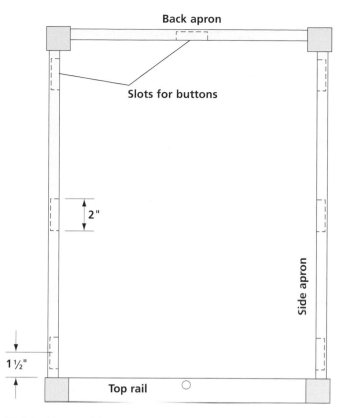

21.5 Button positions

21.6 Thin pieces of wood screwed to glued blocks hold the shelf to the substretchers

21.7 The shelf fixings allow for seasonal movement

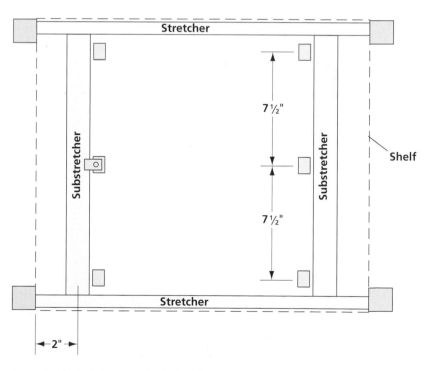

21.8 Shelf, stretchers, and substretchers

DRAWER OPENING

The bottom rail, below the drawer front, must be positioned so that the opening totals the width of the drawer front plus two thicknesses of beading plus a suitable expansion gap. In **21.9**, the bottom rail is $4\frac{5}{8}$" below the top rail to accommodate a drawer front $4\frac{7}{32}$" wide plus two $\frac{3}{16}$"-thick beading strips and an expansion gap of $\frac{1}{32}$".

Before starting work on the table, you must check whether a drawer front $4\frac{7}{32}$" wide will have adequate half-pins when you dovetail it on your dovetail jig. This process is explained in more detail in "Drawer Sizes" in Chapter 7, and at the beginning of the Chest of Drawers project.

If $4\frac{7}{32}$" is not a good drawer width for your dovetail jig, you must change the drawer size to the nearest ideal size for your jig. This adjustment will also call for the following changes:

- Change the bottom rail position to provide the exact opening width for your drawer front plus two $\frac{3}{16}$"-thick beading strips plus a $\frac{1}{32}$" expansion gap.
- Change the positions of the mortises in the front legs to match the new bottom rail position.
- Adjust the widths of the side and back aprons accordingly.

If your drawer width is more than $4\frac{7}{16}$", add the difference to the $5\frac{1}{4}$" and $6\frac{1}{4}$" dimensions shown for the positions of the bottom rail and the leg mortises. Also add the difference to the side and back apron widths, which will be $7\frac{3}{4}$" if the drawer front is $4\frac{7}{16}$". If your drawer width is less than $4\frac{7}{16}$", subtract the difference from each of the three dimensions.

TOP FIXINGS

The top is fixed to the table by wooden buttons with tongues that fit in slots in the side and back aprons **(21.4)**. The button slots are $\frac{3}{8}$" wide, 2" long, and $\frac{5}{8}$" deep, and are centered $1\frac{1}{2}$" from each end of the side aprons as well as at the centers of the side aprons and the back apron. In the front top rail, a central screw hole fixes the top. The tongue at the center of the back apron is glued in place to help keep the top centered.

In regions of dramatic humidity changes, the top might expand in width by as much as $\frac{1}{4}$". Since it is fixed at the centers of the back apron and front rail, the side buttons have to deal with only half the expansion at each side. If the tongues were initially inserted $\frac{7}{16}$" deep, the top can expand by $\frac{3}{16}$" at

21.9 Dimensioned diagram of drawer opening and bottom rail joinery

PART	QTY	SIZE IN INCHES	REMARKS
Legs	4	$1\frac{1}{2}$" × $1\frac{1}{2}$" × $24\frac{1}{2}$"	
Side aprons	2	$\frac{3}{4}$" × $7\frac{3}{4}$" × $11\frac{3}{4}$"	
Back apron	1	$\frac{3}{4}$" × $7\frac{3}{4}$" × $15\frac{1}{2}$"	
Top rail	1	$\frac{5}{8}$" × $1\frac{1}{2}$" × $15\frac{1}{2}$"	
Drawer rail	1	$\frac{3}{4}$" × $2\frac{3}{8}$" × $15\frac{1}{2}$"	
Top	1	$\frac{3}{4}$" × 21" × $17\frac{1}{4}$"	
Shelf	1	$\frac{3}{8}$" × 19" × $11\frac{3}{4}$"	
Stretchers	2	$\frac{3}{4}$" × $1\frac{1}{2}$" × $11\frac{3}{4}$"	
Substretchers	2	$\frac{3}{4}$" × $1\frac{1}{2}$" × $16\frac{7}{8}$"	Length allows for final fitting
Drawer front	1	$\frac{7}{8}$" × $4\frac{1}{4}$" × $15\frac{1}{8}$"	
Drawer back	1	$\frac{3}{4}$" × $4\frac{1}{4}$" × $15\frac{1}{8}$"	
Drawer sides	2	$\frac{1}{2}$" × $4\frac{1}{4}$" × $12\frac{3}{8}$"	
Drawer bottom	1	$\frac{3}{8}$" × 13" × $14\frac{1}{2}$"	
Top-fixing buttons	7	$\frac{5}{8}$" × 1" × $1\frac{1}{4}$"	
Shelf-fixing blocks	6	$\frac{3}{4}$" × $\frac{3}{4}$" × 1"	
Shelf-fixing pads	6	$\frac{1}{4}$" × $\frac{3}{4}$" × $1\frac{1}{2}$"	
Kicker	1	$\frac{25}{32}$" × $\frac{25}{32}$" × 12"	
Drawer bearers	2	$\frac{3}{4}$" × $1\frac{3}{8}$" × 11"	
Drawer guides	2	$\frac{5}{8}$" × 1" × 11"	

Table 7. Bedside Table Parts List

each side before the tongues reach maximum depth. If the top shrinks by $\frac{3}{16}$" at each side, the tongue insertion will still be $\frac{1}{4}$". In practice, the button screw would give a little if necessary, so these allowances are more than adequate regardless of the top's moisture content (MC) at the time of fixing. Nevertheless, good practice requires the initial tongue insertion to be reduced a little if the initial MC is known to be significantly less than 8 percent, and increased if it is known to be higher.

SELECTING THE LUMBER

Most of the comments in the Chest of Drawers project about selecting lumber apply equally to the table, except that the grain pattern of the low tabletop is even more important. In addition, the table has legs with four visible faces each, all of which must be free of defects.

If you wish to, you can make legs with similar patterns on all faces by using lumber that has its growth rings oriented diagonally on the end faces (shown by **1.4** in Chapter 1).

PART	QTY	SIZE IN INCHES	REMARKS
Legs	4	$1\frac{1}{2}" \times 1\frac{1}{2}" \times 24\frac{1}{2}"$	
Side aprons	2	$\frac{3}{4}" \times 7\frac{3}{4}" \times 20\frac{1}{2}"$	
Back apron	1	$\frac{3}{4}" \times 7\frac{3}{4}" \times 15\frac{1}{2}"$	
Top rail	1	$\frac{5}{8}" \times 1\frac{1}{2}" \times 15\frac{1}{2}"$	
Drawer rail	1	$\frac{3}{4}" \times 2\frac{3}{8}" \times 15\frac{1}{2}"$	
Top	1	$\frac{3}{4}" \times 21" \times 26"$	
Shelf	1	$\frac{3}{8}" \times 19" \times 20\frac{1}{2}"$	
Stretchers	2	$\frac{3}{4}" \times 1\frac{1}{2}" \times 20\frac{1}{2}"$	
Substretchers	2	$\frac{3}{4}" \times 1\frac{1}{2}" \times 16\frac{7}{8}"$	Length allows for final fitting
Drawer front	1	$\frac{7}{8}" \times 4\frac{1}{4}" \times 15\frac{1}{8}"$	
Drawer back	1	$\frac{3}{4}" \times 4\frac{1}{4}" \times 15\frac{1}{8}"$	
Drawer sides	2	$\frac{1}{2}" \times 4\frac{1}{4}" \times 21\frac{1}{8}"$	
Drawer bottom	1	$\frac{3}{8}" \times 21\frac{3}{4}" \times 14\frac{1}{2}"$	
Top-fixing buttons	7	$\frac{5}{8}" \times 1" \times 1\frac{1}{4}"$	
Shelf-fixing blocks	6	$\frac{3}{4}" \times \frac{3}{4}" \times 1"$	
Shelf-fixing pads	6	$\frac{1}{4}" \times \frac{3}{4}" \times 1\frac{1}{2}"$	
Kicker	1	$\frac{25}{32}" \times \frac{25}{32}" \times 20"$	
Drawer bearers	2	$\frac{3}{4}" \times 1\frac{3}{8}" \times 19\frac{3}{4}"$	
Drawer guides	2	$\frac{5}{8}" \times 1" \times 19\frac{3}{4}"$	

Table 8. End Table Parts List

MAKING THE TABLE

Cut rough blanks from 4/4 lumber for the side and back aprons, the front top and bottom rails, the stretchers, and the substretchers. Remember that rough blanks are at least $\frac{1}{8}"$ wider and $\frac{1}{2}"$ longer than finished sizes.

Cut leg blanks from 8/4 lumber. Blanks for the top, shelf, and drawer parts can be cut at this time or left until later. If you cut them now, sticker them until they are needed.

Joint one face of each 4/4 frame blank, and then plane them all to $\frac{3}{4}"$ thickness. Continue planing the top rail until it is $\frac{5}{8}"$ thick.

Joint an edge of each planed piece, and then rip them to finished widths. Choose the best face of each piece as the outside face. Decide which edges will be the top edges, and on each top edge, draw an arrow pointing to the outside face.

Cut the planed parts to length as follows:

- Fix a baseboard to the table-saw miter gauge or crosscut sled, as described in Chapter 3, "The Table Saw," to show the exact cutting line. Fit a crosscut blade, and cut a wide piece of material to check that the setup is cutting square. Adjust the sled or miter gauge fence if necessary. When the setup is cutting at exactly 90 degrees to the fence, cut one end of each component square to the edges. Keep the outside faces up to ensure the cleanest possible cut at the outside.
- Mark each component for cutting to its finished length, but mark the sub-stretchers $\frac{1}{8}$" longer than the finished length; doing so will allow them to be cut again later to fit perfectly between the stretchers. Make the length marks on the edges that will face the blade when the outside faces are uppermost. Align each length mark carefully with the baseboard cutting line, and cut each piece to length.

Remove the saw marks from the ripped edges by jointing them lightly. It does not matter that this reduces their widths somewhat.

Joint two adjacent faces of each leg blank square to each other. Plane the legs to $1\frac{1}{2}$" in width and thickness, and then cut one end of each one square to the sides.

Fit an extended fence to the miter gauge, and fix a stop block to it exactly $24\frac{1}{2}$" from the blade. Butt the squared end of each leg against the block and cut the legs to length.

JOINERY

Mortise-and-tenon joints are used for all components of the table base. Some of the tenons can be seen in the partly assembled table shown in **21.10**. Open-topped double mortises and tenons (**21.11**) join the top rail to the front legs in the same way that the stiles and top rails of the bookcase and chest of drawers were joined.

Mortise dimensions are as follows:

Top rail to front legs:
$\frac{3}{8}$" $\times$ $\frac{1}{2}$" $\times$ $1\frac{3}{16}$"
Bottom rail to front legs:
$\frac{3}{8}$" $\times$ $1\frac{1}{2}$" $\times$ $\frac{3}{4}$" deep
Side aprons to front legs:
$\frac{3}{8}$" $\times$ 5" $\times$ $\frac{3}{4}$" deep
Side aprons to back legs:
$\frac{3}{8}$" $\times$ 5" $\times$ $\frac{3}{4}$" deep
Back apron to back legs:
$\frac{3}{8}$" $\times$ 5" $\times$ $\frac{3}{4}$" deep
Stretchers to front legs:
$\frac{3}{8}$" $\times$ 1" $\times$ $\frac{3}{4}$" deep
Stretchers to back legs:
$\frac{3}{8}$" $\times$ 1" $\times$ $\frac{3}{4}$" deep
Stretchers to substretchers:
$\frac{3}{8}$" $\times$ 1" $\times$ $\frac{5}{8}$" deep

21.10 Partly assembled table showing joinery and slots for top-fixing buttons

21.11 Double mortise-and-tenon joint between top rail and leg

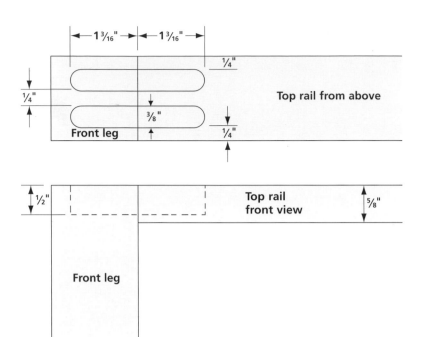

Top rail from above

Front leg

Top rail front view

Front leg

21.12 Top rail joinery

Diagrams **21.12** to **21.16** show the mortise positions.

Mortising with a router and shop-built jig is explained in detail in Chapter 6. The crucial part of mortising is marking the mortise centers on the workpieces. When this is done properly and the jig is correctly set up, little can go wrong.

Review Chapter 6 before marking out the mortise positions on the table parts. It will also be helpful to read through the mortising procedure for the Chest of Drawers project (under "Frame Joinery" in Chapter 19), which is presented in great detail.

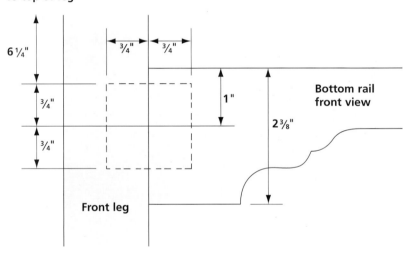

To top of leg

Bottom rail front view

Front leg

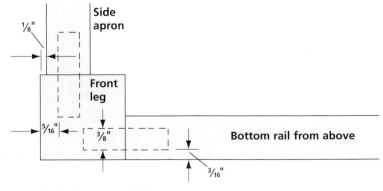

Side apron

Front leg

Bottom rail from above

21.13 Bottom rail joinery

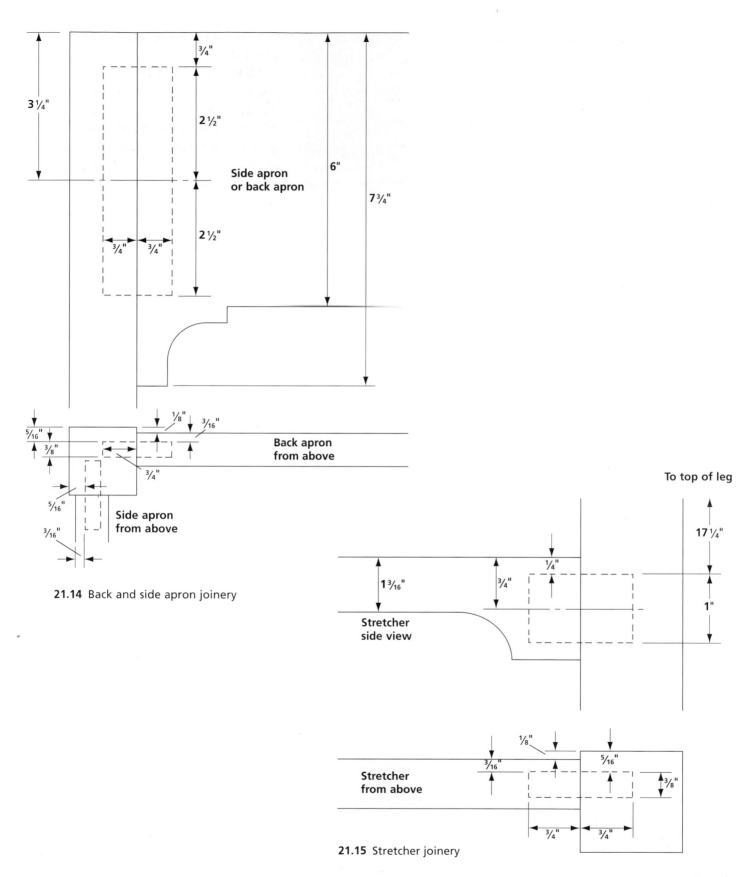

3¼"

¾"

2½"

**Side apron
or back apron**

¾" ¾"

2½"

6"

7¾"

5/16"

⅛" 3/16"

3/8"

¾"

**Back apron
from above**

5/16"

**Side apron
from above**

3/16"

21.14 Back and side apron joinery

To top of leg

17¼"

¼"

1 3/16"

¾"

**Stretcher
side view**

1"

⅛"

3/16"

5/16"

3/8"

**Stretcher
from above**

¾" ¾"

21.15 Stretcher joinery

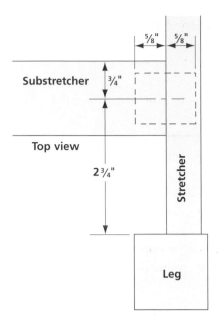

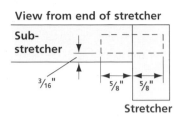

View from end of stretcher

21.16 Substretcher joinery

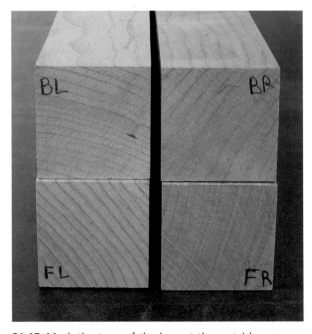

21.17 Mark the tops of the legs at the outside corners

Marking Out

Begin by deciding which corner of the table each leg will attach to; i.e., front left, front right, back left, or back right. Mark the legs FL, FR, BL, or BR. The best positions for the markings are on the top ends in the outside corners (**21.17**) so that the marks will not be lost when the mortises are cut. Placing the marks in these corners also makes it easy to check that the legs are in their correct positions.

Check that the top edges and outside faces of the other carcass components are clearly identified. Mark the mortise centers, as follows, on the ends of the bottom rail and at the corresponding positions on the front legs:

- At one end of the rail, measure 1" down from the top edge, and make a mark on the end with a fine pencil point.
- With a small square and a fine pencil, draw a line from the mark to the outside face of the rail. Do not extend the line all the way across the end. Extending the centerlines only to the outside faces safeguards against positioning a component incorrectly in the mortising jig. Repeat at the other end of the rail.
- Measure $6\frac{1}{4}$" down from the tops of the front legs, on the faces that go to the top and bottom rails. These faces are the right face of the left leg and the left face of the right leg. Make marks at this distance on both legs.
- Using a square, extend the marks in pencil to only the front faces of the legs.
- Draw a $\frac{3}{8}$" × $1\frac{1}{2}$" mortise centered lengthwise on one of the rail marks and set in from the outside face by $\frac{3}{16}$".

The side and back aprons are stepped in from the outside faces of the legs by $\frac{1}{8}$"; hence, the mortises in the legs are set in $\frac{1}{8}$" further from the outside faces than the apron mortises. Thus, you need to draw both a leg mortise and an apron mortise so that the jig can be set for the two different insets:

- Set a marking gauge to $3\frac{1}{4}$" of the distance from the top edges of the aprons to the mortise centers.
- Hold the face of the gauge against the top edge of each apron, and cut a short mark on each end to establish the mortise centers.
- Using a square and a pencil, extend the marks to meet only the outside faces.
- Use the gauge to make corresponding marks on the legs $3\frac{1}{4}$" from the tops. The faces that must be marked are as follows: the back faces of both front legs, the front faces of both back legs, the right face of the back left leg, and the left face of the back right leg, all as viewed from in front of the table.
- Use the square and the pencil to extend the gauge marks to meet the outside faces. Although each leg has two outside faces, a line drawn from any of the marks can meet only one outside face.
- Draw a $\frac{3}{8}$" × 5" mortise, centered in length on one of the apron marks and set in from the outside face by $\frac{3}{16}$".
- Draw another $\frac{3}{8}$" × 5" mortise, centered in length on one of the leg marks. Set this one in $\frac{5}{16}$" from the outside face.

The stretchers have $\frac{3}{8}$" × 1" mortises in their ends. These mortises are centered in length $\frac{3}{4}$" below the top edges. The corresponding mortise centers in the legs are located $17\frac{1}{4}$" from the leg tops. Two mortise drawings are required here as well because the stretchers are stepped in from the leg faces by $\frac{1}{8}$":

- Set the marking gauge to $\frac{3}{4}$", and hold the gauge face against the top edges of the stretchers to mark the mortise centers in their ends.

- Extend the marks to the outside faces in pencil.
- Measure $17\frac{1}{4}$" down from the leg tops, and mark this distance on both the back faces of the front legs and the front faces of the back legs.
- Extend the leg mortise center marks to the outside faces.
- Draw a $\frac{3}{8}$" × 1" mortise, centered in length on one of the leg marks and set in by $\frac{5}{16}$" from the outside face.
- Draw another $\frac{3}{8}$" × 1" mortise, centered lengthwise on the mark on one of the stretcher ends. Set this mortise in $\frac{3}{16}$" from the outside face.

The upper faces of the stretchers and substretchers are flush, so you only need to draw one mortise. Because the wider faces of the substretchers are horizontal, the 1" lengths of the mortises are horizontal on the ends of the substretchers and on the inside faces of the stretchers. The positions of the stretchers and substretchers are shown in the plan-view digram of the table in **21.18**.

Mark the stretcher-to-substretcher mortises as follows:

- With the marking gauge still set to $\frac{3}{4}$", mark the ends of the substretchers from a $\frac{3}{4}$" face; that is, mark the midpoints of the $1\frac{1}{2}$" widths.
- Extend the marks in pencil to reach the upper $1\frac{1}{2}$" faces.
- Measure $2\frac{3}{4}$" from the ends of the stretchers, and mark the inside faces at this distance.
- Extend the marks to reach the top edges of the stretchers.
- Draw a $\frac{3}{8}$" × 1" mortise on the end of one of the substretchers. Center the mortise on the mark, and in the thickness of the substretcher, that is, at $\frac{3}{8}$" from the upper and lower faces.

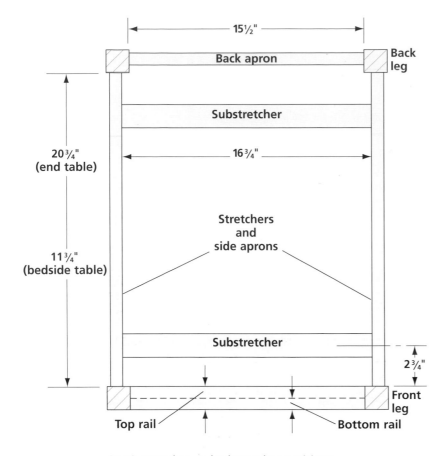

21.18 Stretcher and substretcher positions

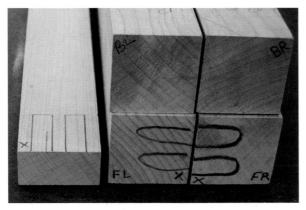

21.19 After drawing one pair of double mortises accurately at each end of the top rail, sketch pairs of mortises on the tops of the front legs

You do not have to draw centerlines for the double mortises in the top rail and leg tops, but two sets of mortises must be drawn on the top rail to assist you in setting the jig fence and side stops:

- Draw a pair of $\frac{3}{8}$" $\times$ 1 $\frac{3}{16}$" mortises on the upper face of the top rail at each end, as shown in **21.12**. Center the mortises at $\frac{7}{16}$" and 1 $\frac{1}{16}$" from the front face. The mortises can be drawn with squared ends.

- Sketch the corresponding pairs of mortises in their approximate positions on the tops of the front legs. Very rough sketches are enough to prevent mistakes when fixing the legs in the mortising jig **(21.19)**.

- Mark an X adjacent to the front faces at each double-mortising position, on the front legs and on the top rail **(21.19)**. The marks will help ensure that you clamp the outside faces to the jig's reference face.

You can also use the jig to make slots in the aprons for the top-fixing buttons. Do the marking for these now, as follows:

- Mark short vertical lines on the inside faces of the side aprons, 1 $\frac{1}{2}$" from each end and at the centers. Extend the marks to the top edges. If you are making the smaller version of the table, omit the marks at the center of the side aprons.

- Make a similar mark at the center of the back apron's inside face. Extend this mark to the top edge.

- Draw the outline of a $\frac{3}{8}$" $\times$ 2" slot, centered in length on one of the apron marks and set in $\frac{3}{8}$" from the top edge.

When all the marking is done, stand the legs in their respective positions and check that the markings are in the right places. Hold each of the aprons, rails, and stretchers close to the legs and check that their markings agree with the leg markings.

Mortising

Clamp the mortising jig to the bench, and fit a ⅜" mortising bit into the router. Take the apron with the 5" mortise drawing on it, and clamp it vertically into the jig. The outside face must be against the jig reference face, and the center mark of the 5" mortise must be aligned with the jig center mark (21.20).

Place the router on the jig, and plunge it so that the cutter touches the apron. Position the cutter within the mortise outline near the midpoint. Then unclamp the jig fence, hold it against the fence guide, bring it up to the router base, and clamp it in position.

Move the router to one side until the cutter is at the end of the mortise outline. Bring the side stop at that side up to the router base and lock it in position. Move the cutter to the other end of the mortise, and lock the other side stop in position against the router base.

Set the router depth stop for a ¾"-deep cut into the apron. Raise the cutter, and then start the router, and cut the mortise in easy stages. Hold the router firmly against the fence at all times.

Cut the other 5" apron mortises using the same settings. Just align the mortise center marks with the jig's center mark.

Next, clamp the leg with the 5" mortise drawn on it horizontal in the jig. Position the leg's outside face to the jig's reference face and the mortise center mark to the jig's center mark. The leg mortises are set in by ⅛" more than the apron mortises, so reset the fence to align the router cutter over the mortise outline. Cut the mortise.

Cut the other 5" leg mortises. (Each front leg has one 5" mortise, and each back leg has two.) Be careful not to cut 5" mortises

21.20 The apron with the 5" mortise drawing is clamped vertically into the jig, with the mortise center mark aligned with the jig center mark

at the ends of the legs where the stretcher mortises have been marked out.

Reset the fence to cut the bottom rail mortises in the inside faces of the front legs and the ends of the rail. Use the drawn mortise to set the fence and to set the end stops for 1½"-long mortises. The fence position will be the same for the rail and the legs, which will both be flush when assembled. Cut the mortises to the ¾" depth already set on the router depth stop.

Now cut the 1"-long mortises into the ends of the stretchers and substretchers. Only the side stops need to be adjusted. As always, the mortise center marks must be against the jig's reference face and aligned with the jig centerline.

Before cutting the corresponding leg mortises, adjust the depth of cut to ⅝" and cut the 1" mortises in the wide faces of the stretchers to match the substretcher mortises. Cover the rabbet in the jig clamp bar by making a ¾" × ¾" × 8" strip of wood and sticking it to the clamp bar with double-sided tape. Make the wood strip flush with the top face of the clamp bar. Clamp each stretcher horizontally in the jig with its top edge to the reference face

21.21 Clamp the top rail into the jig, and align one end with the jig's center mark

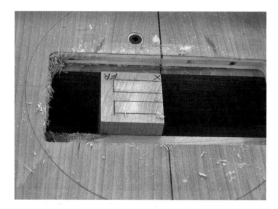

21.22 A front leg clamped into the jig and ready for mortising

21.23 Prepare to make slots in the aprons for the top-fixing buttons by clamping the apron with the slot drawing into the jig

and with a mortise center mark aligned with the jig's center mark. Check to see that you have reduced the depth of cut to $\frac{5}{8}$". Cut the four mortises.

Reset the depth of cut to $\frac{3}{4}$", and adjust the fence for the insets of the 1" mortises near the bottom ends of the legs. Use the mortise drawn on one of the legs to set the fence. Cut the 1" leg mortises.

Before cutting the double mortises in the top rail and the tops of the front legs, reposition the $\frac{3}{4}$" × $\frac{3}{4}$" × 8" strip of wood $\frac{1}{2}$" below the top edge of the clamp bar. Doing so will prevent clamping pressure from being applied at the level of the mortises and thereby avoid collapsing the wood inward as the mortises are cut.

Clamp the top rail into the jig, upper face on top. Put the outside face toward the jig's reference face and align one end with the jig's center mark. Check that the X is nearest to the jig's reference face (**21.21**).

Place the cutter on the $\frac{3}{8}$" mortise outline nearest to the X, and adjust the fence in the usual way to make it parallel to the jig's reference face at the right distance from it. Adjust the appropriate end stop, and set the depth of cut to $\frac{1}{2}$". Cut the mortise.

Slacken the clamps and slide the top rail in order to line up its opposite end with the jig's center mark. Keep the outside face to the jig reference face. Set the other end stop, and cut a mortise at this end.

Clamp a front right leg vertically in the jig with the front face and the X mark toward the jig's reference face and with the open ends of the mortises aligned with the jig's centerline (**21.22**).

With the same jig settings, cut the mortise. Repeat for the other front leg, being sure to place it to the other side of the jig's center mark.

Replace the top rail in the jig, and align one end with the jig's center mark. Move the fence in order to center the router cutter over the second mortise outline. Hold the jig fence to the fence guide so as to make it parallel to the reference face. Check that the X is toward the jig reference face. Cut the second mortise in each end of the top rail.

Cut the second mortise in each of the front legs.

The final operation with the mortising jig is to make slots in the aprons for the top-fixing buttons, as described below.

Remove the strip of wood from the clamp bar. Take the apron with the slot drawing on it and clamp it in the jig (21.23). Make sure that the slot's center mark aligns with the jig's center mark. Set the depth of cut to $\frac{5}{8}$", and set the fence and side stops in the usual way. Cut the slots.

Next, make the hole in the top rail for a top-fixing screw. Drill a $\frac{3}{16}$"-diameter hole through the top rail, at midlength, $\frac{7}{16}$" from the back edge. Countersink the hole in the bottom face of the rail for a #8 FH wood screw.

DECORATING THE LEGS

Each leg has a $\frac{1}{4}$" bead routered along its outside corner (21.24). To help avoid mistakes, first run a crayon line down each leg by the corner that is to be beaded.

You will need a $\frac{1}{4}$"-radius beading bit, not a round-over bit. A round-over bit and a beading bit are shown in 21.25.

If your beading bit has a guide bearing or a pilot guide, fix the router and bit in a router table and set the bit height by trial and error with a test piece. Keep the fence well clear of the bit, and cut a bead on the test piece. When the bit height is correct, switch off the router and hold the beaded test piece against the guide bearing or pilot. Push the fence up against the beaded

21.24 A $\frac{1}{4}$" bead is routered along each leg's outside corner

21.25 Round-over bit (left) and beading bit (right)

21.26 Set up the router table for beading the legs

21.27 A small gap shows between the workpiece and the fence when the workpiece is touching the guide bearing

test piece; then move the fence back about $\frac{1}{32}$" and clamp it in this position. The fence will now protect the end surfaces of the legs when they reach the bit (21.26 and 21.27).

If the bit does not have a pilot or guide bearing, you will need to set the fence precisely to produce the required bead.

Double-check that you have drawn crayon lines down the outside corner of each leg: These are the FL corner of the FL leg, the FR corner of the FR leg, the BR corner of the BR leg, and the BL corner of the BL leg, all as viewed from the front of the table.

Cut the beads down the marked corners of the legs. Cut slowly enough to minimize

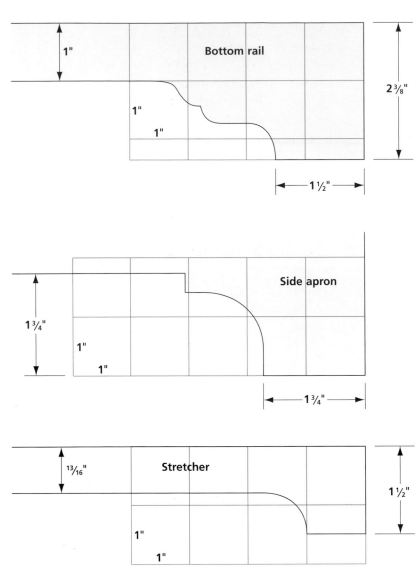

21.28 Draw the shapes at full size onto the parts

the risk of tear-out, but not so slowly as to cause burning. Move the legs from right to left—it is never safe to make a climb-cut on a router table.

SHAPING THE PARTS

Draw a grid of 1" squares on a piece of paper, and transfer the shape of the bottom rail onto it from **21.28**. Do the same for the shape of the side aprons. Cut out the shapes from the paper, and draw around them onto the outside faces of the aprons and rail. Draw the simple shape of the stretchers directly onto the workpieces. The bottom edge of the back rail can either be left straight or shaped like the side aprons.

The best tool for cutting the shapes is a bandsaw with a $\frac{1}{8}$" blade. However, a $\frac{1}{4}$" bandsaw blade will do the job, and even a jigsaw with a narrow fine-tooth blade can be used. Do not cut closer to the line than $\frac{1}{16}$". You can sand or chisel down to the line later. If you are not experienced at cutting curves, practice on scrap material first.

With any method, plan the cuts as described in "Using the Bandsaw" in Chapter 4. Pull back from the cut slightly before changing direction. Slowly does it!

Before shaping the stretchers, drill through them with a $\frac{5}{8}$" Forstner bit close to the curves. After making the straight cuts, the curves can be finished with a small sanding drum.

Smooth the profiles with a small sanding drum fitted in the drill press. A $\frac{3}{4}$"-diameter drum is suitable for these shapes. Do not try to sand closer than $\frac{3}{4}$" from any corner. Be sure to move the workpiece against the direction of the drum's rotation.

Smooth the smallest convex curves with a narrow file or with the toothed edge of a thick file. Alternatively, pare down the

21.29 Sand a chamfer about 1/8" wide around the bottoms of the legs to make them less vulnerable to chipping

curves with a chisel, as described for the plinth of the chest of drawers in Chapter 19, under "Shaping the Parts." Finally, smooth everything with sandpaper, also as described for the chest of drawers' plinth.

SANDING BEFORE ASSEMBLY

Using a random-orbit sander fitted with 120- and 220-grit sanding discs, sand the faces and the straight edges of the aprons, the top and bottom rails, the stretchers, and the substretchers.

Sand all the leg faces at 120- and then 220-grit, but remember to use an uncushioned sanding block on their joinery areas where they meet the aprons, rails, and stretchers. The use of a cushioned block or a random-orbit sander on these areas might result in gaps at the joints (see "Sanding by Hand" in Chapter 15).

Sand the leg beads with narrow strips of sandpaper. Use your fingers to make the strips conform to the bead profile. If you find that sanding the legs has worn down the edges of the bead somewhat, you can quickly add definition to the beads with sandpaper wrapped over a scraper blade.

With a block and 80-grit sandpaper, sand a chamfer about $\frac{1}{8}$" wide all around the bottoms of the legs. This will make them less susceptible to chipping on hard floors (**21.29**). Just a few strokes on each edge is sufficient. Double-check that it is the bottom end before you chamfer it!

ASSEMBLY

Make the tenons, as described in "Making and Gluing Tenons" in Chapter 6. You need the following tenons; in addition, make a couple of spares of each size.

Bottom rail tenons (2)
$\frac{3}{8}$" × $1\frac{1}{2}$" × $1\frac{1}{2}$"
Apron tenons (6)
$\frac{3}{8}$" × 5" × $1\frac{1}{2}$"
Stretcher tenons (4)
$\frac{3}{8}$" × 1" × $1\frac{1}{2}$"
Substretcher tenons (4)
$\frac{3}{8}$" × 1" × $1\frac{1}{4}$"
Top rail tenons (4)
$\frac{3}{8}$" × $\frac{1}{2}$" × 2"

There is no need for the top rail tenons to extend into the radius at the end of each mortise.

The 5"-wide tenons can be made as two $2\frac{1}{2}$"-wide pieces or as single pieces.

Except for the 2" top rail tenons, remember to round the edges of the tenon stock before cutting the individual tenons from it. If you use $2\frac{1}{2}$" stock for the 5" tenons, it need only be rounded on one edge.

Using PVA glue, glue tenons into the mortises in the ends of the side and back aprons, the bottom rail, and the stretchers. Do not glue tenons into the substretchers or top rail at this time. Remove any squeeze-out when the glue has gelled. Leave to set for at least an hour.

Prepare for assembly by using a scraper to create small glue "pond areas" along the leg mortises, except for those where the front rails meet the legs (**6.33** in "Making and Gluing Tenons," Chapter 6).

When the tenon glue has set, assemble the left back and left front legs with a side apron and stretcher; then assemble the right back and front legs with the other side apron and stretcher. Assemble them without glue at first to confirm that everything will go together correctly:

- Measure the mortise depths, and check that the tenons will not hit their bottoms. If necessary, shorten the tenons with a fine-tooth handsaw or by sanding them.
- Insert the apron and stretcher tenons into the leg mortises by hand as far as they will go.
- Check that the outside faces are outside.
- Lay the assembly flat, and place clamping cauls against the legs.
- Use three pipe clamps to pull the tenons fully home (**21.30**).
- Check that the top edge of the apron is flush with the tops of the legs. If it is not, remove the clamps and make it flush. You may need to disassemble everything and check the apron alignments individually with each leg. If the aprons cannot be made flush because the tenon is hitting the end of the mortise, remove a sliver of wood from the tenon with a chisel; use the chisel to round over the tenon again afterward.
- Reassemble the side, and check that the stretcher is at the same distance from the bottoms of both legs.
- When everything seems to fit properly, disassemble the parts and lightly moisten the tenons with water. Apply polyurethane glue to the appropriate mortises, but first check and then double-check that you are about to

21.30 Use three pipe clamps to assemble the side frames

apply glue to the right mortises. When the moisture has disappeared from the tenon surfaces, apply the glue very lightly to these also. Squeeze-out can be difficult to remove from inset aprons, so just scrape glue over them with an almost dry brush.

- Reassemble the side frames, and make the aprons flush with the tops of the legs. Clamp across the legs, using two pipe clamps at the apron end and one at the stretcher end. Before you leave them to set, check to make sure that the outside faces are outside. Unclamp the sides when the glue has set.

Square a line across the right face of the left leg at $5\frac{1}{4}$" from the top. Do the same on the left face of the right leg. The top edge of the bottom rail must be aligned with these marks. Modify this measurement if your drawer opening is not designed to be $4\frac{5}{8}$".

Measure the depths of the mortises and the lengths of the bottom rail and back rail tenons. Shorten any tenons that might hit the mortise bottoms. Insert the back apron and bottom rail tenons one at a time into their mortises in the legs; check that the bottom rail will align with the marks and the back rail will be flush with the tops of the legs. If necessary, reduce the tenon widths with a chisel.

Cut the substretchers to their final lengths, determined as follows:

- Dry-assemble the carcass with only the back apron and bottom rail. Adjust the bottom rail to the $5\frac{1}{4}$" marks on the front legs. Modify the rail tenons with a chisel if you cannot adjust the rail to the marks. With the carcass upside down, use a clamp across the apron and another across the rail to fully insert the tenons. Use cauls to protect the legs.
- Slacken the front clamp, and fit the top rail between the front legs; then retighten the clamp. Do not install the top rail tenons at this time. Apply a clamp across the top rail.
- Hold each substretcher between the stretchers, and mark one end of each to show where the final-length cut must be made. Cut the substretchers to length. Use the table saw and a miter gauge fitted with a baseboard to show exactly where the blade will cut.

Separate the two sides, and moisten the back apron and bottom rail tenons. Also, moisten tenons for the top rail and substretchers. Carefully measure the depths of the mortises in the ends of the substretchers and the corresponding mortises in the stretchers. Make sure the tenons for the substretchers are at least $\frac{1}{32}$" shorter than the combined depths. Remember that two of the substretcher mortises have been reduced in depth.

Apply polyurethane glue to all mortises and to all tenons, except for the top rail tenons. Assemble the sides to the back apron, bottom rail, and substretchers. Adjust the top edge of the bottom rail to

21.31 With the top rail double tenons in place, adjust the rail flush with the tops of the legs and clamp across it

the $5\frac{1}{4}$" marks on the legs. You may need to use an extra clamp across the stretchers to pull in the substretcher tenons.

Remove the clamp across the bottom rail, and place the top rail in position. Then replace the clamp and lay the assembly on its back.

Apply glue to the double mortises in the legs and top rail. Also apply glue to the four top rail tenons. With a mallet, tap the tenons into the rail and leg mortises. When they are in place, possibly after several readjustments, adjust the rail flush with the tops of the legs and then clamp across it. The table can now be stood upright (**21.31**).

AFTER ASSEMBLY

After the glue has set, remove the clamps and check the table for squeeze-out at every joint. With a sharp chisel, carefully remove any squeeze-out.

The double tenons in the top rail will be sticking up above the surface, and dried glue will need to be removed. A hand plane is the best tool for removing glue and making the tenons flush. Take great care to

21.32 The cock-beaded drawer opening

21.33 Make and fix the cock beading; use C-clamps to span the wider parts of the bottom rail

21.34 A drawer stop at the front

avoid damaging the table when you are planing the tenons. If possible, stand the table on something that will bring the top rail to a comfortable height for planing.

The front surfaces of the top and bottom rails may not be perfectly flush with the legs. Although the mortising procedure will have ensured that any discrepancy is very small, they now need to be sanded flush using 120- and 220-grit discs in a random-orbit sander. Before sanding these faces, read "Sanding the Frames" in Chapter 19.

COCK BEADING

This is a suitable stage at which to fix cock beading around the drawer opening (**21.32**). Make the cock bead 1" wide. The total length of fitted cock bead is about 40", but you should make enough to cut at least three 18" pieces and three 6" pieces—about 6 feet total.

Make and fix the beading as described under "Cock Beading" in Chapter 19. You will need to use C-clamps to span the wider parts of the bottom rail (**21.33**).

DRAWER BEARERS AND GUIDES

The drawer bearer (**21.34**) must be installed level with the bottom cock bead. You need to draw guide lines on the inside faces of each side apron at a right angle to the legs and exactly level with the top of the cock bead on the bottom rail, as indicated in **21.35**.

Start by measuring from the top of each leg to the top surface of the cock bead. The distance is awkward to measure and will not be precise. It may also differ slightly on each side. Just measure as accurately as you can. Both measurements should be about $5\frac{3}{16}$" for a $4\frac{1}{4}$" drawer opening.

Draw lines on the inside faces of the aprons at the measured distances down from their top edges.

Make two drawer bearers of the size specified in the parts list. Drill $\frac{1}{4}$"-diameter holes through the widths of each bearer, that is, through their $\frac{3}{4}$" faces, and countersink the holes for #8 FH wood screws. Make the holes at the center and at $1\frac{1}{2}$" from each end.

Transfer the hole centers from the bearers to the aprons by inserting a $\frac{15}{64}$" drill bit into each hole and tapping it while the bearer is clamped level with the line on an apron. Fix the bearers to the side aprons with their top surfaces level with the lines using #8 × 2" FH screws. Check that the screws will not go right through the aprons.

The $\frac{1}{4}$" holes will allow you to adjust the bearer position somewhat. Place a straightedge over the bearer and cock bead. Tap the bearer up or down with a mallet and block to make it exactly level with the cock bead. When the adjustment is right, the straightedge will make contact with the cock bead and the entire length of the bearer. If necessary, enlarge the holes to provide further adjustment. You will do the final adjustment and fixing when the drawer is fitted.

Make two drawer guides. These must be glued onto the bearers so that they are exactly level with the vertical cock bead at each side. Take a piece of waste cock-bead material and clamp it to the inside of a back leg, parallel to the beading on the front leg. Next, place a straightedge against this piece of material and the front vertical beading. The guide is to be positioned against the straightedge (21.36).

Fix the guides to the bearers with epoxy glue, following the procedure detailed under "Drawer Guides" in Chapter 19.

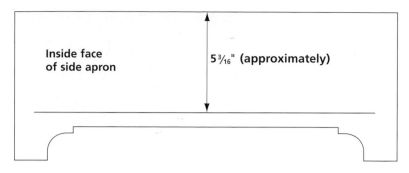

21.35 Draw guide lines on the inside faces of each side apron as shown in this diagram

21.36 A drawer guide is positioned against the straightedge; a small piece of cockbeading strip is clamped to the back leg to keep the straightedge parallel to the side apron

MAKING AND FITTING THE DRAWER

Drawer construction is described in detail in the Chest of Drawers project in Chapter 19. Make the drawer using the procedures described there, except for drilling holes for the drawer pull. The drawer pull for the table is a different size, so refer to the "Drawer Pull" section in this chapter, not Chapter 19. If you are making the smaller version of the table, refer now to the "Drawer Pull" section in this chapter, because you should drill the drawer front for the pull before assembling the drawer.

When you fit the drawer, take advantage of the adjustability of the bearers as follows:

- Sand the drawer sides as described in Chapter 19 ("Sanding the Drawer Sides" under "Drawers"), and fit the drawer into the opening. Tap the bearers up or down with a mallet and block until they make full-length contact with the bottom edges of the drawer. The drawer front should be either lightly touching the cock bead or up to 0.005" above it.
- If you need to remove material from the bottom edges of the drawer sides, proceed as detailed in Chapter 19.

After the drawer has been satisfactorily fitted, remove it and the bearers. Dab a little polyurethane glue on the back faces of the bearers. Replace the bearers and the drawer. Adjust the bearers again by tapping. When they are once more correctly positioned, leave the glue to set. Use only a little glue so that the bearers will not become too permanent. Someone may need to replace them one day.

DRAWER STOPS

The bottom rail has much less area available for installing stops than the rails of the chest of drawers, so the procedure for fixing stops is a little different.

One method is to glue a couple of small blocks to the back apron so that they hit the back of the drawer. To do this, carefully place the drawer with its front level with the front of the carcass so that it is set in $\frac{1}{8}$" from the front of the cock bead. Plane a strip of wood to snugly fit between the drawer and the back apron. Cut two short pieces from the strip, and glue them to the apron at positions where they will clear the drawer bottom.

My preferred method for fixing stops is to put them at the front, where they are placed for the chest of drawers. This entails slightly more work because a piece of wood must first be glued to the bottom rail to provide a fixing surface for the stops. If you choose this method, make a $\frac{3}{4}$" × 1" × 13" strip of wood. Then glue it to the back of the bottom rail with its upper 1" face level with the top edge of the rail, and therefore $\frac{3}{16}$" below the level of the cock bead. Make two drawer stops and glue them to this strip. Follow the procedure described under "Drawer Stops" in Chapter 19. A drawer stop at the front can be seen in **21.34**.

DRAWER PULL

I use two alternative pulls for this table, both from the Horton Brasses catalog (www.horton-brasses.com). They are item number H10S with a $2\frac{1}{2}$" boring, and item number H34S with a 2" boring. I place the fixing holes for either of them $1\frac{5}{8}$" below the top edge of the drawer.

If you are using one of these pulls, draw a line across the drawer front $1\frac{5}{8}$" below the top edge. Mark the drilling positions on this line at $1\frac{1}{4}$" on each side of center for the H10S or 1" on each side for the H34S.

Start the holes with a bradawl, and drill through with a $\frac{1}{16}$" drill bit. Using a $\frac{5}{8}$" Forstner bit, counterbore the hole from the inside to a depth of $\frac{5}{32}$". This will allow the fixing nut to be recessed, and it will allow a $\frac{3}{8}$" socket wrench to be used to tighten the nut. Enlarge the holes for the stems with a $\frac{13}{64}$" drill bit.

Hold the assembled pull against the edge of the drawer to assess how much to shorten the stems. After screwing the nuts onto the stems, cut the stems to length with a small hacksaw. File the cut ends smooth, and then unscrew the nuts to restore the threads if they were damaged by the procedure.

If you are making the small version of the table, carry out the above steps before the drawer parts are assembled, because the small drawer will not allow access for drilling from inside. If the drawer is assembled first, the nuts cannot be recessed, which is also a perfectly acceptable option.

THE SHELF
Making the Shelf

Make the $\frac{3}{8}$"-thick shelf by using the methods described for resawing and for making panels in Chapters 12 and 13. Cut the pieces for resawing at least 1" longer than the shelf, and provide enough extra width to allow for all the edge jointing. Remember that the length of the shelf is its front-to-back dimension. After resawing, either make the shelf immediately or store the pieces in plastic to prevent them from cupping. After gluing the shelf panel, belt-sand it using a 150-grit belt and then cut it to size.

If you are making the bedside table, the piece to be cut is wider than it is long, making it dangerous to cut with the table-saw rip fence. The safest procedure is to use a circular saw for all the cuts, as follows:

- Joint one of the side edges straight and then, on the underside, draw the outline of the other three edges. Make the length $\frac{1}{16}$" less than the distance between the front and back legs of the table, and the width $\frac{1}{2}$" more than the distance between the outside faces of the left and right legs. At this size, the shelf will fit between the front and back legs and extend $\frac{1}{4}$" beyond the legs at each side.

- Clamp the shelf upside down to a bench with one end overhanging the edge. Clamp a straightedge to the shelf, parallel to the cutting line and at the appropriate distance from the shelf to accommodate your circular saw.
- Cut to the line, and then repeat the procedure for the other two edges. Because the shelf was upside down, the saw blade rotation will confine chipping to the underside. You will remove any roughness in the cut later, when you round the edges.

Next, round the edges to a $\frac{3}{16}$" radius. The simplest way to do this is to use a hand plane, followed by a random-orbit sander, and then to complete the job by hand with sandpaper. Begin by planing a narrow facet along each side of an edge at about 45 degrees to the edge (21.37).

On the end-grain edges, you must plane from each end toward the middle; otherwise, tear-out will occur at the ends. It is always best to plane end-grain edges first so that chipping can be removed when the side edges are planed. A slightly slower alternative to the hand plane is a random-orbit sander with an 80-grit disc. You may find it helpful to draw a semicircle on the ends of the edges as a guide (21.38).

Use a random-orbit sander with a 120-grit disc to turn the faceted edges into smooth, semicircular edges. Finish by hand with 120- and 220-grit sandpaper.

When the edges are smoothly rounded, sand the top and bottom surfaces by using a random-orbit sander with 120- and 220-grit discs. Finally, hand-sand a small radius at each corner to remove sharpness.

Fixing the Shelf

Place the shelf in position on the stretchers, and clamp it to them with

21.37 Plane a narrow facet along each side of the shelf edges

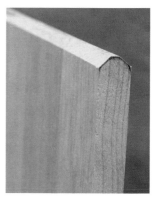

21.38 Round the edges by sanding to a $\frac{3}{16}$" radius; draw a semicircle on the edge as a guide

21.39 Use epoxy to glue the fixing blocks to the underside of the shelf; epoxy avoids the need for clamps

21.40 Roman ogee bearing-guided router bit

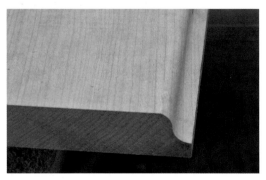

21.41 A test piece with the ogee profile cut into its edge

spring clamps or small C-clamps. Turn the table upside down and draw pencil lines on the underside of the shelf at the inside faces of the substretchers. Make short marks to show where the stretchers meet the substretchers.

Remove the shelf, and then make a $\frac{3}{4}$" × $\frac{3}{4}$" × 10" strip of wood. Check the thickness of the substretchers and plane the strip again to reduce its thickness and width—to $\frac{1}{32}$" less than the thickness of the substretchers, or about $\frac{23}{32}$". Cut six 1"-long blocks from the strip. Glue the blocks to the underside of the shelf along the inside of the pencil lines and about $\frac{1}{16}$" clear of them. Position the blocks at the center and at $7\frac{3}{4}$" each side of center **(21.39)**. Use epoxy glue so you do not need clamps.

Now make a $\frac{1}{4}$" × $\frac{3}{4}$" × 12" strip of wood and cut $1\frac{1}{2}$"-long "pads" from it. At $\frac{3}{8}$" from one end of each of the pads, drill and countersink a hole for a #8 wood screw. When the glue for the blocks has set, reclamp the shelf onto the stretchers and fix it by screwing the $\frac{1}{4}$" pads to the blocks with #8 × $\frac{3}{4}$" FH wood screws (seen earlier in **21.6** and **21.7**). Predrill the blocks for the screws or else they may split. Before fixing the center pads, apply a little PVA glue to the substretchers at those positions; this will keep the shelf centered when it expands and contracts seasonally. Do not glue the pads to the blocks.

THE TOP
Making the Top

Make a glued-up panel for the top. Cut the individual pieces at least 1" longer than the finished length, and allow extra width for all the edge jointing. After belt-sanding the glued-up panel, measure both the outside distance across the front legs of the table and the outside distance across the front and back legs. The first distance should be roughly 18½"; the second should be approximately 14¾" for the bedside table or 23½" for the end table. Cut the top 2½" longer and 2½" wider than these measurements: to 21" × 17¼" for the bedside table or to 21" × 26" for the end table. Use the procedure just described for cutting the shelf, but this time, cut with the top surface uppermost; the circular saw will produce a clean cut at the bottom surface, and any chipping at the top will be removed by subsequent edge shaping.

The edge treatment for the top is a Roman ogee profile made with a ¼"-radius Roman ogee bearing-guided router bit. Photos **21.40** and **21.41** show the bit fitted into a router and a test piece with the ogee profile cut on its edge.

Before cutting the profile, draw a ¾" radius at each corner, and then round the corners by a series of straight cuts with a fine-tooth handsaw, followed by sanding with sandpaper and a block. Or, if your belt sander is not too heavy, you can hold it on its side to round the corners (**21.42**).

You must sand the edges smooth before using the ogee bit, because when you cut the edge profile, the bearing of the ogee bit will follow any unevenness in the edge to produce ripples. Fit the ogee bit in the router, and set the depth of cut until it produces an edge like the one shown in **21.41**. Shape the ends of the top first, moving the router slowly from left to right with minimum downward pressure. Take the router around the radiused corners. Remove any burn marks by repeating the end cuts with increased downward pressure. Move the router fast enough to prevent new burning.

Repeat the procedure on the side edges, but inspect the edge grain first. If it appears to be susceptible to tear-out, raise the bit

21.42 If your belt sander is not too heavy, hold it on its side to round the corners

and make the cut in stages, as explained in the discussion of tear-out in Chapter 5.

The edge profile can be sanded by molding strips of sandpaper with your fingers to conform to the concave part of the shape and then to the convex. However, it is easier to use sandpaper glued to dressmakers' felt (see "Sanding by Hand" in Chapter 15). The felt will be easier to grip if it has sandpaper on both sides.

Start sanding with 120-grit strips held within the concave part of the profile by your fingers. Sand until all marks left by the router bit are removed. Curve the sandpaper over the convex part of the profile and sand this surface. Sand the bottom, straight part of the edge with sandpaper wrapped around a block. Repeat these steps with 220-grit sandpaper.

Sand the top surface with the random-orbit sander fitted with 120- and 220-grit discs. Remove random-orbit swirls by sanding in the direction of the grain with 220-grit sandpaper and a cushioned block.

Fixing the Top

The wooden buttons that hold the top and allow it to expand and shrink can be seen in **21.4**. The buttons are simple, but you must give careful thought to making them

21.43 Use the router table to cut rabbets on the end of the button stock material

safely because making small parts can be dangerous. A procedure like the one described below will keep your fingers away from blades and avoid kickbacks.

The button tongues are formed by a rabbet on one end. The rabbets can be cut on the end of a long piece of wood, from which the buttons can then be cut. If the piece is long enough, your fingers will not need to come close to the cutter, and the buttons can be cut with the table saw and miter gauge without risking any kickbacks. Note that the tongues must be formed at the ends of the buttons so that the grain direction makes them strong.

My preferred method is to cut the rabbets using a router table as follows:

- Mill a piece of hardwood to $\frac{5}{8}$" thick, 1" wide, and at least 15" long.
- Set up a router table with a $\frac{1}{2}$"-diameter mortising bit in the router.
- Adjust the bit height to about $\frac{3}{16}$", and set the fence level with the back of the bit so that the cut will be $\frac{1}{2}$" wide.
- Make a push block approximately $\frac{3}{4}$" $\times$ 6" $\times$ 10". Place the end of the block against the fence of the router table, and hold the button material against it, as shown in **21.43**.

- Cut a $\frac{3}{16}$" $\times$ $\frac{1}{2}$" rabbet into the end of the button material. Use the push block to push it past the cutter and keep it perpendicular to the fence. The push block will also prevent tear-out at the back edge of the cut.
- Carefully compare the depth of the rabbet with the distance from the top of an apron to the button slot (about $\frac{3}{8}$"). If the rabbet equals or exceeds this distance, the buttons will not hold the top tightly. Adjust the bit height and make more cuts until the depth of the rabbet is about $\frac{1}{64}$" less than this distance.
- Clamp a stop block to the table-saw rip fence at least 2" in front of the blade. Adjust the fence for use with the miter gauge to cut $1\frac{1}{4}$" lengths from the rabbeted hardwood piece without trapping them between blade and fence. This procedure for a stop block is described in Chapter 3 under "Miter Gauges and Crosscut Sleds."
- Cut a $1\frac{1}{4}$"-long button from the rabbeted end of the hardwood piece.
- Rabbet the end of the hardwood piece again, and cut off another button. Repeat the process until you have enough buttons.
- Drill a clearance hole for a #8 wood screw through the $\frac{5}{8}$" thickness of each button, and countersink the holes for FH screws. It will very convenient later on if the holes are in exactly the same place in each button. You can ensure this uniformity by setting up a fence and stop on the drill table arranged similarly to the one for drilling the shiplap backboards of the Bookcase project. The arrangement is explained in Chapter 20, under "The Bookcase Back."
- Sand the buttons by rubbing them on a sheet of sandpaper.

Place the top upside down on the bench, and place the carcass upside down on the top. Position the carcass carefully for equal overhangs all around, and then use a felt-tipped pen to draw a line on the top around the inside of the carcass.

Keep the carcass in position on the outline, and place a button in position in one of the slots with the tongue partially inserted. Leave $\frac{3}{16}$" for the top to expand. Place a #8 × 1" FH screw in the button screw hole, and tap it with a hammer to mark its position on the top. Repeat with the other buttons. Also, insert a screw into the hole in the top rail and tap it with the hammer.

Remove the buttons and the carcass, and predrill the top for the screws at the marked positions. If the holes in the buttons are not all identically placed, you will have to number the buttons and the top as you remove each one.

Replace the carcass and screw the buttons into position. Check the final tightness of each one with a screwdriver. Remember that the top must be able to move.

Remove the button from the central slot of the back apron. Put some glue into the slot and replace the button. Take care not to glue the button to the top.

Screw the top rail to the tabletop at the central screw hole.

DRAWER KICKER

Because the table has only a single drawer with no bearers above it to act as kickers, a separate kicker must be installed to prevent the drawer from tipping down at the front when it is pulled forward. All you need is a strip of wood screwed to the underside of the top. In theory, the thickness of the strip should be the same as the thickness of the top rail plus the cock bead, but it is better to make it $\frac{1}{32}$" thinner to ensure that the expansion gap above the drawer is not compromised.

Mill a strip of wood to $\frac{25}{32}$" × $\frac{25}{32}$" × 12" for the bedside table or $\frac{25}{32}$" × $\frac{25}{32}$" × 20" for the end table. Screw the wood to the underside of the top, parallel to the side aprons, with its front end almost touching the top rail. Exactly where it is fixed is unimportant provided that it does not interfere with the fixing buttons and provided that the drawer back will pass directly beneath it.

FINAL TOUCHES

Feel all edges for sharpness and soften them if necessary with a piece of 120-grit sandpaper. Check the edges of the legs, the bottom edges of the top, the bottoms of the aprons, the stretchers, and the front bottom rail. Do not round the edges; just make them comfortable to the touch. Run your hands over everything to check for sharpness or roughness.

Use a bright light to inspect every inch of every surface for dings and scratches.

The table is ready for finishing.

METRIC EQUIVALENTS (to the nearest mm, 0.1 cm, or 0.01 m)

INCHES	MM	CM
1/8	3	0.3
1/4	6	0.6
3/8	10	1.0
1/2	13	1.3
5/8	16	1.6
3/4	19	1.9
7/8	22	2.2
1	25	2.5
1 1/4	32	3.2
1 1/2	38	3.8
1 3/4	44	4.4
2	51	5.1
2 1/2	64	6.4
3	76	7.6
3 1/2	89	8.9
4	102	10.2
4 1/2	114	11.4
5	127	12.7
6	152	15.2
7	178	17.8
8	203	20.3
9	229	22.9
10	254	25.4
11	279	27.9
12	305	30.5
13	330	33.0
14	356	35.6
15	381	38.1
16	406	40.6
17	432	43.2
18	457	45.7
19	483	48.3
20	508	50.8

INCHES	MM	CM
21	533	53.3
22	559	55.9
23	584	58.4
24	610	61.0
25	635	63.5
26	660	66.0
27	686	68.6
28	711	71.1
29	737	73.7
30	762	76.2
31	787	78.7
32	813	81.3
33	838	83.8
34	864	86.4
35	889	88.9
36	914	91.4
37	940	94.0
38	965	96.5
39	991	99.1
40	1016	101.6
41	1041	104.1
42	1067	106.7
43	1092	109.2
44	1118	111.8
45	1143	114.3
46	1168	116.8
47	1194	119.4
48	1219	121.9
49	1245	124.5
50	1270	127.0

Conversion Factors

1 mm = 0.039 inch	1 inch = 25.4 mm	mm = millimeter
1 m = 3.28 feet	1 foot = 304.8 mm	cm = centimeter
1 m^2 = 10.8 square feet	1 square foot = 0.09 m^2	m = meter
		m^2 = square meter

Index

Stability, of furniture, 26–27. *See also* Moisture
    content (MC); Shrinkage/expansion

T
Table saw(s), 42–55
    adjusting, 53–55
    blade position, 44, 53–55
    blades, 48
    crosscut sleds, 50–51
    crosscutting boards on, 43–44, 50–51, 52–53
    cupped wood and, 51
    cutting rough lumber, 52–53
    extended miter gauge fences, 49–50, 51
    featherboards for, 47
    functions of, 42
    guarding arrangements for, 46–47
    miter gauges, 43, 44, 49–50, 51
    mitering on, 44, 208–211
    outfeed support, 52
    pushsticks for, 44, 45, 46–47, 131, 132, 133, 183
    resawing on, 130–133
    rip fences, 48–49
    ripping boards on, 42–43, 51–52
    safety precautions, 44–46, 131
    sanding discs, 150, 198
    table inserts, 47–48
    using, 42–44, 51–55, 130–133

Tops
    Bookcase project, 252, 257–260
    Chest of Drawers project, 185, 223–229
    edge thickeners (strips) for, 224–225, 257, 258,
        259–260
    End Table/Bedside Table project, 290–293
    fixing, 228–229, 291–293
    Roman ogee edge on, 290, 291
    screw holes for, 185, 252

W
Warp, 17, 24–26
Wood. *See also* Grain
    buying/selecting lumber, 23–26, 169–171
    changes, 13–17. *See also* Shrinkage/expansion
    grades of, 23–24
    log (growth-ring) orientation and, 13–15
    measuring standards, 13
    moisture content, 18–23
    sawn board types, 14, 15
Woodworking process, 10–12

ABOUT THE AUTHOR

PETER ANDERSON lives in New Hampshire, where he works at his custom woodworking business. During his life in England, his father, a woodworker, taught him to use hand tools, and although he turned to engineering for his first profession, woodworking remained a lifelong interest. In 1993 he changed careers to become a custom furniture maker, at which point he discovered the joys of power tools. Their precision appealed to his engineer's instincts, and the reduction in physical work that they offered had an even deeper appeal. In this book, he shares with readers the techniques he uses to obtain the full benefits of the power tools available to amateur woodworkers.

Much of Peter's time now is spent making commissioned custom pieces. He also offers woodworking lessons tailored to individual needs. His Web site is www.andersonfurniture.com